DATE DUE

The Achuar Indians live in the remote forest reaches of the Upper Amazon and have developed sophisticated strategies of resource management. Philippe Descola, who has gathered material over several years of fieldwork, documents their rich knowledge of the environment. He explains how this technical knowledge of the increasingly threatened Amazonian ecosystems is interwoven with cosmological ideas that endow nature with the characteristics of society. Combining a symbolist approach with an ecological analysis, the book contributes a new theory of the social construction of nature.

"This work is not only an historical and ethnographic contribution to the study of a particularly important area of the New World, at the hinge of Amazonian and Andean high cultures; it is also a work of undoubted theoretical and methodological value, one that opens up new paths for anthropological thinking."

Claude Lévi-Strauss

Cambridge Studies in Social and Cultural Anthropology
Editors: Ernest Gellner, Jack Goody, Stephen Gudeman,
Michael Herzfeld, Jonathan Parry

93

In the society of nature

A list of books in the series will be found at the end of the volume

IN THE SOCIETY OF NATURE

A native ecology in Amazonia

PHILIPPE DESCOLA

Translated from the French by Nora Scott

CAMBRIDGE
UNIVERSITY PRESS

Published by the Press Syndicate of the University of Cambridge
The Pitt Building, Trumpington Street, Cambridge CB2 1RP
40 West 20th Street, New York, NY 10011-4211, USA
10 Stamford Road, Oakleigh, Victoria 3166, Australia
and Editions de la Maison des Sciences de l'Homme
54 Boulevard Raspail, 75270 Paris Cedex 06

Originally published in French as *La nature domestique.*
Symbolisme et praxis dans l'écologie des Achuar
by Editions de la Maison des Sciences de l'Homme 1986
© Fondation Singer-Polignac 1986
First published in English by Editions de la Maison des Sciences
de l'Homme and Cambridge University Press 1994 as *In the
Society of Nature. A native ecology in Amazonia*
English translation © Maison des Sciences de l'Homme
and Cambridge University Press 1994

Printed in Great Britain at the University Press, Cambridge

A catalogue record for this book is available from the British Library

Library of Congress cataloguing in publication data

Descola, Philippe.
[Nature domestique. English]
In the society of nature: a native ecology in Amazonia / Philippe
Descola; translated from the French by Nora Scott.
    p.   cm. – (Cambridge studies in social and cultural
anthropology; 93)
Includes bibliographical references and index.
ISBN 0 521 41103 3. – ISBN 2 7351 0511 3 (Maison des sciences de
l'homme)
1. Achuar Indians–Agriculture.   2. Achuar Indians–Social
conditions.   3. Achuar Indians–Religion and mythology.   4. Human
ecology–Amazon River Region.   5. Subsistence economy–Amazon River
Region.   6. Conservation of natural resources–Amazon River Region.
I. Title   II. Series.
F3430.1.A25D4713   1994
304.2'089'983–dc20 93-1045   CIP

ISBN 0 521 41103-3 hardback

ISBN 2 7351 0511 3 hardback (France only)

Contents

Illustrations

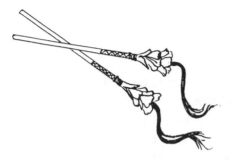

Part title illustrations

Chapter drawings

Preface

The present book is both a description and an analysis of the technical and symbolic relations entertained by an Upper-Amazonian Indian tribe with its natural environment. The result is a degree of ambiguity, which the unsuspecting reader might ascribe to some awkwardness in the construction or vagueness in the conception of the theme expounded. And yet this ambiguity is a basic constituent of the anthropological approach, which has always oscillated between a subtle geometric mentality and an *esprit de finesse*. The contradiction is usually resolved by a division of labor: while some favor a type of intuition rendered demonstrative by the consistency of the logical sequences it permits, others – less numerous, it is true – concentrate on detecting patterns which can be confirmed empirically by means of statistics. The theme I chose precluded such disjunction, since any system whose aim is the socialization of nature inextricably combines material as well as conceptual aspects. The analysis of energetic exchange flows calls for rigorous quantification of food production and time allocation, while the study of symbolic relations with the environment depends on the interpretation of myths, taxonomic systems, and magical techniques and rituals.

Unfortunately quantification and hermeneutics rarely make a happy match, and each member of this unlikely couple tends to be self-sufficient in its particular sphere of objectivation. Whatever the economy of the text, the description of production techniques, the measure of their efficacy, and the analysis of the social actors' representations of them seem doomed to discursive divorce. Each part of the development takes on a sort of internal coherence of its own, which persists like a faint echo when it comes to showing that these are not separate, autonomous objects, but merely discrete approaches to a single object. No doubt this unfortunate dissociation of the various ways of analyzing praxis is inevitable, however, and the present work is no exception. But beyond the methodological constraint of disjunction, I propose to show that it is illusory and useless to draw a hard line between technical and conceptual determinations. I have therefore given equal heuristic weight to quantitative and qualitative data in this analysis of the relations between one society and its natural environment. The nature of the subject dictates that the book be bound by the rules of the ethnographic monograph; but the reader must judge for him- or herself whether its ambition – to avoid the snares of dualism – is, in the end, fulfilled.

Any undertaking of this sort is obviously conditioned by the intellectual milieu in which it was conceived. As a young philosophy student, I succumbed, like many of my contemporaries, to the "scientistic" fascination of Althusserian Marxism. Ethnology shook me out of this dogmatic lethargy and gave me a lesson in both humility and hope. Instead of a totalizing theory that promised to render reality absolutely intelligible, to my naive stupefaction, I discovered the existence of strange, exotic institutions for which no number of reductionist incantations of "determination in the last instance" could account.

Whereas Marx himself minutely detailed precapitalist socio-economic systems, we thought we could simply pronounce on the scientific worth of his labors, never addressing the question of their operative fruitfulness. To break out of the circular exegesis of *de jure* questions, I had personally to undergo the painful test of the facts; I had to take leave of the lofty community of philosophy and descend into the dark depths of empiricism.

The ethnological exile turned out to be promising, however, for, if it humbled the neophyte, it also gave him reason not to despair. Predictably for a philosopher, it was Claude Lévi-Strauss' work that greeted me on the threshold of my new world and was soon joined by Maurice Godelier. Of these authors, our little group of doctoral students generally knew just enough to hold forth with brio on the notion of structure, but that was about all, and it was very little. I suddenly discovered that what we had until then regarded as an idealism without a transcendental subject, or as a metastasis of Marxist epistemology could also be used to solve some thorny ethnographical problems. In his structuralist study of Amerindian mythology, Lévi-Strauss showed that the logic of the concrete was amenable to rigorous analysis, thus shaking the comfortable certainties of the reflection theory of myth. Grounding his thinking in a reinterpretation of Marx and in a vast body of literature on economic anthropology, Godelier challenged Althusserian mechanical causality by revealing the conditions in which certain elements of the "superstructure" could also function as relations of production. From Godelier and Lévi-Strauss alike I also learned that an ethnographer must be attentive to the slightest detail, however lowly. Resituated in a meaningful context, the plumage of a bird, the revolution of a planet, the productivity of a field or the construction of a fence become crucial elements for interpreting social and cultural reality. This scrupulous attention to the concrete fabric of material life was paradoxically lacking in the would-be Marxist ethnological works of the day. With a few exceptions – in particular André-Georges Haudricourt – ethnologists of a materialist stripe seemed to favor a morphological approach to relations of production over in-depth analysis of systems of productive forces. Both Lévi-Strauss and Godelier, each in his own area, made me see that the way to understanding social logics necessarily led through the study of the material and intellectual modes of socializing nature. Like exchange or ritual, the ecology of a society appeared as a total social fact that synthesized technical, economic and religious elements following a pattern whose deep structure was isomorphic with the other structures underlying the social whole.

This rather long preamble was meant to show the extent of my intellectual debt to those who pointed me towards the type of anthropological approach illustrated in the present work. But even when marked by gratitude, a declaration of filiation does not guarantee recognition of paternity; therefore I alone take the responsibility for any deformations that may have occurred in the thought of those who inspired my undertaking.

The initial intellectual fecundation led to the birth of an ethnographic study, which Lévi-Strauss and Godelier encouraged wholeheartedly. My ethnographic knowledge suffered from numerous gaps, and when, in 1973, Lévi-Strauss kindly accepted to direct my thesis, my entire apprenticeship still lay before me. I acquired the rudiments of my trade at the Sixth Section of the Ecole Pratique des Hautes Etudes (now the Ecole des Hautes Etudes en Sciences Sociales), and particularly in the seminar on research methods in anthropology. I became acquainted with Amerindian anthropology in Simone Dreyfus-Gamelon's seminar, which drew the whole generation of young ethnologists interested in the lowlands of South America. Her teaching and advice were valuable assets when it came to drawing up my research project. Maurice Godelier's seminar initiated me into the *arcana* of economic anthropology and to the techniques of measuring and quantification he had perfected in the course of his fieldwork among the Baruya of New Guinea. From him I learned that reading Polanyi and Schumpeter did not obviate the necessity of knowing how to measure a field or to time a task.

Finally, in 1976, I was able to leave for Ecuadorian Amazonia and to live among the Achuar, thanks to funding from the Centre National de la Recherche Scientifique, obtained through the Laboratoire d'Anthropologie Sociale of the Collège de France, whose director at the time was Claude Lévi-Strauss. I would like to thank the many people who helped me over the course of my fieldwork. Mr. Dario Lara, adviser with the Embassy of Ecuador in France, saw to the administrative formalities for my stay and provided me with a warm recommendation to the authorities of his country. A supplementary stipend from the CNRS and a Paul Delheim scholarship from the Collège de France enabled me to spend nearly all my time, from September 1976 to September 1978, with the Achuar. From September 1978 to September 1979, I divided my stay between fieldwork and teaching in the anthropology department of the Pontificia Universidad Católica del Ecuador, in Quito. This extension was made possible by a scholarship from the Mission de la Recherche, which Professor Olivier Dollfus was kind enough to obtain for me. My courses at the Catholic University gave me the opportunity to establish a true working relationship with my Ecuadorian colleagues, the only concrete way of showing them my gratitude for their warm welcome. From them I learned a great deal about the social and political realities of Ecuador, and about the art of living that characterizes Quito and which I dearly miss. I have in mind more particularly Segundo Moreno, Diego Iturralde, Marcelo Naranjo, Jose Pereira, and Jorge Trujillo, who have done so much to ensure that anthropology is recognized in Ecuador as both an important scientific discipline and an instrument for lucid social criticism.

I would also like to thank the civilian, military, and church authorities as well as the native organizations which gave me continuous support. I am especially grateful to Mr. Hernan Crespo Toral, director of the Instituto Nacional de Antropología e Historia, for having granted me a permit to conduct ethnological research, and which served as a safe-conduct pass in many circumstances. The Federación de Centros Shuar took an interest in my project and gave me permission to proceed as I saw fit. I treasure memories of my conversations with a number of its leaders: Domingo Antun, Ernesto Chau, Ampam Karakras, Rafael Mashinkiash, and Miguel

Tankamash, who are struggling to preserve their cultural identity while facing the present with courage and realism. Without the support of this outstanding native organization and its Salesian advisers – in particular Juan Bottasso and Luis Bolla – I could never have realized my project. I also owe a debt of thanks to Lloyd Rogers (Shell-Mera Evangelist Mission) and to the North American pilots of the Alas de Socorro company, who organized most of my air trips around the Achuar territory.

To Antonino Colajanni and Maurizio Gnerre, pioneers in anthropological fieldwork among the Achuar, I am indebted for having guided my first steps in the forest; I would like to thank them here for that handsome gesture, which was the beginning of a long friendship. Professor Norman Whitten was constantly forthcoming with advice and encouragement; his familiarity with the places and people of Ecuadorian Amazonia, as well as his keen anthropological perception made him an ideal mentor for a beginning anthropologist. I received a warm welcome from my ORSTOM compatriots based in Quito, who gave me the benefit of not only their scientific aid but their generous hospitality.

In 1980 I returned to France and turned to writing my thesis, which constitutes the main matter of this work. During this period many colleagues and friends gave me their support. I am especially indebted to Mr. Clemens Heller, director of the Maison des Sciences de l'Homme in Paris, for his timely financial assistance on many occasions. Nor shall I forget the exceptional working conditions provided by King's College in Cambridge. But my gratitude goes first and foremost to my real and classificatory families, to use an expression common to ethnologists and the Achuar. By sharing his interest in Indian America with me, my father oriented my research towards the New World, while my mother devoted several months to typing my manuscript. With my wife, Anne-Christine Taylor, I shared the joys and trials of life with the Indians as well as the uncertainties and enthusiasms of work *in camera*. To say that this book owes much to her is an understatement. It is every bit as much the fruit of our complicity as of my own labors. Out of sight, but close to heart and mind, my Achuar classificatory family was formed little by little by the mythic ties of adoption. From Wisum, the first man to call me "brother" and to treat me as one, I inherited a vast kindred that extends to the limits of the tribe. This book is dedicated to all those Achuar who took me in and educated and protected me because they pretended to take the duties of our imaginary kinship seriously. I hope that, when the grandchildren of my brother Wisum are able to read this *apachiru Yakum papiri*, the world it attempts to describe will not have vanished forever.

Preface to the English edition

Although the original edition of this book appeared in French in 1986, I finished writing it in early 1984. In the ten years that have elapsed since then a great amount of material has been published on the cultural ecology of Amazonian Indians as well as on the ethnography of the Jivaro. Faced with the choice of either extensively rewriting the book to include and discuss this new material, or to let it stand as it was, I chose the second solution. Indeed, most of the data published in the last decade on native adaptation to Amazonian habitats appears to substantiate the hypotheses I set forth in this work rather than contradict them. As for the theoretical approach to the question of the relations between nature and society which I advocate here, I have every reason to believe that it has lost nothing of its actuality and relevance.

Paris, 1993

A note on spelling

The Achuar terms used in this work are spelled according to the traditional transcription of Jivaro adopted by agreement between the Federación de Centros Shuar, the Salesian Mission, and the Summer Institute of Linguistics. This transcription is based on the phonetic system of Spanish and is not entirely rigorous; nevertheless, it seemed legitimate to choose a standardized system of transcription used in alphabetizing those for whom Jivaro is the native tongue.

	Standard Jivaro*	Phonetic transcription		Standard Jivaro*	Phonetic transcription
consonants	ch	/ č /	vowels	a	/ a /
	j	/ h /		a̲	/ ã /
	k	/ k /, / g /		e	/ ɨ /
	m	/ m /		e̲	/ ɨ̃ /
	n	/ n /		i	/ i /
	n̲	/ ŋ /		i̲	/ ĩ /
	p	/ p /, / b /		u	/ u /, / w /
	r	/ r /		u̲	/ ũ /
	s	/ s /		y	/ i /, / ɟ /
	sh	/ š /	diphthongs	au	/ ɔ /
	t	/ t /, / d /		ai	/ ɛi /
	ts	/ c /, / ts /, / dz /		ei	/ ɛ̃i /
	w	/ w /, / ß /			

*In standard Jivaro an underlined phoneme indicates nazalization (see above); to simplify the typography, I have omitted the underlinings in the text.

General introduction

Nature and society: lessons from Amazonia

Devoted to the theme of the socialization of nature, the present book attempts to navigate between two conceptions of the world usually presented as mutually exclusive: the one sees nature as an animate twin of society, the other conceives it as the set of phenomena occurring outside the realm of human action. It is the signal privilege of ethnologists to tread this line, between a silent *physis* subjected to mathematization and a cosmos telling its tale through the illusory voice of those who make it speak, as they would walk a familiar road between two grassy banks, looking now to one side, now to the other. At once consenting trustees of a rationalist tradition and patient students of exotic systems of thought, they thread their way along the seam between two worlds. The pages that follow chronicle one such trek as it tacks between two representations of the relations one society entertains with its natural environment.

The setting is Amazonia, a region of the globe whose diversity of plant and animal life has excited the curiosity of the native inhabitants as much as that of the men of science who have visited the area. To the latter goes the responsibility of having transformed the great Amazonian forest into a major site for the naturalist projections of Western imagination. From Oviedo to Buffon, scholars have looked upon this original world as a sort of botanical and zoological conservatory, only incidentally inhabited by

1

humans. Thus reduced to appendages to the realm of nature, the Amerindians could hardly be credited with a cultural approach to this domain. Only two years after the discovery of the New World, a Spanish doctor who had sailed with Columbus wrote: "Their bestiality exceeds that of any beast" (quoted by Fernandez de Navarrete 1825: 371). Nearly two and a half centuries later, this stubborn prejudice was vehemently illustrated by Buffon, for whom the American Indian "was in himself no more than a first-class animal and, for nature, merely an inconsequential being, a sort of impotent automaton incapable of bringing her reform or succor" (*Œuvres complètes*, VX: 443). It is to the immense credit of the pioneers of South American ethnography that they invalidated this approach by revealing to the Western World the richness of the symbolic productions of these "impotent automata" and the sophistication of their techniques for exploiting the environment. But naturalist ideology brooks no proof to the contrary; and so it is not surprising to see, as of late, the Amazonian Indians pressed by the distant heirs of Buffon into service as an unwitting illustration of the implacable determinism of ecosystems.

Present-day ethnography advances contradictory interpretations of man's relationship with his environment in the Amazon Basin. Briefly, two main approaches can be identified, the mutually exclusive character of which often has to do more with polemics than with reality. One approach sees nature as an object upon which to exercise thought, as the privileged matter, the springboard, for the taxonomic and cosmological imaginings of forest peoples. Environmental features are an unavoidable methodological constraint if the internal organization of the systems of representation is to be accounted for with any rigor. Nature and the way it is used are invoked as mere demonstrative props of the main undertaking, to wit: establishing the semiology of native discourse.

Starkly contrasting with the first approach, concerned mainly with symbolic morphology, ecological reductionism wildly attempts to explain all cultural manifestations as epiphenomena of nature's "natural" work. Postulating that society is totally determined by its environment, this utilitarian interpretation rejects any specificity that might obtain in the symbolic and social sphere. If these opposing perspectives may at times have been seen as two forms of monism, reproducing the aporias of an abusive mind–matter dualism, it is perhaps because both concede only a subservient role to practice. In one case, attention is focused almost exclusively on productions of the mind: any reference to practice is only as one of the ways of deciphering different types of encoded discourse (myths, taxonomies . . .); in the other case, practice is entirely reduced to its alleged adaptive function, thereby forfeiting all meaningful autonomy. And yet techniques of using the body, nature, and space are often the bearers of rich symbolism. But this symbolism is often implicit and not necessarily visible in the normative ideological productions – such as myths – usually called upon to explicate culture. In societies which, like the Achuar, have no coherent canonical theories of the world, the structures for representing practices must be pieced together from a motley collection of clues: an avoidance practice, a magical chant, or the way game is handled.[1]

I have attempted, using an ethnographic case, to analyze the relations between humans and their environment from the standpoint of the dynamic interactions between the techniques used in socializing nature and the symbolic systems that organize them. I have tried to isolate the principles that structure a praxis – the praxis itself being non-reducible – but, in so doing, not to prejudge the levels of causality or their hierarchy, a certain form of methodical doubt being needed if the snares of dualism are to be avoided. Materialist empiricism views representations of material life as secondary elaborations, mere ideological reflections of modes of appropriating and socializing nature. To me this perspective is unacceptable, for there is no justification for assigning causal or analytical preeminence to the material over the conceptual. Every action, every labor process begins with a representation of the conditions and procedures necessary for its execution. Or, according to Maurice Godelier's formula, "the conceptual part of reality" is no less concrete than its material part (1984: 167). A practice is thus an organic totality, in which material and conceptual aspects are closely interwoven; if it is an oversimplification to say that the latter are no more than deformed reflections of the former, it is still perhaps not impossible to assess their respective roles in the structuring of practices.

I am aware of the enormous difficulties raised by such an approach, and my ambition is not so much to map the problem as to mark some of the trails leading to it. As I said in the foreword, the object I have outlined is particularly difficult to construct, since the point is to avoid creating a separation between the ways the environment is used and the forms of representations these are given. It is on this one condition that we can show how the social practice of nature hinges at one and the same time on the idea a society has of itself, the idea it has of its material environment, and the idea it has of its intervention in that environment. My task was facilitated by the fact that the Achuar go about their socialization of nature in a primarily domestic setting. And so the household suggested itself as one pole of analytical continuity to which the different ways of using and representing the environment could be attached. Each household, standing alone in the forest, thinks of itself as an individual independent center where the relation to nature is constantly being acted out. The household's autonomy in the use of production factors is echoed by its autonomy with respect to the symbolic preconditions of this use, since no outside mediator is needed to perform the rites of propitiation.

Part One of this work, "The Sphere of Nature," describes the Achuar's environment and their representations of it (excluding the uses to which it may actually be put). This is pure author's artifice; if, upon occasion, it is possible to analyze the components of an ecosystem, while leaving aside a human presence that contributes ever so slightly to its modification, it is arbitrary to study the ways this system is represented outside the context of the techniques and ideas the Achuar use to interact with it. The choice was dictated by the necessities of synthetic exposition; it also allowed me to show that, contrary to the claims of neofunctionalist theses, the Indians' knowledge of nature is not governed exclusively by utilitarian consider-ations. Leaving the theme of abstract environmental knowledge, Part Two analyzes the various domains of concrete practice of nature in their material and conceptual forms. I have taken over the spatial divisions used by the Achuar themselves to differentiate the ways of socializing nature according to the metaphorical form and the place of practice (house, garden, forest, river). To a detailed, quantified description of the various subsistence techniques I have thus added an interpretation of the symbolic specificities of the practice used in each of the autonomous domains in which it manifests itself in a distinctive way. Chapter Eight, a thematic study of Achuar categories of practice, attempts to draw a parallel between the time allocated to the different sectors of activity and the indigenous model of the sexual division of labor. The last chapter is a detailed study of the productivity of the Achuar economic system which advances some hypotheses for the interpretation of its homeostatic character.

This type of analysis implies certain constraints which it is only fitting to state at the outset. The Achuar are new arrivals on the ethnographic scene, and the extreme scarcity of historical documents restricted my study to a strictly synchronic framework. The result is a snapshot, as it were, of the relations between the Achuar and nature taken at a given moment in their respective courses of development. The synchronic perspective demands in exchange that the object chosen be of homogeneous composition.[2] When Anne-Christine Taylor and I began our field study, however, a fraction of the Achuar population was beginning to undergo certain socio-economic mutations, sparked by episodic contact with missionary organizations (see Chapter One). Although the effects of these mutations were scarcely noticeable in daily life, I thought it preferable not to introduce into the study of the system of resource usage an analysis of the possible origins of its transformations. I therefore decided to use, in the framework assigned to this work, only the ethnographic material we had collected in those parts of the Achuar territory not yet penetrated by missionaries. But even given this methodological precaution, I am not so naive as to think that the subsistence techniques used by those Achuar who are the most sheltered from outside contact are still of an aboriginal type. However isolated it may be, no refuge area in the Amazon Basin is a true isolate; there is no Amerindian population that has not to some extent borne the technological, epidemiological, and demographic consequences of the European presence. Nevertheless, the fact remains that the system of socialization of nature presented here was, in 1976, one of the best preserved in Amazonia. Many Achuar were still fortunate enough to have no regular relations with the dominant national society, something quite rare at that time. Their lives were therefore free of all those constraints normally imposed upon indigenous nations by the internal colonial apparatus.

So that misunderstandings do not arise, I would also like to state the nature of my enterprise as it relates to the problematics of such fields as human ecology and economic anthropology. It is already clear that I have eschewed a naturalist perspective and, while I have undertaken to analyze the Achuar ecology, I will not be using biologists' techniques. I use the term ecology in its broadest meaning to designate the study of the relations obtaining between a community of living organisms and its environment. Employed as a shortcut, the word does not imply any affiliation on my part with the theoretical positions held by the proponents of geographic determinism, quite the contrary; one of my objects is to refute the reductionist theses of ecological anthropology. Moreover, considering the complexity of the problems encountered by biologists in studying symbiotic interactions on a tiny scale, it is evident that an ethnologist can hardly deal with the ecology of a whole human society in anything but an almost metaphorical form. The anthropological analysis of the relations between a society and its environment thus requires that two methodological precautions be observed. In the first place, the existence of many ecological chains of determination and the fact that they are tightly intertwined demands that great care be taken in the assignment of causes: the system of constraints an ecosystem is thought to exercise on the ways humans adapt can be elucidated only conditionally. But it must also be emphasized that the relations a society entertains with its environment are not univocal and cannot be conceived exclusively in terms of adaptive responses; ethnology's contribution to an ecological approach – in the broad sense of the term – consists rather in showing the creativity each culture brings to its manner of socializing nature.

If it is to fulfill its aim, such a project should consider those relations that people contract with one another in the process of production and reproduction, and especially those that organize the forms of access to resources and the way they are used; it should therefore encompass the entire sphere of social relations. I chose not to do this here for reasons of ease of exposition, not of principle. In order to justify my hypotheses and give the reader a chance to judge for him- or herself, I needed to make the ethnographic description of the intellectual and material techniques of utilizing nature as complete as possible. Therefore this did not seem the place to go into a serious analysis of Achuar social structure as well. In the interests of keeping the text to a reasonable length, I also decided to leave aside the description and analysis of the techniques used in producing certain artefacts, of which it may be said that they represent a later stage in the socialization of nature. Pottery manufacture, the weaving of cloth and baskets, and the fabrication of ornaments are complex activities, and their products are loaded with very rich and partially esoteric symbolic values; too hasty a treatment would not have done them justice.

This book is not really a monograph in economic anthropology, then, despite the detailed measurements it contains of both allocations of labor and returns of subsistence techniques. If the term economy is meant to designate that structure which combines, in a different way for each society, the system of energetic exchanges consciously organized within an ecosystem with the system of sociocultural devices which makes it possible to reproduce these flows, then it is clear that this work will be dealing primarily with the first term of the pair. The way the Achuar organize domestic production legitimizes the separation. Without being exactly autarkic, each isolated domestic unit nevertheless constitutes an autonomous center of production and consumption which depends on its social environment only to reproduce its labor power, renew some of its means of labor, and ensure the conditions of its access to natural resources. As households depend only minimally upon each other for the concrete process of socializing nature, it seemed justifiable provisionally to leave aside the supralocal social relations of production. In sum, although this book is a totality with a goal of its own, it is also the first stage of a vaster undertaking, the basis for a future analysis of the forms and conditions of social reproduction found in Achuar society.

Achuar and Jivaro: an illusory state of nature

The Achuar are one of the four dialect groups that make up the Jivaroan linguistic family (the others being the Shuar, the Aguaruna, and the Huambisa). With a population on the order of 80,000, the Jivaro are probably at present the largest culturally homogeneous indigenous nation in the Amazon Basin. Scattered throughout the forests covering the eastern foothills of southern Ecuador and northern Peru, they occupy a territory greater than that of Portugal, one endowed with a rich ecological diversity (Figs. 1 and 2). Prior to the Spanish conquest, the Jivaro held sway – linguistically at least – over an area larger than they do today, since it extended all the way to the Pacific coast (Descola and Taylor 1981). Within the Jivaro group, the Achuar represent a small bloc of some 4,500 individuals sprinkled along either side of the border between Ecuador and Peru (Fig. 3).

Although the popularity of shrunken heads in the West earned the Jivaro dubious fame, paradoxically the group remained little known to ethnologists. Of the huge number of publications devoted to the Jivaro over the past two centuries, we found only three monographs, during our exploratory study in 1974, that offered any appreciable guarantee of ethnographic diligence (Karsten 1935; Stirling 1938; Harner 1972); and two of these were written before the last World War. All three provide only sketchy information on the economic and social organization of the Jivaro groups. Finally, the verdict which, in 1945, concluded the review of Jivaro sources in the *Handbook of South American Indians* still seemed valid thirty years later: "Present needs include adequate studies of technology (which are now only partially available), clarification of social structure and function and of marriage practice through a genealogical approach, verification of the patterns of religion and shamanism, analysis of property rights, and study of agricultural methods" (*Handbook of South American Indians*, 3: 619). Harner's book on the Shuar, published in the interval, fell far short of filling in all the blanks, and those remaining thus provided a clear outline for a program of research.

Preliminary investigation revealed that, as of the early 1970s, the Achuar were the last of the Jivaro groups still to be spared the destructuring effects of Western contact. They maintained the most salient features of a traditional way of life, fast vanishing in the other dialect groups. Moreover, no description of the Achuar had ever been published; some urgent "salvage ethnography" seemed in order if one of the last unacculturated societies of the Amazon Basin was to become known.[3] The idea of gaining a more intimate understanding of these paradoxically little-known Jivaro, which first germinated in the remote calm of a library, eventually led us to share the Achuars' daily life for the better part of three consecutive years.[4]

The Achuar are a perfect synthesis of those enigmatic inclinations peculiar to many societies of Amazonian Indians. They are a near carica-ture of zero-degree social integration and the living illustration of the inadequacy of functionalist conceptual models to account for the facts of a society. The lack of those institutions that Africanists have taught us to regard as the sociological axes of classless societies – chiefdoms, village communities, unilineal descent groups – does not seem to hamper the Achuar to any degree. Internal conflict is permanent, but it does not follow

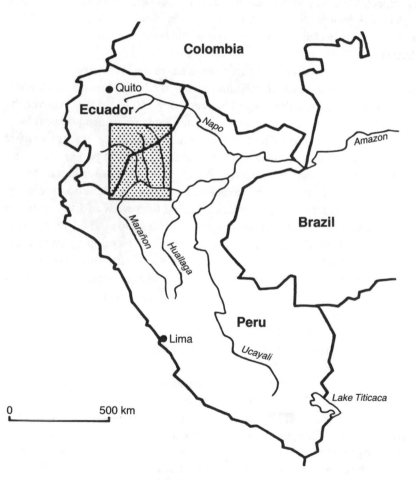

1. Location of the Jivaro Group in Upper Amazonia

the fine segmentary logic dear to ethnologists. In view of the extreme atomization of these quasi-autarkic households engaged in endemic feuding, it is obviously tempting to evoke the presocial condition in which, according to the well-known formula, "every man is Enemy to every man" (*Leviathan*, Everyman Library, 1970). It is with reference to a Hobbesian state of nature, then, that Chagnon proposes to interpret certain warlike societies, like the Jivaro or the Yanomami (1974: xi, 77). In the case of the Achuar, the state of generalized anomia is more apparent than real, however; and it can be reduced without risk of a philosophical misconstruction

In point of fact, their residential atomism is tempered by a supralocal structure for which the Jivaro have no name and which we will call the "endogamous nexus" (Descola 1982b). An endogamous nexus consists of from ten to fifteen households scattered over a relatively well-defined territory, whose members are closely and directly related by kinship and affinity. The concept of endogamous nexus has no formal existence in Achuar thought, unless it is as an echo of the prescriptive norm to marry "close to home" (both geographically and genealogically). Prescriptive marriage between bilateral cross-cousins reproduces the parents' and grandparents' marriages, following the classic Dravidian model (Dumont 1975; Kaplan 1975; Descola 1982b; Taylor 1983a). Polygyny, preferably sororal, is widespread; residence is strictly uxorilocal and levirate is systematic. Nexus are never completely endogamous, the highest rates of endogamy being found in those with the highest demographic density; many exogamous unions stem from the abduction of women in the course of raids on neighboring nexus.

The territorial axis of an endogamous nexus is the river or stretch of river whose name is used to designate all members of one nexus as being part of a geographic whole (e.g. *Kapawi shuar*, "the Rio Kapawi people"). Although the scattered households of a nexus are strung out, more or less uninterruptedly, along the river and its main tributaries, the territorial divisions between endogamous zones are fairly clear. There is generally a no-man's-land of at least a day's walk or canoe trip between adjacent nexus. The abstract unity of each nexus is thus based on territory and on the interlacing of ego-focused kindreds, but also on the sphere of influence of a great man or a pair of great men, most often two brothers-in-law who have exchanged sisters. The Achuar great man is a tried and tested warrior who, because of his ability to manipulate vast networks of alliances, is capable of organizing the offensive or defensive strategy of a nexus. He assumes a directive role only in times of conflict, and then in military matters alone; any allegiance to him is personal, temporary, and not codified by any institution. Moreover this war leader derives no particular economic or social advantages from his status, even though his fame generally enables him to capitalize prestige, making him much sought as a partner in trading networks. The great man is thought of as temporarily embodying the unity of a nexus and, by virtue of this, the territory he represents sometimes carries his name ("the land of X").

Serious conflicts within a nexus are rare; when one does break out, the opponents are often a native of the territory and a resident relative-by-marriage from another nexus. Usually ignited by a real or imaginary infraction of the marriage rules, this type of clash, individual at the outset, rapidly escalates into a conflict between nexus. The male affine returns to his kindred for help and protection, and spreads highly alarming rumors about the belligerent intentions of the nexus he has just left. The most frequent pretext for transforming a *casus belli* into declared war is a sudden death in one or another of the factions present, which is attributed to a shaman's attack. Indeed, Achuar shamans are credited with being able to kill from a distance, and their death-dealing capacities are often called upon in confrontations between nexus (Descola and Lory 1982). As the two sides recall more and more unpunished murders yet to be avenged, the shared responsibilities become inextricable. Both sides then launch a series of expeditions, the aim of which is to kill as many of the other side as they can.

When a conflict threatens to spread, the great men of each camp gather their factions into big fortified houses capable of sheltering up to six or seven domestic units. For the duration of the war, which can last up to two or three years, the assembled Achuar live in a state of siege, broken by periodic sorties into enemy territory. When the most deadly phase of the conflict is past, each unit regains its former place of residence. Whatever the outcome, a clear military victory of one nexus over the other does not imply territorial annexation. The object of armed conflict is therefore not local sovereignty. Achuar society lives in a perpetual state of war, and it is no doubt significant that their vocabulary has no term for peace; daily life swings between times of out-and-out warfare and periods of latent hostility. This endemic feuding has important demographic consequences, since something on the order of one out of every two male deaths can be attributed to war, as compared to one in five for women.

This rapid sketch of the Achuar sociological armature brings out the highly labile character of a system of social relations organized around factionalism and institutionalized feuding. Although it is periodically re-affirmed through "fortress life" and drinking parties, solidarity among close kin never takes the form of lasting segmentary identity. The nexus is but a warp into which is woven, as the cases arise, a fluid network of affinal solidarities and military alliances that can come unraveled at the slightest provocation. Even at the heart of the nexus everything contributes to keeping social life in a mild state of anarchy. Each man individually acquires the symbolic power to reproduce himself as a warrior, and is obliged to engage in an upward spiral of murders in order to preserve this power. Abstract kinship obligations do not always coincide with the prosaic necessities of war, and no man is ever sure he will not be treacherously assassinated by his classificatory brother or brother-in-law. A general climate of suspicion is maintained by the multiplication of shamans, strange healers whose ability to kill is reputedly as great as their ability to cure. In these circumstances, it is easy to see why the house is one of the rare poles of stability in an otherwise turbulent world; its central position in this book is a reflection of the role it plays in structuring Achuar society.

PART I

THE SPHERE OF NATURE

Down river on a balsa raft, Numpaimentza

Introduction I

The modern traveler who descends Ecuador's eastern cordillera towards the Amazonian reaches of the Rio Pastaza is following a trail opened at the beginning of the seventeenth century by Dominican missionaries en route to found Canelos, on the upper Rio Bobonaza. In place of the former mule path, he takes a dirt road that runs from Baños, the last little town in the Sierra before the Oriente, twisting and turning between the steep cliffs that wall the tumbling Pastaza. Water runs off the mountains and down the rutted road; a persistent fog hangs half-way up the slopes, masking the last ranks of the great forest that cling to the precipitous faces dominated by the volcano Tungurahua. This invisible world towering above the road is the *ceja de montaña*, lying at an altitude of between 2,000 and 3,500 meters, perpetually covered in clouds that roll in from Amazonia and pile up here against the cordillera. It was in this uninhabited area that expeditions used to come to gather cinchona bark, in the thick forest, rich with epiphytic plants but showing little stratification (Grubb *et al.* 1963: 596).

As the altitude falls, the approaching jungle increasingly gives signs of its impending presence: a mild, damp heat replaces the dry air of the high plateaux, the croaking of frogs provides a basso continuo, and a faint odor of rotting organic matter hangs in the air. As he follows the gorge of the Pastaza, the traveler scarcely notices that he is crossing the *montaña*, the humid forest zone adjacent to the *ceja*, which forms a continuous band covering the better part of the Andean foothills. According to Hegen's typology of Upper Amazonian forest zones, the 2,000 to 1,000 meter belt is characterized by montaña; this band forms a transition zone between the ceja and the *hylea*, the true Amazonian forest (Hegen 1966: 18–19). The montaña thus corresponds approximately to what Grubb and Whitmore, in their classification of vegetation zones of the Ecuadorian Oriente (Grubb and Whitmore 1966: 303) call "lower montane forest." The central portion of the Ecuadorian foothills is mountainous, with sharply rising ridges cut by narrow straight-sided valleys that gradually subside into a huge alluvial fan. Rainfall is high and diminishes with the altitude, falling from an annual mean of more than 5,000 mm in the foothills proper to 4,412 mm at Puyo (elevation 990 m). The montaña forest is more stratified and diversified than the ceja, but the trees do not grow to more than 30 meters (Acosta-Solis 1966: 407).

Rounding a bend, the steep Pastaza canyon comes to an abrupt end, and the traveler discovers a broad, gently rolling green plain stretching to the horizon. This will be his only chance to glimpse a panoramic view of the hylea, the tropical rain forest that covers most of the Amazon Basin, reaching from an altitude of 1,000 meters in the foothills of the Andes all the way to the Atlantic shore. This stretch of the Pastaza still flows swiftly, sweeping logs down through impressive whirlpools; but once free of the constraining cliffs, it sprawls out into a multitude of branches separated by pebble beaches and small bamboo-covered islands. There where it surges into the Amazon forest, the Pastaza is too dangerous for canoes, and so the Dominicans took to land in order to break a trail directly to the upper Rio Bobonaza, the only eastward-flowing river navigable from its headwaters.

Today's road follows the old missionary trail, at least as far as the town of Puyo, where it comes to an end. Situated at an altitude of some 1,000 meters, that is at the limit between hylea and montaña, Puyo is the capital of the province of Pastaza and the bustling center for would-be traders from the Amazonian hinterland. This big little town where the majority of houses are still built of wood has, in the past thirty years, become the site of large-scale spontaneous colonization by migrants from the Ecuadorian Sierra. Based on extensive stockraising, the settlement frontier forms a continuous band of cleared land that is gradually advancing eastward, driving before it the Quichua populations of the forest (Canelos Indians or *sacha runa*), who, during the first half of the century, had settled in the vicinity of Puyo, occupied until then exclusively by the Jivaro.

If the traveler continues on foot along the old Dominican Trail in the direction of Canelos, he will eventually leave the grazing areas and engage in a sea of low, rounded hills covered in thick forest. His eastward progress now takes him through a region typical of the upper Amazon Basin interfluve. At this altitude (between 500 and 600 meters), the temperature is never excessive, but the rugged terrain makes walking difficult, a hardship augmented by the many small streams that cut the path and which must be forded on foot. At last the trail comes to an end at the Canelos mission, built on a broad esplanade overlooking the tranquil course of the Bobonaza. Canelos is the name of the mission station itself, the exact location of which has varied over the centuries, but it has come to designate the Quichua Indians living in the area. The Dominicans had named their mission after a tree extremely common in the region (*Nectandra cinnamonoides*, in Quichua: *ishpingu*), whose dried flowers taste exactly like cinnamon bark.

Downstream from Canelos, the Bobonaza is easily navigable and is used as the main line of communication by the Quichua Indians who live along its banks between Canelos and the other side of the Montalvo mission. Despite the many nearly circular meanders that make the descent interminable, the river is free of rapids and dangerous whirlpools. From the second half of the seventeenth century, the Bobonaza served the occasional contacts between the Canelos region and the middle course of the Pastaza, where the Jesuit missionaries from Maynas had established a small number of "reductions." Beyond, the Bobonaza shortcut provided access to the Marañon Basin – at that time under the jurisdiction of the Audiencia of Quito – and thereby to the Amazon catchment. But until the end of the eighteenth century, navigation on the Bobonaza remained the preserve of a handful of particularly stout-hearted Jesuit and Dominican missionaries, sometimes accompanied by a civilian or military escort.

The Bobonaza region was largely spared the effects of the rubber boom of the second half of the nineteenth century, which devastated the native populations of the upper Amazon. The center of extraction lay north and northeast of the Bobonaza, around Curaray and Villano. The Zaparo Indians, who inhabited the region at that time, bore the direct brunt of the horrors of forced labor and were almost entirely exterminated. At this time, with the exception of the Dominican missionaries, the only people on the Bobonaza were a few traveling merchants (*regatones*), who traded with the Canelos Indians. The river was also used periodically by Ecuadorian soldiers sent out to relieve the tiny malaria-ridden frontier posts on the Pastaza. But Ecuador's nominal jurisdiction over these remote territories was especially difficult to maintain. The Peruvians, on the other hand, controlled the Marañon river system and regularly piloted their small steamboats up the Santiago, Morona, Pastaza, and Tigre rivers into the territories north of the Marañon, over which Ecuador did not have the means to ensure its sovereignty.

By 1941, Peru had eaten its way so far into Ecuador's territory that war broke out between the two countries, enabling Peru to annex a large portion of Ecuadorian Amazonia, which it had already partially infiltrated. The *fait accompli* was ratified by the 1942 Protocol of Rio de Janeiro, which shifted the border between the two countries some three hundred kilometers to the north, northwest of the Rio Marañon. Although it was subsequently declared invalid by Ecuador, the Protocol did actually establish a border, manifested by the presence of military detachments from the two sides along the principal rivers. This border now impedes any official passage on the Pastaza beyond its junction with the Bobonaza; the former direct access to the Marañon via the Bobonaza and the Pastaza is thus, for the time being, blocked by a political barrier. And it appears to be a serious one, not likely to be dismantled in the near future if the regular skirmishes between the two armed forces along their respective Amazonian borders are any indication.

From the end of the nineteenth century until the Second World War, the Bobonaza was also traveled by a small number of explorers, naturalists, and ethnographers, some of whom continued down the Pastaza to the Marañon. They have left a few picturesque descriptions of their canoe trips, notably the accounts of Abbé Pierre (1889: 19–154), Bertrand Flornoy (1953) and Rafael Karsten (1935: 21–47). But none ever ventured into the region bounded by the south bank of the Bobonaza, which remained *terra incognita* until the late 1960s. If he had a taste for adventure, then, our traveler could continue on his way from Canelos, choosing a different route from that taken by his predecessors. Rather than descending the Bobonaza to its junction with the Pastaza, he could haul his canoe onto the bank at the end of the second day of navigation and plunge directly into the forest, in a southerly direction. He would come to a plateau covered in thick jungle and incised by numerous clearwater rivers coursing through steep, narrow gorges. After four days of hiking up and down a succession of steep climbs and descents, he would emerge onto the alluvial plain of the Pastaza, far upstream from its confluence with the Bobonaza. Striding down an abrupt rim of some thirty meters, our traveler would suddenly discover an entirely different landscape from the one he had so recently been crossing.

The rugged hills of the interfluvial forest are supplanted by dry arms of the river, which form a network of pebble-strewn avenues along which white egrets serenely stalk. Impenetrable stands of giant bamboo arrayed in ramparts edge beaches of black sand. Progress is often slowed by the large swamps that must be crossed by wading through black, stagnant water. These permanently flooded depressions are almost entirely covered in a peculiar type of vegetation: colonies of *Mauritia flexuosa* palms, variously called *aguaje*, in the upper Amazon, and *moriche*, in Venezuela. By derivation, the swamps in which the palms grow are known in Spanish as *aguajal* or *morichal*; they constitute a biotope typical of the riverine zones and deltas of the Amazon and Orinoco Basins. Standing on a small rise at the edge of a marsh or on a river terrace, our traveler will notice here and there large oval-shaped houses surrounded by manioc gardens. If he happens to know that the Jivaro name for the marsh palm is *achu*, he will understand why these Indians of the *aguajales* call themselves *achu shuar*, "the people of the *aguaje* palm" or more often, by the contracted form, *achuar*.

1

The territorial space

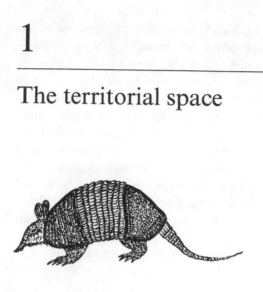

The Achuar inhabit a huge territory in the heart of upper Amazonia covering two degrees of latitude (from 1° 40′ south to 3° 30′ south) and more than the same number of degrees of longitude (between 75° and 77° 30′ west). The northwest–southeast diagonal is formed by the Rio Pastaza, from its junction with the Rio Copataza some fifty kilometers to the east of the first foothills of the Andean cordillera to where it joins the Rio Huasaga two hundred and fifty kilometers further south (Fig. 2). The Achuar zone is bounded on the north by the Rio Pindo Yacu, which becomes the Rio Tigre after its confluence with the Rio Conambo at the Peruvian border. Where it comes into Peru and down to its junction with the Rio Corrientes, the Tigre is the eastern limit of Achuar expansion. The western boundary is set by the Copataza, to the north of the Pastaza, it then curves south along the southern bank of the Rio Bobonaza, as far as the Montalvo mission, where it again turns north along the seventy-seventh parallel to the Rio Pindo Yacu. South of the Pastaza, the western boundary is defined by the Rio Macuma, until its confluence with the Rio Morona, then by the latter to where it is joined by the Rio Anasu. Slightly west of the Macuma, a large tectonic fault running north–south for more than sixty kilometers creates an abrupt drop of some one hundred meters; this fault is traditionally regarded as the natural boundary between the Shuar Jivaro, to the west, and the Achuar Jivaro, to the east. No natural boundary defines the southern limit of the Achuar zone of expansion; but it can be visualized as an imaginary east–west line connecting Lake Anatico to the Morona at the point where it joins the Anasu.

The Achuar region is drained by an immense river system, then; the whole hydrographic network slowly works its way downhill from northwest to south-southeast, where it feeds into the Marañon. The altitude gradually decreases as one goes east, dropping from 500 meters in the western part of the territory to under 200 meters in the Marañon Basin. With the exception of the upper Bobonaza valley and the land lying between the upper reaches of the Macuma and the Huasaga, mean elevations are almost always under 300 meters.

But the Achuar did not always inhabit so vast a territory, and their present expansion is the product of important historical movements that have repeatedly affected upper Amazonia since the sixteenth century (on this subject, see Taylor 1993, Chaps 3–5). At present, however, and no doubt due to their reputation for ferociousness in war, played up in the popular media of Ecuador and Peru, the Achuar have this gigantic region almost entirely to themselves. Unlike the Shuar Jivaro in Ecuador or the Aguaruna Jivaro in Peru, at no point do they have any direct contact with a solid frontier of colonization. In this territory nearly the size of Belgium, the Achuar population in 1977 numbered approximately 4,500 individuals. In Ecuador the total Achuar population at the same time was around 2,000; the figure was slightly higher for Peru: some 2,500 individuals, according to the census taken in 1971 by the Summer Institute of Linguistics and updated on the basis of an annual growth rate of 3% (Ross 1976: 17). Achuar country is a sort of human wasteland, then, few the likes of which still exist elsewhere in Amazonia. Scattered as they are over this immense void, the Achuar seem unaware that they may one day have to share their territory with invaders. Yet the insidious encroachment of outside elements around the edges and along the main navigable waterways becomes more noticeable with each passing year.

Around the northwestern, southern and northeastern edges, the forest-dwelling Quichua populations, who have long occupied the adjacent territory, are now penetrating deeper and deeper into Achuar lands and settling there (Fig. 2). The result is bi-ethnic population zones in which the settlement sites are either completely integrated (e.g. on the upper Conambo) or ethnically separated but quite close together (on the upper Corrientes in Ecuador and the upper Tigre in Peru). The pluri-ethnic concoction found along the northwestern edge of the Achuar territory is a very old phenomenon in its own right, since the Canelos Indians are one

such composite group, comprised more particularly of gradually transcul-
turated Achuar and Zaparo elements. Behind the ethnogenesis of this
heterogenous group of refugees turned Quichua-speakers under Dominican influence, is an ongoing process of assimilation of alien populations.
After the extinction of the Zaparo as a separate ethnic entity, the integration continued with the step-by-barely-perceptible-step transculturation

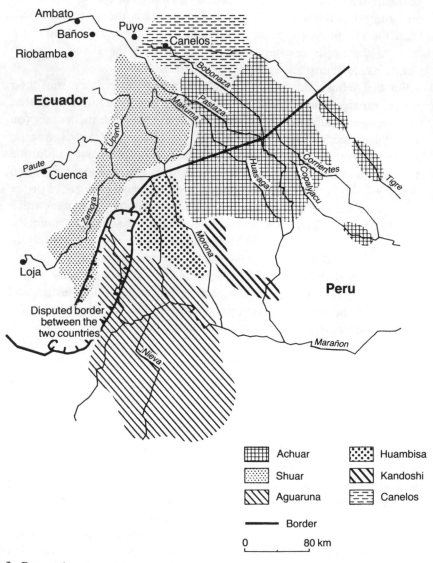

2. Present location of Jivaroan dialect groups

of those Achuar living in contact with the Canclos. Thus, along the upper Conambo, the upper Corrientes, and the upper Copataza, nearly all Achuar speak both Achuar and Quichua.[1]

Moreover, the Canelos Indians have long been the right arm of the Ecuadorian army when it comes to establishing posts in the center of the Amazonian territory. Faced with what it saw as Peru's expansionist designs, the Ecuadorian army decided, in the early seventies, to send small detachments of soldiers to this border zone inhabited by the Achuar and until then devoid of any military presence. As they were unable to make contact with the Achuar – whom they regarded at any rate as savages and to be avoided – the army used Canelos Quichua in organizing the infrastructure of these border posts. From the soldiers' point of view, the Canelos Indians offered the advantage of knowing the forest and, at the same time, speaking Spanish; they also appeared to be docile, the result of decades of continual interaction with the whites. Entrenched in these little posts linked by plane with the foothill garrisons, the soldiers depended entirely on the Quichua for everything to do with the surrounding environment. Each detachment of soldiers was thus encircled by a half-dozen Canelos Quichua families, who served as guides, boat pilots, purveyors of fish and game, manual labor for the construction and upkeep of the landing strips, and so on. In 1977 there were four military establishments of this type on Achuar land, each of which acted as a pole of attraction for little colonies of Canelos. This as yet larval migration is due in great part to the eastward progress of the frontier of pastoral colonization from the vicinity of Puyo. Driven from their lands by the settlers, some Quichua are seeking refuge in the forest, on Achuar lands, as far as possible from the whites.

A similar situation prevails on the western edge of the Achuar's territory, also under heavy pressure from another expanding native group, the Shuar Jivaro (Fig. 2). Over the last thirty years or so, the latter have seen their best lands in the Rio Upano valley gradually occupied by colonists arriving from the Sierra. There, too, the development of the pastoral colonization frontier has generated an eastward flow of native migration: some Shuar are now seriously contemplating settling east of the Macuma, which has until now been the inviolable dividing line between the two dialect groups. Furthermore, in 1964, the Shuar formed a Federation which has gradually become the most important native organization of its kind among the Amerindians of the South American lowlands (on this subject, see Descola 1982b; Salazar 1977; Santana 1978). With a praiseworthy concern for ethnic oecumenicalism, the Shuar invited the Achuar – despite their hereditary enmity – to join the Federation. In the triangle of Achuar territory defined by the Pastaza, the Macuma, and the border with Peru, a number of households regrouped into semi-villages, designated as *centros*, thereby benefiting from the services offered by the Federation and, in particular, bilingual educational programs taught by Shuar instructors. These generally very young men exhibit every sign of a prestigious acculturation: flashy clothes, transistor radios, fluent Spanish. In the eyes of the non-acculturated Achuar, the bachelors constitute highly desirable sons-in-law. And so these young Shuar instructors tend to stay on and found a family with a local Achuar girl. In so doing, they earn the right to establish themselves near their father-in-law, according to the logic of uxorilocality common to both Shuar and Achuar (Descola 1982b). Such a settlement mechanism would have still been unthinkable in the late 1960s, when any Shuar who ventured into Achuar territory was, *ipso facto*, risking his life.

Last of all, still on the western edge of the Achuar area, two mini-centers of continually expanding colonization could, in the long run, spill over onto Achuar land. In effect, at Taisha and San José de Morona, the Ecuadorian army has built large military garrisons with landing strips big enough to accommodate large planes. Taking advantage of this means of communication in a region that has no roads, several dozen white and mestizo families have settled in Taisha and Morona in order to farm cattle under the protection of the army. These centers of colonization are, in all likelihood, bound to expand in the years to come, since the soldiers – ever wary of the Achuar – would like to stabilize the border with Peru by establishing a permanent cordon of non-native settlements.

In the Peruvian portion of their territory, the Achuar's neighbors to the west, along the Rio Morona, are the Huambisa. Until the end of the 1950s, most of the Huambisa lived even further west, in the Companquiz cordillera; but since then, pressed by missionary organizations, they have colonized the upper Morona (Ross 1976: 20–1). Between the last Huambisa dwellings on the Morona and the first Achuar settlements along the eastern tributaries of this river lies a sort of forest no-man's-land some thirty kilometers wide. But, as in the case of the Shuar Jivaro and the Canelos, intermarriage between Huambisa and Achuar has become common practice along the edges of the two territories.

The Peruvian Achuar lands abut, in the south, on those of the Candoshi Indians, an ethnic group of around a thousand members whose language is unintelligible to the Achuar (unlike Shuar and Huambisa, two dialects of the Jivaro family). The Candoshi live along the lower tributaries of the Pastaza and Huasaga and around Lake Anatico and Laguna Rimachi (Amadio and d'Emilio 1982: 1). There are also a few communities of Shapra

Indians, close relatives of the Candoshi, living along the middle course of the Morona, to the southeast of the Huambisa. No doubt due to the linguistic barrier, the Achuar seem to have fewer contacts with the Candoshi-Shapra Indians than with their other native Jivaro- or Quichua-speaking neighbors. And so the Achuar's immediate neighbors, in both Ecuador and Peru, are other indigenous groups, generally more acculturated and thereby serving as relays for the spread of Western influence (Descola and Taylor 1977).

The penetration of non-native elements is more emphatic in the Peruvian part of the Achuar territory than on the Ecuadorian side. In the first place, the army has established small detachments of soldiers, as in Ecuador, with a view to stabilizing the border. The Peruvian soldiers adopt the same attitude towards the Achuar as their Ecuadorian counterparts: they live in complete autarky within their border posts and refrain from intervening in the life of the indigenous communities (Ross 1976: 54–6). In neither country does the presence of military detachments inside Achuar territory seem to have a major effect on the Indians' daily life. As their function is essentially to affirm their respective sovereignties through their symbolic presence, Ecuadorian and Peruvian soldiers usually avoid becoming involved in feuds. For the Achuar, the border is permeable in both directions, then, and, except when it coincides with the major rivers, is a border in name only. If they are careful to avoid certain stretches of the Huasaga and Pastaza, they can circulate perfectly well without ever encountering a military patrol.

There is, however, among the Peruvian Achuar, a very old form of non-indigenous settlement that has no parallel among the Achuar of Ecuador. This institution is known as the *patrones*. The *patrón* is a white or mestizo trader who leases a sort of logging concession (*habilitación*) that he runs in part with the help of native labor. Each patrón exercises his activity on one river or well-marked stretch of water, and his influence extends to all Achuar living within his sphere of control. The system is founded on voluntary but unequal exchange, the Achuar providing the patrón with rough timber (notably *cedro*: *Cedrela* sp., and *lupuna*: *Ceiba pentandra*), in order to pay off debts occasioned by advances of manufactured goods (shotguns, machetes, axes, knives, cartridges. . .). Practically speaking, the debt is never cancelled, since it is constantly reactivated by new advances. Trading in pelts is one of the patrones' subsidiary activities, but unlike logging, the Peruvian Achuar do not hunt skins as an independent labor process. They merely kill the desired animals (ocelot, peccary, otter, caiman) if they chance upon them while hunting or trekking.[2]

The main reason for the near century-long presence on the Peruvian side of Achuar territory of a mini-frontier of extraction is the ease with which their territory is accessible from a major river, the Marañon, by way of its highly navigable tributaries. This is also part of the reason why the border between the two countries is where it is today;[3] during the 1941 war, Peruvian soldiers pushed upstream until the rivers became unnavigable. Correlatively, the Ecuadorian Achuar found themselves protected from Western penetration because the waterways crossing their territory were inaccessible to navigation, both from downstream in Peru and from upstream in the Andes. The little town of Andoas, which has stood on the upper course of the Pastaza since the eighteenth century, symbolizes this non-indigenous infiltration into what is now the Peruvian part of Achuar territory (Taylor 1993, Chap. 4). Nevertheless, the number of white and mestizo settlers in Andoas was never very high and, in 1961, only some sixty remained (Ross 1976: 63).

International economy also penetrates the Achuar's territory in the form of big multinationals that come in search of oil. Ecuador has long been the site of oil exploration, dating from before the Second World War, when the Shell company opened a drilling operation at Taisha and built an air strip, which now serves the military post. But the results were inconclusive, and the drilling, in the 1970s, by the American company Amoco, north of the Bobonaza in Ecuador, was just as unrewarding. Most of the exploration was conducted outside Achuar territory or around the perimeter.

The search for oil was longer in coming to the Peruvian sector, but also more disruptive for the Indians; for, unlike what happened in Ecuador, the exploration was carried out in the very heart of Achuar lands. By 1974, the Petty Geophysical Company had already "shot" over 3,500 km of seismic lines, for the most part in the zone situated between the Huasaga and the Pastaza (Ross 1976: 85). Fortunately for the Achuar, these trials turned out as disappointingly as they had on the Ecuadorian side, and it now seems probable that no oil wells will be drilled on their lands.

It was only because the Indians had been partially "pacified" by the missionaries by the late 1960s that Achuar lands themselves (in Peru) or the perimeter of their territory (in Ecuador) could be explored for oil. This means that, if the oil companies left few traces of their fleeting passage, the effects of their evangelical correlate, on the contrary, will be felt for some time to come. In Peru, it is the Protestant missionaries from the Summer Institute of Linguistics (SIL) who, with their customary efficiency, have taken in hand the Achuar's "pacification." It is true that this job was facilitated by longstanding commercial transactions between the Achuar and the patrones, which had accustomed the Indians of this region to interacting with non-natives. The SIL used a technique derived from the antique *reducciones*, a classic tactic used by missionaries when confronted with highly mobile, widely dispersed native populations. To persuade the Achuar to settle in one place, the SIL encouraged them to form small communities, semi-villages, concentrated around landing strips served by the organization's planes. The missionaries do not themselves live with the Achuar, but in a station at the edge of the territory, on the lower Huasaga (Ross 1976: 81). From this base, they make regular visits to the Achuar communities, gradually establishing commercial exchange circuits, which tend to replace those controlled by the patrones and the regatones (river traders). As a consequence, the Peruvian merchants' influence over the Achuar seems to be declining while the ascendency of the SIL missionaries grows (Elke Mader: pers. commun.). Their hold is far from complete, though, and many isolated Peruvian Achuar remain hostile to the presence of the SIL.

Among the Ecuadorian Achuar, missionary penetration has taken other, somewhat different forms. In the first place, unlike their Peruvian brothers, who have long lived side by side with the patrones, the Achuar of Ecuador, for all intents and purposes, refused non-natives access to their territory until the late 1960s. It was not until somewhere between 1968 and 1970 that Catholic and Protestant missionaries were able to establish the first stable, peaceful contacts. Two rival missionary organizations were vying in their attempts to evangelize the Jivaro: the Salesians, whose presence among the Shuar Jivaro dates back to the end of the nineteenth century; and the American Protestants from the Gospel Missionary Union (GMU), also established in Shuar territory, at Macuma, since the 1940s.

Over and beyond any theological disagreements, the ideology, methods, and "style" of the two groups are profoundly dissimilar (on this subject, see Taylor 1981). From the outset, the Protestants from the GMU, like their SIL counterparts, disposed of a well-established infrastructure (single-engine planes, radio communications), and this influenced their approach to the Achuar. Some time around the early 1960s, a fleeting contact was made which resulted in the construction of an airstrip next to the house of Santiak, the first Ecuadorian Achuar to have accepted the missionary presence (Drown and Drown 1961). But Santiak, a well-known war leader, was soon assassinated in a raid, and relations between the Achuar and the Protestant missionaries were broken off. It was not until the early 1970s that the latter managed once more to penetrate the Achuar territory, with the help of Shuar Jivaro evangelists. Their "pacification" techniques were those of the SIL: concentrate isolated households into sedentary semi-villages laid out around a landing strip and bring in converted Shuar instructors to conduct a program of alphabetization and indoctrination. Some of the semi-villages have been provided with a few head of cattle, the meat being marketed on the colonization frontier by the missionaries, thanks to their aircraft. But the American missionaries continue to live at their station in Macuma and visit the Achuar communities in their precinct only about once a year.

The technique initially employed by the Salesians for gaining acceptance by the Achuar community affords a striking contrast with GMU methods. Towards the beginning of the 1960s, a new generation of young Italian missionaries began to question the highly conservative approach of their elders. Rejecting the traditional method of evangelization that had been used on the Shuar since the beginning of the century, the "young Turks" advocated delegating political and religious responsibility to the Indians themselves and participating with them in the sometimes violent struggle against the encroaching settlement frontier. It was during this period that the Federación de Centros Shuar was created under the auspices of the Salesian mission. The new method implied that the missionaries involve themselves more closely in the daily life of the Shuar instead of barricading themselves into their missions and their boarding schools redolent of paternalism (Bottasso 1980).

It was by putting these precepts into practice that, at the end of the 1960s, Father Bolla finally won acceptance by the Achuar at Wichim. It was to his advantage that he had a reasonable command of Shuar Jivaro and, above all, that he identified with the Achuar to the extent of adopting their way of dress and covering hundreds of kilometers on foot to preach the gospel in remote regions where the Indians had probably never seen a white man. In contrast to the considerable technological means employed by the Protestants, this itinerant style of evangelization did not upset the traditional Achuar life style. The results obtained by Father Bolla were hardly conclusive, though: despite the missionary's objurations, the Achuar, as in the past, went on feuding (Arnalot 1978).

At some point in the mid-1970s this situation was to undergo an abrupt change. By this time the Federación de Centros Shuar had grown to considerable size, numbering among its members the near total non-Protestant Shuar population of Ecuador (Federación de Centros Shuar 1976). Like the Protestant missionaries, the Federación Shuar and the Salesians had come around to the practice of encouraging the formation of *centros*, those sedentary semi-villages built around a landing strip and organized into cooperatives. With the help of Catholic missionaries and

Ecuadorian laymen, the Federación had even set up a domestic air link served by two small one-engine planes, thereby entering into direct competition with the Protestant monopoly in this domain. And so, although their goals were entirely different, the Federación Shuar and the Salesians had, in the end, come to adopt the same techniques (planes and radios) and the same spatial disposition (sedentary semi-villages) as the GMU. It is in this new context that, around 1975, the leaders of the Federación Shuar and their Salesian advisers envisaged allowing the Achuar into the Federación. The itinerant ministrations of the early days no longer seemed sufficient, and the Achuar were invited to regroup into sedentary semi-villages, served by airplanes and affiliated with the Federación. As we saw earlier, the implantation of the Federación on Achuar territory was accompanied by an initial influx of Shuar migrants, acculturated Shuar with a tendency to think that the theoretical membership of all Jivaro-speakers in one "native nation" partially abolished internal territorial boundaries between dialect groups.

This brief overview of the Achuar social environment provides a fair indication of the wide variety of local situations coexisting within the territory. Between 1976 and 1979, we were able to discern some four sectors, each defined by a distinct mode of interaction between Achuar and adjacent indigenous or non-indigenous social groups. The first major division between internal sectors is the national boundary separating Ecuador and Peru. Of course this boundary is relatively permeable to the Achuar, and so they do not suffer from the presence of the soldiers defending the two sides. But if it is only a nominal reality for the Achuar, for all those, ethnologists included, who do not want to incur the risks of a clandestine crossing, it is very real. In other terms, and for the geographical reasons we have already reviewed, the sort of symbiotic balance between Achuar and patrones that has long existed in the Peruvian sector has never spilled over onto the Ecuadorian side. The Peruvian Achuar are alone in having undergone the very special form of selective acculturation engendered by the practice of a market system. Their articulation with an international market by way of the controlled production of commodities has had no effect on the most obvious aspects of traditional life (dress, architecture, kinship system, feuding. . .). But it has had noteworthy consequences for certain fundamental elements of economic life that are the object of this study (transformation of the nature and the duration of labor input, of technology, of habitats). Conversely, the Achuar living in the Ecuadorian sector remained on the fringe of this mini-frontier of extraction, and so the ways they adapted to their environment were unchanged by the demands of small-scale market production. It is largely for this reason that we decided to conduct our study in this sector rather than among their Peruvian neighbors; but the existence of the national border played its part by forcing us to choose sides from the outset.

The other three sectors of interaction all lie within the Ecuadorian part of Achuar territory; henceforth we will be speaking of this part only (Fig. 3). These sectors can be defined basically by the type and intensity of the relations the Achuar entertained locally with missionary organizations in

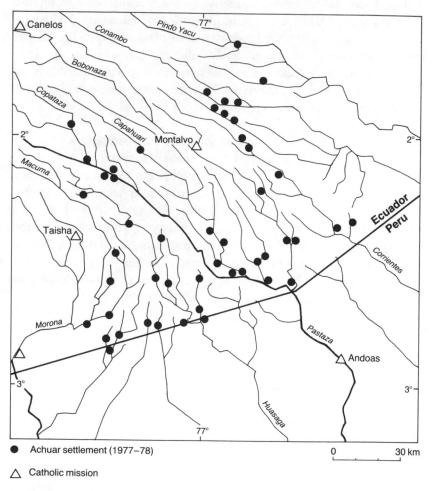

● Achuar settlement (1977–78)   0   30 km

△ Catholic mission

— Border

3. Achuar territory in Ecuador: map of human settlements

1977: relations with the Salesians and the Federación de Centros Shuar, relations with the American Protestant evangelists, and total absence of relations with whites. If we make a distinction between the two missionary organizations here, it is because the goals of their work among the Achuar are very different (Taylor 1981). In the case of the Federación Shuar and the Salesians, there is an effort to bring about the same type of conscious integration of the Achuar into the national society as was obtained earlier among the Shuar. But integration does not mean assimilation, and the education and health programs that have been set up respect traditional Achuar values. In fact, these programs have been developed by Shuar who, though highly acculturated – and sometimes even university graduates – still belong to the same cultural and linguistic community as the Achuar.

GMU missionaries take a radically different stance. Their somewhat primary fundamentalism admits of no other method of evangelization than total deculturation and the eradication of all elements of the traditional culture that they perceive as "satanic" (polygyny, shamanism, native religion, feuding...). Paradoxically, this position of principle is so ethnocidal that it moves the Achuar to only superficial conversion, a façade that they don for the rare visits of the American missionaries. As soon as the latter have gone home to their remote bases, traditional "satanic" life resumes its course. The corollary of this paradox is that the "soft" assimilation practiced by the Federación Shuar and the Salesians results in a much more efficient acculturation of the Achuar, since it is conducted very intelligently in the form of insidious but deliberate syncretism.

In 1977 the missionaries' respective sectors of influence were separated by the Rio Pastaza: the Achuar to the south fell to the Salesians and the Federación Shuar (with the exception of two small isolated Protestant centers), while the American missionaries reigned supreme north of the Pastaza. But this dichotomy of sectors of influence and methods of acculturation must not be allowed to mask the objective convergence of the Federación Shuar and the Catholic and Protestant organizations on the new means of organizing Achuar settlements. As we have seen, the establishment of missions results in the relocation of traditionally dispersed households into semi-villages, *centros*, concentrated around airstrips cleared by the Indians. The term "semi-village" was chosen because only three or four houses are usually built next to the landing strip, the others being in more remote spots, sometimes two or three kilometers from the *centro*. Moreover, in 1975, the Federación Shuar and the GMU missionaries began a program of cattle raising in the Achuar *centros* of their respective zones of influence. Although the experiment was in its early stages at the time we began our study, in the long run this small-scale pastoral production threatened the Achuar with economic, ecological, and social upheavals, the first signs of which were already showing (see Taylor 1981; Descola 1981a,b; 1982a,b).

In 1977 five Achuar *centros* were affiliated with the Federación Shuar, all south of the Pastaza (Pumpuentza, Makinentza, Wichim, Ipiakentza, and Wampuik). Their respective populations were between over a hundred individuals (Pumpuentza) to under fifteen (Wampuik). Only two (Pumpuentza and Wichim) had any cattle. At the same time, the Protestant missionaries controlled eight Achuar *centros* (two south of the Pastaza: Mashumar and Surikentza; and six to the north: Copataza, Capahuari, Bufeo, Conambo, Corrientes, and Sasaime), three of which (Copataza, Capahuari, and Sasaime) had already received some cattle. At the time of our fieldwork, slightly fewer than three quarters of the two thousand Ecuadorian Achuar had been affected by the nucleation of their settlements into *centros*. In some cases, the process was not yet completed, and the airstrip itself had not been cleared. In other cases, as at Bufeo, Sasaime, Surik, or Wampuik, the *centros* comprised no more than five households scattered over a radius of two kilometers, and therefore did not constitute a form of settlement radically different from the traditional system of dispersal in which three or four houses might decide to associate for a time. However, in *centros* dating from the early 1970s, like Pumpuentza or Capahuari, the concentration could reach up to ten households, that is, a much higher density than was usually found in normal settlement sites immediately prior to white contact.

Whatever may be the case and the density of their population, these *centros* differ from the traditional mode of settlement in one essential point: their sedentary character. Indeed, for the Achuar, clearing a small landing strip with the rudimentary tools at their disposal (axes and machetes) implies such an investment of labor that the families responsible for the undertaking are very likely to remain in the vicinity. Thus the landing strip imposes a constraint of sedentariness, which is more or less flexible, since the houses and gardens can still be moved within a radius of a few kilometers of the airstrip. This semi-sedentary existence contrasts with traditional forms of territorial occupation characterized by the periodic relocation of dwellings (every ten to fifteen years, on average). And so even though, in 1977, most of the Achuar *centros* numbered only a handful of households, had no cattle, and saw a white man only once a year, they already constituted a pattern of human settlement different from the traditional norm. The new pattern of settlement in *centros* is not without consequences for our study since it introduces an outside constraint – sedentariness – into the system of relations the Achuar entertain with their environment. Even if this constraint does not affect many aspects of the indigenous process of learning about and transforming nature, it is nevertheless a limiting factor which could distort the analysis. And since we chose to exclude from our present study the diachronic phenomena of the Achuar's transition (the broad lines of this analysis have already been published by A-C. Taylor and myself: Taylor 1981; Descola 1981a,b; 1982a,b), it was only fitting that we clearly identify the external variables that could influence the aboriginal system of adaptation to the environment. This is why we decided to collect our data on the traditional economy within the fourth sector, the one in which, aside from the introduction of metal tools, the Achuar mode of production has remained practically untouched by Western influence.

This sector, which had not yet been penetrated by missionary organizations in 1977, was located primarily north of the Pastaza, that is in the American Protestant nominal zone of influence. In this region, where GMU missionaries had already established five Achuar *centros*, some fifty households still lived in dispersed settlements, scattered far from the *centros* over a vast, underpopulated territory. It is almost exclusively in this part of the zone of Achuar expansion, drained by the Rio Pastaza and its tributaries to the north, as far as the Rio Pindo Yacu, that we conducted our fieldwork. For everything concerning the settlement sites, then, the ethnographic present refers to 1977, the year we conducted an exhaustive census of the Achuar living in this area.

Within an overall area of 12,000 km² occupied by the Ecuadorian Achuar, our sector, which lies north of the Pastaza, constitutes the largest region, with an area of some 9,000 km² (including the Pastaza Basin). In this immense expanse live 1,110 Achuar, compared with 900 in the zone south of the Pastaza (A. Colajanni, pers. commun.), or nearly the same population for a territory three times the size. Of these 1,110 individuals, around half live in the five *centros* of Protestant obedience (Capahuari, Copataza, Conambo, Bufeo, and Corrientes); the other half are strung along the banks of the Pastaza, on the lower Kapawientza and Ishpinku, on the lower Corrientes and its tributaries, the lower Bobonaza and its tributaries, the mid-Conambo and its tributaries, the mid-Pindo Yacu and its tributaries, and the upper Copataza.[4]

Looking at this brief description of the Achuar settlement pattern, one cannot help being struck by one remarkable feature: the extremely low population figure for the expanse of territory. In Ecuador, some two thousand Achuar are scattered over an area greater than Corsica; even if we add fifty or so Canelos and Shuar Indians having recently infiltrated the region, the general population density is still very low, on the order of 0.17 persons/km^2, which is a little less than two Achuar per 10 km^2.[5] Such a low density is unusual for an indigenous population in the Amazon Basin; it is, for example, one seventh the estimate advanced by Harner for the Shuar Jivaro (1.2 persons/km^2) who, towards the end of the 1960s, lived east of the Cordillera de Cutucu, a region not yet under pressure from the advancing colonization frontier and where the traditional pattern of dispersed settlement still existed (Harner 1972: 77). Furthermore, the considerable disproportion between the density of these two neighboring dialect groups throws a new light on the reasons behind the present flow of Shuar migrants to Achuar territory.

The global population density must be weighted as a function of local settlements; it is noticeably higher for the Achuar living south of the Pastaza (0.3 persons/km^2), and slightly lower for the Achuar north of the river, the region covered by our study (0.12 persons/km^2). Within this last sector, the situation can vary widely with the pattern of settlement, since nucleation into semi-villages naturally concentrates the population into a smaller space. If we take as a basis for comparison the area of forest actually exploited and traveled by a given group of people that considers itself to have exclusive usage rights to this territory, we obtain an order of magnitude quite revealing of the variations in the population density: around 1 person/km^2 for the Copataza *centro*, as compared with 0.1 person/km^2 for the three isolated households on the Rio Wayusentza (a tributary of the Pindo Yacu). Finally the population density must be corrected for local ecological features, as the Achuar consider certain parts of their territory to be unfit for habitation, particularly the zones dominated by *aguajales*.

Despite local variations, the extremely low human density already tells us that the Achuar do not exploit their environment in an intensive manner. The ways they have adopted for socializing nature cannot fail, therefore, to contrast sharply with the more intensive forms of production that prevail among some tropical horticulturalists with a very high population density. And thus the representations of the forest space and the techniques for its use cannot be the same for swidden horticulturalists who, like the Achuar, number fewer than one inhabitant per square kilometer, and for populations who, like the Taino of Hispaniola (Dreyfus 1980–1) or the Chimbu of New Guinea (Brown and Brookfield 1963), manage their environment in such a way that it will support densities of over 100 persons/km^2. From the standpoint of a simple arithmetic ratio of population to area, the Achuar are closer to hunter-gatherer societies living in a semi-desert habitat than to most societies of tropical swidden horticulturalists, even in Amazonia.[6]

From the air, this impressive forested vastness begrudgingly reveals to the alert eye of the airborne traveler a few inhabited clearings, sometimes so tiny that they might well have been a trick of the imagination after all. Although they are scarcely visible in the midst of the interminable forest that shelters them from the outside world, the Achuar have been able to domesticate it for their own purposes. Nearly untouched by human hands, but profoundly socialized by human thought, it is this sphere of nature that we are now about to explore.

2

Landscape and cosmos

Terrestrial water, celestial water

Like other Amazonian groups, the Achuar make a clear lexical distinction between celestial water, *yumi*, and terrestrial water, *entza* (Lévi-Strauss 1964: 195). *Yumi* designates the rainwater that falls in a relentless drizzle for days on end or the water that buckets down in the late afternoon, and from which those out of doors take refuge as they can under an umbrella fashioned from a banana leaf. *Entza* is both water from the river and the river itself; it is the clear water of fast-flowing streams, the brown boiling flood waters, the slack, low waters of the river, and the stagnant waters of the swamps. By some curious paradox, the Achuar use *yumi* to designate the cooking water used in making manioc beer and for boiling the tubers; and yet they fetch this celestial water from the river in a gourd they also call *yumi*. *Entza* becomes *yumi* by virtue of its final destination, then, since an Achuar, even when very thirsty, rarely stoops to drink directly from the river. *Entza*, river water, is good only for bathing, fishing, navigating; it is used for washing dishes and clothes; it even serves as a public convenience for the men, who go down to the river before dawn to defecate; it is impure water that cannot be drunk *in situ*. If, in spite of everything, terrestrial water is used for cooking, it is only after a semantic detour whereby it becomes domesticated. This is a two-step process: when the water, *entza*, has been drawn from the river, it becomes *yumi*, drinkable celestial water, but not drunk as such; then from *yumi* it goes on to become *nijiamanch* (manioc beer), by the magic of fermentation, which makes it at last socially fit for consumption. True rain water, *yumi*, is never used in cooking, for lack of suitable receptacles in which to catch it. Thus for the Achuar, this water ubiquitous in all rainforests appears in two distinct aspects, which we propose to adopt as analytical categories for describing the physical environment.

Entza

Terrestrial water is that which, spilling down the Andes as it has for millennia, helps shape the landscape, carrying alluvium and sediments, slicing through plateaux and seeping deep into the ground.[1] We know that, a very long time ago, and more precisely, until the late Cretaceous period, water dominated the region presently occupied by the Achuar, since it was covered by a huge freshwater sea. When the eastern cordillera of the Andes emerged during the Eocene, the sea withdrew, depositing in its wake sediments comprised mainly of conglomerates, fine sandstone, and red, gray, and yellow clays. Somewhere between the late Miocene and the Pliocene, a huge alluvial fan began to form at the foot of the eastern Cordillera; it spread out and, during the Plioquaternary, was gradually extended and built up by detrital deposits rich in volcanic elements (graywackes). Tectonic action has caused a transversal break in the structural continuity of this alluvial fan, forming a north–south anticlinal corridor, which in part constitutes the natural western boundary of the Achuar territory. To the east of this longitudinal corridor, the alluvial fan has been deeply dissected by erosion, leaving a mesa relief with an overall monoclinal structure. Beyond the eastern edge of the alluvial fan stretches a landscape of flat-topped convex–concave hills. These hills are what is left after erosion of the former subhorizontal (Premiocene) sedimentary clay structure. The prevailing gentle slope of the hills gives them an air of peneplain.

The Achuar territory south of the Pastaza features a large plain that has been filled in by the meanderings of the river. This ancient flood plain is composed primarily of andesitic volcanic material deposited on the original clay bed. Waterlogging is progressively turning the eastern and southeastern parts of this plain into marshlands. More recent and not as vast as the ancient flood plain, the Pastaza alluvial plain changes width with the course of the river; on the north bank, the alluvial plain has cut deeply into the Plioquaternary deposits, producing a steep-sided plateau.

The beds of secondary rivers have numerous meanders, which form valleys rarely more than two kilometers across. Depending on the nature of the geological formations encountered by the rivers, the pedological features of these valleys can differ widely. Small rivers rising in old weathered clay massifs (around the anticlinal corridor and in the mesa region) have a capacity of transport inferior to their capacity of concentration, which makes for constant erosion of the banks and an absence of alluvial deposits. By contrast, water courses rising in the ancient flood plain or further west, in the rugged zones covered in volcanic ash, deposit excess sediment along their banks, thereby building up fertile alluvial terraces.

The region occupied by the Achuar can thus be split into five broad geomorphological and/or pedological regions: the mesa region (produced by erosion of the alluvial fan); the hill region (produced by the dissection of tertiary sediments); the Pastaza ancient flood plain; the recent alluvial plains and terraces and their swamps; and the non-alluvial valleys (Fig. 4). This five-category typology is necessarily something of a reduction from a strictly pedo-geomorphological standpoint, and, if we have restricted the range of landscapes and soils to five, it is because the specificity of each of these is clearly perceived by the Achuar.

Nearly one third of the Achuar territory, the northern and northwestern portion, is characterized by plateaux. These mesas are elongated and almost horizontal ridges rising some hundred meters above the valley floor. Depending on the degree of dissection and weathering, the plateaux take two forms: either a gently rolling surface, convex toward the top, with gradients of not more than 40%, or a more dissected surface that rises to a peak, with gradients of up to 70%. Between the main valleys (Bobonaza, Capahuari, Conambo, and Corrientes), the plateaux are grooved by numerous small clear-water streams that have cut narrow gorges (*quebradas* in Spanish) to a depth of five or ten meters. The nature of the soils varies with the type of volcanic materials from which they have evolved. On volcanic sandstone the soil is a compact, coffee-colored sandy clay, Oxic Dystropept, which can be as much as five meters thick.[2] On clays and conglomerates, the soil is also a compact Oxic Dystropept, but less evolved or deep than the former, its color verging on brick red.

To the east and southeast of the mesa region, and generally below an altitude of 300 meters, stretches a sea of flat-topped hills, for the most part less than 50 meters high, with gently sloping sides rarely exceeding 30%. Once again the soils are red, compact Oxic Dystropets, resulting from the intense laterization of the clayey sedimentary substratum. The red Oxic Dystropets of the hills and certain parts of the mesa region are typical clay-based, highly leached lateritic soils. They usually have a very acid pH and are calcium and potassium poor with a high level of aluminum toxicity. These soils are very mediocre with a minimum fertility potential. The brown Oxic Dystropepts that prevail in the plateau region are no richer, despite the presence of graywackes. These too are highly leached clay lateritic soils with high percentages of exchangeable aluminum and a slightly less acid pH than the red Oxic Dystropepts. With the exception of the valley system this vast region of hills and plateaux that typifies the

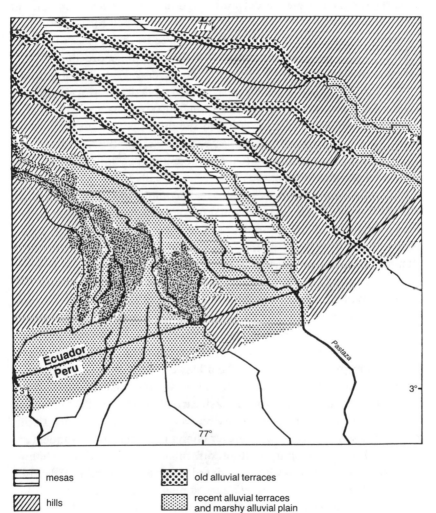

 mesas   old alluvial terraces

hills   recent alluvial terraces and marshy alluvial plain

ancient floodplain   border   0   30 km

4. Achuar territory in Ecuador: relief map of soils

northern part of the Achuar territory has an extremely low agricultural potential.

Within the valley network, a distinction should be made between two very different pedological zones, the characteristics of which are determined by the altitude, gradient, and composition of the geological formations encountered by the waterways that cross the area. Often the soils at the head and the mouth of a valley will be entirely different; this is the case of the Bobonaza and Capahuari valleys, for instance. Upstream, that is in the mesa region, rivers have cut deep into high terraces formed from ancient sandy-loam alluvium. The regime of these rivers, which for the most part rise below the eastern cordillera, is characterized by the absence of marked seasonal variations and by "flash" flooding. Lying more than twenty meters above the thalweg, these old terraces never receive alluvial deposits; on the contrary, they are constantly being eroded by the swift-flowing waters. The rivers crossing the mesa region fall 300 meters over a distance of barely 100 kilometers. That is equal to the drop they will make over the nearly 5,000 kilometers remaining before they flow into the Atlantic Ocean. These valleys are undergoing intense erosion, and their soils are considerably less fertile than those of the recent alluvial valleys.

Within the old alluvial valley system, soil composition varies principally with the level of erosion. In the main, it presents a mosaic of predominately lateric soils with a high proportion of volcanic sandstone (close to the brown Oxic Dystropepts of the plateau region). Although the levels of aluminum toxicity are usually lower in these soils, and their pH less acid than in red Oxic Dystropepts, they have a rather low level of fertility. The old terraces of erosion valleys therefore cannot sustain permanent monoculture and tolerate only the temporary practice of swidden polyculture.

On the eastern edge of the alluvial fan, the general slope of the land levels off, and the turbulent rivers that had, up to that point, been channeled by the sandstone plateaux, soon slow to a lazy crawl, forming broad alluvial valleys in the Tertiary sediments. The sandy materials picked up in crossing the mesas combine with the volcanic ash carried down from the foothills to form low alluvial terraces, constantly rejuvenated by new deposits. In this region of low reliefs, rivers are forever changing course; the meanders are intersected by sand spits, cutting off inland ox-bow lakes; shallow depressions form swamps when inundated in flood season, alluvial deposits build up into natural levees (*restingas*), sometimes completely isolated in the middle of waterlogged depressions. Unlike the mediocre soils of the old alluvial terraces, the constantly regenerated soils of these low-lying valleys can be very fertile.

The structure of the alluvial soils varies with the origin of the sediments.

In the Pastaza alluvial plain, the deposits are composed of volcanic sands washed down from the detrital formations of the eastern cordillera. On the other alluvial terraces along the lower stretches of the Macuma, Huasaga, Capahuari, Conambo, and Corrientes, the soils are more loamy and less marked by their volcanic origins. In every case, these alluvial soils are deep, loose packed and a varying shade of black, depending on the proportion of volcanic ash. Their physico-chemical characteristics make them the best soils in the Achuar region: the pH is only very slightly acid (5.5 to 6.5 in water), the level of exchangeable aluminum is low, and, when not regularly flooded, their upper layer is rich in organic matter. Nevertheless, there are relatively few of these alluvial terraces in the Achuar region (less than 10% of the total area), and waterlogging often makes them unfit for cultivation. Even in the absence of actual flooding, the water table is never far from the surface.

To simplify mapping, we have grouped together recent alluvial terraces and marshy alluvial plain, for, even if the origin of the soils is perceptibly different, their composition is nearly identical. The most characteristic feature of these alluvial plains is the existence of large shallow depressions (*aguajales*) filled either part or all of the year with water. Unlike ox-bow lakes, regularly renewed by feeder channels (*igarapés*), *aguajales* can be located a fair distance from a water course. *Aguajales* are clay-bottomed depressions which retain precipitation and are therefore more or less under water, depending on the volume of rainfall and degree of evaporation. The soils are usually Tropofibrists, extremely rich in organic matter, which sustain natural hydromorphic vegetation comprised mainly of *aguaje* palms. The soils in the best-drained portion of these alluvial plains, as in the ancient flood plain (the Pastaza fossil delta), have a not negligible agricultural potential, albeit generally lower than that of true alluvial terraces. Their structure varies, with predominating deep, brown-colored clay soils, of the Umbriorthox and brown Oxic Dystropept types. In hydromorphic conditions, the latter type may evolve into Tropacuepts or Tropaquents, soils valued by the Achuar because they are fertile and perfectly suited to high-moisture-tolerant cultigens.

The thick cover of vegetation almost uniformly blanketing this small portion of Amazonia that is home to the Achuar harbors a wide variety of soils and reliefs. More than anyone else, the Achuar are aware of the geomorphological and pedological diversity of their territory. If their empirical knowledge of their surroundings is not rooted in paleogeographical abstractions, it is nonetheless based on centuries of observation and agronomical experimentation, which have given them a detailed knowledge of the various components of their inorganic environment. Thus, native taxonomy of reliefs makes a clear distinction between the various types of hills (*mura*) and plateaux (*nai*), between trough-shaped alluvial valleys (*chaun*) and shallow basins (*ekenta*) and narrow steep-sided canyons (*japa*), between water-logged depressions (*pakui*) and marshy ox-bow lakes fed by rivers (*kucha*).

The Achuar generally associate each of these topographical elements with one or more of the principal forms of running or standing water. *Entza* is the generic term for waterways and as such enters into the composition of names of rivers and streams as a suffix to proper or common nouns (e.g. Kunampentza, "squirrel river"). Within the generic category *entza*, however, the Achuar distinguish several specific forms: *kanus* denotes the major river flowing in a broad alluvial valley and is used only to refer to the Pastaza; *kisar*, on the other hand, designates clear-water streams confined by steep-sided canyons (*japa*); while the term *pajanak* indicates a particular type of stream that becomes a distributary when the river is in flood. With the exception of *kisar* streams, which rise in the sandstone plateaux or in the sea of hills to the east, all waterways in the Achuar region are typical *rios blancos*, white-water rivers. These are opaque watercourses of a variable shade of milky-brown, that carry large quantities of suspended sand and minerals from their headwaters in the Andean foothills.

The Achuar generally associate a specific type of soil with each combination of relief and limnology. Their typology is built on the association of differential parameters: color, location, depth, texture, drainage (Fig. 5).

This typology is articulated by a system of explicit and implicit categories which we will see at work in many other Achuar taxonomic orders. The first internal division separates the visible components of the soil into three explicit categories: stones (*kaya*), sand (*nayakim*), and earth (*nunka*). The latter is in turn divided into eight explicit types by qualifying it with a color, texture, or location. Clays, mineral colors, and magical charms, each designated by a name of its own, seem not to be included in this ternary classification, but form a separate collection. In reality, however, this mixed collection is connected in a non-explicit manner to the three primary categories. The three mineral colors and the magical charms are identified with stones (*kaya nunisan*), because of their density. Moreover, they are found mainly on eroded river banks where the subsoil has been exposed by water action. By their compactness and their association with running water, they combine with the pebbles found in rivers and the boulders that stand in their beds to become implicit elements of the primary category *kaya*. The same is true of clay types, which, although each is designated by a specific name and usage, are all conceived as individual forms of the category *nunka*, earth.

The Achuar have a pragmatic and theoretical knowledge of the diversity of their inorganic environment, then, and this knowledge is put to use in the ways they utilize nature, and particularly in their agricultural techniques. The choice of house and garden sites depends mainly on the potentials that the Achuar assign with great precision to each type of soil found on their territory (Chapter Five). We have analyzed this complex pedological mosaic at length because we wanted to emphasize the variety of possibilities of adaptation afforded by this area of the upper Amazon. We also wanted to indicate from the outset that any understanding of indigenous settlement patterns and resource management could not stop at abstract generalities

Indigenous nomenclature	Description
Pakui nunka "Dirty earth"	Dark hydromorphous soil, characteristic of alluvial terraces and *aguajales*
Kanus nunka "River earth"	Alluvial soil over silt; dark and loamy
Shuwin nunka "Black earth"	Sandy black alluvial soil
Nayakim nunka "Sandy earth"	Compact lateritic soil made up predominantly of volcanic sandstone; brown with sandy clay-like texture
Kante nunka "Dense earth"	Lateritic soil made up predominantly of volcanic sandstone; brown and clayey
Keaku nunka "Red earth" *Muraya nunka* "Hill earth"	Compact red lateritic soil characteristic of the hills; clay texture
Kapantin nunka "Reddish-orange soil"	Highly laterized soil
Nayakim "Sand"	Black sand characteristic of Pastaza beaches
Kaya "Rock"	The term denotes either the volcanic rocks (*pampa*) protruding from riverbeds or the pebbles that build up on the beaches (*kayan-matak*: "pebble beach")
Nuwe	White clay used for pottery
Maajink	Small surface deposit of white clay often used as a wallow by peccaries
Kitiun	A chip of rock caked with brown clay that takes its color from ferrous oxide (a coloring used for pottery)
Pushan	*Idem*, but yellow
Pura	*Idem*, but red
Namur, nantur	Flint chips used as magical charms

5. Achuar soil and mineral typology

concerning the properties of tropical soils; this would do justice neither to reality nor to the knowledge that the Indians have produced. And yet such generalities have been the basis upon which many ethnographers thought they could construct totalizing theories, in the hope of reducing the different Amerindian approaches to socioterritorial organization to a single explanatory paradigm founded exclusively on the action of ecological limiting factors and, at times even, on strictly pedological factors alone (we have in mind more particularly Meggers 1971 and Carneiro 1961).

Yumi

Yumi, celestial water, is that climatic element which, in the form of regular precipitation and high atmospheric humidity, combines with sunlight to promote the continual vegetative growth of the forest. The Achuar region has a typical equatorial climate, which corresponds, in Köppen's system of classification, to the Af group: constantly humid, no dry season, and a monthly rainfall always over 60 millimeters (Dresch 1966: 614). Two degrees south of the equator, days and nights are nearly the same length and, as the sun hardly deviates from the zenith, temperatures remain constant throughout the year. The apparently uniform sunlight and rainfall characteristic of equatorial climates should not, however, be allowed to obscure significant local variations. Regional climatic differences as well as seasonal cycles of fluctuation, however modest, have a direct influence on the techniques the Achuar employ on their natural environment.[3]

One of the most striking climatic features of the equatorial zone of the Andean foothills is the gradual drop in rainfall coupled with the regular rise in temperature as the altitude decreases. The Andean barrier plays a decisive role, for it alters the general circulation of intertropical low-pressure fronts by retaining dense, moist air masses on its eastern slopes. Thus the increase in temperatures and the decline in rainfall progress regularly and inversely along an altitudinal axis, with the exception of a relatively sharp spike in the 1,000–500 meter range: between Puyo (elevation 990 m) and Taisha (elevation 510 m) the mean yearly temperature jumps from 20.3°C to 23.9°, while annual rainfall drops from 4,412 mm to 2,943 mm.

Despite their proximity to the Andean barrier, the Achuar are not directly affected by the special meteorological conditions of the foothills. In the low-lying regions they inhabit, the climate is closer to that of the town of Iquitos, more than 400 km to the east, than to that of Puyo, which is less than 70 km to the west. The disparity is worth noting, for the Jivaro are often used in comparative ethnography as an illustration of a group that has adapted to a montaña ecosystem. While this geographical description is correct in the case of the Shuar Jivaro of the Upano valley, it is completely erroneous when applied to the Achuar. By its topography as well as its climate, the region occupied by the Achuar can be assimilated more readily to the Peruvian lowlands than to the immediately adjacent strip of foothills where the Shuar live.

The first noteworthy feature of the Achuar climatic zone is the extent of solar radiation: mean annual daytime temperatures vary between 24° and 25°C, depending on the altitude. The amount of sunlight is fairly constant throughout the year, with a difference of less than two degrees between the highest and lowest monthly means. The annual average low for daytime temperatures fluctuates between 19° and 20°C, depending on the altitude, while the average annual highs are between 29° and 31°C; the monthly variations within the two are also less than two degrees. In short, it is always hot, the temperature variations over the year being too small to allow distinction of a hot and a cold season. At most it might be said that it is marginally hotter from October to February, that is, during the months when the average temperature is always slightly above the annual average.

Relative atmospheric humidity varies little, but does show a tendency to drop slightly during the hottest months (minimum 85%) and to rise during the less hot months (maximum 90%). It would seem logical then that the months with a mean temperature below the annual average and with the highest relative humidity would also be the rainiest. And yet, uniquely on the basis of rainfall data collected by the three weather stations closest to the Achuar territory, it seems all but impossible to detect any meaningful pattern. Rainfall varies considerably from one year to the next, and the available measurements cover too short a period (five years) for any representative series to be established. Of course a few overall constants can be identified. For instance, the annual average is never more than 3,000 mm for the highest sectors (Taisha), nor less than 2,000 mm for the lowest (Soplin). Furthermore, average precipitation for the rainiest month seems to vary little as a function of altitude (292 mm and 270 mm, respectively, for the two stations mentioned above), but the average for the least rainy month shows a wider variation as a function of altitude (174 mm and 135 mm). Within these broad upper and lower limits, there is, then, a slight tendency for rainfall to decline with a drop in elevation.

A closer look at seasonal and micro-local contrasts reveals a much more complex situation however, for, from one year to the next at the same station, or at different stations in the same year, differences of up to plus or minus 700 mm can be seen. Furthermore, the month with the highest average rainfall over a five-year period is not necessarily the same for each of the three stations (April, March, or June), nor is the month with the lowest average (December, August, and August). The unpredictable character of monthly rainfall in the Achuar territory is not without its effects on the environment. For example, a micro-region can experience a temporary severe dry spell, while neighboring micro-regions receive heavy rainfall for the same period. In 1979 on the upper Pastaza, we witnessed an exceptional dry spell during the months of January and February, when it rained only three times in thirty-two days. And yet the adjacent regions to the northwest and the southeast were practically untouched by the phenomenon.

Such periods of too little or too much precipitation have no noteworthy effect on the vegetative activity of wild and cultivated plants, since the duration is too short to have any long-term influence. By contrast, an abrupt, temporary change, in one direction or the other, in rainfall is enough to have a direct consequence for the fragile balance of energy flows within animal populations. Drought rapidly dries up secondary branches of rivers and depressions normally filled with water, asphyxiating the fish that live there. The mammals that water at these holes must range far afield in search of new spots, especially in the case of naturally gregarious and highly mobile species like the peccary. In the opposite case, heavy continuous rainfall tends to accelerate the decomposition of organic bedding, rapidly destroying the fruit and seeds eaten by large terrestrial herbivores such as the tapir or the peccary. In this case, too, but for the opposite reason, herds of peccary tend to migrate to more hospitable regions. So even a short but severe drought or exceptionally heavy rains have an impact on the availability of certain animal species that play an important role in the Achuar diet. It is true that, in the long term, the risks are spread over the whole population: as no micro-region of the Achuar territory seems safe from these freaks of weather, the consequences for any one locality will, statistically, be felt by all residential units at one time or another.

The apparent absence of regular seasonal contrasts can partially be corrected if the analysis of rainfall data is extended to all eleven stations in the south- and central-eastern parts of Ecuador. When this is done, a homogeneous climatic region can be seen south of the second parallel (i.e. in the latitude occupied by the Achuar), which shows identical seasonal differences in rainfall despite internal variations in the volume of precipitation due to altitude. A period of heavy rains can be observed from March to July, while there is a relative decline in rainfall between September and

February, with a fairly clear minimum in December. August is a transitional month, since, depending on the year, it can be either rainy, thus extending the season of heavy rains, or dryer, thus announcing the onset of the season of lighter rains. And so for five months of the year – from October to February – the rise in temperatures and the drop in rainfall are clearly perceptible, and yet this season cannot be called dry in any strict sense of the word.

The Achuar have developed a model of the annual weather cycle that goes into much more detail than the meteorologists' model. Their year is divided into two seasons: the rainy season, or *yumitin* ("in rain"), which begins in mid-February and goes on until the end of July, and the dry season, or *esatin* ("in sun"), which starts in August and ends at the beginning of February (Fig. 6). But within this general binary framework, the Achuar, having observed their weather over a very long time, have also identified a series of micro-seasons, the actual existence of which is impossible to detect from meteorological tables.

According to the Achuar model, the rainiest part of the wet season is the month of May, when the rivers rise (*narankruatin*, "flood season"); this they attribute to the action of the Pleiades. Towards the end of April, the Pleiades constellation (*musach*), which until then could be seen every evening just after sunset, sinks below the western horizon. This is a phenomenon found throughout the equatorial band of the Amazon Basin and has been interpreted in various ways by the Amerindian populations of this zone, for whom it always functions as a seasonal marker (Lévi-Strauss 1964: 203–61). The Achuar themselves maintain that the Pleiades fall into the river near the headwaters (*musach yakiniam ejakmawayi*) and that every year they thus drown. Their rotting corpses cause the rivers to become turbulent, and this movement produces the high waters downstream. In June, new Pleiades (*yamaram musach*) are reborn in the east, emerging from the now appeased downstream waters.

A second period of exceptional flooding is caused, according to the Achuar, by an identical phenomenon of putrefaction, which they situate oddly enough at the onset of the *esatin* dry season. These are the *wampuash* or kapok (*Ceiba trischistranda*) floods, named for the typically riparian tree that begins flowering in mid-June and goes on until August.[4] The Achuar use the fibers of the *wampuash* flower as wadding, which they wind around the end of their blowgun darts to form an air foil, and they keep a close eye on the growth cycle of this tree so that, when the time comes, they can gather their supply of kapok. When the tree has finished blooming, the *wampuash* flowers fall into the passing waters and drift lazily along with the current. This sprinkling of white fluff floating on the surface of the rivers is a classic late-August sight. But light as they may be, the kapok flowers always sink in the end; like the Pleiades, their decomposition due to the action of the water is thought to make the rivers churn, which in turn produces high waters and flooding.

But why do the Achuar situate the "kapok floods" (*wampuash narank-ruatin*) at the beginning of September, that is to say, theoretically already one month into the *esatin* dry season? This apparent anomaly has to do with the transitional status of the August rains, which, as we mentioned above, can be either very light or very heavy depending on the year. The Achuar call this period *peemtin* ("lightning season"), an expression that denotes the constant presence of storm fronts. High morning temperatures favor air

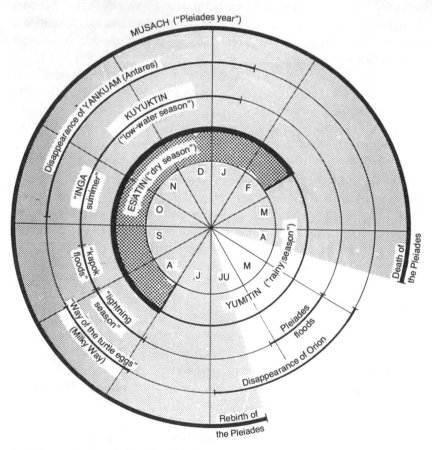

6. Astronomical and climatic calendar

convection, and enormous cumulo-nimbus clouds (*yurankim*, in Achuar) build up towards late afternoon. But the storms do not always break, and many times during this season thunder (*ipiamat*) rumbles for days without producing a drop of rain. When the storm does break, several inches of rain pour down on the forest within a few minutes, rapidly raising the level of the rivers. In contrast to *yumitin*, when the rainfall is generally regular, the month of August is hot and sunny, but broken by sporadic violent storms in the course of which the overall volume of rainfall can exceed that of a normal rainy month. The extent of the early September "kapok floods" thus depends largely on the intensity of the August storm activity.

The actual connection between celestial water and terrestrial water does not appear in the Achuar meteorological model as a direct circular, causal link. Indeed, the cause–effect relation between rainfall and flooding – a relationship that the Achuar formulate explicitly in their everyday commentaries – is completely obscured in the general theory of seasons by an organicist explanation. The high waters are attributed to a process of cosmic fermentation for which the metaphorical model is the making of manioc beer. Just as enzymes found in saliva cause the manioc mash to ferment and rise, certain organic bodies (clusters of stars and white flowers), as they decompose, set the rivers churning. The appearance of these organic bodies is not unlike the white curds of manioc that line the bottom of the fermentation jars (*muits*) and serve as starter.

This idea of flood as fermentation should be placed in parallel with the indigenous theory concerning the inverse phenomenon, the production of rain from river water. The Achuar attribute the formation of celestial water to a change of state in terrestrial water; however they do not think of the relation in terms of the natural phenomenon of evaporation, but as the direct result of human intervention. Etiquette demands of adults that they be careful not to offend terrestrial water, and that, when bathing, they behave in a dignified and unambiguous manner. Couples who engage in shameless erotic play in the river bring about persistent rains. Similarly, the collective drunkenness that is usually the hallmark of drinking parties is thought to engender torrential rains. Finally, every time fish poison is used, it seems that a downpour follows, for the celestial water must "wash" the river of the last traces of any plant poison that might subsist. In other words, rain is almost always the consequence of a human action performed in or on a liquid (terrestrial water, manioc beer), whether the action be a normal activity or a violation of etiquette. In contrast, the seasonal regime of rivers depends on a recurring cosmic event upon which humans have no bearing, even though the way it functions is modeled on a technique of transformation of the liquid element. Rain has its origins in a process linking terrestrial water (or its socialized form, manioc beer) and celestial water; flooding has its origins in an analogical process which places on the same plane two natural phenomena, one of which is controlled by humans, while the other is not.

The *esatin* dry season is determined negatively with respect to the rainy season, that is, by its relatively deficient rainfall rather than by the amount of sunlight it receives. As the Achuar define climate in terms of the state of water in its two forms, the elements used to characterize the contrasts within the dry season are purely descriptive. Not long after the "kapok floods" at the end of September, fruit appears on the *tserempush* (*Inga marginata*), one of the few trees whose fruit ripens at this time of year. Like the *wampuash*, the *tserempush* grows almost exclusively along river banks and it begins bearing fruit just after the kapok tree has finished flowering. The ripening of the *Inga marginata* fruit thus provides a convenient temporal indication which permits an automatic correlation with the level of water in the rivers. The initial portion of the dry season is marked by the generalized subsidence of flood waters and is called by derivation *tserempushtin* ("in *tserempush*"). The abatement becomes quite noticeable from November to the end of January, a period called *kuyuktin* or "low-water season." It is at this time of year that the highest temperatures are recorded, and the Achuar also use the term *tsuertin* or "heat season" to designate this period. Although these seasonal contrasts are designated with great precision by the Achuar, they actually fall within a very narrow range, especially when compared with the regular climatic fluctuations over the year in the eastern portion of the Amazon Basin.

The more or less constant combination of abundant solar radiation and high humidity is particularly conducive to the continuous growth of a spectacular climax rain forest. Except for the swamps, this thick, humid forest grows in an unbroken blanket over the whole Achuar territory. It differs from other types of forest, and particularly the forest of the foothills, by the typical presence of three main stories of trees (Grubb *et al.* 1963). The top story is formed of trees that have grown to a height of between 40 and 50 meters, like the *Ceiba pentandra* (*mente*, in Achuar) or the *Calathea altissima* (*pumpu*), with straight trunks as much as several meters in diameter at the base and flat, spreading crowns. These giants of the forest are particularly vulnerable to sudden gusts of wind (*nase*, in Achuar), which, from March to May, sometimes take on the aspect of veritable tornadoes. To anchor themselves, the tallest trees often put down tabular roots or grow pyramidal buttresses; these "flying buttresses" form woody panels, from which the Achuar make doors for their houses and mortars for pounding manioc. When one of these giants is felled by natural causes, it takes its neighbors with it, creating a temporary natural clearing in the heart of the forest. The middle story is the thickest, with trees from 20 to 30 meters tall, whose top branches intertwine to form an unbroken canopy. The understory is populated with the slender trees typical of undergrowth, which, together with the saplings of the taller species, grow in a highly humid carbon-dioxide-rich atmosphere. This last level also contains many species of palm, the most common of which are: *ampaki (Iriartea ventricosa), chaapi (Phytelephas* sp.*), iniayua (Maximiliana regia), kumai (Astrocaryum chambira)*, and *tuntuam (Iriartea* sp.*)*. The ground is carpeted with dead leaves and organic matter, enlivened here and there by some ferns or very young saplings. At every level of the forest, liana and epiphytic plants form a dense tangle, which becomes practically inextricable wherever daylight manages to penetrate the understory.

The main floristic feature of this tropical forest is the large number of species represented and the very small number of individuals of each species. Except in swamps or along rivers, it is rare to encounter more than four or five individuals of any one species per hectare. The best represented families of the several hundred common species identified and named by the Achuar are the Palmae, the Rubiaceae, the Leguminosae, and the Moraceae. By contrast, forest growing on hydromorphic soils is much more homogeneous, for it harbors only a few species specifically adapted to spending some or all of their life in water. Besides the garlands of kapok and *Inga marginata*, stands of various species of *Cecropia* and bamboo grow on the frequently flooded river terraces. The *achu (Mauritia flexuosa)* dominates the flooded depressions, often in association with other species of palm, like the *awan (Astrocaryum huicungo)* or the *kunkuk (Jessenia weberbaueri)*, while the only trees capable of surviving in several meters of water are the likes of the *tankana (Triplaris martii)* or the *kasua (Coussapoa oligoneura)*. Finally, natural windfall clearings, abandoned garden plots, and the margins of forests and rivers are colonized by a small number of sun-loving intrusive plants always associated with this type of habitat. The most frequently found are *sua, sutik*, and *tseek* (three species of *Cecropia*), *kaka (Trema micrantha), yampia (Visima* sp.*)*, and *tsenkup (Scleria pterota)*.

From an ecological standpoint, this type of humid forest is in a state of dynamic equilibrium, as its system of energetic exchange operates theoretically in a closed circuit (Odum 1971: 104). The organic matter and minerals are continually recycled by a complex network of microorganisms and specialized bacteria; as a consequence, non-alluvial soils have only a poor capacity for storing nutrients. The humic layer is very thin and, once the protective plant cover has disappeared, the topsoil is rapidly destroyed by the combined action of rain and sun. With the exception of river terraces and alluvial plains, much of the region occupied by the Achuar is made up of nearly sterile lateritic acid soils. Dense forest can develop on such poor soils only because it produces its own conditions of reproduction, on the one hand, by providing its own nutrients, and, on the other hand, by protecting such soils from the devastating effects of leaching. The wide diversity of plant species also results in a mixture of individuals whose nutritional needs are very different; this means that each species does not need to compete to optimize its symbiotic interaction with its habitat. In other words, such a forest manages to feed itself more or less independently of the prevailing local pedological conditions; in this environment, as Fittkau says, "a new tree can grow only from the corpse of a dead one" (Fittkau 1969: 646). When a man clears a garden in this forest, he temporarily taps into the small store of nutrients that the forest had built up for its own consumption. But the humic layer of these nutrient-poor soils disappears very fast, and intensive leaching finishes off what is left of the nutrients, making any long-term agriculture impossible. On naturally fertile alluvial soils, deforestation does not engender such drastic consequences provided the soil can partially be protected from leaching and solar radiation by a well-structured cover of cultivated plants.

And so, despite the diversity of soils on a micro-regional level, the trophic structure of the forest is practically the same wherever the soil is not hydromorphic. On the hillsides, the plateaux, and the best-drained portions of the terraces and flood plains, the only internal differences in forest composition are the minimal variations in the density of the trees. The Achuar are well aware of the relatively homogeneous character of their forest and are quite capable of saying how it differs from the forest growing at an altitude of over 600 meters, which is the habitat of their Shuar neighbors. The presence or absence of certain characteristic species constitutes ethnic habitat markers, of which the *achu*, from which the ethnonym Achuar is taken, is the best example. Such palms as the *awan, kunkuk, tuntuam, chaapi,* and *iniayua,* and trees such as the *mente, wampuash* (see above), and *chimi* (*Pseudolmedia laevigata*) are virtually non-existent in the Shuar habitat, while species that are extremely rare in the Achuar habitat abound on Shuar land, for instance the *kunchai* (*Dacryodes* aff. *peruviana*), *kaashmumi* (*Escheweilera* sp.), *tsempu* (*Dyalyanthera* sp.), and *mukunt* (*Sickingia* sp.).

It is probably because of this structural and floristic homogeneity that the Achuar did not develop a very complex typology of the major types of forest in their territory. And yet they identify with precision the various plant associations which, as we have seen, characterize certain micro-habitats (natural clearings, flooded forest, river banks. . .) and are perfectly capable of reciting the complete list of species that make up the first stage of secondary growth on an abandoned garden plot. The taxonomy of forest types proper, however, is restricted to five elements. The generic term for a climax forest is *ikiam*, and when it grows in a flooded area, it is called either *tsuat ikiam* (literally: "garbage forest") if it is very dense, or *pakui ikiam* ("forest on sticky soil") if the ground is very marshy. By contrast, natural clearings are not perceived as part of the category *ikiam* and are designated by the expression *tsuat pantin* ("clear garbage"), while the portions of the understory colonized by tree ferns are called *saak*, to differentiate them from the surrounding forest. Finally, even if they do not classify the local types of vegetation into broad categories, the Achuar are extremely sensitive to the slightest variations in their organic environment, such as we would have been incapable of detecting on our own had we not enjoyed their patient collaboration.

Upstream and down

Descending a waterway like the Bobonaza, the Capahuari, or the Huasaga, in a canoe, one cannot help being struck by the contrast between the upstream regions and those further down. Geomorphological analysis of the Achuar territory has already shown the evolution of the reliefs and soils along the main valleys as the current loses speed. Near the headwaters, the rivers flow between high terraces of extremely lateritic soil, while downstream, they sprawl over the broad floors of alluvial valleys dotted with marshes. Even the vegetation changes: while the forest along the upstream banks is in every way identical to that covering the nearby hills, the forest on the downstream terraces is dominated by such characteristic species as kapok, *wachi* bamboo (*Bambusa* sp.), or *kinchuk* palms (*Phytelephas* sp.). Overwhelmed by the two impenetrable walls of green that sometimes join overhead, the traveler descending the narrow upper reaches has difficulty detecting any animal life. At best he may hear the occasional distant ruckus of a band of howler monkeys or the cry of a toucan. But once he reaches smooth water, the river suddenly seems alive with the constant comings and goings of animals: otters (*uyu* in Achuar) swim along holding their pointed brown heads well out of the water, a capybara (*unkumi*) wallows in the mud, sometimes even a freshwater dolphin (*apup*) plays gracefully around the canoe. And insects are not absent from this animal kingdom which has so suddenly sprung into view; a wide range of parasites, from horseflies (*ukump*) to anopheles mosquitoes (*manchu*), completely unknown upstream, makes its presence painfully felt.

The contrast between the landscapes and animal life of the upper and the lower stretches of the same river is sufficiently systematic to imply the coexistence of two distinct biotopes within the Achuar territory. Upstream (*yaki*) and downstream (*tsumu*) are the terms the Achuar themselves use to designate the two habitats, whose differential specificity is determined less by their location with respect to an isometric line of altitudes, temperatures, and rainfalls than by a unique combination of geomorphological, pedological, and limnological factors. The upper Pastaza valley is a typical lowland biotope, even though it is several hundred meters higher than the eastern hills, themselves a typical interfluvial biotope. It is true that its alluvial plain makes the Pastaza an exceptional case; as a rule, alluvial river terraces and swamps are found downstream and at elevations of less than 300 meters (Fig. 7).

It has been only in the past twenty years or so that specialists in Amerindian cultures of the Amazon Basin have begun to notice the diversity of the ecosystems that make up this huge region so seemingly uniform on first sight. Even Julian Steward, the founder of cultural ecology, did not seem clearly to appreciate the consequences on the indigenous systems of adaptation to the ecological differences between river margins and forest zones when, in the 1940s, he decided to establish a typology of the cultural areas of the South American forest. In the end, his diffusionist interpretation uses ecology to show that evolved cultural forms imported from highland regions are not sustainable in the lowlands due to limiting environmental factors (Steward 1948). It was not until the pioneering work, in the 1950s, of Felisberto Camargo and Harald Sioli on the Brazilian Amazon that a clear distinction emerged between the ecological attributes of riverine habitats – alluvial plain – and those of forest habitats – interfluvial regions (Camargo 1948, 1958; Sioli 1950, 1954, 1957). This basic duality would subsequently be expressed by a variety of paired terms: *terra firme/várzea* (B. Meggers 1971), *ete/várzea* (Hegen 1966), interfluve habitat/riverine habitat (Lathrap 1968, 1970), or tropical forest/flood plain (A. Roosevelt 1980). But whatever lexical form may have been used to contrast the two ecotypes, Amazonian specialists now agree that the opposition has significant consequences for indigenous modes of living.

Opinions differ widely, however, on what actually characterizes these two biotopes and therefore on what portions of Amazonia can legitimately be assigned to each. B. Meggers' definition of *várzea* is highly restrictive, being limited almost exclusively to the alluvial plain of the middle and lower Amazon, from the mouth of the Japura to the littoral delta; the rest of the Amazon Basin, that is, 98% of its area, is, in her opinion, characteristic of a *terra firme* biotope (Meggers 1971: 28). Meggers' *várzea* is limited, then, to the narrow, low-lying band along the Amazon which receives a yearly layer of rich alluvial deposit washed down from the Andes; regions of the Amazon Basin that do not strictly fit this criterion would be automatically classified as *terra firme*, despite the wide variety of their soils, their flora, and their fauna. We personally prefer to follow Lathrap (1968), Hegen (1966), Fittkau (1969), and Denevan (1970), and use less narrowly limnological parameters (annual sediment deposition by flooding) in defining the riverine habitat.

There can be no doubt that the prime characteristic of a riverine biotope must be of a geomorphological order, since only the broad alluvial valleys irrigated by rivers carrying Andean volcanic matter can be qualified as riverine. These rivers build up alluvial levees that separate them from the flood plain which is inundated regularly; but the river bed is constantly on the move, and, within a few years, the cut-offs form crescent-shaped ox-bow lakes. On either side of the erratic river bed lie zones of more or less marshy land broken by ridges (*restingas*) built up from alluvial deposits. But this type of landscape is not confined to the middle and lower course of the Amazon; as Lathrap has shown, it is also typical of the lower valleys of the major Andean tributaries of the Amazon, from the Putamayo, to the north, to the Ucayali, to the south (Lathrap 1970: 26–7). Even in Ecuador the lower courses of the Napo, Pastaza, and Morona are typical enough of this type of environment, as in the case of the Pastaza, above.

But as its name indicates, a biotope cannot be defined exclusively in terms of pedology and geomorphology; its particularity stems as much from the specific fauna and flora that have managed to adapt to the constraints imposed by a given type of soil and relief. The riverine biotope is thus characterized by a particularly rich and abundant fauna, paradoxically better represented today in the alluvial valleys of the upper Amazon than on the Amazon flood plain proper. In effect, over the past few centuries, the Brazilian *várzea* has been subjected, by the colonial and neocolonial societies, to intensive commercial exploitation of its natural resources. As a consequence, while the species that had once been emblematic of the riverine habitat – the large river turtle (*charap*: *Podocnemis expansa*), the black caiman (*yantana*: *Paleosuchus trigonatus*), or the large *paiche* fish

(*Arapaima gigas*) – have almost vanished from the Brazilian *várzea*, they are still quite common in those zones which, like the Pastaza valley, are still unaffected by mercantile pillaging.

The major rivers and the lower courses of the secondary waterways are remarkable for their animal life, which includes some of the largest freshwater fish in the world: the enormous *paiche* (*paits* in Achuar), several species of Pimelodidae (generic name: *tunkau*), weighing up to 80 kilograms, and a large variety of sizeable Cichlidae and Characidae. At certain times of the year, huge schools of *kanka* (*Prochilodus nigricans*) make their way upstream, while from August to November, *charap* turtles lay delicious eggs by the thousands on the sandy beaches of the Pastaza.[5] When the rivers flood, great quantities of fish are swept into the ox-bow lakes (*kucha*) where they remain when the waters abate, constituting fabulous fishing grounds. This Garden of Eden is not limited to fishing, however; the riverine biotope also provides a highly favorable habitat for several species of herbivorous and carnivorous mammals. The aquatic plants and the vegetation growing along the river banks (especially the *Cecropia*) attract tapirs, deer, capybara, and sloths; while the fish and crustaceans provide food for otters (*Lutra annectens*), giant otters (*wankanim*: *Peteronura* sp.), crab-eating raccoons (*entsaya yawa*: *Euprocyon* sp.), and raccoons (*putsurim*: *Procyon aequatoralis*). There are countless numbers of aquatic birds (kingfishers, herons, egrets, ducks, grebes), and their eggs, like those of the turtle, are a favorite food of the black and the spectacled caiman (*Caiman sclerops*, *kaniats*, in Achuar).

With the exception of freshwater dolphins and river turtles, this highly characteristic fauna does not keep to the Pastaza and the lower course of its principal tributaries; it is also found in a vast region which does not have a regime of regular flooding. In this sense, the riverine biotope cannot be defined exclusively in terms of pedology, since the low-lying marshlands along the Peruvian border also harbor a typically riverine fauna, even though it does not answer the criteria for a flood plain. *Aguajales* and forests flooded by the build-up of rainwater rarely communicate with the hydrographic network, and yet the wooded swamps of the interior are a favorite habitat of peccaries, tapirs, and capybaras, which can be found in great concentrations. Inversely, the fertile terraces of much of the Macuma and Bobonaza valleys, although formed by recent alluvial deposits of volcanic origin, do not have the fauna and flora typical of the riverine biotope, which appear only further downstream.

In these circumstances it is understandable that our mapping of the riverine biotope (Fig. 7) is not absolutely isomorphic with our mapping of

the alluvial plains and terraces (Fig. 4). In defining the contours of the
riverine biotope, we have largely adopted the distinctive criteria used by the
Achuar themselves in differentiating upstream and downstream regions.
Over and above attributes of the soils and reliefs (hydromorphic or alluvial
soils, regularly flooded valleys, marshes. . .), we used as diacritical markers
the simultaneous presence of all or some of several animal and plant
species. For the animals, we used the known range of the freshwater

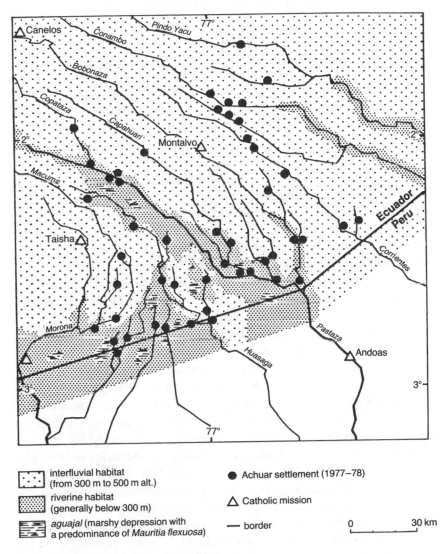

interfluvial habitat
(from 300 m to 500 m alt.)

riverine habitat
(generally below 300 m)

aguajal (marshy depression with
a predominance of *Mauritia flexuosa*)

● Achuar settlement (1977–78)

△ Catholic mission

— border   0   30 km

7. Achuar territory in Ecuador: habitat map

dolphin, the *charap* turtle, two species of caiman, the *paiche*, and especially the anopheles mosquito. These mosquitoes carry malaria (*chukuch*), and the epidemiological map of this disease among the Achuar coincides almost perfectly with the riverine biotope. The wild plant markers we used were the *wachi* bamboo, the kapok tree, and the *achu* (*Mauritia flexuosa*) and *kinchuk* (*Phytelephas* sp.) palms.

The interfluvial biotope contrasts sharply on all points with the riverine biotope. The rich alluvial soils fertilized by the annual floods that prevail downstream give way upstream to the mediocre lateritic soils of the hills and mesas. The density of animal life in the riverine valleys is matched by its dispersion in the interfluvial forest. The upper reaches of the major rivers are as rich in fish as the lower stretches, though the larger Pimelodidae do not make it upstream. But the small acidic clear-water streams of the interior do not favor the development of an ichthyological potential.

The density of non-aquatic animals is strongly conditioned by the availability of plant resources. Terrestrial herbivores are particularly scarce, since leaf mulch contains almost no elements that can be used by animals (Fittkau 1969: 646). The only possible food sources are the seeds and ripe fruits that fall to the ground, but these are never concentrated in one place, the plant species being highly dispersed (Fittkau and Klinge 1973: 10). Such constraints entail two types of consequence for terrestrial herbivorous populations (peccaries, tapirs, rodents, and deer): on the one hand, an overall low density due to the dispersion of edible vegetable matter and, on the other hand, a tendency to roam, particularly for the gregarious species, which are obliged to forage over vast areas. Usually comprised of at least thirty animals, a horde of white-lipped peccaries (*untsuri paki*) must stay on the move in order to satisfy its food needs. The situation is appreciably better for the arboreal vertebrates, which eat the fruits and seeds they require directly from the trees, and thus do not have to be content with whatever falls to the ground. The canopy is much richer in vegetable resources than the groundstory and, as logic would have it, it is the exclusive habitat of the great majority of the specifically Amazonian species of mammals (Fittkau 1969: 646). But here again, abundance is only relative: the fruits eaten by birds and primates are scattered, and their availability is subject to wide seasonal variations. If we add that many terrestrial and arboreal mammals are nocturnal, and that some of them, like the sloth, are so perfectly camouflaged as to be virtually undetectable, and that more of half of the Amazonian biomass is made up of insects (Fittkau and Klinge 1973: 2–8), it will be readily understood that it is entirely possible to spend hours in the interfluvial forest without encountering any animals other than flies and ants.

Many anthropologists and archaeologists now maintain that the ecological differences between the Amazonian riverine and interfluvial biotopes provide an explanatory key to the nature and variability of native forms of socio-territorial organization (Lathrap 1968; Carneiro 1970; Denevan 1970; Lathrap 1970; Meggers 1971; Siskind 1973; Gross 1975; Ross 1976, 1978; Roosevelt 1980). But if specialists are unanimous in stressing the opposition between the two biotopes in terms of differential agricultural productivity, they disagree completely on how to assess the contrasts in natural resource availabilities. For some authors, the scarcity and dispersion of edible animals in the interfluvial forest mean that procurement of the protein required by the human metabolism must be regarded as an absolute limiting factor (Harris 1974; Gross 1975; Ross 1976, 1978). These anthropologists point out that the staple cultigens in general, and manioc in particular, are poor in protein and that most of the dietary protein must be gotten from animal populations. This limiting factor would drive the native populations to institutional mechanisms adapted to a situation of protein scarcity, the function of which would be to maintain at an optimum stable level the population that theoretically could be carried by the environment. From this perspective, systematic infanticide and warfare would make it possible to maintain overall population growth at a tolerable level. Factionalism and local intergroup hostility would contribute to a highly dispersed settlement pattern and thus would justify maximal dissemination of human predators, a pattern adapted to the faunal dispersion. Finally, the purpose of food taboos and animal taxonomies would be to regulate the rates of animal capture, thereby avoiding overhunting local areas and causing certain animal species to disappear. Such adaptive mechanisms are held to be "cultural" responses to the scarcity of animal and plant protein in the interfluvial biotope. But were this the case, there would be no reason to find such mechanisms among the indigenous populations occupying a riverine habitat. As these populations have access to extremely fertile agricultural lands and a rich aquatic and riparian animal population that is diversified and readily available, they could exploit their environment much more intensively than the groups in the hinterland. Following the same line of reasoning, unlike their neighbors in the interfluve, who are reduced to a highly dispersed settlement pattern, the riverine populations of the Amazon Basin should always be found concentrated in large sedentary, politically stratified villages.

Without going into the epistemological problems posed by this type of geographical determinism, it can be noted that the thesis of scarcity of protein sources in the interfluvial biotope is far from being shared by all experts on Amazonian ecology. Some authors have rightly pointed out that the amount of animal protein available to humans in Amazonia has heretofore been largely underestimated because of ethnocentric prejudices tending to exclude from the edible zoomass all non-mammals (birds, fish, reptiles, invertebrates), which are widely consumed by the Amerindian populations (Beckerman 1979; Lizot 1977). The very idea of a scarcity of terrestrial mammals was called into question by Lizot (1977), Smith (1976), and Beckerman (1978, 1979); in fact, Beckerman has pointed out that the quantified data ordinarily used for calculating the density of certain South American animal populations were obtained in nonrepresentative locations. These were, in fact, either isolates with very special attributes, like Panama's Barrio Colorado Island or the El Verde Forest in Porto Rico, or hunted-out regions like the forest studied by Fittkau and Klinge some sixty kilometers from the town of Manaus (Beckerman 1979: 536–7). Finally, all anthropologists acquainted with the eating habits of the Amerindian societies of the interfluve are fully aware of the important dietary role of certain protein-rich wild plants (see in particular Lévi-Strauss 1950: 469–72). In the end, given the lack of adequate scientific instruments for analyzing the composition of the animal biomass of a territory measuring several thousands of square kilometers, it seems that the only way of assessing the availability of protein sources in the interfluvial biotope is to measure the average amounts of amino acids the native populations procure in one form or another from their natural environment (see Chapter Nine).

In view of the controversy over both the respective economic potentials of the interfluvial and riverine habitats, and the hypothetical socio-cultural differences engendered by allegedly distinct adaptive mechanisms, the Achuar can be considered an altogether exceptional test case. In effect, over the past several centuries, this tribe has been exploiting both types of ecological niche (see Taylor 1993, Chaps. 3 and 5). The analysis of the ways the interfluvial and the riverine Achuar relate to their respective ecosystems should yield conclusions that are not only useful in this particular ethnographic case, but pertinent for a better overall understanding of the indigenous societies of the whole Amazon Basin. The comparative examination, within a single social and cultural group, of the synchronic variations in the techniques of exploiting and the systems of representing nature as a function of habitat type is no doubt a more epistemologically plausible undertaking than the abstract juxtaposition of societies which, a priori, have nothing more in common than their simultaneous presence in the Amazon Basin. The effect of any difference in the ways of socializing nature, according to the various ecotypes, can thus be determined by using parameters that are clearly defined, quantifiable, and ethnographically irrefutable. This is not the case, however, when the comparison is done using data from disparate sources, a perilous exercise of which Betty Meggers gave us an exemplary demonstration when, with no regard for historical context and on the basis of vague and sometimes erroneous information, she decided to use the Jivaro, on the one hand (described by Karsten in the 1930s), and the Omagua, on the other hand (described by Father Fritz at the beginning of the eighteenth century when they were already living in missionary "reductions"), as archetypes of different modes of cultural adaptation to two Amazonian biotopes (Meggers 1971).

Even at this early stage of our analysis, simply establishing a geographical boundary between the two types of habitat focuses our attention on a disturbing phenomenon. When the Achuar contrast upstream and downstream regions, or flatlands (*paka*) and hills (*mura*), they are aware that the difference is one not only of landscape, but also of potential utilizations. They know perfectly well that the land is better on the alluvial terraces along the major rivers, that there are more peccaries there, that turtles abound and that the fisheries yield miraculous catches. One might think that, given its known potential, the riverine biotope would be densely populated, since the interfluvial forest would seem to be little more than a deserted refuge zone. It would be easy to see this hinterland as a place where the smallest local groups hide out for a time because their reduced numbers deny them the military means of imposing their permanent presence along the major rivers. But when the actual demographic data are analyzed, this somewhat simplified view begins to look questionable.

When it comes to overall area, the interfluvial portion of the Achuar territory (in Ecuador) is nearly two and a half times that of the riverine part; if the flooded zones and the *aguajales* unfit for human habitation are subtracted from the total (approximately 700 km²), the ratio rises to three to one. Now around 1,250 Achuar inhabit the 2,800 km² of utilizable riverine habitat, compared with 750 inhabitants for the 8,500 km² of interfluvial forest. The contrast is striking, and it is echoed by the huge discrepancy between the population densities: 0.44 person/km² in the riverine biotope and 0.08 person/km² in the interfluve; in the latter case, the density approaches that of the central Australian Aborigines (0.06 person/km² for the Murngin), whereas the former is close to that of typical Amazonian interfluvial populations like the Barafiri Yanoama. It is precisely this type of homology that is a problem, for above and beyond the stark contrast between the two densities, one cannot help wondering why the population density of the riverine Achuar is not greater than that of interfluvial populations in other areas. In other words, how is it that all the Achuar of Ecuador do not live together in an ecological strip which, of their own admission, has more resources than the interfluvial forest? The density implied by such a concentration would, moreover, be derisory: 0.7 person/km², or less than the density of those populations who, like the Machiguenga (0.8 person/km²) and the Campa of Gran Pajonal (1 person/km²) inhabit rugged regions typical of the interfluve. The situation is even more clear cut for the Peruvian Achuar, who live almost exclusively in the interfluvial forest, leaving the river plains uninhabited (Ross 1976: 144–5).

The hypothesis of the strongest local groups militarily controlling the riverine zones and thus forbidding local interfluvial groups access to the best lands is not at all plausible. Indeed, the settlement pattern in the riverine strip is extremely dispersed, human habitations sometimes being separated by uninhabited zones of several dozens of kilometers (2–3 days by canoe). Moreover, the intense feuding endemic among the local riverine groups precludes any build-up of forces and thus any global strategy on the part of riverine Achuar against Achuar in the interfluve. Finally, certain local interfluvial groups live only a dozen or so kilometers from the uninhabited parts of the riverine habitat without ever dreaming of migrating. It is clear then that contemporary Achuar do not fit the classic upper Amazon settlement model as formulated by Lathrap (1968), since local groups do not compete for access to the flood plains. And so we must try to understand why, long ago, the Achuar chose to occupy simultaneously the interfluvial forest and the major river valleys, despite the fact that they had the possibility of occupying an exclusively riverine biotope.

The cosmos and its markers

The Achuar's world is marked by a network of highly diversified spatio-temporal coordinates: astronomical and climatic cycles, seasonal periodicity of various types of natural resources, landmark systems, and the organization of the universe into layers as defined in mythic thought. When the observer has the patience to piece together these different topological and chronological grids, a global cosmological vision emerges; but this vision takes on real coherence only when looked at through the prism of the observer's eyes. The general gridmapping of the biosphere exists only as a synthetic possibility for creating meaning; it is never actually expressed in a discourse on the world. The Achuar do not spontaneously comment on the organization of their cosmos, unlike other Amazonian societies, in which philosophical questions on the origin and meaning of the universe seem to comprise the main matter of daily palavers (see Bidou 1972). Moreover, whereas we see space and time as two quite separate categories of experience, the same is not true for the Achuar, who constantly combine the two orders into a highly varied system of empirical references.

If one wants to structure this incongruous cluster of statements on space and time, one needs an analytical grid by means of which the individual networks of coordinates can be made congruent. The Achuar cosmos can be plotted along a conceptual scale which lays out the various systems of spatio-temporal markers according to their position in a field that runs from the implicit to the explicit. At one pole are the most concrete ways of dividing reality – measuring systems – while, at the other, appears in filigree an image of the universe which is never openly stated in Achuar commentaries, but must be reconstructed from odds and ends of myths and popular sayings. We shall take this hierarchy of positions as the guideline for our exposition. Moreover the gradual transition from the explicit to the implicit also assumes the form of a progressive passage from the human to the non-human, the spatio-temporal markers being represented as a continuum from which anthropocentric references progressively disappear.

In an environment as uniform as that of the equatorial forest, it is not altogether surprising that direction is most often indicated with respect to Ego, or determined by the subject's location in space. And yet the concepts of right (*antsur*) and left (*chawa*) are rarely used to designate a directional axis; they are above all used to specify relative position, particularly in the course of military operations, when each warrior must be assigned his place in a deployment or an encircling maneuver. Most of the time a vigorous thrust of the chin accompanied by an "*au*" are enough to indicate the rough direction of the object, place, or animate being referred to, whether it be a few meters or a few dozen kilometers away. The lexical poverty of the number system – one through five – makes it difficult to give exact distances, which are always evaluated in terms of the time needed to cover them. For short jaunts, an Achuar will indicate the length of the trip by showing approximately where in the sky the sun will be upon arrival, it being understood that trips always begin at dawn.

Beyond a day's walk or canoe trip, distance is counted in days (*tsawan*), and when the goal is more than five days away, people say simply, "it's very far." The notion of proximity itself is in fact extremely elastic, since it is defined contextually as a negation of distance. The expression *arakchichau* (literally: "not very far") can also designate places anywhere between half an hour and seven or eight hours' walk from where the speaker stands. The only exception to the rule of distance being expressed in terms of travel time is canoe trips, which afford the possibility of counting the number of meanders traveled. But this is valid only for short runs during which the number of meanders between two settlements can be counted on the fingers and, if need be, the toes. Finally, although measuring rods are used in the building of houses (Chapter Four), stepping off distances is unknown and the dimensions of a future garden are determined by rough reckoning.

As the duration of a trip can be estimated only for routes that are already familiar and used fairly often, it is nearly impossible to refer clearly to the location of a specific place that has never been visited using parameters of distance alone. In this case, a system of landmarks must be used which is common to the whole Achuar territory and can be immediately read in the landscape by anyone. The hydrographic network is just this system, whose every feature from the smallest feeder stream to the most remote waterhole has its own name. And yet, knowledge of the topography of the waterways also depends on individual empirical experience of a section of the network. In this way any Achuar is able to reconstruct, in the abstract, the mesh of the portion of the network with which he is familiar, either in a linear fashion, by naming off the successive tributaries of a river as though he were encountering them on a canoe trip, or in a transverse fashion, as though he were crossing them in the course of a trek. Giving verbal directions to a settlement is therefore easy: as the houses are necessarily built along a waterway, the coordinates of the site are defined "longitudinally" by its location along a given river and "latitudinally" by its position along a section bounded by two tributaries.

And so the portion of the hydrographic network frequented by each individual Achuar could be represented as a spider web of which each house-territory is the center. On the periphery, the mesh is naturally not as tight, and the only familiar names are those of the truly major rivers which constitute recognized boundaries between local or dialect groups. To designate the location of a distant local group with which relations are on the whole hostile, people will say "they live on the other side (*amain*) of such-and-such a river." Waterways, then, are the only landmarks that can be used to locate with any precision settlements and territorial limits. Of course, in the eastern plateau region, a few larger-than-ordinary mesas have sometimes been given proper names, but these are known only by the local population. Strictly speaking, the only integrated toponymic system that exists is the hydrographic network.

On the scale of a micro-region irrigated by a very small number of waterways, this absence of toponyms makes it difficult to talk about a specific forest site if no reference can be made to either a river (toponym) or a human settlement (anthroponym). In this case a system of esoteric markers must be called upon which requires an intimate knowledge of the salient elements of the micro-region in question: a peccary wallow, a salt lick regularly visited by animals, a deposit of pottery clay, an exceptionally large tree such as the *mente* (*Ceiba pentandra*) or localized stands of palms, tree ferns, or *ishpink* (*Nectandra cinnamonoides*). Upon returning home in the evening, a hunter gives a detailed account of the day's erratic itinerary, referring to such indications, leaving it up to the listener mentally to follow the trail being meticulously described. The trail markers used can be situated only by the small community of individuals who know this portion of the forest as well as the narrator for having frequently traveled its width and breadth. Now, because of the dispersed pattern of residence, this community is necessarily very limited; in most cases it is made up of the members of the residential unit alone. Every member of the household is thus perfectly acquainted with each acre of the circumscribed territory from which natural resources are procured. But, as the distance from home increases, the forest gradually becomes a *terra incognita*, devoid of familiar markers.

In order to advance in this forest without becoming lost, the Achuar use two types of trail: paths running between houses (*jintia*) and hunting trails or tracks (*charuk*, from the verb *charuktin*, "to cut"). For an outside observer unaccustomed to following a trail, these are hard to distinguish, on first view, from the riot of vegetation. With a little experience, the ethnographer can manage to follow a house path by paying attention every minute; but the hunting trail remains irremediably invisible. The Achuar do not clear their *jintia* paths, and so these are gradually formed by the nearly imperceptible trampling of the vegetable litter under travelers' feet. Whenever an obstacle blocks the way, (impenetrable windfalls, marshes, unfordable rivers), the path makes a wide detour. Because they are winding, the distance between two points on a path is sometimes three or four times the distance as the crow flies. Moreover, when a path is infrequently used, it tends to "close": any hint of its presence vanishes.

The *charuk* trails are not even perceptible on the ground, as they are marked by contrasting shades of green produced by branches broken at intervals. Many plants have leaves that are shiny one side and dull on the other; by bending back a branch so that the shiny side stands out against the dull background, or vice versa, hunters are ensured of a marked alignment that is, so it seems, perfectly visible. In this manner, each man creates for himself a labyrinthine network of marked trails that cover his hunting territory and which he navigates with ease. It should however be noted that, while Achuar have no difficulty in following an unfamiliar *jintia* path – even if it is barely beaten or is interrupted in places – a trail of broken branches can rarely be followed by anyone other than the person who created and maintains it. Now, anyone tracking game must necessarily leave the beaten path and scour the forest in every direction; and so when a hunter ventures into unfamiliar areas which he has not previously marked, he always runs the risk of not finding his way back. An Achuar may easily become temporarily lost when, visiting in an unfamiliar region, he decides to go hunting alone. Similarly, a group of warriors advancing by reckoning through unfamiliar parts to attack a house may wander for several days before coming upon their target.

Because Achuar may become lost in the forest, an important part of gathering trips is devoted to instructing children in orientation and alimentary survival techniques. The main directional axis by which one may orient oneself is the daily trajectory of the sun from east to west. The various points of this trajectory make it possible, first of all, to split the day into clearly defined periods: *tsawastatuk ajasai*: "day is almost coming" (first glimmer of dawn), *tsawas ajasai*: "day is breaking," *nantu yamai tsawarai*: "day broke a little while ago," *nantu tutupnistatuk ajasai*: "the sun is almost at its zenith," *nantu tutupnirai*: "the sun is at its zenith," *teentai*: "it has passed the zenith," *nantu pukuntayi*: "the sun is starting to decline" (4 o'clock p.m.), *mushatmawai*: "the light is growing dim," *kiawai*: "it's dusk," *kiarai*: "the sun has just set." As we have seen, these times of day are also used to express distance in terms of approximate travel time. When it is not cloudy and the canopy is not too thick, the trajectory of the sun can also be used to gauge general direction. Paradoxically, however, it is not this trajectory that defines the two principal cardinal points. When visibility is poor, the Achuar rely on another directional axis. Questioned on the vernacular words for east and west, the Achuar do not answer with reference to the path of the sun, but rather with reference to the flow of the waterways. East and west are indeed designated by specific terms (*etsa taamu* and *etsa akati*, respectively), but the pair downstream–upstream (*tsumu–yaki*) is preferred for indicating direction. In effect, the hydrographic regime flows in an overall northwest–southeast direction, which makes the two bipolar systems roughly equivalent. And yet, for a number of reasons, the celestial east–west trajectory turns out to be of much less importance for the Achuar than the symmetrically inverse course of the rivers as they flow from the headwaters to the mouth.

In fact, though, I have made the distinction between trajectory and path for purely analytical purposes, for, according to the Achuar conception of the world, the heavenly plane and the aquatic–terrestrial plane are a continuum. The earth is represented as a disc entirely covered by the vault of the heavens (*nayampim*); the terraqueous disk and the celestial hemisphere are joined by a band of water, the source of all rivers and their final destination. Now there is one heavenly body which combines, in an exemplary fashion, the aerial and aquatic paths along an east–west axis and this is the Pleiades constellation. When the Pleiades vanish from the western sky in mid-April, they fall into the upstream waters, causing the waters to rise as they make their way downstream, where they finally appear in the June sky, just above the eastern horizon.

This aquatic–celestial revolution, accomplished each year at the same time, is the cosmic repetition of the initial journey made by a group of orphans, whose story is recounted in a myth. Variants of the tale differ as to the circumstances surrounding the birth of these children, but all agree on the conditions in which they ascended into the sky.

The myth of the Musach orphans

The orphans, named Musach, lived with their adoptive parents and, as is often the case among the Achuar in such circumstances, they were unhappy and felt neglected in their adoptive home. And so they decided to run away and to this end made a raft out of balsa wood. One day when their adoptive parents had gone into the forest, the orphans caused the river to rise and embarked upon their raft, which began to drift swiftly downstream. But just then their adoptive father, Ankuaji, returned from his forest expedition and caught sight of the raft far down stream; he decided to pursue the orphans in his canoe and bring them home. The chase lasted several days, the orphans always managing to stay one jump ahead of Ankuaji. Finally the children came to the place where the waters and the heavens meet; they scrambled up some *wachi* bamboo and into the sky. A short time later, Ankuaji followed them up by the same path.

The Musach became the Pleiades, their raft is now the constellation Orion (*utunim*), while Ankuaji (literally: "eye of the evening") continues his vain eternal pursuit as the star Aldebaran.

The Achuar are far from being the only ones to postulate an association between the Pleiades, Orion, Aldebaran, the celestial and the terrestrial waters; Lévi-Strauss has shown these to be a feature common to both Amerindian and Ancient mythologies (1964: 203–87). In the first place the Pleiades and Orion can be defined diachronically by the near simultaneity of their co-presence and co-absence (231); in the Achuar region, the constellation Orion disappears at the end of April, two weeks after the

Pleiades have vanished from sight, and reappears at the end of June, two weeks after the "new Pleiades" (*yamaram musach*) have become visible once again. But the two constellations also oppose each other in the synchronic order "as a clear-cut division of the field and as ill-defined shape in the field" (232), since for the Achuar they illustrate respectively a rectangular raft and a group of children. According to Lévi-Strauss, it is this twofold contrast, both diachronic and synchronic, which makes the Orion–Pleiades pair "a preferential signifier of seasonal alternation" (232). It is a preferential signifier indeed: not only do the Achuar identify the disappearance of the Pleiades with a period of rains and high water, but they endow the term *musach* with the status of a unit of time denoting the span between two reappearances of the Pleiades. The *musach*-year begins in mid-June when the Pleiades once again appear downstream, a discrete sign that a new calendar cycle is starting up.

The annual cycle of the Pleiades is a good symbol of the compenetration in Achuar thought between categories of time and those of space, a phenomenon we glimpsed when analyzing the representation of meteorological cycles. Here, as in mythic thought in general, units of time can be defined by the paths traveled by a variety of moving bodies: humans; celestial, aquatic, or terrestrial mythological beings; anthropomorphized animals and plants. There are as many periodic cycles as there are specific paths traveled by these moving bodies. The Achuar are no exception to the rule when they use astronomical coding to divide time. Aside from Orion, the Pleiades, and Aldebaran, the Achuar have names for very few heavenly bodies: the sun (*etsa*, also called *nantu*), the moon (*kashi nantu*, literally: "night sun"), Castor and Pollux (*tsanimar*, literally: "the pair"), the Milky Way (*yurankim*, "cloud" or *charapa nujintri*, "turtle eggs"), and lastly Antares (*yankuam*). All the named stars lie close to the line of the ecliptic; the rest of the undifferentiated starry bodies answer to the generic name of *yaa*. But a detailed analysis of cosmology and astronomical mythology would take us beyond the scope of our study, and so we will therefore indicate only briefly the systems of heavenly bodies in opposing phases which the Achuar have perceived as being significant enough to constitute temporal markers.

The first phase opposition is naturally enough the division of day (*tsawan*) and night (*kashi*) into two periods of identical length. This opposition did not always exist, and a myth relates how the alternation between day and night came about.

The myth of how day and night came to be

Long ago it was always day because the two brothers, Sun and Moon, lived on earth. Since night never fell, people could not sleep, and life was difficult for everyone: the women could never rest from making manioc beer, nor the men from hunting. Now that Moon has gone up into the sky, night falls regularly and we can sleep. When Moon lived on earth, he was married to Auju (the great potoo: *Nyctibius grandis*). One day before he set out hunting, Moon asked Auju to cook some *yuwi* squashes (*Cucurbita maxima*) for his return. So she picked some ripe squashes, cooked them, and ate them all up, she did not leave a single one. Shortly before Moon came home, Auju fetched some green squashes and fixed them for her husband. Furious that all he had been served was green squashes, he suspected his wife of having eaten the ripe ones. The next day, Moon decided to hide near the house to see what his wife was up to. Once again Auju picked the ripe squashes, which she cooked for herself, while she saved the green ones to serve her husband. Then her husband came home and called his wife a glutton; but Auju had cleverly sewn her mouth up with thorns from the chonta palm, and she replied: "How could I have eaten all those squashes with my tiny little mouth?" Enraged by his wife's impudence, Moon decided to climb the vine that used to link the earth with the heavenly vault and go up into the sky. Auju was quick to follow, but when Moon had nearly reached the sky, he asked Squirrel *wichink* (*Sciureus* sp.) to cut the vine below him, causing Auju to fall. In her terror, she began to defecate wildly, and each piece of excrement turned into a deposit of *nuwe* pottery clay. Auju changed into a bird, and Moon became the night star. When Auju gives her characteristic moaning cry on nights of the full moon, she is weeping for the husband who left her. The heavenly vault has risen considerably since that time, and, because there is no more liana, it is no longer possible to go walking in the sky.

In this mythic version of the genesis of the alternation between day and night, the opposing phases are caused either by the presence of the sun or by the presence of the moon. Night is engendered not so much by the absence of the sun as by Moon's rising and the daily repetition of the original ascension. The Achuar are obviously aware that some nights the moon cannot be seen, since they always watch it carefully. The moon is a source of omens, the most feared of which is the threat of war, prefigured by a halo (*nantu misayi*) around the full moon. When this occurs, it is said that Moon has donned his feather crown (*tawasap*) as warriors do when going on the war path. But even when Moon refuses to be seen in the night sky, the Achuar say, and rightly so, that he is still there. Like all men, Moon is a hunter, and his fortunes vary; when he has not found any game, he has nothing to eat, and he grows so thin that he cannot be seen. At the first crescent, Moon is said to have eaten a blue-throated piping guan (*Pipile pipile*), then a deer for the first quarter, a tapir for the gibbous moon, and that he is as round as a ball (*tente*) at the full moon. Moon's phases are identified then with the lump in the serpent's belly which varies in size according to the nature of its prey.

The period between two new moons constitutes a unit of time known as *nantu*. But the Achuar do not count moons any more than they do days. They frequently speak of going to visit someone "at the new moon" (*yamaram nantu*) or the day after tomorrow (*nui kashin*), but no one ever says "I will do something or other in three moons" or "in ten days." The Achuar do not express the date something is to happen by adding up temporal units, be they days (*tsawan*), moons (*nantu*), or Pleiades years (*musach*), unless the date immediately follows one of these units. This imprecision of temporal assignation is even more patent when they are referring to the past than when they evoke the future. There is an expression, *yaunchu*, which is used in the temporal order in somewhat the same way as *arak* ("far") in the spatial order. *Yaunchu* designates anteriority with respect to the present moment; it may be used to qualify mythic times as well as to speak of an event that occurred a few seconds ago. Taken out of context, it is therefore impossible for the listener to tell exactly how much time has elapsed, which is not without posing a few problems for the ethnologist anxious to establish chronological sequences.

The Achuar do, however, have a division halfway between the moon and the year, which allows them to divide the latter into two distinct parts. Although this division is coded astronomically, it constitutes not so much a unit of time as a means of marking periods; this is the annual disappearance of *yankuam* (the star Antares in the constellation Scorpion), which in the calendar stands symmetrically opposite the disappearance of the Pleiades.[6] Still visible at nightfall in late September, Antares vanishes from the night sky at the beginning of October to reappear shortly before dawn in mid-January. Antares' disappearance occurs then during the *esatin* dry season and is, term for term, the counterpart of the Pleiades' disappearance, which, on the contrary, marks the height of the *yumitin* rainy season. The reappearance of Antares heralds the heavy rains, while the reappearance of the Pleiades announces the beginning of the light rains. Moreover, during the Pleiades' absence, from the end of April to the middle of June, Antares can be seen both in the evening on the eastern horizon and at dawn on the western horizon. For the duration of this period, Antares takes the place of the Pleiades in a twofold movement of inversion: on the one hand, it comes out at dusk, as the Pleiades did previously, but at the opposite pole of the sky; on the other hand, it takes the Pleiades' place in the very spot from which they vanished, but at the end of the night rather than at the beginning. And so Antares–*yankuam* and the Pleiades–*musach* form a preferential pair, articulated by a regular series of opposing phases and polarities. Their respective periods of presence and absence allow the Achuar to divide their year into two astronomical stages, each of which is characterized by a contrast in climate (Fig. 8).

There is one more heavenly body to which the Achuar assign the function of periodic marker, but its pertinence as a temporal reference stems less from any astral trajectory than from climatic conditions. It is well known that the Milky Way can be seen only on very clear, moonless nights; when, on the contrary, the atmosphere is saturated with moisture, it becomes very difficult to detect. It is easy to understand, then, why the Achuar claim that it is invisible during the rainy season; and when, every now and then, it shows itself during this season, it is simply dismissed as clouds (*yurankim*). The heavy rains come to an end in August, and the Milky Way can once more be seen on almost any night of the dry season. Now this is also the period when the *charap* turtles (*Podocnemis expansa*) begin laying their eggs in the upstream regions. And so the Milky Way is depicted by the Achuar as being a swath of eggs of turtles (*charapa nujintri*), who climb the heavenly vault to lay in the sky.

The association between a meteorological-astronomical phenomenon and the seasonal periodicity of a natural resource is fairly typical of the twofold nature of Achuar representations of temporality. Two time scales exist side by side, one of which serves to indicate fixed times, while the other divides the year into a series of significant periods. The first scale uses an astronomical coding, in itself quite precise, but wanting in pragmatic value, for lack of an extended number system which could combine the three main classes of time units (days, moons, years). By contrast, the second time scale – the calendar of seasonal resources – overlays the entire year with a dense network of tangible signs whose succession is ineluctable, but whose local appearances may fluctuate (Fig. 8).

Paradoxically, this calendar of natural resources revolves around the seasonal periodicity of a plant cultivated in every Achuar garden, the chonta palm (*Guilielma gasipaes*, or *uwi* in Achuar). It is the only species of palm tree in upper Amazonia that is a true cultigen, that is, whose reproduction depends entirely on human action (Lathrap 1970: 57). The chonta bears large racemes of reddish-orange fruit from mid-February to mid-August. The exact date of first fruiting varies with the nature of the habitat; as a rule, it is later in the lower zones than in the interfluve, a difference that can be as much as three weeks. The Achuar do not attach as much symbolic importance to the chonta palm as their neighbors, the Shuar, and the highly elaborate ritual which the latter celebrate each year for this plant has no equivalent among the Achuar (Pellizzaro 1978b). For the Shuar, the periodic fruiting of the chonta is even the model for the annual cycle: they designate the year by the term *uwi*, preferring this agronomic coding system to the Achuar's astronomical system. But even if the Achuar do not surround the chonta with any such symbolic apparatus, they still consider the six-month period during which this palm tree bears

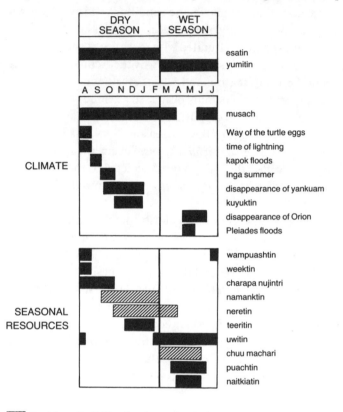

▨ Best times for fishing, hunting, and gathering
namanktin: "fish season"
teeritin: "fish-egg season"
charapa nujintri: "turtle-egg season"
chuu machari: "woolly-monkey-fat season"
weektin: "flying-ant season"
puachtin: "frog season"
neretin: "fruit season"
naitkiatin: "late-fruit season"
wampuashtin: "kapok season"
uwitin: "chonta season"

8. Calendar of seasonal resources

fruit (*uwitin*, "chonta season") to come under the sign of abundance. In effect, chonta season coincides in part with the end or the beginning of other natural resource cycles (Fig. 8) the temporary conjugation of which makes this a particularly lavish time of year.

Around three months before chonta season, the "wild-fruit season" (*neretin*) begins, and goes on until mid-April, when the "late-fruit season" takes over, lasting into June. The height of abundance falls between February and April, during which time some thirty wild species are all bearing succulent and sometimes huge fruits. The most common, that is those that, during this season, are eaten every day in all Achuar homes, are those from the wild mango *apai* (*Grias tessmannii*), the *aguaje* palm, the *kunkuk* palm, the wild sapote *pau* (*Pouteria* sp.), the different varieties of *Inga*, the *tauch* tree (*Lacmella peruviana*), and the *chimi* tree. By contrast, the "late-fruit season" is relatively poor, as only a half dozen species bear fruit at this time of year; the most important are the *chaapi* palm, the *sunkash* tree (*Perebea guianensis*), and the *shimpishi* tree (*Solanum americanum*). The *neretin* season is also the time of the year when three different species of bee make their honey (*mishik*) in hollow trees.

The periodic abundance of wild fruits has direct consequences for the animal populations that feed on them, especially birds and primates. *Neretin* season is the time when monkeys build up the body fat and muscle that see them safely through the relatively lean period beginning in July. These fruit-eaters are very thin at the onset of the fruit season and need three or four months to reconstitute their stores, so that it is not until March that the *chuu machari* ("woolly-monkey-fat") season really begins. This expression comes from the fact that, from March to July, the woolly monkey carries a layer of fat (*macha*) several centimeters thick under the skin of its thorax. Now the Achuar are exceedingly fond of fat, and this seasonal trait of the woolly monkey thus becomes the symbol of a period of plentiful animal fat.

February is also the time when many species of bird hatch, since the abundance of available fruit makes it easy to feed the nestlings. The beginning of *chuu machari* season is therefore the best time to go nest robbing, especially for parrot and toucan eggs and young. Skewered and roasted over the fire, these little birds are a favorite delicacy, for, while the flesh of the adult bird is normally on the tough side, that of the young birds is tender and tasty. From April to June is also the time when a succession of various species of frog come down from the trees in which they normally perch. With the heavy rains of *yumitin* season, puddles and ponds proliferate, and frogs gather by the thousands during *puachtin* ("frog season") to lay their eggs in the water-filled depressions. Drawn by the croaking choruses, the Achuar visit these batrachian assemblies to better their daily fare.

Because of the abundance, the quality, and the variety of easily available natural resources, the period from January to June is the best time for hunting and gathering fruit. These two activities do not cease with the month of July, but the harvest falls off sharply in quality or in quantity: the game is thin and stringy, and the wild fruits become so scarce that people must fall back on palm hearts (*ijiu*), the only vegetable resource available all year round.

That the end of "frog season" practically coincides with that of "woolly-monkey-fat season" does not, however, mean the onset of a period of generally scarce natural resources. Come August, the "turtle-egg season" (*charapa nujintri*) begins together with "flying-ant season" (*weektin*). *Charap* turtles lay their eggs in the sand from August to December, that is when the heat and the dry air provide optimum conditions for incubation. Each animal lays up to fifty eggs in a hole it has dug on the beach, above the water line, and which it carefully covers, then abandons. The Achuar have only to walk along the beach until they see the characteristic tracks made by the turtles when they drag themselves out of the water to lay. At the height of *charapa nujintri* season, any well-exposed sand bar will yield several hundreds of these appetizing and highly nutritious eggs. The beginning of the dry season is also the time male warrior ants (*week*) leave the anthill in flights of hundreds of individuals, after having paid their respects to the queen. This seasonal migration takes place only once a year in each colony, and so the Achuar watch closely for the warning signs. At the right moment, a shallow ditch is dug around the anthill and enclosed with a light fence. The night the *week* seem set to swarm, the Achuar affix copal torches to the top of the breastwork; the ants fly into the flames, burn their wings and fall in large numbers into the trench. The Achuar are very fond of these roasted ants, and the *weektin* season is eagerly awaited.

If the dry season provides a chance to vary the daily diet with such delicacies as ants and turtle eggs, it is also the best time of year for fishing; the size of the catches during this period generously makes up for the scarcity and thinness of land game. Between October and February, the generally low river levels (*kuyuktin*) make fish highly vulnerable to the various devices used by the Achuar. Fish poisoning, for instance, is practicable only when the water is low, since one must be able to wade in to collect the asphyxiated fish. When the rivers are at their lowest, it also becomes easy to block off a branch with a weighted net (*neka*) and harpoon the trapped fish at leisure. As they are hungry for oxygen and food in the shallow waters, the fish are always jumping, thereby signaling their presence to the watchful fisherman. These starved fish will take any bait, and fishing with a hook at this time of year is more like hauling fish from a stock pond. From December to February, that is to say towards the end of "fish season" (*namanktin*), the females spawn. This "fish-egg season" (*teeritin*) is joyously hailed by the Achuar, as the last delicacy from the aquatic world heralds the opening of the good-hunting season.

And so the ways of using nature change with the seasons, and if she liberally showers the Achuar with her blessings, they are not the same from season to season. This is worth pointing out, for the absence of seasonal contrasts in the agricultural cycle of the societies native to the upper Amazon all too often makes us forget those that characterize their foraging activities. Each time of year is marked by a preferential relationship between man and one particular natural domain: the forest, dispenser of fruits, insects, and arboreal game; or the river, purveyor of fish, turtles, and aquatic game. But the duality is not only diachronic, for, depending on the habitat, the use of the environment inclines toward one or the other of these resource spheres. Upstream Achuar lean more towards the forest, while downstream groups look to the river.

Each of these areas of daily praxis is itself linked with yet other levels of the cosmos: with the heavenly vault rising out of the inaccessible headwaters of the rivers and with the underground and underwater worlds peopled with a host of spirits. The Achuar are well aware that they dwell on the surface of a universe the upper and lower levels of which are ordinarily closed to them. The layer to which they are confined lies within very narrow limits: above their heads, the tops of the trees they climb to rob toucan nests form one impassable boundary, while beneath their feet or beneath the hull of their canoe stretch strange, unknown worlds. Only the Achuar living on the upper course of the Pastaza have an episodic experience of the netherworld, because they sometimes descend into chasms that afford nesting grounds for thousands of *tayu* birds (*Steatornis caripensis*). The young of these cave-dwelling nightjars contain prodigious amounts of fat, and it is the prospect of a Pantagruelian fat feast alone that persuades certain Achuar to surmount their repugnance for the chthonian world.

And yet this stratification of the cosmos is not as irrevocable as it might seem at first glance; passageways existed in mythological times, and, in exceptional circumstances, some of them are still practicable. The world above has become definitively inaccessible since Moon commanded the celestial liana to be severed. But before that, they say the Achuar used to go walking in the sky. The celestial vault used to be much lower than it is today and, before getting there, one had to beware of the slate-colored hawk, *jiishimp* (*Leucopternis shistacea*), who divebombed travelers to make them release their hold. In order to pass this test, the traveler had to shut his eyes and continue climbing; the traveler who looked directly at the bird was changed into a hawk on the spot. These celestial strolls seem to have been the prerogative of one and all, and to this day the Achuar regret their definitive disappearance.

The descent into the worlds beneath the ground or the waters has an entirely different status from the celestial ascent; if no cosmic catastrophe has actually barred the way, the journey is nevertheless now made by only a handful of daredevils, and only in very special circumstances. Translation to the lower realms is not accomplished in the waking state (*tsawaramti*), but in the course of journeys made by the soul when dreaming or in a hallucinatory trance (*nampektin*) induced by narcotic plants. These peregrinations of the soul (*wakan*) make it possible at times to catch sight of those strange populations that lead underground and underwater lives very like those of the Achuar on the face of the earth. Divided into several clearly separate races, these beings are the tutelary spirits which ensure that hunting and fishing are performed in the proper way; some of them also act as shamans' helpers. But these spirits do not always keep to the lower layers; when they surface on the plane where the Achuar live, they constitute a real threat to human life. Beneath the ground and the waters, then, lie inhabited worlds parallel to the surface world and with which one must endeavor to remain on good terms. It is on this condition that the spirits renounce their natural aggressiveness and allow the Achuar to take from the different domains of the biosphere what they need for their living. Throughout the year, upstream and down, above and below, beneath the ground and beneath the waters, nature appears as a great continuum of sociality. In this way these peripheral sites inaccessible from the domestic sphere are conceptually annexed by human praxis as the sources likely to nourish man's condition of possibility.

3

Nature's beings

The limited types of landscape that make up the humid forest contrast
sharply with the extreme variety of animal and plant species found there.
The jungle appears monotonous, not because the species are all the same,
but because an identical mixture of species is repeated ad infinitum. When it
is possible clearly to distinguish landscapes, this is done by contrasting
growth that is characterized by diversity (dense forest) with monospecific
growth (flooded forest, riverine forest, stands of tree ferns. . .). If then they
wanted to produce an operative classification of such uniformly varied
organic elements, the Achuar had no choice but to name them all
separately. The procedures for identifying and classifying plant and animal
species constitute an important sector of Achuar representations of the
environment. But their knowledge as naturalists falls far short of exhausting reality, for the organic world cannot be reduced to simple taxonomic
systems. And so the Achuar identify each plant, each animal as belonging to
a class; but they also endow each with human affects and a life of its own.
Thus every living being in the world of nature has its own personality, which
distinguishes it from the other members of its species and enables humans
to deal with each individually.

The taxonomic order

Flora

On a forest walk, it is extremely rare that an adult Achuar is unable to provide the ignorant ethnologist with the vernacular name of any plant he may point to. Several experiments with patient informants show that a man knows the name of nearly all the trees he encounters on a trip of several kilometers or in a large tract of forest that is to be cleared. Proceeding in this manner, we were able to catalogue 262 different Achuar names of wild plants; but our list is certainly not complete and could no doubt be extended by a systematic ethnobotanical survey. The distinctive criteria for identification are first of all morphological; for trees it is shape, the texture and color of the bark, the leaves and fruit, the bearing of the crown, and the aspect of the roots. When shape and color are not enough to identify one species of tree morphologically very like another, the Achuar make a cut in the trunk and remove pieces of bark and sapwood; identification is then made by smell and often by taste. The Indians' scientific curiosity is always on the alert; when someone comes across a species he does not recognize, he will take a bark sample in order to submit his own interpretation to the sagacity of more experienced botanists.

The completeness and precision of the vernacular nomenclature varies with the family of plants; while all trees specific to the region have vernacular names, only a few species of epiphytic plants and mosses are identified. And yet the inclusion of a plant in the native system is not determined by strictly utilitarian criteria, and many plants that are of no use to humans have been given names. Of the 262 wild plants identified, no more than half are of any practical use to the Achuar: some sixty species bear edible fruit or are used in medicinal or cosmetic preparations, some thirty are used in building houses and making various artefacts, and roughly the same number are used for firewood. Certain wild plants, in particular the palms, are polyvalent and, as the circumstances demand, contribute their leaves, their fruit, their wood, their bark, or their latex.

As a rule each vernacular name corresponds to a species in Western botanical nomenclature. Some species, however, are given two names, employed alternately depending on the context in which the plant is used; this is the case with the common chambira palm (*Astrocaryum chambira*), which is called *mata* when referring to its edible fruit, or *kumai*, when speaking of the leaf fibers, used for making string. Inversely, sometimes a single vernacular term designates different species having similar botanical characteristics; for instance, *chinchak* denotes several species of *Miconia* and *Leandra*, of the Melastomaceae family, whose berries are relished by toucans. It also happens that a single name is used for two morphologically similar species, one of which is wild and the other cultivated. For example, *paat* designates both sugar cane (*Saccharum officinarum*) and a nearly identical riparian cane (*Gynerium sagittatum*), while *winchu*, the generic name for the domestic banana (*Musa* sp.), also denotes a wild Musaceae (*Heliconia* sp.). In both cases, it seems that the name of the wild plant was used, by derivation, for non-indigenous cultigens introduced long ago.

There are a number of systems for naming plants. Most often the plant has an individual name that distinguishes it from all the other lexemes of the language. But a plant may also be designated by a descriptive metaphor; this expression does not constitute a lexeme in its own right, even though the specific combination of terms is peculiar to this plant. The most frequent examples are produced by affixing a determiner to the generic term "tree" (*numi*): for instance *taishnumi*, "yellow-tailed-oriole tree," designates a tree whose fruit is a favorite food of these weaver birds, which nest there in colonies; *ajinumi*, "pimento tree" (*Mouriri grandiflora*), has berries that resemble this spice; while the star apple, *yaas* (*Chrysophyllum caimito*), grown in every garden, is used as a determiner to make the name of a very similar wild species, *yaasnumi* (*Pouteria canito*). Or the metaphor may be entirely descriptive and illustrate one of the plant's morphological features: for instance, *panki nai* ("anaconda's fang") and *pamasuki* ("tapir's scrotum") are two legumes whose fruits allegedly look like these parts of the anatomy.

The names of some plants are the same as the objects made from them: for instance *karis* designates the decorative tubes that men stick through their ear lobes as well as the slender bamboo from which they are made; *taun* denotes the boatman's pole and the tree (*Aspidosperma megalocarpon*) used in its making; *paeni* means both the posts of a house and the tree (*Minquartia punctata*) usually employed. And finally, the proper name of a plant is sometimes specified by a term indicating its purpose or use: for example, *uum kankum* ("blowgun *kankum*") is a vine used mainly for wrapping blowguns. Aside from a few phonetic variations, there is little difference between the Achuar and Shuar names for wild plants. Nevertheless, certain species have entirely different names in the two dialect groups, and in this case act as ethnic markers: for example, (Ach.) *naship* = (Sh.) *shimship* (*Licania* sp.), (Ach.) *kuunt* = (Sh.) *teren* (*Wettinia maynensis*), or (Ach.) *wapa* = (Sh.) *iwianch jii* (*Mucuna huberi*).

The Achuar have no term for plants in general, and their classification within this unnamed group is meagre. The three main taxonomic systems can be seen in Achuar ethnobotany: a system of explicit conceptual categories, a system of explicit categories determined by their pragmatic destination, and a system of implicit or latent, underlying categories. By explicit categories, we mean named categories that can be used as a generic term in place of the species name in a performative utterance. For example, if an Achuar wants to designate a tree whose proper name he does not know, he will say "*ju numi*" ("this or that tree"). Besides *numi*, the explicit conceptual categories are: *nupa* ("grassy plant"), *cesa* ("flower," e.g. for orchids), *shinki* ("palm tree"), *naek* ("thin vine"), *kaap* ("thick vine"), and *jinkiai* ("berry bush," but also "berries," "pits," "seeds"). As in the case of *numi*, these explicit categories are often used as generic terms in the composition of species names: for instance *saar nupa* ("whitish grass") or *tanish naek* ("thin fencing vine"). We qualify these categories as conceptual in that they divide the plant kingdom into morphological classes irrespective of any notion of practical utilization.

Inversely, the system of pragmatic explicit categories subsumes into a single named class all species of plant used for the same purpose. Sometimes the two systems overlap, particularly in the case of the category *shinki*. Indeed, *shinki* designates the class of palm trees as a whole, but the term also denotes the highly typical type of wood provided by palm trunks. Because of the density and the particular structure of their wood, palm trees are used for making a wide variety of objects, from beds to blowguns. Depending on the context, then, the term *shinki* is used in a conceptual mode (the class of palm trees) or a pragmatic mode (the class of plants that yields a certain type of wood). Another class is that of firewood, *jii* (literally, "fire"), which includes some twenty species whose properties are identical: slow combustion, high heat production, and high density. Except in rare cases, the Achuar always use *jii* trees for their home fires; the most prevalent are: *chimi* (*Pseudolmedia laevigata*), *tsachir* (*Mabea argutissima*), *tsapakai* (*Guarea* sp.), *tsai* (a legume), and *ararats*.

The latent categories are obviously much more difficult to detect than the explicit ones, as the ethnologist always runs the risk of plucking them from his own imagination. We have therefore taken the precaution of considering implicit plant classes to be made up only of those species always associated in the same way in certain types of unsolicited commentaries accompanying the answer to a question from the ethnologist. For instance, when asked the name of a certain palm tree, an Achuar informant will often add "*ijiu yutai*" ("the heart is edible"). It is thus permissible to postulate that the species of palm trees with an edible heart – which is not the case for all species – form an implicit pragmatic category. The existence of such an unnamed category seems confirmed by the fact that, when an Achuar is asked what species of palm trees have edible hearts, he automatically reels off the list: *tuntuam, kunkuk, sake* (*Euterpe* sp.), *achu, iniayua, katiri,* and *kuyuuwa* (unidentified).

Most of these latent categories are structured by utilitarian concerns. The most immediate of these is the division of all plants into two mutually exclusive classes according to their food potential: *yutai* ("edible") and *yuchatai* ("non-edible"). This alimentary determiner is not reserved for those species that provide edible elements for human consumption. We also postulate the existence of at least two latent categories that subsume plants whose fruit or seeds are eaten by animals: that of toucan trees, denoted by the commentary "eaten by toucans" (*tsukanka yutai*), and that of woolly-monkey trees. In both cases the trees in these categories provide prime natural blinds for stalking game. Another latent category of a pragmatic order seems to be formed by the set of trees used for house frames (see Chapter Four).

Latent pragmatic categories are fairly easy to identify because of their obvious use in the context of certain spheres of practice. The existence of implicit, conceptual categories, on the other hand – that is, categories not determined by the potential use to which they may be put – is harder to affirm with certainty. In an article on the ethnobotany of the Aguaruna Jivaro, Brent Berlin posits the existence of latent native categories ("covert categories") corresponding more or less to Western botanical genera (Berlin 1977). The idea is certainly attractive, even though the interpretation the Aguaruna may have of the distinctive features that define each of these "covert categories" is not set out in any detail. It is certain that, like the Aguaruna, the Achuar perceive morphological similarities between different species of plant with distinct names. These similarities are sometimes clearly indicated by lexical derivation, as in the case of *yaas/yaas numi*, but this is far from being the rule. There is no doubt however that certain floristic associations are perceived as such by the Achuar, whether they be defined in terms of botanical or of spatial proximity (e.g. intrusive secondary growth species). Nevertheless, with the exception of a few instances (in particular *Ingas*, see Chapter Five), it would be risky systematically to transform these empirically observable associations into implicit analytical categories.

Fauna

If there are a few gaps in the mesh of terminology the Achuar have developed to classify the flora of their habitat, by contrast, the fauna is covered by an extensive system of names and articulated by a host of generic categories. The Achuar have a lexicon of around six hundred animal names, of which 86 are for mammals, 48 for reptiles, 47 for amphibians, 78 for fish, 156 for birds, and 177 for invertebrates (42 different names for ants alone). Of all the species distinguished by the Achuar, only slightly over a third (around 240) are considered edible and less than a tenth are eaten on a regular basis. In the case of the fauna, even more than in that of the flora, it is clear that Achuar ethnoscience is not governed primarily by utilitarian concerns. In effect, the meticulousness with which they apply themselves to taxonomy is independent of the potential use-value they ascribe to the species under consideration; it is, for example, hard to see what economic benefit could possibly accrue from differentiating between thirty-three different species of butterfly, not one of which is put to any practical use by the Achuar. Taxonomic knowledge is just as much an instrument of pure knowledge for bringing order to the world as a practical instrument for acting effectively upon it. Although this principle has on the whole been accepted since Lévi-Strauss first advanced it in *The Savage Mind*, acceptance has not been unanimous; American ecological materialism continues to relegate its proponents to the obscure idealistic realms of "mentalism."

That certain animals are every bit as good to think with as they are good to eat stands out in the extraordinary development of such areas of Achuar ethnozoology as ethology or comparative anatomy. And the native knowledge of animal behavior and morphology is as broad for non-hunted species as for those they hunt. While it is essential to observe the habits of game, fish, and predators in order to hunt and fish effectively, it is of no immediate pragmatic significance when it comes to animals not directly either useful or harmful to humans. And yet the Achuar are well acquainted with the latter, and the notion of any selective knowledge of species based on their usefulness can only lead to paralogism. Indeed, it would be difficult to explain how the Achuar could temporarily suspend their faculties of observation, which are continually solicited by myriads of natural objects.

Not only are the Achuar capable of describing the minutest details of the habits and habitat of each species they identify, they can also imitate their calls. Almost all animals are attributed a mode of expression that takes the linguistic form of a stereotyped onomatopoeia: for example, the call of the spider-monkey is "*aar*" and that of the toucan "*kuan-kuan*." When a myth relates the transformation of a human being into an animal of the same name, the change of status is often marked by the loss of spoken language and the acquisition of a specific call. Certain variants of the Auju myth specify that, when *auju* woman changed into a potoo bird and then attempted to plead with her husband, the only sound she could utter was the characteristic cry "*aujuuu-aujuuu-aujuuu*." Their remarkable knowledge of animal behavior goes well beyond mere taxonomy, then, and sometimes even stands in its stead. When identifying birds from color plates, it was often the case that an informant would say: "This one is diurnal, lives in the canopy, eats such-and-such foods, is hunted by this or that animal, lives in bands of seven or eight, sings this way, but I've forgotten its name."

As a rule, each vernacular animal name corresponds to a species in our own zoological nomenclature, but the exceptions here are more numerous than for plant names. In particular, the Achuar frequently distinguish several species where zoologists only recognize one. In effect, the Amazonian fauna is still relatively little known, and the Achuar have the considerable advantage over naturalists of being able constantly to observe animals in the wild. For example, the Achuar distinguish twelve species of feline, more than half of which are not clearly identified by scientific zoology. Furthermore, because of native hostility towards whites, Jivaro territory has long been a *terra incognita* for Western naturalists; it is likely that a scientific survey would turn up some unidentified species or some reputed not usually to be found in this type of habitat.

Unlike the flora, for which species names are sometimes formed from metaphors drawn from the animal kingdom, each element of the fauna recognized by the Achuar has a name of its own. The one exception to this rule of lexical univocity is the firefly, called *yaa*, like the stars. An animal's name is often formed simply by reproduction of the characteristic sound it makes: this is the case, as we have seen, of the *auju* bird or of the noisy *achayat*, which designates both a type of manakin (*Teleonema filicauda*) and its peculiar cry. An animal may also be called alternately by its proper name or by the lexeme that imitates its call: this is the case, for example, of the slate-colored grosbeak (*Pitylus grossus*), called either *iwianch chinki* (literally, "bad-spirit sparrow") or *peesepeesi*. Even in the case of avifauna, in which sexual dimorphism is often strongly marked, the Achuar are quite capable of recognizing in both the male and the female the characteristics common to the species. It rarely happens, then, that male and female are identified as two different species, even if their secondary sexual attributes make them morphologically quite dissimilar. The only case worth mentioning is the hummingbird *Florisuga mellivora*: the male is called *maikiua jempe* (*jempe* is the generic name for hummingbirds), while the female is called *tsemai jempe*.

Within a single species, the Achuar may bestow a proper name upon certain individuals whose function or morphology or habits set them clearly apart from the others. Such is the case, for instance, of solitary members of a gregarious species or, inversely, of herd leaders. Similarly, with Amazon ants (*yarush*), the Achuar make a distinction between winged males (*week*), soldiers (*naishampri*), female workers (*shuari*, literally "the people"), and the queen (*shaasham*). Species that go through post-embryonic metamorphoses are often given a different name for each developmental stage; for example the palm grub (*Calandra palmarum*) is called *tsampu* in the adult stage, while the larvae – which the Achuar relish – are known as *muntish*. On the other hand, tadpoles are given a generic name, *kutuku*, regardless of the species of batrachian they will turn into as adults (the Achuar distinguish some fifty species).

Cases in which the scientific nomenclature is more discriminating than the vernacular system are extremely rare; in one instance, the Achuar use the name *saserat* for a red-crested woodpecker that systematic ornithologists divide into two species (*Campephilus melanoleucos* and *Dryocopus lineatus*) because of differences that are difficult to see at first glance. The same holds for the *jaapash*, a nocturnal heron – and therefore both hard to observe and inedible – which, it seems, should in reality be split into two very closely related species (*Nyctanassa violacea* and *Nycticorax nycticorax*). Lastly, certain names designate families for which the terminology recognizes no individual species: for example, owls, *ampush* (Strigidae), nightjars, *sukuyar* (Caprimulgidae), puffbirds, *shiik* (Bucconidae), and vultures, *yapu* (Cathartidae). The Achuar are obviously aware of the morphological differences between the various species in these families, but these are pushed into the background by common generic attributes: to wit, the horns and the circles around the eyes of owls, and the tufts around the beak of puffbirds.

The Achuar do then perceive the distinctive features by which species can be grouped into named generic classes, the outlines of which, in fact, rarely correspond to those of the families of Western zoology. The vernacular terms that designate these generic categories constitute root names to which a determiner is added in order to identify a particular species. The rules governing inclusion in a generic category are sometimes elusive. For example, the category *yawa* includes a number of carnivorous mammals that, at first sight, seem quite dissimilar. Among the Felidae, we find the jaguar, *Pantera onca* (*juunt yawa*: "big *yawa*"), the black jaguar (*suach yawa*), the puma, *Felis concolor* (*japa yawa*: "deer-*yawa*"), and an unidentified animal the size of a jaguar but with a slightly different coat (*yampinkia yawa*). But this category also includes small carnivores very different from cats: two types of wild bush dog, *Speothos venaticus* (*patukam yawa*: "Huambisa *yawa*") and *Atelocinus microtis* (*kuap yawa*), the huron, *Gallictis vittata canaster* (*entsaya yawa*: "water-*yawa*"), a species of tayra (*amich yawa*: "tayra-*yawa*"), and the domestic dog (*tanku yawa*: "domestic-*yawa*"), a hound, probably descended from the Estremaduran greyhound, introduced among the Jivaro shortly after the Spanish conquest.

Among the members of this motley collection, the jaguar and the dog are almost always designated, in a performative context, by their basic generic name, *yawa*, without the appropriate qualifying prefix. It is therefore permissible to regard them as two distinct archetypes, of which other kinds of *yawa* would be derivatives. A number of clues seem to confirm that the dog and the jaguar have a matrix-like function in constituting the category *yawa*. In the first place, the domestic dog is always symbolically associated with the bush dog, which becomes its wild counterpart (Chapter Six); this is a purely conceptual association, and the Achuar are fully aware that it is not founded on any process of genetic derivation. Now all the non-feline *yawa* are morphologically very similar to the *Speothos*, even if morphologically they differ considerably from the Achuar domestic dog. Furthermore, the black jaguar enjoys supernatural status and is regarded by the Achuar as an aquatic equivalent of the spotted jaguar, acting as watchdog for the spirits of the water-world. According to coat color, solid or spotted, the physical conformation of the feline *yawa* species identifies them with one or the other of this original jaguar pair. The rule governing subsumption into the *yawa* category seems to rest on two inverted conversions of animal pairs articulated by the nature–culture axis. In one case, the wild jaguar is socialized into a supernatural domestic dog, the resulting pair constituting the matrix from which the feline *yawa* are derived; while in the other case, the domestic dog is transformed into a wild dog, the latter becoming the emblem of all non-feline *yawa*.

But as is often the case when analyzing taxonomic systems, it is much easier to speculate on the general structural principles that govern inclusion in a class than to understand where this inclusion stops. Thus a whole series of felines whose coats are spotted like the jaguar's, or solid, like that of the black jaguar, are nevertheless not designated by the generic *yawa*, but each by its own name; among these we find, in particular, two species of ocelot, *Felis pardalis* (*untucham*) and *Felis wiedii* (*papash*), the margay, *Felis tigrina* (*wampish*), and the jaguarundi (*shishim*). Also excluded from the category *yawa* are certain carnivores morphologically similar to the bush dog, like the skunk, *Conepatus* sp. (*juicham*), the giant otter (*wankanim*), or the common tayra, *Tayra barbara* (*amich*). In the latter case, it is even harder to understand how, of two closely related species of tayra, one is *yawa* and the other is not, unless we postulate that here *yawa* is not the generic name but, on the contrary, the determiner affixed to qualify *amich*, itself a generic category of tayras.

So the basic classifications cannot be said to function merely as a totalizing explanatory logic, and the ethnologist must of necessity accept a certain degree of arbitrariness in matters of taxonomy. The rules for assigning determiners to root names however seem to be entirely consistent. Within the category *yawa*, for example, two types of determiner are used: one specifies the basic category by means of a habitat qualifier, the other uses morphological homology. Members of the first type are names like *entsaya yawa*, "water-*yawa*," or *patukam yawa*, "Huambisa *yawa*," sometimes also called *mayn yawa*, "Mayna-*yawa*." *Patukam shuar* is the ethnonym used by the Achuar to designate the Huambisa Jivaro, while *mayn shuar* denotes an Achuar subgroup living in Peru along the tributaries of the Rio Corrientes. Here the determiner refers not so much to the purported ethnic origins of the bush dog as to the particular biotope he is thought to occupy together with these two dialect groups. The second type of operator of determinations specifies by similarity of appearance. For instance, in the name for puma, *japa yawa*, the determiner *japa* (the generic name for the Cervidae) evokes the fact that the coat of this feline and that of the brocket deer (*Mazama americana*) are the same color. In this instance, the root name and the determiner are also generic names, as is the case, too, for *amich yawa*; the operator *yawa* specifies a variety of tayra by its alleged resemblance to the bush dog.

Because of their morphological characteristics, certain species or certain families become preferential signifiers of categorial distinction and are thus systematically used as determiners. For instance, *chuwi* designates a class of the Icteridae family that includes several species of cacique and oropendola whose common trait is a bright yellow belly. The species type of this class and the one that gives it its name, is the very common crested oropendola (*Psarocolius decumanus*). Within this class, the Achuar go on to distinguish a green oropendola with a large beak (*Psarocolius viridis*), called *chuwi tsukanka* ("toucan-*chuwi*") by homology with the outsized beak of the toucan.

In the animal order, the Achuar distinguish and name twenty-seven categories, of which only two correspond to what Western zoology calls suborders: bats (*jeencham*) and spiders (*tsere*). These generic categories exhibit highly diverse properties (Fig. 9). They can, for example, comprise species whose morphology is either very dissimilar, as in the case of the *yawa*, or very close, which is the case for the seventeen generic categories of bird. Some of the categories are inclusive; for instance all Ophidia are divided between two mutually exclusive classes: constrictors, *panki*, the type species of which is the anaconda (*Eunectes murinus*), and non-constrictors, *napi*. On the other hand, frogs are the only generic category of tailless batrachians that have a name (*puach*) used in composing the names of particular species. Toads are named by individual species but not subsumed into a generic category. If most of the generic categories are used as root names for the formation of species names, some however are not integrated into the naming system. For example, the category *pinchu* encompasses five species of bird of prey of the Accipitridae and Falconidae families, only one of which, the type species, is designated by the root name *pinchu* plus determiner: *pee pee pinchu* (the hook-billed kite, *Chondrohierax uncinatus*) is thus placed with *kukukui* (the forest falcon, *Micrastur*), *kauta* (the laughing hawk, *Herpetotheres cachinnans*), *makua* (the black-collared hawk, *Busarellus nigricollis*), and *jiishimp* (the slate-colored hawk, *Leucopternis shistacea*) to make up the group *pinchu*.

The category *tsere* (spiders) is an interesting case, for it also designates a species belonging to a different zoological phylum; in effect, *tsere* is also the vernacular name of the capuchin monkey (*Cebus capucinus*). Indigenous commentary maintains that the terminological homology is founded on a disturbing behavioral homology. According to the Achuar, both animals feign death when they are threatened, curling up into a tight ball and tucking in their legs; then they literally jump on the first occasion to bite their aggressor. Here the Achuar taxonomical imagination has selected a highly discrete behavioral homology between the capuchins and spiders rather than the much more obvious morphological homology that led Western travelers to give the name spider monkey to another species of primate, the *Ateles belzebuth*. Moreover, by an amusing paradox, the spider monkey (Ach. *washi*) itself serves as a determiner in the compound name of yet another type of spider called *washi tsere*. Taxonomic systems bear witness to the peculiar way the logic of material things functions, as not only the principles of like habitats or morphological features are pressed into service as categorial operators of distinction, but also the principle of same behavior, as illustrated here. Certain animal species are emblematic of a particular quality, and this distinctive quality becomes the determining feature, signified by the name of the species that embodies it best.

And yet, there are few generic categories, and they leave out whole areas of inexplicably neglected qualities. For instance, some very common species which would seem to belong to one class by virtue of the particularly characteristic physical features that they share are nevertheless not incorporated into generic categories. The prominent bill of Cuvier's toucan

Suprageneric categories

Vernacular name	Common name	Zoological identification
Kuntin	"Game"	—
Chinki	"Sparrows"	—
Namak	"Big fish"	—
Tsarur	"Minnows"	—

Generic categories

Ampush	Owls	Strigidae
Charakat	Kingfishers	Alcedinidae
Chinimp	Swallows, purple martins	Hirundinidae
Chuchup	Antbirds	Formicariidae
Chuwi	Oropendolas, caciques, orioles	Icteridae
Ikianchim	Cuckoos	Cuculidae
Jinicham	Flycatchers, tyrants	Tyrannidae
Jempe	Hummingbirds	Trochilidae
Kawau	Macaws	—
Patu	Ducks	Anatidae
Pinchu	Kites, falcons, hawks	—
Shiik	Puffbirds	Bucconidae
Tinkish	Wrens	Troglodytidae
Turu	Woodpeckers	—
Yampits	Doves	—
Sukuyar	Nightjars	Caprimulgidae
Tunkau	—	Pimelodidae
Nayump	—	Loricariidae
Panki	Constrictors	Boidae
Napi	Non-constrictors	Non-Boidae
Puach	Frogs	—
Japa	—	Cervidae
Paki	Peccaries	Tayassuidae
Jeencham	Bats	Chiroptera
Tsere	Spiders	—
Yawa	Certain carnivorous mammals	—

9. Generic names of the animal kingdom

(*tsukanka*) makes this bird the bearer of an original quality which, as we have seen, qualifies it to specify a species of Icteridae. Nevertheless, the Ramphastidae family, all members of which closely resemble Cuvier's toucan, does not as a whole constitute a vernacular class. Each of the five species of toucan has its own name, and the tiny differences that set them apart are enough to prevent the Achuar incorporating them into a single category. Another exemplary case is the armadillo, with its odd morphology. The Achuar identify five species of Armadillo: *sema* (*Cabassou* sp.), *shushui* (*Dasypus novemcinctus*), *yankunt* (*Priodontes giganteus*), *tuich* (*Dasypus* sp.), and *urancham* (*Dasypus* sp.). At first glance, what sets one type of armadillo apart from another (size, number of plates in the armor) seems less important than what sets armadillos as a group apart from other animals. But here again the Achuar eschew placing all armadillos into a generic category. And we could find other examples, for such generic gaps affect all orders of the animal kingdom.

The field offered by these obvious possible groupings is far from being integrally covered by vernacular generic categories, and the more classification proceeds from the particular to the general, the more imprecise the taxonomic divisions become. Unlike the Western system of classification, Achuar zoological taxonomy distinguishes neither phyla (vertebrates, molluscs. . .), nor classes (mammals, fish. . .), nor orders (primates, rodents, carnivores. . .). They have, for example, no named category for birds, monkeys, or insects. And yet the Achuar use four general categories, the peculiarity of which is to classify certain animals by the way they are captured rather than by their morphological traits: *kuntin* ("game"), *namak* ("big fish"), *tsarur* ("minnows"), and *chinki* ("sparrows").

Kuntin designates all animals with fur or feathers that can legitimately be hunted; this category embraces all vertebrates not prohibited as food, with the exception, naturally, of fish and batrachians. *Namak* is the term for all fish that are caught with harpoon or hook and line, while *tsarur* refers to small fish caught by fish poison. The two categories encompass most fish, since, with the exception of the electric eel (*tsunkiru*), all species may be caught, and each, of necessity, can be defined by its membership in one or the other class. As large fish are sometimes taken when streams are dammed and poisoned, the *namak*/*tsarur* classification is further refined by differentiating the ways of preparing the catch. Big fish are generally cut into slices or filleted, and boiled; while minnows are cooked whole in *papillottes* of banana leaves. *Chinki* are a somewhat special case, as this is both a generic and a suprageneric category. Any small bird too far away to identify by its proper name will be designated as *chinki*. But *chinki* also denotes a very broad generic class embracing several species of the order of Passeriformes; each species is qualified by the basic name *chinki*, plus a determiner. All four suprageneric categories designate distinct groups of edible animals and, in everyday usage, are as much a way of classifying food types as they are zoological taxonomies.

Just as we postulated the existence of implicit categories that divide up the plant kingdom as a function of pragmatic ends, so it seems that the same type of latent categories can be identified in the animal kingdom. As in the case of the flora, these categories are implicit in that they can never be substituted in an utterance for a particular species; but it is possible to detect their existence and function by analyzing spontaneous comments made by the Achuar. Of all the latent generic categories, one in particular, *tanku* ("domestic"), marks the point where the implicit and explicit intersect, for the quality it expresses is used as a determiner in forming the name of certain species. Generally speaking, *tanku* is the opposite of *ikiamia* (literally, the adjectival form of "forest"), and the Achuar use the epithet to qualify a permanent state of domestication as well as the temporary state of "being tame." In the name of the domestic dog, *tanku yawa*, the element *tanku* defines a very particular species of the category *yawa*, the physical and ethological characteristics of which remain stable over time. Like the dog, the other domestic animals are not aboriginal, and their names are borrowed from Quichua (*atash*: chicken) or Spanish (*patu*: duck).

Tanku also qualifies the state of certain more-or-less tame wild animals – particularly primates and birds – that the Achuar frequently keep as pets. Some are remarkably easy to tame, and trumpeters, piping guans, tamarins, and marmosets soon become so used to people that they are allowed to roam freely. It is also not unusual to see a young peccary trotting at its master's heels like a dog. The everyday presence of pets testifies to the fact that the domesticated state is necessarily derived from the "forest" state. When new species of domestic animals are introduced to the Achuar, they are therefore categorized in terms of the wild species from which they are supposed metaphorically to be descended. The most recent example is the cow, which is called *tanku pama* ("domestic tapir") by assimilation to the largest wild terrestrial herbivore in Amazonia. The tangible sign that characterizes *tanku* is their capacity for friendly cohabitation with humans, in other words, their acclimatation to a socialized space separate from their real or hypothetical original environment. We will have the occasion to see that wild plants that have been transferred to gardens are perceived in exactly the same way.

Unlike explicit categories, all implicit suprageneric classes are dichotomous and therefore defined by pairs of symmetrically opposed qualities. This is the case of the division of animals into diurnal and nocturnal species, itself homologous with a series of explicit and implicit opposing pairs. The game category *kuntin*, for instance, is a subset of the category of diurnal animals, for the Achuar do not hunt at night, with the exception of the nocturnal curassow, *ayachui* (*Nothocrax urumutum*) or rodents which are ambushed, as it were, when they come into the gardens at night to root up manioc tubers. Inversely, most predators come out at night, and when men give up the hunt at the end of the day, they are relieved by their animal competitors which pursue their prey in the dark. The opposition diurnal/ nocturnal animals is then in part equivalent to the opposition hunted/ hunting animals, both pairs being in turn split into the dichotomy edible/ non-edible animals, since edible game is diurnal, while the Achuar declare nocturnal predators unfit for consumption.

But the class of non-edible animals (*yuchatai*) is much larger than the category of predators, and lumped into this class are animals that have so-called "sickening" meat (*mejeaku*), as well as those that are generally prohibited as food because they are thought to be the reincarnation of a dead person's spirit. Not all "sickening" animals are really that, though, and the meat of many in this group could perfectly well be eaten. It is easy to understand why the Achuar abstain from eating carnivorous mammals, opossums, birds of prey, carrion-eaters, hoatzins and most waterfowl. On the other hand, it is surprising that they regard as inedible a number of animals much appreciated in other Amerindian cultures, such as the capybara (*unkumi*), the giant armadillo (*yankunt*), the two-toed sloth (*uyush*: *Choloepus hoffmanni capitalis*), or the spectacled bear (*chae* : *Tremarctos ornatus*). The Achuar are revolted by the very idea of eating these animals and openly scorn those who, like their Quichua neighbors, do not hesitate to do so. According to the Achuar, the Quichua are as undiscerning in their eating habits as dogs and chickens, who will eat anything, including excrement.

The inclusion of certain animals in the "sickening" category is dictated less by empirical experience than by cultural serendipity. Thus *mejeaku* may be seen as synonymous with impure, a taxonomic operator of every system of classification in the world. Whereas, when applied to flora, edible and non-edible are defined basically by their utilitarian function (no edible plant is ever said to be "sickening"), when applied to fauna, they mean something quite other than whether or not they can be used as food. An animal is reputed to be inedible because the Achuar endow it with certain extrinsic qualities of which it then becomes the preferred signifier. This emblematic function is particularly visible in those animal species that are forbidden on the grounds that they are the metamorphoses of human beings.

As is generally the case with eschatological theories, the Achuar conception of metempsychosis does not comprise a unified corpus of normative beliefs, but is the object of highly varied, idiosyncratic individual interpretations.[1] Nevertheless, there seems to be a general consensus that certain parts of the deceased's body take on a life of their own (*ankan*) and after death assume the bodies of certain species of animals. The lungs turn into butterflies (*wampishuk*), the deceased's shadow, a brocket deer (*iwianch japa*: *Mazama americana*), the heart, a slate-colored grosbeak (*iwianch chinki*: *Pitylus grossus*), and the liver, an owl (*ampush*). The tapir and spider monkey, too, are reincarnations, but opinion diverges as to their status: are they animated by the whole person or only by certain anatomical parts? Whatever the case may be, all six species fall into the generic category of *iwianch*, a type of vaguely malevolent supernatural spirit.

Iwianch are the materialization, in the form of an animal or a human-like form, of the soul (*wakan*) of a person who has died; if, at the moment of death, the soul finds itself in one of the above-mentioned organs, it changes into its animal counterpart. It is generally a bad sign to encounter an *iwianch*, but, despite their negative charge, these spirits represent no real danger for humans. In their human form, it seems they have an unfortunate tendency to abduct children, either for companionship or to torment Achuar spending the night in the forest. But no one remembers them having deliberately killed anyone. *Iwianch* are impersonal and dumb, and so when one is encountered, there is no way of knowing who it is. If an Achuar shoots an animal *iwianch*, he always runs the risk of doing grievous harm to a recently deceased relative, as eating the animal's flesh can be assimilated to a form of cannibalism (*aents yutai*).

And yet, there is a gulf between the official norm and actual practice; while no Achuar deliberately sets out to hunt tapir, some do not hesitate to shoot when they come across one by chance. The temptation is all the greater as no social or supernatural sanction punishes the consumption of animals in which the dead are embodied.[2] Inversely, the violation of a temporary prohibition on a specific animal (applicable for instance to pregnant women or shamans undergoing initiation) is supposed to have detrimental consequences for those responsible. And so *iwianch* animals only appear to be animals, and if they form a zoological category as well, it is partly due to a distortion of meaning. The human attributes with which the Achuar taxonomy of nature's beings endows taboo animals show clearly enough that these are not classified solely according to morphological and ethological criteria.

The anthropocentric order

Until now we have been speaking of nature as an autonomous sphere in which humans are present only in the knowledge they produce about it; this is so because our categories for describing the Achuar world have been frozen into a conceptual stand-off between nature and the man-made world ever since the "Greek miracle." And yet it is obvious that the idea of nature as the domain of all phenomena occurring independently of human action is completely foreign to the Achuar. For them, the natural is no more "real" than the supernatural. (Lucretius' old distinction between reality and Chimera makes sense only because one is posited as the reflection of the other.) Unfortunately, our traditional concepts are tainted with an implicit naturalism which makes it tempting to see nature as a reality outside the human sphere, something that mankind organizes, transforms, and transfigures. Accustomed as we are to thinking with our inherited categories, we find it especially difficult to avoid such deep-rooted dualism. And yet that is what must be done if we are to account for what the Achuar claim is a continuum between human beings and nature's beings.

The Achuar do not see the supernatural as a level of reality separate from nature, for all of nature's beings have some features in common with mankind, and the laws they go by are more or less the same as those governing civil society. Humans and most plants, animals, and meteors are persons (*aents*) with a soul (*wakan*) and an individual life. Seen in this light, it is easier to understand the lack of named suprageneric categories to designate the set of all plants or all animals, since the denizens of nature form a conceptual whole whose parts are homologous by virtue of their properties. Nevertheless, only humans are "complete persons" (*penke aents*), in that their appearance corresponds fully to their essence. If nature's beings are anthropomorphized, it is because they are assumed to have the same faculties as humans, even though their appearance differs.

But it has not always been so; in mythical times, nature's beings had a human appearance too, and only their name contained the idea of what they would later become. If these human-looking animals were already potentially possessed of their future animal destiny in their name, this is because their common predicate as nature's beings is not man as species, but humankind as condition. When they lost their human form, they also, *ipso facto*, lost their speech organs and therefore the capacity to express themselves in spoken language; they did retain several features of their former state, however, to wit, consciousness – of which dreams are the most direct manifestation – and, for certain species, a social life organized according to the rules of the world of "complete persons." Achuar mythology is concerned almost entirely with how nature's beings came to look the way they do. The corpus of myths appears as one long commentary on how speciation came about, as a meticulous statement of how the undifferentiated became differentiated. One of these myths is of particular interest because it clearly places the animals into human social categories, thereby providing a better understanding of the type of social life the Achuar ascribe to nature's beings.

The myth of the war between the forest animals and the water animals

Once upon a time animals were people like us; the animals of the forest, like the *tsukanka* (Cuvier's toucan), the *kerua* (*Ramphastos culminatus*), the *kuyu* (*Pipile pipile*), the *mashu* (*Mitu tomentosa*), the *shiik* (puffbird), were all persons and they covered the face of the earth. In the water lived many anacondas and they ate people; as they were meat eaters, their breath stank. Along with the anacondas were a host of *chunka* crabs (*Potamon edulis*), *wampi* fish (*Plagioscion squamosissimus*), and *tunkau* fish (Pimelodids). These water creatures were also persons. The animals of the forest could no longer go down to fetch water or bathe because they were in constant danger of being eaten; and so they decided to declare war on the people of the waters. The *kuyu* undertook to dig a ditch to drain the lake where their enemies lived, the better to fight them. But the anaconda sent countless *katsaip* ants that overran the excavations, and nearly all the *kuyu* were wiped out. Seeing that, a crowd of *mashu* came, shaking their spears, to take their place, but as they lacked courage, they too were decimated. Next came flocks of *chiwia* (trumpeters), shaking their spears; but in spite of their numbers, the anaconda killed nearly every one. Then *tsukanka*, the "stabber," came to the rescue along with a host of *kerua*, equipped with digging sticks to dig the ditch. They dug with might and main, and the ditch grew; and they said among themselves, "We will take on the anaconda." But once again *katsaip* ants overran the ditch and, little by little, the diggers were exterminated. Some of the animals of the forest had waited to see the outcome; this was the case with the momot *jurukman* (*Momotu momota*), the *piakrur* bird (*Monasa atra*), the *shiik* (puffbird), the *tuich* armadillo, the *shushui* armadillo, and the giant *yankunt* armadillo. *Tsukanka*'s widow scolded those who had hung back, and they were ashamed. Then *shiik* said: "I am going to take them on." *Shiik* called together the others of his species as well as the *yankunt*, who root in the earth, to perform the *anemartin* (the ceremonial combat before going into battle). *Tsukanka*'s widow served the warriors manioc beer and said to them: "You are a bunch of fools, you swagger and strut doing the *anemartin*, but you are all going to get yourselves killed; my husband was a famous 'stabber' and yet he was killed, what are you going to do?" Then *piakrur* spoke: "I've got a bellyache, I'm sick." The others exhorted him: "Don't pretend you're sick, be brave, go on, *piakrur*!" The tiny *shiik* leader took over and told *piakrur* to stay put, then he gave out the tasks: "*Yankunt*, you will gut; *jurukman*, you will gut; *shushui*, you will gut; *tuich*, you will gut; *chuwi* (crested oropendola), you will stab." Then they set off towards the lake; but as their numbers had shrunk, they stomped their feet to create the impression of a large troop. When the people of the lake heard the noise, they fell into a frenzy; hosts of fish swam in circles slapping the water noisily with their tail, and the anaconda shook the ground;

all cried: "To battle, to battle, let's go now"; they raised a horrible racket. Then *tseap-tseap*, the parrot (*Pyrrhura melanura*), breached the thin wall of earth still separating the lake and the ditch and the people of the waters were washed onto the dry land. The forest animals slaughtered fish with their spears and machetes. They stabbed the enemy *tunkau* who jumped and flapped about, then strung them onto poles. They stabbed the *wampi* fish, too. The *kusum* (Anostomids) and the *tsenku* fish that are usually poisoned and gathered by the handful, these, too, they stabbed with their lances. And they stabbed the Anaconda. When the lake was drained dry, a host of crabs could be seen crawling on the bottom, but *chuwi* was there with his forked spear and he pinned them to the mud and dismembered them there. *Unkum* (*Cephalopterus*), the umbrella bird, the "cutter," cut the heads off the fish and his hair turned blue. Then he hung the heads around his neck and carried them off to smoke them over the fire to make little *tsantsa* (shrunken heads). This is the story my mother Chinkias told me when I was a child.[3]

This myth sheds a particular light on the problem of taxonomy, as it brings into play two opposite categories of animals: water creatures (anacondas, fish, shell fish) and forest creatures (birds, armadillos). Aside from their habitat, the basic characteristic of aquatic animals is that they are carnivores and even cannibals, since the animals of the forest that they eat are themselves human. If some of the animals in the myth, like the pencil-fish, *kusum*, no longer devour live prey, this is because the forest animals cut their mouths and they have lost their teeth. The archetypal aquatic animal at their head is the anaconda, *panki*, the most dangerous of nature's beings, according to the Achuar. The anaconda is one of the shaman's powerful helpers; he is said to live in underwater dens in riverbanks; when he flies into a rage, as in the myth, he writhes furiously and causes the earth to quake, which in turn causes landslides. The anaconda commands creatures, like the *kaitsaip* ants, who do not live in the water. And yet these insects do have some points in common with aquatic beings: like the anaconda, they live underground, they have dangerous pincers like crabs and they are known to be carnivorous.

On the other hand, the forest animals in the myth have no teeth, but are equipped with sharp appendages (claws or beaks), which several use to dig or scratch out food. They live on the ground (armadillos, curassows, trumpeters) or in the lower layers of the forest canopy, and none of them can swim. In terms of their methods of warfare, the myth makes a clear distinction between the water beings that devour and the forest beings that gut and stab. Armed with real or metaphorical (in the case of the toucan) spears, the latter put their enemies to death in the culturally accepted way for belligerent confrontations. In this they distinguish themselves from the cannibalistic creatures who do not kill like warriors, but devour their victims as, metaphorically, shamans are thought to do.

The protagonists of this First War do not behave in a haphazard manner. Whence the moving posthumous homage paid to *tsukanka's* courage by his widow which is symptomatic of the Achuar's conception of the toucans' domestic life. They say that these birds form lasting couples and that there is a strong bond between the male and the female. When one member of the couple is killed, the other cries out heartrendingly for several days and then hastens to find a new mate. Such behavior, far from being stigmatized, is regarded as entirely legitimate, for widowhood must not drag on, since man can fulfill himself only within marriage. Toucans are perceived as the model of the happy couple, and as such, are one of the main characters in the *anent* songs sung to strengthen the bond between husband and wife (see Taylor 1983b). The couple's happiness is synonymous with sexual relations, and the toucan's reputed sexual prowess makes the bird a much sought after ingredient in the manufacture of love potions.

The highly socialized behavior imputed to the toucan is also attributed to the woolly monkey, which is supposed to observe scrupulously the rules prescribed for contracting a marriage. In effect, this type of monkey breeds only with his authorized mate (*waje* in kinship terminology), in this case his bilateral cross cousin. This behavior contrasts with that of other monkeys like the howler who have what seems to be a frantic sex life, coupling unhesitatingly with mother or sister. Similarly the hummingbird is contrasted with the toucan for his impenitent Don Juanesque behavior and because he is not faithful to any of his conquests. This trait of the hummingbird is well known, and a young man who has numerous amorous adventures is said to be "playing the hummingbird" (*jempeawai*). Animals' social lives are not restricted to their mythic past, then, and some of them retain distinctive behaviors inherited from their former condition. While the myth seeks to account for the phenomenon of speciation, it does not make a clean break with the past, since, even in their new form, some animals continue to obey human social codes. But just as there are a few shameless individuals among the Achuar, so too certain species of animals evidence their asocial character by behaving like beasts.

But social life cannot be reduced to rules for choosing a mate; it also implies maintaining good relations with people who are only distantly related. Nowhere is this obligation more imperative than in times of war, and the myth clearly shows the advantages that flow from a strategy of military alliances. Here the Achuar maintain that certain animals form permanent associations for purposes of mutual defense, the best example of which is Cuvier's toucan and the *yakakua* crow. The *yakakua* are called "toucan's mothers," "mother" here denoting not so much domination as benevolent protection, albeit not devoid of authority. Apparently the *yakakua* serve as guides, conducting the toucans on their peregrinations and acting as lookouts. *Yakakua* are not considered edible, and their loud crowing, which alerts the toucans to the approach of hunters, therefore does not expose them to any danger.

This "mothering" association may take very odd forms. Anopheles mosquitoes are reputed to live on a "mother-animal" that looks like a big dog, for which they provide a living coat, as it were. They feed on the blood of this mother, which they constantly suck without harming the animal and proceed in symbiosis wherever it goes. *Tete* sandflies, too, have a similar live host, and the presence or absence of the two species of insects in any region is attributed by the Achuar to the unpredictable wanderings of their exemplary mothers. Sometimes the association is contracted between an animal and a plant, and it is said that the Icterids *chuwi* hold long conversations with the trees in which they intend to establish their colonies. Only when they are sure that the tree is going to accept their presence do they come in and weave their pouch-shaped nests. *Chuwi* are very sedentary, and the tree is thus ensured that it will be left standing, for a hunter prefers to use it as a regular blind than to fell it in order to rob the nests. In turn, the *chuwi* are apparently assured that their host will maintain the solidity of its branches from which they hang their garlands of nests. Man often represents the third term of these associations, the common denominator that makes them necessary, either because he is a threat or because he himself is an alternative prey.

This is clearly the case of certain associations based on dangerous complicities. For instance, the innocuous freshwater dolphin is supposed to procure prey for his partner, the anaconda, carrying unlucky bathers off into deep waters where he turns them over to the voracious great snake. This evil couple are themselves associated with a group of animals the cohesion of which is ensured by their collective allegiance to the *tsunki*, or water spirits. The anaconda, dolphin, jaguar, turtle, and caiman are familiars of these water spirits, which sometimes delegate the most dangerous of these (the anaconda and jaguar) to assist shamans in their criminal undertakings. And if the ethos and sociability of some animals are grounded in specific myths, this is far from true in all cases. The human behavior the Achuar ascribe to nature's beings is a convenient way of condensing into universal rules the fruits of constant empirical observation of the various interactions occurring in the biosphere. By attributing human-like behavior to animals, the Achuar endow them with a language readily capable of expressing the whole complexity of natural phenomena.

The anthropomorphization of plants and animals can be seen then as just as much the manifestation of mythical thinking as a metaphorical code that serves to translate a form of "popular knowledge."

Although we do not propose to inventory all the social behaviors the Achuar identify in nature's beings, we would like to raise a few questions concerning the rules that govern not only the sociability of creatures and natural phenomena, but also the relations the latter entertain with the properly human sphere of "complete persons." By maintaining that the Jivaro endow all of nature's beings with a soul, Karsten is able to subsume all native representations of the material world into the single fetishized category of "animistic philosophy" (1935: 371–85). But such universalization of essences is no doubt a simplification of the very different ways in which the Achuar conceive the spiritual existence of animals, plants, heavenly bodies, and meteors. Within the vast continuum of postulated consubstantiality there are internal borders marked by differences in mode of communication. It is according to their capacity or incapacity to establish an exchange of messages that all denizens of nature, including man, are divided into watertight categories.

Out of reach in their cyclical rounds, heavenly bodies are deaf and dumb to human words. The only clues they leave to their spiritual existence are certain physical signs that the Achuar interpret as so many omens or temporal markers. Addressed to no one in particular, these messages are there to be read by one and all. Heavenly bodies are indeed persons, whose behavior is predictable, but over which man has no influence. Here mythology introduces a break between the world above and the world below; all communication between the two levels was irrevocably interrupted with the cutting of the vine that once linked the two. On the other hand, some meteors establish very close relationships with humans, as shown by the example of thunder. For the Achuar, lightning, *charimp*, is a separate concept from the distant rumblings of thunder, *ipiamat*. *Charimp* dwells in the earth, whence from time to time he emerges in a devastating flash of lightning, *peem*, to silence his sons, *ipiamat*, who are raising a rumpus in the sky. Every man is endowed with his personal *ipiamat*, the main function of which is to warn his male kin when he is in mortal danger. It is a sort of alarm that sounds independently of the will of the person it benefits. The relation of communication is indirect, since no information is exchanged between the *ipiamat* person and the man it guards; the rumble of thunder is the autonomous outward vector of a wordless message.

The relations between humans, plants, and animals are much more complex, for different modes of communication are used by the ones and the others depending on circumstances. Just as the Achuar express themselves in a language peculiar to them, each animal species has its own language which was assigned to the species when it acquired its final form. The Achuar understand some elements of these individual languages inasmuch as they are stereotyped expressions of conventional feelings familiar to humans, such as fear, pain, joy, love. All species then have a register that, in principle, is made up of a basic sound message, sometimes accompanied by cries or songs for special situations. Moreover, each species can express itself only in its own language, although humans are capable of imitating other animal sounds and use these, for instance to lure or to reassure the prey they are stalking. Nevertheless, and unlike the various human languages, of which the Achuar are aware, languages that translate into one another and permit an exchange of meaning providing one has mastered them, animal languages can be reproduced by voice or by a game call, but cannot be used to converse. There are therefore a number of cases in which the audible message is inoperative: no species of animal speaks the language of another species, humans can only imitate elements of animal languages but cannot use these to convey information; as for plants, they do not emit any perceptible audible signal.

If, in spite of everything, nature's beings manage to communicate among themselves and with humans, it is because they have other means of making themselves understood than by emitting sounds that can be heard by the ear. In effect, intersubjectivity can be expressed by speech from the soul, which transcends all linguistic barriers and transforms every plant and animal into a subject capable of producing meaning. Depending on the way in which communication is to be established, this soul speech can take any of a number of forms. Normally humans speak to plants and animals by means of incantations, which are supposed to go straight to the heart of whoever they are addressed to. Although they are formulated in ordinary language, these songs can be understood by all of nature's beings, and we will often have the occasion, in the course of this work, to look more closely at their content and the way they work (see especially Chapters Five and Six). This sort of sung metalanguage is also used by the various species of animals and plants to communicate with each other, thus overcoming the solipsistic curse of separate languages. But, although humans in their waking state are able to send messages to plants and animals, they are not able to intercept either the information these beings exchange or the answers they send back. For a true interlocutory relation to be established between nature's beings and human beings, their respective souls must leave their bodies and free themselves of the material constraints of speech by which they are ordinarily bound.

Soul journeys occur mainly during dreams or trances brought on by hallucinogenic drinks made from *Datura* (*maikiua*) or *Banisteriopsis* (*natem*). Shamans are particularly adept at controlling the wanderings of their conscious double, as they have a great deal of practical experience in sending out their souls. But this is not an exclusive prerogative of shamans, and anyone, man, woman, or child, under certain circumstances, is capable of sending his soul beyond the narrow confines of the body in order to dialogue directly with the double of another of nature's beings, be it human, plant, animal, or supernatural spirit. Nevertheless, and contrary to Michael Harner's interpretation (1972: 134), we do not feel we can set up an absolute opposition between the field in which the dematerialized doubles act and the ordinary conscious waking state. Harner contends that the Shuar Jivaro see the normal world as a lie and an illusion, since the only real world is that of supernatural forces, to which only the soul has access as it journeys. The daily course of affairs, according to Harner, is a reflection of structuring causes secretly at work in the supernatural realm. By ascribing this platonic brand of idealism to the Jivaro, Harner is only a step from remaking their conception of the world into a realism of essences in which philosophical endeavor is supplanted by the taking of hallucinogenic drugs. And yet what is needed here, if we are to understand how the different states of awareness are related, is not a metaphysics of being but a logic of discourse.

For the Achuar there is no world of pure idealities divorced from the world of epiphenomena, but two distinct levels of reality created by distinct modes of expression. And so the animals one was conversing with in a dream do not disappear from one's perceptual field upon awakening; their language merely ceases to be comprehensible. The condition for the existence of the other, on either level of reality, comes down to whether or not dialogue can be established. Dialogue is the normal form of Achuar verbal expression. An Achuar always addresses a specific interlocutor, however many individuals may be present. But the normal speech of "complete persons," which is codified in a host of set rhetorical dialogues, does not have the power to make itself understood by the rest of nature's beings. It is therefore necessary to accede to another level of expression in order to attain this other level of reality on which ordinary language is inoperative. It is of little concern that this metalanguage is identical to daily speech, since what makes it fundamentally different is the alteration of the subjective conditions in which it is uttered. We are not dealing with some existential philosophy that would define Ego and Other through intersubjectivity as it is realized in the use of language, but with a way of organizing the cosmos by specifying the modes of communication that humans can establish with each of its component parts. The perceptible universe is seen by the Achuar as a many-sided continuum, now transparent, now opaque, now eloquent, now dumb, depending on the mode of apprehension chosen. The natural and the supernatural, human society and animal society, material sheath and the life of the spirit are conceptually on the same plane, but methodologically, they are separated by the respective conditions that govern their access.

PART II

ON THE PROPER USE OF NATURE

Inside an Achuar house, Numpaimentza

Introduction II

The Achuar are constantly drawn towards the fragmented atomistic form of society engendered by a social life built wholly upon the notion of autonomy; this deeply embedded tendency to dissociate finds its natural expression in a highly dispersed pattern of dwelling. As the only readily visible unit of Achuar society, the house and its surrounding territory are the epitome of the closed microcosm that for Aristotle embodied the virtues of *oikonomia*. In this little self-sufficient world, the social and material reproduction of each isolated household is felt to be truly harmonious – Aristotle used the term "natural" – only if accumulation is excluded and the constraints necessarily engendered by commerce with others kept to a minimum.

Of course there is no such thing as absolute self-sufficiency, no more in the wild than in the *polis*; but the idea is so firmly entrenched in the Achuar representation of the good life (*shiir waras*) that we will adopt it for the moment as a working hypothesis that enables us to break down the area under study.

To alleviate any misunderstanding, I would like to stress that the preeminence of the domestic economy theme in this study in no way indicates a theoretical orientation. If indeed the order of *oikonomia* – or simple reproduction, if you prefer – governs the way the Achuar economic system works in appearance, it remains that the self-sufficiency paradigm that we have adopted here is a manner of methodological fiction. The term "domestic economy" is a simple descriptive notion and not a theoretical concept, or in other words, we are not using it as the criterion of some historical stage of economic development (domestic mode of production, natural economy or economy of the *oikos*), but as a convenient term by which to designate a configuration of production factors and they way they are geared to actual consumer practices in the framework of the domestic unit, which we will consider for the needs of our hypothesis to be autonomous.

If, in spite of the foregoing it were still necessary to qualify this household-scale domestic economy, we could refer back to those old Germanic populations, isolated in their own sylvan expanses, of whom Marx wrote in his *Pre-capitalist Economic Foundations* (transl. by J. Cohen, ed. by E.J. Hobsbawm, New York, International Publishers, 1965) "basically the whole economic sphere is contained within each house, which constitutes its own autonomous center of production". Therefore, to say that the object of the second part of this work is the Achuar "domestic economy", is one way of signifying again that, within the limits we have set ourselves, we have deliberately left aside the sphere of relations of production, that is, both the ways in which the labor force renews itself and the intentional and unintentional relations between household units as they go about appropriating nature.

In restricting this section to the study of what we call the "proper use of nature", it is not our intention to take on the description of what is commonly called the subsistence sphere. Rather we will be attempting to analyze the specific ways in which Achuar households combine a system of resources with a system of means. Setting aside for the moment the relationships that link the people who occupy a territory in a given way and, for methodological reasons, making believe that the reproduction of the labor force is ensured by incest, we will try to describe Achuar work processes and their material and conceptual technological frameworks (tasks and skills), and to measure the output of labor by the yardstick of the needs set by the Achuar system of values. In fact, the two tasks are inseparable, as production and consumption are but two sides of the same process. It is easy enough to recognize, behind the study of the "proper use of nature", a basic description of what Marxists term the "nature of productive forces", in other words that building-block of every mode of production a detailed knowledge of which is indispensible if a study in economic anthropology is to be more than an abstract morphology of the relations of production.

Domestic or household economy centers on the house and spreads outward from there; one must yield to this tautological fact when deciding on the order of exposition. We will therefore describe the ways of using nature in terms of concentric zones – house, garden, forest – set out in the classic ethnographic model, which in this case is homologous with the Achuar representation of spatial segmentation. Besides the fact that it conforms to a logic that divides the physical world into ever less socialized segments, this expository order has the advantage of respecting the equivalence between acquiring knowledge and refunding the results of this process. Indeed, what first strikes the novice observer is the scrupulous materiality of household etiquette. While verbal communication is still strewn with pitfalls, he familiarizes himself with the techniques for transforming nature; and so as his despair of ever collecting a myth grows over the months, he works off his impatience on quantitative measurements. When the garden seems to have yielded up its secrets, it is time to make his first foray into the menacing forest and attempt to hunt for himself. So the evolution of the fieldwork takes the form of a gradual letting go of the mirages of domestic security, and it may be that the attempt to espouse in one's analysis the progression of knowledge that accompanied it is not a mere figure of rhetoric.

4

The world of the house

The household is the smallest unit of Achuar society, and the only one explicitly conceived as a normative form of social and residential grouping. Because of the extreme fluidity of the categorial outlines of a system of social classification based uniquely on prescriptive rules of marriage and overlapping unbounded kindreds, the house – and the temporary social circumscription that it creates within its material precinct – represents the only effective principle of enclosure in the Achuar social system. There is no social and territorial grouping between household and tribal group based on an explicit, univocal, durable rule of ascription. Even though the Achuar have no lexical term for the actual concept of domestic unit, the household is the basic unit of a nebulous social world which lacks corporate groups, villages, or descent groups.

An isolated residential unit of production and consumption, the household is ideologically turned in upon itself, bathed in a freeflowing private sociability that strikes a sharp contrast with the formalism prevailing in interhousehold relations. A household is always made up of one family, sometimes nuclear but more often polygynous, plus resident sons-in-law and single relatives of the head of house or his wives. These satellites, usually widows and/or orphans, are taken in because they are directly related by blood or marriage to one of the various elements that comprise the composite family. This means that, apart from young couples' extended period of uxorilocal residence, it is exceptional under normal circumstances for two families, especially if they are polygynous, to occupy the same house for any length of time.

Even in the case of prolonged uxorilocal residence, one can speak of a multiple family household only in a purely descriptive sense. The strongly subordinate status of the son-in-law seems to individualize his presence and efface the autonomy of the family unit that revolves around him. In this sense, the position of an Achuar son-in-law more closely resembles that of an unmarried satellite than that of a normal family head: he appears more as some extension of his wife's family than the axis of a second parallel family.

The Achuar seem to be particularly refractory to the very form of conviviality that favors communal living in the large multifamily *malocas* of northwest Amazonia. They readily spell out the many causes of friction that could arise when two families live together for too long: quarrels between children which degenerate into quarrels between their respective parents, the temptation of adultery, disputes over which family head takes precedence when both are necessarily equal, jealousy over success in hunting or gardening, et cetera. Two brothers or two brothers-in-law may sometimes share a house for a short time, but this is usually a temporary arrangement, designed to accommodate one of the families for the time needed to build a new house on a nearby site.

The social parasite is most exceptional, for a married man who obtains the full-time hospitality of one of his male relatives places himself in the same tacit tutelary relationship as that which characterizes son-in-law–father-in-law relations. The absence of autonomy and independence that comes with freely accepting this status is seen as such a blatant admission of weakness and lack of self-confidence that adult men usually feel authorized to behave as they please with the parasite and, within the bounds of formal etiquette, make him feel that he has regressed to the category of unmarried adolescent. Even fairly serious physical handicaps are not considered sufficiently incapacitating to justify parasitism. For instance, two families of deaf-mutes – one deaf-mute couple with no children and one couple with children of which only the man was afflicted – each had their own house and in no way manifested any external difference that might have deprived them of their independent status. It may be said then that, when two families occupy a single house for any time, there is always at the root of this cohabitation a statutory or acquired relation of subordination (son-in-law/father-in-law and, in exceptional cases, father/married son and host/parasite), even though this relationship is not always obvious from the system of attitudes alone.

The usually one-family household undergoes a complete transformation during the periods of open hostility characteristic of brewing feuds. At these times, several families closely related by blood or marriage regroup into a single house behind a stockade, which provides shelter during the most lethal phases of the conflict; it is easier to plan concerted attacks and to defend the group if the factional kin group is all under one roof. For the duration of the conflict – which never lasts more than three or four years – the fortified house may contain up to sixty or seventy persons.[1] The unifying leaven provided by the sense of shared dangers and enemies usually keeps the inevitable minor frictions of daily life from growing into causes for open conflict within the extended household.

It is not unusual for certain sites to have a cluster of two or three houses (i.e. situated within a radius of not more than two kilometers) in which relations involving mutual assistance and visits are more crystallized than is normally the case. These aggregates are articulated around direct relations of consanguinity and/or affinity (a group of brothers, brothers-in-law, or son-in-law/father-in-law), but their spatial and social proximity in no way imply – except very partially in the last case – the sharing of resources and skills among the households. Furthermore, these aggregates rarely last; since the Achuar household, in its constant reassertion of independence, can only demonstrate its difference in relative isolation, the bias against cohabiting under one roof extends to excessive relations between neighbors. As a rule, then, each residential unit corresponds to one household producing and consuming independently, whatever may be the nature of their topographical situation. Whether the house is part of a small residential aggregate or particularly isolated (i.e. more than a half-day's walk or canoe trip from another house), it is always the household unit that provides the immediate framework for the transformation, if not the appropriation, of nature.

Architectonic elements

Standing free of the surrounding forest, the inhabited area extends from its center in three concentric circles that form as many stages in decreasing degrees of the fashioning of space. Although clearing and planting are chronologically anterior to building the house, it is the presence of the latter, in the midst of its gardens, that symbolizes human occupation; the house is the logical point from which its inhabitants begin marking out space. The house, *jea*, is surrounded by a large yard, *aa* (the "outside-around"), carefully kept free of weeds and embellished with a scattering of small medicinal or narcotic shrubs, fruit trees, and chonta palms. The yard is itself encircled by the garden or gardens, *aja*, which are in turn edged with rows of banana trees, the last outposts of cultivated land that seem to be just managing to stave off the advancing forest, *ikiam*.

The house is always erected on a slightly raised, level terrace and next to a river or lake. When the slope of the bank leading down to the water is too steep, log stairs are made to give access without danger of slipping. For reasons of defense, however, the Achuar avoid building directly on a large river navigable by canoe; when they do settle close to a waterway, they usually choose a site along a secondary branch or, even better, on one of the small tributaries some distance from the main arm. In the latter case, the canoes are tied up on the main course and a path made between the tie-up and the house, which remains invisible from the river.

Although the Achuar are on the whole expert boatmen and, when they have the choice, would rather travel by canoe than on foot, for daily domestic use they prefer shallow clearwater streams with a regular flow, as flash flooding on the larger waterways makes bathing quite dangerous, especially for children, who spend much of the heat of the day playing in the water. Furthermore, the larger rivers are completely opaque, thus concealing their most nocuous residents: the highly dangerous sting ray, *kaashap* (*Potamotrygon hystrix*), the electric eel, *tsunkiru*, and the anaconda, *panki*. Although the latter is infinitely more rare than the ray, the Achuar regard it as the principal danger present in every river because of the supernatural powers they attribute it. Finally, maintaining a short distance from major waterways makes it just about possible to bear the persistent presence of the anopheles mosquitoes, *manchu*, and the sandflies, *tete*, that infest the riverbanks.

The Achuar house is a large, harmonious, almost oval-shaped building, usually without outer walls (to allow constant ventilation of the living space), covered by a high roof with straight sides and semi-circular ends which descend to approximately man height. When the head of the house judges that a conflictual situation has developed and is generating insecurity in his vicinity, he prefers to forego the fresh air and enclose the house within walls, *tanish*, built of large vertical palm staves (from the *tuntuam* or *uwi*), lashed to crossbars themselves attached to the posts that support the eaves. When the insecurity spills over into specific threats of attack, a stockade, *wenuk*, some three meters high, is erected around the house, built along the same lines as the walls, the support posts consisting of stakes driven deep into the ground. The staves used for the *wenuk* are much thicker than the wall staves and tightly joined, leaving no opening through which an enemy could fire into the house. The stockade is sometimes entirely lined on the inside by yet another row of staves to consolidate the fortification.

One enters a house enclosed within walls or a stockade by solid

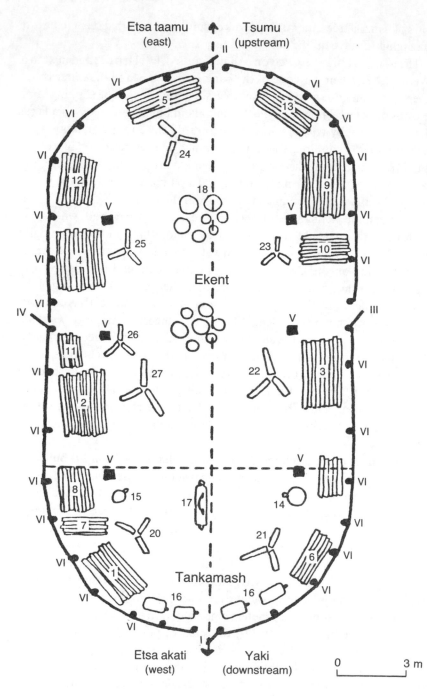

10. Floor plan of an Achuar house (upper Pastaza)

Key

Upper course of the Rio Pastaza, south bank at junction with the Rio Sasaim
Composition of the household

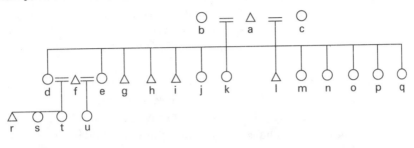

1. Visitor's *peak* (bed)
2. *peak* of *b* (45 years old), house owner's co-wife, and of her children *j* (7 years old) and *k* (8 years old); a wide slat-work shelf (*peek*) hangs overhead
3. *peak* of *c* (40 years old), house owner's co-wife, and of her children *o* (5 years old), *p* (4 years old) and *q* (7 years old); overhead, a *peek*
4. *peak* of *d* (20 years old), daughter of *a* and *b*, and her children *r* (3 years old), *s* (2 years old) and *t* (1 year old); overhead, a *peek*
5. *peak* of *e* (18 years old), daughter of *a* and *b*, and her child *u* (1 year old); overhead, a *peek*
6. *peak* of *I*, adolescent son (18 years old) of *a* and *c*
7. *peak* of *g*, adolescent son (12 years old) of *a* and *b*
8. *peak* of *h*, adolescent son (13 years old) of *a* and *b*
9. *peak* of *m*, adolescent daughter (17 years old) of *a* and *c*
10. *peak* of *n*, adolescent daughter (15 years old) of *a* and *c*
11. platform for *b*'s dogs
12. platform for *d*'s dogs
13. platform for *c*'s dogs
14. *a*'s *chimpui* stool
15. *f*'s *chimpui* stool
16. *kutank* stools for visitors
17. *tuntui* (signal drum)
18. *b*, *d* and *e*'s *muits* (storage jars for manioc beer)
19. *c*, *m* and *n*'s *muits*
20. *f*'s fireplace
21. *a*'s fireplace
22. *c*'s fireplace
23. *m* and *n*'s fireplace
24. *d*'s fireplace
25. *e*'s fireplace
26. *j* and *k*'s fireplace
27. *b*'s fireplace

I   *tankamash waiti* (door)
II   *ekent waiti*
III–IV side *waiti*
V   *paeni* posts
VI   *nawe* posts

Note: Furniture and utensils not drawn to scale

rectangular doors, *waiti*, usually fashioned from a *wampu* tree (*Ficus insipidia*); these swing on two pivots carved from either end of one side. The pivots are set into two pieces of wood that form the lintel and the threshold, respectively; and depending on the location of the door, either two roof posts or two stakes of the stockade serve as door posts. The doors are secured on the inside by either a crossbar or a stake driven into the ground and wedged against the door.

The size of the house and its degree of refinement depend on the social position and the number of wives of the household head as well as on the size of the workforce he is able to muster for its construction. The ambition of every adult male is to have many wives, many sons-in-law, a spacious house, and big gardens that will produce an abundant supply of the indispensable manioc beer, *nijiamanch*, that he offers his guests. All of this means that the size of the house is one of the signs that indicate a *juunt* (a "great man"). His house is always noticeably larger than required for his family's everyday needs, and so allows him liberally to accommodate a number of visitors.

It is easy to calculate the size of the house one wants, for it is a function of the distance between the four or six house poles, *paeni*, that support the entire framework; the longer the sides of the square or rectangle staked out on the ground, the bigger the house. The most common dimensions for a house are some fifteen meters long by ten wide and five or six meters high. Some houses, however, are particularly spacious, such as the one in Fig. 10; this dwelling measured twenty-three meters in length, twelve in width, and seven in height, and could house twenty people on a permanent basis.

The two most common types of house are the *naweamu jea* ("house with legs," i.e. with posts around the sides) and *tsupim jea* ("cut-off house," i.e. without the side posts). The latter is smaller than the former because the roof does not extend as far; otherwise both use the same type of framework (see Figs. 11 and 12, types of house frames). A third type, the *iwianch jea* ("bad-spirit house"),[2] is fairly rare and is distinguished from the other two by its conical rather than elliptical shape; this type of framework is sometimes used by isolated young couples because the frame is easier to raise.

A house is not built from any preset formal representation; the materials are selected, fashioned, and assembled following an automatic sequences of phases, the proportions being determined, as we have seen, by the initial height and spacing of the *paeni* posts. Each time several pieces need to be cut to the same length, a specially calibrated "measuring" stick (*nekapek*) is used.

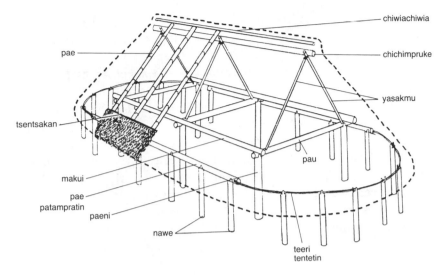

11. Framework of a *naweamu jea* house

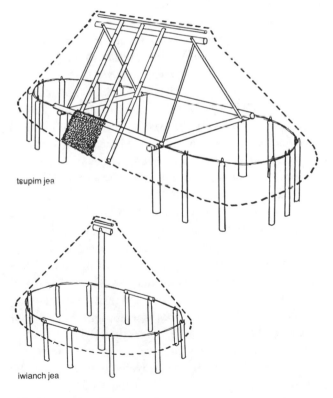

12. Two types of framework

When the *paeni* have been sunk, two tie-beams (*pau*) are laid across the tops and held in place by diamond-shaped teeth carved out of the top of the post. The side beams (*makui*) are lashed to the ends of the *pau* and support the main rafters (*yasakmu*) which simply abut the *makui*. At this point, the height of the roof can be chosen with great precision by fixing the angles at which the principle rafters meet; once this has been established, the crossed ends of the rafters are lashed together, and the roof pole (*chichimpruke*) laid onto the saw-horse thus formed. The armature of the semi-circular ends of the house (*teamu*) remains to be built; the ends are determined by tracing an arc with a string held at the midpoint of either end. Along the two half-circles traced on the ground, support posts are planted at regular intervals, and the tops are carved, like the *paeni* posts. Flexible slats (*teeri tentetin*) are laid into the grooves, these receive the rafters (*teeri*) that cover the rounded ends of the house. The side rafters, *pae* or *awankeri*, are then laid up and lashed onto the roof beam, *chichimpruke*, and the lengthwise beams, *makui*.[3]

The materials most commonly used for house timbers (i.e. the *paeni, pau*, and *makui*) are two species of palm, *tuntuam* and *ampaki*, and half a dozen other trees, *paeni, chikainia* (*Talauma* sp.), *atashmatai* (*Iryanthera juruensis*), *chimi, yais* (*Cymbopetalum tessmanii*), and *wantsunt* (a legume). The rafters are usually made of *kenku* bamboo (*Guadua angustifolia*) or the *kaya yais* tree (*Oxandra xylopiodes*); for the laths and the staves, *teeri tentetin*, the *kupat* palm (*Iriartea exorrhiza?*) is used; for the main rafters, *kaya yais*, as we have said, and the *chiwiachiwia* tree (*Aspidosperma album*). Pieces subject to high mechanical stress are lashed with the inner fibers from the bark of the *shuwat* (*Gustavia hexapetala*), *kakau* (*Miconia elata*), and *yunkua* (*Lecythishians*) trees, while lighter pieces like the staves or laths are lashed preferably with *kaap* vines (*Heteropsis obligonfolia*).

The nature of the roofing materials varies with the biotope and strongly affects the lifetime of the house. In the interfluve, two closely related species of palm tree are used: *kampanak* (*Hyospatha* sp.) and *turuji* (*Hyospatha tessmannii*); each frond is aligned along the slope of the roof and attached by its petiole to one of the roof laths, *tsentsakan*, that are laid up the rafters. These fronds are especially resistant to both rot and parasites, and the way in which they are fastened ensures that the roof is watertight. Such a roof can last up to fifteen years and keeps, as a rule, longer than the house posts, which begin to rot at the base after six or seven years; the posts can nonetheless last a few more years before definitively compromising the stability of the structure. Also, it is not unusual for the roof fronds to be reused on a new house built in the immediate vicinity of the old one, the lifetime of a *turuji* or a *kampanak* roof being nearly twice that of the timbers.

In the riverine habitat, by contrast, there are almost no *turuji* or *kampanak*, and the palm tree most commonly used in roofing is the *chaapi* and, occasionally, the *kuunt*. These fronds are less resistant, but the work progresses slightly faster, since they are affixed longitudinally directly to the rafters without the use of roof laths, using the central vein as the armature. Each frond is prepared by folding it down the middle, along the center vein, then the two halves are brought together and the lobes interwoven; these woven fronds are laid up by packets of four. The overall quantity of fronds used by this roofing technique is slightly lower than that required when roofing in *kampanak* palms. The lifetime of a *chaapi* roof, however, rarely exceeds five or six years, and the occasional repairs do not prolong it by much. Since the house has no chimney holes, smoke constantly filters through the roof, thus helping protect it from plant-eating insects. Furthermore, on some houses, leaves from the fish poison *timiu* (*Lonchocarpus* sp.) are added at regular intervals to the roofing fronds, where they are supposed to keep away parasites.

The difference the type of roof makes to the lifetime of a house does not necessarily imply a difference between the two biotopes in the rate at which dwellings are relocated. In effect, roofing a large house in the interfluvial biotope practically exhausts in one fell swoop the entire supply of *kampanak* in the immediate vicinity; when it becomes necessary to construct a new house a few years later, it must automatically be built on a new site in order to be close to new stands of palm trees. By contrast, a house in the riverine habitat makes up for its shorter life-span by taking fewer roofing fronds, so that two successive houses can be built on the same site before exhausting the local *chaapi* palm supply.

One way or another, however, at the end of a fifteen-year period, there is no choice but to change sites for the new house, the only alternative being endless laborious treks between the building site and the distant spots where the palm fronds must now be gathered.

Erecting an Achuar house is no small undertaking, then, as the roof area (often more than 250 square meters) and the complex assembly of the frame demand both strict attention to detail and a heavy labor input. The construction of a good-sized house requires around 150 man-days of work, including the gathering and fashioning of materials from the forest. The duration of the construction in relative time – it varies between 3 and 9 months – depends not only on the dimensions desired, but also on the number of men among whom the individual days can be divided and on the number of times their collaboration can be obtained.

Raising the frame and roofing are exclusively male activities; the only tasks that are sometimes partially left to the women are carrying and weaving the palm fronds. The time it takes to build a house is therefore a function of the sociological and topographical environment; the more isolated a site is, the harder it will be to organize frequent work parties made up of the homeowner's kinsmen living in the region, as the latter are naturally reluctant to make too many long trips.

Of course collective labor speeds up construction, but, however difficult certain phases of the assembly may be – particularly placing and fitting the heaviest pieces – and however tiring it may be to transport the bulky palm fronds and the heavy posts from where they were gathered and cut, there are no specifically technical constraints which demand the use of an extended workforce. The minimum requisite for the transport, raising, and assembly of the framing timbers is two grown men, a condition that is fulfilled by all the completely isolated residential units that we visited; these always included, besides the head of the house, at least one son or son-in-law over the age of eighteen. Some of these remote households had managed to build a house relying almost exclusively on their own labor capacity, thus satisfying in an exemplary way the self-sufficiency principle that governs the socio-economic life of Achuar residential units.

Symbolic topography of the house

There is no ritual for the building of a house or for its inauguration; the highly profane character of the conditions of production of dwellings is also apparent in the lack of formal structuring of the explicit symbolic associations connoting the house as a material object. In both mythological and everyday discourse, the Achuar house carries a fairly low semantic load, especially when compared to the richness and variety of the native symbolic interpretations of the house in other upper-Amazonian societies (see among others Hugh-Jones 1977; Guyot 1974; Gasche 1974).

On the most immediate level, that of technical architectural terminology, the equivalents or homologies between the name of certain material elements of the house and other semantic categories of the language fall into a dual system of references: on the one hand, functional or metonymic equivalents (a piece of the frame is designated by the name of the tree from which it is usually fashioned) and, on the other hand, metaphorical equivalents of both an anthropomorphic and zoomorphic nature (for

Part of frame	Native architectural term	Anthropomorphic or zoomorphic reference	Other references
House	*Jea*	*Uchi jeari*: placenta	
Side rafters	*Pae* or *awankeri*	*Pae*: ribs	
Lengthwise beams	*Makui*	*Makui*: thigh	
Peripheral eavepoles	*Nawe*	*Nawe*: leg	
Diamond-shaped teeth on heads of house- and side posts	*Wenunch* *Charapa nuke*	*Wenunch*: sternum *Charapa nuke*: turtle head	
	Yantana nuke	*Yantana nuke*: caiman head	
	Nanki		*Nanki*: war spear
Ridge beam	*Chichimpruke*	*Chichimpruke*: crest particularly of the harpy eagle	
Roof sides		*Nanape*: wing	
Rafters that fan out at the two ends of the roof	*Teeri*	*Teeri*: fish eggs	
Finishing laths around the eaves	*Jea shikiri*	*Shiki*: urine (*jea shikiri*: house urine)	
Principal rafters	*Yasakmu*		*Yasakmu* from *yasak* (to inhale tobacco juice through the nostrils) and *mu* (passive substantival suffix) denoting the flow of the tobacco juice into the sinuses
	Tijirsari		*Tijiras*: from the Spanish *tijeras* (scissors); recent
House posts	*Paeni*		*Paeni*: *Minquartia punctata* (Oleac.)
Tie beam	*Pau*		*Pau*: *Pouteria* sp. (Sapotacae)
Laths	*Tsentsakan*		*Tsentsakan*: fishing spear
Ridge pole	*Chiwiachiwia*		*Chiwiachiwia*: *Aspidosperma album* (Apocynacae)

13. House vocabulary

details, see Fig. 13). Now all our attempts at exploring this metaphorical system of references, that is, all our efforts to elicit a consistent, explicit global image to which the composite anatomical fragments could be referred, met with patent incomprehension on the part of the Achuar. When we undertook to obtain a term-by-term semantic commentary on those elements of the house whose names also designated a (human or animal) body part, it was our impression that they thought of their metaphorical referents in the same way as they did the metonymic equivalents also used in speaking of architecture, that is, as functional homologies based, in the event, on morphological similarity. That explains the fact that, because of their function as much as because of their placement, rafters are called ribs, the ridge beam a crest, and the lengthwise beams thighs.

Nevertheless, even if we admitted the purely functional status of meta-phorical equivalents, there remained the subsidiary problem of why anatomical metaphors so prevail in Achuar house vocabulary over simple metonymic equivalents. In other words, even though, in nearly all cultures, the body is one of the prime sources of metaphors, this still does not explain its systematic use as a morphological reference for the bulk of the architectural elements of the Achuar house. Our inability to obtain from informants a formal, global, metaphorical image of the house stemmed from the simple fact that it is not so much the symbol of a living being whose model had previously been provided by nature as the model of organic life in its broadest sense.

The contradictory, composite character (even from the standpoint of native anatomical taxonomy) of the representation obtained by bringing together according to their place in the house the various architectural elements designated by anatomical terms is therefore amenable to a twofold explanation. To the extent that the designation of these elements is based on morphological homology, it is normal that these iconic signs (in C.S. Pierce's sense of the term) refer to a very broad corporal vocabulary, their combination constituting a syntagm the semantic scope of which bisects several animate species (humans, birds, fish). But at the same time, because the predominance of anatomical terms in architecture works as a simple symbolic marker for the house, overdetermining its implicit organicism, the architectonic structure of these elements is in no need of the same anatomical coherence as a flesh-and-blood being.

The organicist connotations associated with the house are highly plastic, then, and the idea that the house has a life of its own has no counterpart in some explicit native model that accounts for its physiological workings.

The organicist analogy is actually formulated in only one instance, in the case of the metaphorical equivalence between *jea* (house) and *uchi jeari* ("the child's house": placenta). This correspondence is bi-univocal: the placenta is to the fetus what the house is to the man and vice versa. After the birth, the placenta is buried, thereby becoming a form without an occupant, just like the house, which is abandoned after the death of its owner. Now, after death, the *nekas wakan*, the "true soul" of the deceased, may choose to re-occupy the placenta and to lead a sort of second *intra utero* existence, underground, which is described as being identical with that of a man in his house.

There is obvious continuity, then, between the life of the embryo in its placenta-house, *post-partum* life in the house-placenta, and the life of the "true" soul after death, again in its placenta-house. In this organic analogy, the house is not seen as a womb, that is as one part of an anatomical whole, but as a sheath or envelope, endowed with an organic life of its own, since the placenta continues to lead an underground existence after being expelled from the uterus. In this sense, it is clear that the house is not the analogical image of a living being, or a part of a living being, but the paradigmatic image of organic processes in general; the house is endowed with a life of its own, but the Achuar are able to formulate the stages of this life only in terms of homology with other organic processes for which nature provides the model.

Although mythic discourse has little to say on the house – and is, in this, in logical agreement with the generally vague way the theme is represented – it nevertheless provides an opportunity to explore other dimensions of the subject. Even a rapid overview of the mythology reveals an implicit image of the house as a mediating space, a passageway between the celestial and subterranean worlds. Two fragments of separate myths are particularly revealing; the versions we give here are highly condensed and do not take into account their many variants.

Summary of the first fragment:

Etsa ("Sun"), during his earthly life, kills Ajaimp ("glutton": cannibal) and burns down his house. But Ajaimp does not really die and, apparently harboring no ill feelings, asks Etsa to help him rebuild his house; Etsa agrees and, while he is bent over the hole he is digging to set the *paeni* posts, Ajaimp runs him through with one of the posts and pins him to the ground. Thereupon Etsa asks the *paeni* to empty itself out and he climbs up the middle of the hollow post and out the top and from there makes his way to the sky where he turns into the sun.

Summary of the second fragment:

When some people ask Nunkui if she will please share with them the domestic plants of which she has exclusive use, she gives them her baby daughter Uyush ("sloth"); when the people get Uyush home, she makes all the domestic plants appear, one after the other, by simply pronouncing their names. Uyush is mistreated by the household; she takes refuge on the roof of the house which is close to a grove of *kenku* bamboos. Uyush calls a *kenku*, chanting: "Kenku, kenku, come and get me, let's go eating peanuts"; blown over by a sudden gust of wind, one of the *kenkus* falls on the house and Uyush climbs into the tree; she descends inside the *kenku* all the way into the earth, defecating regularly as she goes (the bamboo joints are called Nunkui's excrement).

In mythic times as now, *paeni* and *kenku* are the building blocks of the house; the *paeni* are the house poles and the *kenku* bamboo – which, in the myth, are not part of the house proper – are the rafters, that is, they occupy on the roof of the house the same place as the *kenku* of the myth, which fell onto the roof. In Achuar mythological discourse, the house does not appear as a microcosm, for it is first and foremost a passageway to two other worlds – the sky and the netherworld – which are co-extensive with it, but henceforth irrevocably external, since the way is now closed to humans. After having come to the end of their earthly existence and gone to their respective domains, Etsa and Nunkui (Nunkui and her daughter Uyush–sloth are metaphorically equivalent) go on playing a large and beneficial role in people's daily lives (Chapters Five and Six).

And so even today the house attests to a former material continuity between the celestial, terrestrial, and chthonian worlds, which, once broken, inaugurated a new order of things; but the old order was never fully effaced and remains forever inscribed in the architectonics of the house frame. As the vestige of an axis transcending several layers of space and time, the Achuar house is thus a symbol of mediating verticality, elegantly condensing in its one ground floor the Bachelardian topoi of cellar and attic.

Moreover, both myth fragments affirm the organic nature of the house, since they stress that natural autonomous and conscious beings comprise its substance. The *paeni* tree and the *kenku* bamboo, through the intercession of the myth, thus become the archetypes of this bustling yet invisible life that inhabits the skeleton of the house. In this sense, the building process is not so much the simple reproduction of an original form, but a sort of act of re-creation, in which the Achuar produce a new life form by combining in a set way the atomized lives that are already present in each constituent element of the house.

The latent vertical axis is intersected by two perfectly explicit horizontal axes. An imaginary line divides the house crosswise into two clearly differentiated parts: the *tankamash*, the men's area of sociability, and the *ekent* ("wife"), the women's area of sociability (Fig. 10). Both areas are left by an exit located at the far end of each part. When the house has no walls, the *waiti* doorways are indicated by the space between two posts supporting the eaves which are set closer together than the rest; when there are walls, the doors are made, as we have seen, of moveable panels.

In principle, the ridge beam runs along an east–west axis thus bisecting the transverse axis and the two parts of the house that it delineates. The *tankamash* faces the setting sun (*etsa akati*) and the *ekent*, the rising sun (*etsa taamu*), the two doorways standing opposite each other on the same axis. In the great majority of cases, however, it must be said that the houses are not laid out according to the prescribed east–west orientation; rather, their true situation depends on the direction of the watercourse that bounds them. The most common house orientation is parallel to the river, or at right angles, with the *tankamash* on the water. There is no doubt that this orientation has a practical function: the *tankamash* being the only part of the house that visitors may enter, it is normal for it to face onto the river if the house is reached preferably by water. And yet the quasi-general non-respect of the east–west norm has to do with other reasons.

As we saw in Chapter Two, the most significant directional axis for the Achuar is not the east–west course of the sun, but the inverse, approximately west–east orientation of the river system. Although the categories *yaki*, upstream, and *tsumu*, downstream, are more or less the equivalent of *etsa akati*, west, and *etsa taamu*, east, the fact remains that this directional axis is inscribed on the face of the earth, as the rivers flow, and not in some heavenly trajectory. When they orient their house with the *tankamash* facing upstream and the *ekent* downstream, the Achuar are aware that it is situated on an imaginary axis running counter to the path of the sun, even though, in reality, this is often not the case, owing to the erratic course of the river.

The orientation parallel with the river is the best possible spatial approximation of the latent model of the house traversed from one end to the other by a stream. The Achuar do not spontaneously formulate this interpretation of the house as a segment of river: rather it constitutes an unconscious master-image the existence and operative fecundity of which can be verified by the fact that they combine into one coherent set a multitude of atomized symbolic associations none of which has independent meaning, even for the Indians themselves. Those houses set perpendicular to the river are not anomalies, they are simply topological conversions of the master-image; if one considers that, in this type of organization, the *tankamash* is the part of the house nearest the river, it is immediately clear that it is symbolically connected to the waterway, thereby becoming the port of entry for the aquatic flow.

Tsunki is the generic name of a category of male and female spirits which appear human and dwell in rivers and lakes, where their social and material lives are identical to those of the Achuar. They exercise their influence in a broad sphere, in particular, they are the source of shamanic powers, and mythology pictures them as a sort of model for intrahousehold sociability and its rules of etiquette. Now it happens that many material elements of the house reinforce this association between the Achuar household and the Tsunki's aquatic family. The homeowner's *chimpui* stool and the small *kutank* benches for the use of visitors or the rest of the household represent respectively the *charap* turtle and the *yantana* black caiman on which the Tsunki normally sit in their underwater house. Likewise, *tuntui*, a large signal drum made from a hollowed-out log, is associated with *panki*, the anaconda, who entertains the same faithful relationship with the Tsunki as dogs do with man. The turtle and the caiman also feature as counterpuntal constituent elements of the house, since the diamond-shaped teeth of the *paeni* are called "*charapa*'s head" or "*yantana*'s head."

Moreover, the *tuntui* as well as the *chimpui* and the *kutank* are made from the *shimiut* tree (*Apeiba membranacea*), a semi-soft-wooded Tiliaceae. Now Lévi-Strauss has shown that, in Amerindian mythic thought, this family (like the closely related Bombaceae) is an invariable term connoting shelter and refuge, and playing on a dialectic between container and content, on the one hand, and water and fish, on the other (Lévi-Strauss 1967: 337–8 and 167–8). Finally, it is not unusual to hear married men talking freely about their apparently seamless double life with, on one side, their legitimate terrestrial family and, on the other, their adulterine aquatic Tsunki spirit family. It thus seems that, through a series of linkages operating on several levels, the world of the house and the aquatic world work on a single principle of continuity.

Certain aspects of the funeral ceremony shed more light on this master-image of the house–river. The most common way of burying the dead is to place the corpse in a hollowed-out log – a *shimiut* once again – which is shaped like a small canoe and is explicitly called *kanu*. When the canoe is used as the coffin of the head of the household, it is buried in the center of the house along the longitudinal axis, the corpse's head toward the *ekent*.

The explicit function of the funeral ceremony is to protect the family and those present from the harmful consequences of death, which can affect the living on two levels. The *nekas wakan* ("true soul") of the deceased leaves the body before clinical death and wanders around the house and the immediate vicinity trying to lure the *nekas wakan* of the survivors to keep it company in its new solitude. Part of the funeral ceremony then consists in preventing it from carrying out its plan which would obviously set off a chain reaction of deaths.

There is also another type of exorcism which no longer addresses the potential danger posed by the soul of the deceased, but one which emanates directly from the lifeless body. Although it is now seen as devoid of any active principle of its own, since its soul has left, the cadaver is nevertheless still regarded as dangerous because it harbors the alien principles that caused its organic death. These active principles which survive clinical death are usually magic darts, *tsentsak*, shot by a shaman, or more rarely the contamination of some Western disease, *sunkur*, the epidemic and contagious nature of which are clearly perceived by the Achuar. Several parts of the funeral ceremony are intended to cleanse those present of the harmful influence of these independent active principles, *pausak*, by sending them into various substances which are then committed to the river to drift away on the current. It would therefore seem that burial in the canoe-coffin belongs to that part of the ceremony designed to eliminate the deceased's *pausak*. It is as though the *kanu* itself were set invisibly adrift on the river that symbolically flows through the house in order to carry downstream and away the bodily sheath of the deceased, which now endangers the living.[4]

Domestic sociability and its spaces

In addition to being an undifferentiated organic process and the symbolic projection of a system of explicit and implicit directional coordinates, the house is the center of social life. The rules for conduct in the house are meticulously regulated, and the inhabited space is marked off by this etiquette and encoded in a number of ways; we will be analyzing the protocol concerning this space the better to track down the principles that actually govern the workings of the household.

The exact site upon which a house is erected is never referred to by anything but the spatially vague waterway that bounds it and which forms not the point but the line of reference. In Achuar topography, the only way of marking space is with respect to Ego, that is starting from where the speaker stands. The house is therefore not appended to some socially defined and geographically delineated territory whose limits and substance continue from one generation to the next; on the contrary, it is the periodically displaced center of a network of forest paths and trails, the temporary focus, the starting point for using the surrounding space.

In the absence of an abstract grid of territoriality, in the absence of any system of land tenure that would mark the preeminence of appropriation over use, the house and the surrounding transformed space are not designated by a place name, but by the name of a man ("so-and-so's house"). It is the head of the family who built the house (*jea nurintin*, "the houseowner") who gives the household its social and material coherence. That is why a house is inhabited, socially speaking, only when the household head is physically present, and that is also why the chance visitor will never enter a dwelling when the master is temporarily away, even if his wives and children are all there.

The decision to extend hospitality – or in exceptional cases to refuse it – is always incumbent upon the household head; a house to all appearances bustling with domestic activity and ringing with children's laughter and games is, in fact, socially empty, *itiarka*, if the master of the house is not there to mark it as an inhabited place. Unless a visitor is a very close relative, etiquette demands that, when passing near a house thus abandoned by its "active principle," he pretend not even to notice the existence of the inhabited structure and that he behave as though the occupants were transparent. Such an attitude is partially justified by a puritanical sexual code that demands that occasions for unsupervised encounters between outside men and married women be kept to a minimum, as the latter are reputed to have an instinctive and irrepressible tendency to commit adultery. On a deeper level, the protocol of avoidance would seem to signify that it is only by the presence and will of its head that the household exists and endures.

The guiding function of the household head is thrown into a clearer light by its absence when he dies, and the social and physical fabric of the configuration of which he was the center suddenly dissolves and vanishes. Once he has been buried in the middle of his house, it is abandoned;[5] a few decades later, nothing tangible will remain to show that in this place a man had built a house and won from the forest a small space of sociability, no pilgrim will come to honor his memory now gone like the site he once fashioned. The material destruction of the house is accompanied by the disintegration of the household, whose members will be incorporated willy nilly into other domestic units, the wives and children of the deceased generally attaching themselves to his brothers, in accordance with the custom of levirate, placing their labor and their fecundity at the service of the illusory independence of a new family head.

The *tankamash* is the focus of male sociability, which extends out from the immutable seat of the houseowner, his *chimpui*, or stool, that stands beside one of the two *paeni* posts marking the boundary of the male side of the house. Seated on his *chimpui*, the head of the family receives his visitors, takes his meals, and drinks manioc beer; it is there that he weaves the *chankin* carrying baskets or makes a quiver; in short, it is his physical occupation of the *chimpui* that most clearly denotes that a house is inhabited. If the owner is away for any period of time, his *chimpui* will usually be turned on its side, thus signaling to passing visitors that no one is home. As the *chimpui* is reserved for married men, a resident son-in-law will be allowed to make one for himself (in fact, that is often one of the first things he will do to mark his new status), but he will make it smaller and less ostentatious than his father-in-law's. Like a scale model, the son-in-law's *chimpui* will stand symmetrically opposite that of the master of the house, at the base of the other *paeni* post (see floor plan, Fig. 10).

It is in the *tankamash* that the men do their talking: their style of speech is public and agonistic, characterized by formal rhetoric that precludes any hesitation or slip of the tongue. Seated on the low *kutank* benches, male visitors, *irar*, exchange with their host, *pujaku* ("he who is present"), the interminable ritual dialogues that are the preamble to any normal conversation.[6] The master of the house and his guest sit stiffly facing each other, gun between the knees ready to hand, eyes systematically averted. The more distant genealogically and geographically the visitor's region is from his host's, that is the more difficult it is to uncover his true status as ally or enemy, the longer the coded dialogues will go on and the more charged the verbal exchanges will be with formalism and latent tension, each of the speakers retiring behind protective rhetoric for as long as it takes to form an opinion of the other.

If the visitor has come to convey important information or to discuss a serious matter – such as taking part in a raid – he will wait until the wee hours, just before dawn, to expose the affair in detail. This period from waking until sunrise is a time of relative intimacy during which the men gather around the host's *chimpui* and fire to drink a decoction of *wayus* (a plant of the *Ilex* genus). They converse in low voices, telling stories or discussing their dreams, while consuming great quantities of the sweetish emetic. In effect, it is unseemly for a man to start the day with a full stomach and the *wayus* helps him cleanse his bowels.

In the early hours of dawn, the circle breaks up; each guest goes out to the edge of the garden to vomit in a concert of retching and throat clearing, then all return, the host to his *chimpui*, the guests to their *kutank*, for a new session of daylight formalities. If the exceptional spatial proximity engendered by the *wayus* ceremony excludes recourse to ritual dialogue, the air is no less often tense, and the highly controlled intonations can still be heard as proof that host and visitors remain wary of each other. In effect, it is precisely that moment of relative intimacy that guests most often choose treacherously to assassinate their host, counting on a lapse of attention at the only moment in the entire day when the rules of conviviality demand that he lay down his weapon.

The fireplaces in the *tankamash* are not for cooking, or at least are not for cooking food; they are used exclusively to warm the coldest, dampest late-night hours and to prepare the mixtures and decoctions that are the exclusive province of men: heating the *wayus* or the curare vessels, softening the resin to be used on blowguns, or heating to incandescence a sliver of metal that will be used to engrave a quiver. It is also in the *tankamash* that the *tuntui* is hung, the big signal drum whose hollow voice informs the neighbors of important events in the household – a death for example – and calls the *arutam* souls to the *natematin* feast.

The *tankamash* is a place of physical non-contact, since only unmarried adolescents sleep there on a permanent basis together with occasional visitors. This male space is for most purposes off-limits to the women and they put in an appearance only in the line of their duties to the men: serving manioc beer in the *pininkia*, thin, elegantly decorated earthenware bowls, or bringing in the food they have prepared in the *ekent*. Sometimes, if the master of the house is in a jovial mood, he will invite one of his wives – usually his first wife, called *tarimiat* – to share the meal she has set at his feet, but this privilege is usually reserved for the young boys of the family.

Little girls who inadvertently wander into the *tankamash* when there are men present are sharply reprimanded; from an early age they learn never to cross the imaginary line that separates them from the male domain unless they have been invited. When serving manioc beer in the *tankamash* in the presence of guests, a young woman will stand silently and carefully avoid looking directly at the men. Only a *tarimiat* or the experienced wives of a *juunt*, will sometimes join in the conversation, if it is not a ritual dialogue, or interject caustic remarks from time to time, which the men pretend not to hear although they listen closely.

No woman will ever enter the house through the *tankamash* entrance, and the wife of a distant visitor – be she the wife of the ethnologist – must stand or squat outside, on the outskirts of the men's domain, until the various phases of the ritual dialogue her husband is conducting with the master of the house are over. This temporary period of exclusion – which denotes the subordinate character of the woman's social role as soon as she is no longer at home – lasts until the women of the house at last invite her to come around into the *ekent*, where she is in turn served manioc beer.

Although the *ekent* is the focus of women's sociability within the house, it is not only that, since the prohibitions that codify the presence of women in the *tankamash* do not apply symmetrically to the *ekent*. In other words, the *ekent* is a space open to the comings and goings of the men of the house, although it is generally closed to male visitors. This part of the house is basically reserved for private life, for cooking and sleeping, where the formalism that prevails in the *tankamash* is left behind.

Every woman, whether married or widowed, has a large bed in the *ekent*; this is a platform, *peak*, consisting of a rectangular frame across which are laid slats of split *kenku* bamboo or one of a variety of species of palm. In a polygynous household, in the interests of privacy the *peak* is often partially surrounded by slats of the same type. Above the *peak* in most cases and constructed in the same manner is another slat platform, *peek*, used to store each co-wife's cooking utensils along with small household objects: dyes for pots and cotton, the spindle, needles and thread, and so on. It is there too that the block of salt, obtained by trading with the Shuar, is kept, as well as small stores of such foods as beans or ears of maize.

In the center of the *ekent* stand the large jars, *muits*, in which the manioc mash for the *nijiamanch* ferments. Next to the *muits* is a large flat, round mortar, *pumputs*, made, like the doors, of *wampu* wood; this is used by all the women of the house to mash the boiled manioc. Baskets, *chankin*, full of peanuts, are often hung from the *ekent* tie-beam out of the reach of voracious rodents and greedy children. At the foot of each sleeping platform smolders a cooking fire, *jii*, consisting of three logs laid end-to-end star fashion, that must be rekindled each time there is cooking to be done.

In the case of a polygynous domestic group, each co-wife and her children create around her *peak* and cooking fire a tiny, autonomous, clearly separate matricentric socio-economic cell. With the exception of the *pumputs* mortar used by everyone, all of a woman's tools and utensils have been made by her or are for her exclusive use. A co-wife sleeps with her offspring on her own *peak*, and the baby's hammock hangs at the foot of the bed. She ties her dogs under her own bed or to a small *peak* next to it; they are kept tied in the house. She does the cooking for herself, her children and her husband at the foot of her own bed, where she also prepares her manioc beer and weaves cotton cloth or makes pots. And one day she and perhaps some of her children will be buried beneath that same *peak*.

The spatial differentiation of each matricentric unit is clearly illustrated on the floor plan in Figure 10, which shows how two co-wives go about distributing, within clearly circumscribed spaces, their married and unmarried children and the zones of their daily activities.

The master of the house has no bed of his own in the *ekent* – he often has a resting bed in the *tankamash* where he naps during the hottest part of the day and which may serve as a guest-*peak* – and each night he honors the *peak* of a different wife, following a generally even-handed system of rotation. The son-in-law, too, sleeps in the *ekent* with his wife; and his *peak*, the only place he can call his own, is to a certain extent the symbol of his integration in the domestic group. In a society that does not do much bodily touching, the *peak* appears as the chosen place for physical intimacy, a small island in the night where bodies of all ages pile together in uninhibited tenderness.

If the *peak* is the usual stage for marital and maternal caresses, it is only rarely – especially in polygynous households – the scene of regular sexual commerce. Sexuality and love play are engaged in freely only in the forest, usually on the occasion of a hunting trip, since one wife nearly always accompanies the head of the house to carry his kill. There too fair-handed rotation is the rule: the master of the house setting out for the forest at the crack of dawn will usually take along the wife with whom he has just spent a chaste night.

Pursuing into the forest the principles governing gender relations within the house, it becomes clear that the internal duality of the house is founded on something other than the spatial reification of a male order (*tankamash*) and a female order (*ekent*). In effect, although the forest is a predominantly male space (see below, Chapter Six), like the *ekent*, it permits the conjunction of the sexes that is forbidden by the *tankamash*. By contrast, gardens are exclusively female places, structurally equivalent, even though the poles of exclusion are reversed, to that space of sexual disjunction, the *tankamash*. Male and female areas of sociability are not topographically contiguous, then; rather the spaces are interwoven according to the order dictated by the principles of conjunction and disjunction: the *ekent*, a conjunctive space, is to the *tankamash*, a disjunctive space, as the forest is to the garden (Fig. 14).

The area around the house, *aa*, and the river that bounds it, do not fit this pattern of opposing pairs. From the standpoint of the spatial dichotomy engendered by relations between the sexes, the *aa* has no specificity of its own; this zone becomes a disjunctive space where it is an extension of the *tankamash* and a conjunctive space where it is an extension of the *ekent*. The *aa*, therefore, dwindles to the attenuated projection, restricted to the perimeter of the house, of the principles of sexual conjunction and disjunction that govern the space inside the house. As for the river, it is not annihilated, but it does lose its materiality, its extension, becoming a simple axis running through the totality of these concentric spaces (Fig. 15). In effect, the river cannot be reduced to a binary system, for it allows at once the conjunction and the disjunction of the sexes depending upon the use made of it and the nature of the space on which it borders. And so the guiding function it ensures within the house orientation system enables the river to transcend these concentric places, while preventing it from constituting a space in its own right.

If we now see the house not as a matrix of gender relations within the domestic group, but as a matrix of relations between the domestic group and the surrounding social world, we observe that the coefficients of

Within the domestic group			
Conjunction male–female		Disjunction male / female	
Forest (*ikiam*)	*Ekent*	*Tankamash*	Garden (*aja*)
male–female space predominantly male	female–male space predominantly female	male space	female space
Sexual relations	–private sociability –private speech –body contact –cooking fire –no segregation of sexes –sexual relations	–public sociability –formal speech –gestural formalism –non-cooking fire –segregation of sexes	–giving birth

Between domestic group and outsiders			
Conjunction household-outsiders male space		Disjunction household / outsiders female space	
Forest (*ikiam*)	*Tankamash*	*Ekent*	Garden (*aja*)
Place of accidental conjunction with predominantly hostile outsiders (feuding)	Place of formal conjunction with predominantly friendly outsiders (visits)	Off-limits to outside men, except if they are integrated (marriage alliance)	Entry permitted to outside women providing they work there (visits)
		Entry permitted to outside women (visits)	Off-limits to outside men, except for adulterine sexual relations (alliance broken, motive for war)

14. Spatial organization of relations of conjunction and disjunction

conjunction and disjunction may permute their attributions within the
household, while remaining constant in the outside space. In this model, the
ekent, a disjunctive space, is to the *tankamash*, a conjunctive space, as
gardens are to the forest (Fig. 15). The river and the house yard are still
excluded from this binary model; they lose their spatial specificity for the
reasons we gave earlier: the *aa*, because it is a mere extension of the house,
and the river because it is always a combination of conjunction (linear
conjunction between separate houses along a single waterway) and disjunction (private, domestic use of a segment of river). This second model is also
a fair demonstration that relations between houses (conjunction) are
mediated as a rule by male spaces, while sociability within the household

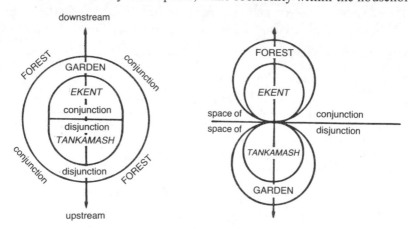

Relations of conjunction and disjunction between the sexes within the domestic group

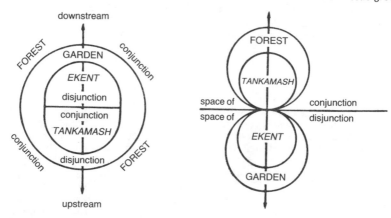

Relations of conjunction and disjunction between the domestic group and outsiders

15. Social structuring of space

(disjunction) revolves around the *ekent*, that is a predominantly female space.

The pair conjunction/disjunction is a constant of the space inside the house despite the inversion of poles that occurs with the passage from one model to the other. Such permanence is significant in that the house subsumes into one unified matrix several different systems of spatial division, which have in common only the fact that they are based on norms of social conduct flowing from the general paradigm provided by "house etiquette." Clearly the house is not organized according to the classic mode of concentric circularity, which proceeds from the innermost to the outermost, on the periphery, but according to a more complex model, which articulates two sets of circles on either side of a tangent. If one converts the empirical topographical representation of the house and its territory from the two models (intrahousehold sociability and interhouse sociability) into two logical schemas organized by twos around the pair conjunction/disjunction, one goes from a figure in which all circles are concentric to one in which the circles are tangential (Fig. 15). But this topological conversion is more than a formal exercise, for it shows the logical structure of a space coordinated by the social forms of its use. In the concentric topographical representation, cosmological continuity is depicted by the river axis that bisects the set of recognized spaces; in the schematic conversion it is combined with a fundamental discontinuity which distributes these same spaces on either side of a plane separating the areas of conjunction and disjunction. This plane introduced into the dwelling by the artifice of the diagram is of course the level of social relations, that is male–female relations or domestic group–outsider relations.

In a society that places a high value on control of the body and its functions and in which, especially for men, will-power and fortitude are demonstrated by mastery of one's physical needs, the house is the privileged focus of self-restraint. The first instance of this control over nature is the regulation of one's own natural dispositions within a tight network of bodily habits. The house is first and foremost that place where no natural impropriety must occur.

Frugality and the ability to go without sleep are virtues prized by the Achuar; the first is a leitmotif running through an otherwise laxist attitude to child-raising. The condemnation of gluttony is not linked to any obsession with a lack of food; it is drummed into children as the basic principle that is the source of the capacity to control one's instincts. To subject oneself to eating little, sleeping parsimoniously, bathing in the cold river before dawn after having purged oneself is to submit to the constraints indispensable for purifying the body of physiological wastes. It is no doubt not capitulating to a dualist Cartesian conception of man to see this constant control as the result of a typically Achuar tendency to introduce ever more cultural and social elements into the manifestations of man's animal nature.

Self-restraint in young men often takes a theatrical turn, the spectacular aspect of which is meant to mark the existence of a norm and to signify the young person's observation of it over and above what is normally demanded. To show everyone his disgust for gluttony, an adolescent will protest loudly each time a kinswoman brings him food, demanding that it be withdrawn immediately. Similarly, he will sleep as little as possible, rising in the middle of the night to go noisily about trivial occupations, to be sure that the whole house, now awake, sees how little sleep he needs.

And so the house, the only physically enclosed space in this society, also calls for enclosure of the body, or more precisely, for an explicit demonstration of clear limits on corporeity, through the control of physiological attitudes, expressions, and substances. In the presence of visitors, in particular, retention is extremely strict: one must never look a visitor straight in the eye on pain of signifying hostility (between men) or desire (between men and women); during ritual dialogues, the hand, held over the lower part of the face, hides the teeth and the moving lips, giving the impression of disembodied voices; the face, practically hidden beneath a mask of achiote, becomes a painting on an inscrutable support.

The nearly hysterical reaction of men upon catching sight of any excrement left by children or domestic animals to soil the packed earth floor testifies eloquently enough to the fact that the house is a place in which nothing must recall the disorder found in nature. This is where the constant socialization of humans and pets takes place; without many illusions, it is expected of parrots, macaws, or curassows that they will control their bowels like the other domestic animals.

Of all the body substances whose emission is controlled by will-power only saliva is freely and publicly expelled within the confines of the house. Women's saliva is the prime principle of the fermentation of manioc beer, and liberal use is made of it during the preparation. Men's saliva in the form of long streams elegantly directed between two fingers pressed to the lips forms the counterpoint to any dialogue or conversation. Punctuating the speeches, the cadence of emissions keeps pace with the mounting tension between the speakers. Principle of alimentary transformation and phonic lubricant, saliva is a body substance that is both instrumental and highly socialized, being an adjunct to speech.

The differentiated social functions of saliva, distinguished according to whether they are exercised in the *ekent* or the *tankamash*, bring us back, after a long detour, to the representation of the house as organic process. In effect, the house clearly synthesizes the various operations performed by the digestive tract; once again, though, the metaphor is not explicit and merely combines into a single image the different uses that can be made of the dwelling. The *tankamash*, associated with male saliva, evokes the upper extremity, that is the mouth, connoted essentially by its faculty of speech. It is also through the doorway of the *tankamash* that the men go outside to vomit shortly before dawn, and it is in this part of the house that the men produce the instrumental music that is assimilated to singing.

The *ekent*, associated with women's saliva, is the locus proper of an artificially initiated cultural digestive phenomenon – the fermentation of manioc and the cooking of food – which precedes organic, natural digestion and enables it to take place. Moreover, the schematic orientation of the *ekent* facing downstream, *tsumu*, is significant, for *tsumu* also designates the buttocks. Now all household waste is evacuated by the women from the *ekent* to the section of the river downstream from the house, where it is thrown either directly into the water or onto the river bank. It is also into the river that the men defecate at dawn, slightly downstream from where the women normally go to bathe or draw water. The master-image of the house as a segment of river is now taking shape, since it is as though the water, as it follows its ideal course through the house, were changed by metaphor into the contents of the intestines.

It appears then that, although the Achuar have no highly structured corpus of representations of the house, it is nevertheless coded on a number of levels – sociological, topographical, and organic – which underpin indigenous speech and practices, albeit in a mainly unconscious fashion. Spatial matrix of several systems of conjunction and disjunction, anchor for inter- and intrafamily sociability, model for articulating the coordinates of the world, and final segment of a nature–culture continuum, every Achuar house is at the same time like all others and irreducible in its singularity. All houses are alike, for in a world where singularity is not proclaimed by eccentricity, each household is a reflection of all others and the materialization of a general model repeated ad infinitum. But each house is also irreducible, for as both material substance and social body, each stands as the image of an autonomous whole, controlling its piece of territory with the illusion of free will that comes from the long practice of solipsism.

5

The world of gardens

The garden world encircles the house like a belt, forming a space temporarily wrested from the invasive grasp of the jungle. One might even say commandeered once human action has replaced the natural ecosystem by an artificial ecosystem resembling a scale-model forest. But the wresting comes first, not only in the chronological order of making a garden, but also in the way the Achuar see this process. The term *aja*, which we have been translating as "garden," does not actually designate the plantings but the man-made clearing (from the verb *ajak*: "to clear"). What primarily characterizes the *aja* then is the initial annexation of a portion of nature more than its subsequent transformation. The preeminence of the idea of man-made clearing over that of garden plot is quite clear in the *denotata* of the *aja*; this stems in particular from the fact that the Achuar practice what has been called "pioneering slash-and-burn cultivation," that is they always use for swidden sites parts of the forest that have never been cleared before.[1] Each new garden is therefore the result of an act of predation committed on the forest; it is man marking the environment and not the reclaiming of land, that is the reappropriation of a once-socialized space.

Clearing and gardening

Choosing the site

Having no toponyms associated with concrete landmarks and no historico-genealogical memory which would enable them to pass on the memory of the exact site of former gardens, the Achuar must certainly upon occasion mistake for primary forest what is actually very old secondary growth. Even though phytographers generally estimate that the complete reconstitution of a dense rain forest requires several centuries (Schnell 1972, t. 2: 694), in fact, only a few decades after the appearance of a man-made or a natural clearing, trees have grown back into something closely resembling the aspect and composition of a climax forest. In northwest Amazonia, for example, some hundred years after the trees were cut, it is now nearly impossible for a professional botanist to tell the secondary growth from the surrounding primary forest (Sastre 1975). The Achuar use a series of signs to recognize relatively recent secondary growth. The first is the presence of certain cultigens that resist the invasion of forest species for a period of some twenty years after the garden has been abandoned (*uwi, wakamp*: *Theobroma subincanum; timiu, wayus, tsaank: Nicotiana* sp.; and *wampa*: *Inga edulis*); the second is the abundance of sun-loving intrusive plants (*suu*: *Cecropia sciadophylla*; *tseek*: *Cecropia* sp.; *wawa*: *Ochroma pyramidale*) and the presence of trees typical of secondary growth (*takatsa: Jacaranda copaia* and *uruchnum: Croton*), and finally the absence of epiphytic plants and liana. A tract in the process of regeneration, whether the product of tree-felling or natural causes, is generally called *tsuat pantin* ("clear garbage"). The idea of "garbage" connotes the density of undergrowth, which forms an inextricable tangle of brush, shrubs, and tree ferns, making progress all but impossible. The idea of "clear" refers to the luminosity characteristic of such a tract: the upper story has not yet grown back, and there is therefore a sharp contrast with the surrounding forest, where the broad crowns form an almost continuous canopy that lets through little light. After some thirty years, the secondary growth begins to blend in with the structure of the climax vegetation, and then the Achuar distinguish old clearings by the absence of large trees and eventually by the presence of hardwood stumps that have not yet rotted.

The pioneering character of Achuar horticulture does not mean that they always make their clearings in true climax forest then, but simply in one whose morphology leads the Indians to believe that it has not been cut for at least three generations. Such a forest – or tract of forest – is called *takamchau* ("that which has not been worked"), that is, virgin, the expression being used without distinction for the earth and women. The "work" (*takat*) can be sexual or horticultural, for, in both cases, it actualizes potential fertility by socializing it. Similarly, a girl is "educated" (*unuimiam*) by the work of male sexuality, in other words, she is socialized by her husband, just as the random fertility of a tract of virgin forest is recruited by human action, which employs it to social and cultural ends.

This predilection for climax forest can be confirmed empirically by analyzing the remains of natural vegetation left in recently cleared gardens. Counting and identifying all stumps more than 10 centimeters across in five 10 × 10 m sampling units located in five separate clearings in the first stage of planting indicate that the squares never contain fewer than eleven different species and no more than two members of each species. The results of this survey fit the usual structure of climax rain forest which, except for swampland and river banks, is characterized by a great diversity of species and a small number of individuals per species. The only exception to this rule of always using "primary forest" are the small clearings planted entirely in maize which, as we shall see, are sometimes made on land that was cleared five or six years earlier and where the secondary growth is especially easy to cut.

As a rule, the Achuar do not show much concern for forest regeneration and have no specialized vocabulary for the various stages of secondary growth. When a garden is no longer weeded, it becomes *arut aja* ("old garden"); when the secondary growth is over a man's head, the clearing becomes *tsuat pantin*, until it finally blends in with the climax forest. Such indifference can be explained, for, given the low density of human population and the highly dispersed pattern of settlement, the probability that two clearings would be made in the same spot more than once in a century is practically nil. In other words, the Achuar do not take great pains to choose a tract of absolutely "primary" forest since, in any given part of their territory, the risk of happening on a piece of secondary forest, even a very old one, is minute.

The low population density makes competition for horticultural lands unnecessary, even if all soils are not equally suited to cultivation. When the head of a domestic group selects a new house site, the choice is not dictated strictly by agronomic criteria, but rather by those having to do with his assessment of the natural resources available in the micro-region in which the household will be doing its foraging. He first chooses a space conducive to hunting, fishing, and gathering before going on to select the best site for the gardens and house. The latter choice is usually made in the course of a hunting expedition.

The main factors weighed by domestic units when choosing a foraging territory are the quantity and variety of plant resources, the game supply, and the presence of a stream with a more or less steady flow. The plant species whose presence is a determining factor are first of all palm trees, particularly those used for roofing and which often grow in small stands in natural semi-clearings (*saak*). In regions where trading exists, the local concentration of species gathered for their commercial value is a fundamental motivation in the choice of a dwelling site. The main species are the "cinnamon tree" *ishpink*, whose dried flowers are used in certain culinary preparations in the highlands of Ecuador; the *kinchuk* palm, whose fibers are used to make brooms; and the *kunkuk* palm, whose seeds are used to make oil.

By contrast, a plentiful supply of game is an important criterion only in the interfluve, where the bulk of dietary meat comes from birds and land- and tree-dwelling mammals. In the riverine biotope, a lake (*kucha*) or the dead arm of an old meander (*kanus tsenken*) are decisive; the considerable ichthyological potential of this type of aquatic micro-environment often permits even the presence of a small cluster of houses. And yet the riverine environment is hampered by one limiting factor for the human occupation of large areas: the flooded *aguajales*, *tsuat ikiam* ("garbage forest"), the only spaces in the Achuar ecosystem unfit for human habitation. A secondary but non-negligible limiting factor in certain regions is the presence of thick stands of *kenku* bamboo, which make impregnable retreats in which fleeing peccaries invariably take refuge, thus frustrating the hunter of his game after a long pursuit.

Once the household has chosen its foraging territory, the selection of the garden and house sites depend almost entirely on the prosaic necessities of daily life as described in the preceding chapter. Once again, agronomic criteria recede into the background; a site is chosen first of all for its convenience, for its strategic location or because it is close to a stand of palm trees that can be used for roofing. Of course, the Achuar do not consider all sites to be good for gardening, but among the many suitable sites, the final choice is made on the basis of extra-agronomic criteria.

The indigenous criteria for evaluating the agronomic potential of a site are generally threefold: the relief, the soil, and the vegetation. The ideal site is a flat, well-drained terrace, free of rocks, above flood level, covered in "primary" forest, yet without really big trees which represent an important labor input if they must be felled. In effect, gardens only rarely contain stumps and fallen logs over 1.20 cm in diameter. Whereas these particular reliefs and types of vegetation are fairly common all over the Achuar territory, the soils considered truly suitable for cultivation are not as widespread.

In order better to understand indigenous agricultural criteria and to assess the parameters used in selecting a garden site, we will briefly analyze the phytological and pedological features of three different representative residential sites. The first two are genuine riverine micro-regions, but which differ in their settlement pattern: relatively concentrated on site n° 1 and highly dispersed on site n° 2; the third site is typical of the interfluvial biotope. In each case, we relied on the native categories for identifying the various elements of the terrain and soils that the Achuar distinguish in their reading of the landscape.[2]

At all three sites and irrespective of the nature of the biotope, the zones regarded by the Achuar as most suitable for horticulture are highly restricted. While it is true that the only absolutely decisive limiting factors for horticulture are the inundated *aguajales* and hills with too steep a slope (a gradient of more than 55%), it remains that certain potentially workable zones are considered marginal by the Achuar because of low productivity and the labor that would be needed to keep them growing. This is an important point, and it conditions any rigorous analysis of territoriality, inasmuch as demography must be seen, and the horticultural carrying capacity assessed, with respect to indigenous criteria of effective land use, and not as a function of the absolute limiting factors of the ecosystem. These problems will be discussed at greater length in Chapter Nine, but even now a number of lessons can be drawn from the analysis of the three sites.

In the first place, analysis shows that the indigenous agronomic choices denote an excellent empirical knowledge of differential soil fertility, confirmed by pedological analyses performed on sites 1 and 3. The Achuar typology of soils suited to cultivation recognizes three broad categories, by order of increasing fertility: *keaku nunka*, "red earth," *nayakim nunka*, "sandy earth," and *shuwin nunka*, "black earth." The red lateritic soils of the hills, *keaku nunka* (Oxic Dystropepts), are only very occasionally used, for if they are quite well tolerated by sweet manioc, they are, on the whole, incompatible with more demanding cultigens like bananas, yams, peanuts, or maize. Furthermore, if the sandy soils with a predominance of volcanic sandstone (*nayakim nunka*) are the most fertile that the interfluvial terraces have to offer, they are nonetheless relatively mediocre in comparison to the black alluvial soils (*shuwin nunka* and *kanus nunka*) of the riverine biotope.

While a garden with alluvial soil will sometimes grow manioc for over ten years with no noticeable decline in productivity, the production of a garden with sandy soil will fall off rapidly after the second year. The extreme fertility of riverine alluvial soil makes for highly flexible planting strategies: with the guarantee of a very productive main garden, there is no danger involved in playing on a broader pedological spectrum and making "experimental" secondary gardens. This was the case, for instance, at site n° 1,

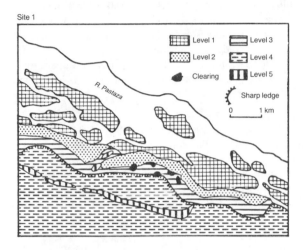

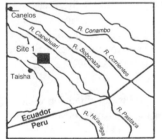

16. Garden site: no. 1

Key
Upper course of the Rio Pastaza, south bank; approximate coordinates at center of map: 2°10′ latitude south by 77°20′ longitude west.

Level 1:
Indigenous name: *kaanmatak* ("pebble beach") or *nayakim* ("sand beach"). These are very low alluvial terraces over recent alluvial deposits less than 3 m higher than the present thalweg. The materials accumulated are gravel, coarse and fine sands and sedimentary deposits. The soils are usually Tropofluvents (pH 5–6). This level is flat and often flooded. The natural vegetation is sparse and comprised chiefly of

riparian species: *wawa, pumpu, paat: Gynerium sagittatum; naship, kenku, suu, winchu: Heliconia* sp.

Level 2:

Indigenous name: *pakui* ("dirty," "sticky," "waterlogged but non-marshy" terrain). These are low alluvial terraces over recent alluvial deposits more than 3 m above the present thalweg. The granulometry of these deposits is sandy-loam. The alluvial soil (*kanus nunka*: "alluvial river earth") is black, deep (60–80 cm) and loose, Tropaquent and Tropaquet. The pH is moderately to slightly acid (5.5–6.5) with a minimum level of aluminum toxicity. High soil fertility is counteracted by bad drainage (no slope). This level rarely undergoes seasonal flooding. The vegetation resembles on the whole that of level 1, but in addition comprises an upper story dominated by several species of *Inga* and by *wampuash*. Although this level may sometimes be used for gardens, it is never used for settlements.

Level 3:

Indigenous name: *paka* ("flat"). These are medium-height alluvial terraces more than 5 m above the present thalweg. The alluvial soil (*shuwin nunka*: "black earth") over silt deposited by flooding is quite loamy, deep and loose with a moderately to fairly acid pH (5.8–6.5) and a minimum level of aluminum toxicity. The high fertility and good drainage of the soils on this level make the *paka* the prime choice for gardens and dwellings. The vegetation is typical of climax forest, and it is not unusual to find trees over 40–50 m, such as the *mente*.

Level 4:

Indigenous name: *mura* ("hill"). These are high or very high alluvial terraces over old alluvial deposits, which rise above the preceding level and are separated from it by a sharp drop. The soils (*keaku nunka*: "red earth") are clayey, deep and hard packed with a strong to very strongly acid pH (4.5–5.5) and mediocre fertility. The vegetation does not grow as tall as that of level 3, but it is thicker.

Level 5:

Indigenous name: *tsuat ikiam* ("garbage forest"). These are water-filled depressions that form permanent marshes (*aguajales*). The most common vegetation on this level is a near monospecific formation: stands of *achu* palms; *tankana* and *kasua* can also be seen fairly frequently.

The gardens were cleared on level 3, *paka*, which has the best soils, relief and drainage. Technically speaking, secondary gardens can also be made on level 2, *pakui* (limiting factor: bad drainage) or on level 4, *mura* (limiting factor: poor soil). The disadvantages of these two levels are partially off set by a number of specific advantages: ease of clearing trees on level 2 and fewer weeds on level 4, but their potential utilization (one clearing was made on level 2) always comes after level 3. As the map shows, level 3 is quite narrow, but long enough for a string of houses. To give some indication: the houses closest to this site along the river are 8 km upstream and 60 km downstream; they, too, stand on level 3.

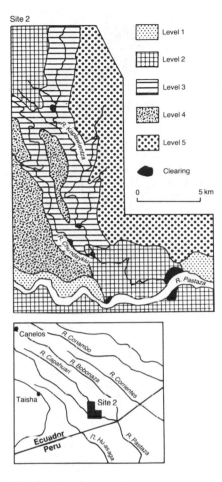

17. Garden site: no. 2

Key

Lower course of the Rio Kapawientza, where it joins the Rio Pastaza; approximate coordinates at center of map: 2°20′ latitude south by 77°10′ longitude west.

Level 1:
Indigenous name: *pakui*; these are very low alluvial terraces subject to flooding, in every way like level 2 of the preceding site.

Level 2:
Indigenous name: *paka*; this is a low alluvial plain but not subject to flooding, pedologically and phytologically like level 3 of the preceding site.

Level 3:

Indigenous name: *paka*; these are medium-height alluvial terraces, pedologically and phytologically like level 3 of the preceding site.

Level 4:

Indigenous name: *mura*; this is a very high alluvial plain towering some 40 meters above the alluvial terraces; the soils are Dystropepts and Dystrandepts of mediocre fertility (no analyses available); the natural vegetation is like that of level 4 of the preceding site.

Level 5:

Indigenous name: *mura*; these are mesas, rising some 50–80 m above the valleys. The clay soils formed over graywakes are Oxic Dystropepts (*keaku nunka*: "red earth") of mediocre fertility. The vegetation is roughly the same as that of the preceding level.

The clearings were made on levels 2 and 3, the only difference between these being the altitude and the better soil and drainage. The very large clearings that can be seen on either side of the Rio Pastaza are not Achuar gardens; these correspond to the zone occupied by a small military border guard.

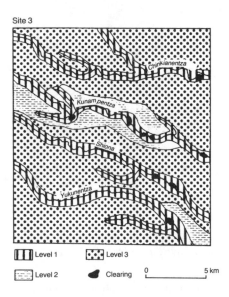

18. Garden site: no. 3

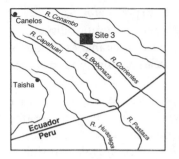

Key

Middle course of the Rio Kunampentza (Rio Conambo); approximate coordinates at center of map: 1°50′ latitude south by 76°50′ longitude west

Level 1:

Indigenous name: *paka*; these are level terraces about 5 m above the thalweg, composed of laterite soil with a predominance of graywakes. The soils (*nayakim nunka*: "sandy earth" or *kante nunka*: "dense earth") are deep, compact Aquic Dystropepts ranging from heavy to sandy clay with a very acidic pH (5.1–5.6), high level of aluminum toxicity and mediocre fertility. The vegetation is dense, well-structured climax forest; among the most common species encountered: *apai, shimiut, tinchi: Nectandra* sp.; *chinchak, tuntuam, shuwat.*

Level 2:

Indigenous name: *mura*; these are small, low (generally under 20 m) hills made up of red clay soils over clay deposits. The soils (*keaku nunka*: "red earth" or *kapantin nunka*: "red-orange earth") are Oxic Dystropepts, lateritic, clayey to very clayey, shallow and compact with a strong to very strongly acidic pH (4.5–5.5), very high level of aluminum toxicity and very low fertility. The vegetation is climax forest, on the surface not very different from that of level 1; among the most common species encountered: *paeni, tiria, tsachir, apaich numi: Himatanthus sucuuba.*

Level 3:

Indigenous name: *mura*; these are mesas towering some 50–80 m above the valleys. The tops are divided into almost horizontal ridges, separated by small, secondary thalwegs; the mesas often fall off sharply. The clay soils on graywackes are Oxic Dystropepts very like those of level 2; in fact, the Achuar make no distinction between the two. The vegetation, too, is like that of level 2.

All the clearings were made on level 1, *paka*, which has the least unfavorable soil conditions and the only level areas. The width of the terraces varies with the course of the river, but never exceeds a kilometer on either side.

where a small garden devoted exclusively to the fish poison *timiu*, a cultigen which apparently likes very acid soils, was made on the lateritic hillsides. At the same site, another garden was planted in maize and bananas on highly fertile but poorly drained alluvial soil, both species having good tolerance for high soil humidity.

The relative fertility of a piece of land is perceived by the Achuar as a constant specific attribute of a soil category, and the signs denoting this fertility are themselves clearly conceived as soil attributes. Forest species generally representative of certain edaphological levels are taken as simple identification marks; the nature of the soil is determined by the Achuar first and foremost by means of purely physical qualities: color, texture, and porousness.

The agronomic characteristics of a fertile soil are clearly defined by the Achuar: manioc produces longer there than elsewhere, the tubers are bigger and more plentiful; maize, yams, and peanuts grow easily; banana trees reproduce spontaneously by shoots from the main stem (which is not the case on poor soils). The paradigm of a fertile soil type is *shuwin nunka*, and it is said that it is *susutin*, "bearded," the beard and hair being directly associated by the Achuar with the idea of fecundity and sexual potency, as is also the case in many other societies (Leach 1958).

From the standpoint of the organization of labor, Achuar slash-and-burn horticulture fits the classic sexual division of labor, as it is most commonly practiced in Amazonia: clearing the undergrowth and felling the trees are exclusively male activities, while planting, weeding, and harvesting are done almost entirely by women, with the exception of a few particular cultigens that are handled by men only. Theoretically every married woman has her own garden clearing, or at least a patch clearly marked off by paths or rows of banana trees within a larger garden subdivided into as many plots as there are married women in the domestic unit. Strictly speaking then, the co-wives do not exploit the garden in common, and the matricentric individualization of household chores that prevails within the house extends to the garden as well: each woman is responsible for planting, cultivating, maintaining, and harvesting her own plot.

Clearing and planting a garden are the preliminary phases of site occupation: the house is built and the final move made only once the garden can feed the domestic unit, that is when the manioc can be harvested, eight to ten months after planting. In most cases the house is erected in the middle of the clearing or on the edge, near the temporary shelter that housed the family during the months needed to make the garden and build the house.

When a site is first occupied, the most common layout is a single garden clearing, subdivided or not into individual patches, depending on whether or not the house is polygynous (see Figs. 19 and 20). The initial topographical arrangement may change over the years under the impetus of two factors: in the first place, bringing new married women into the household necessarily involves increasing the surface under cultivation; and in the second place a serious drop in production and the concomitant increase in the number of weeds – particularly on the less-productive interfluvial soils –

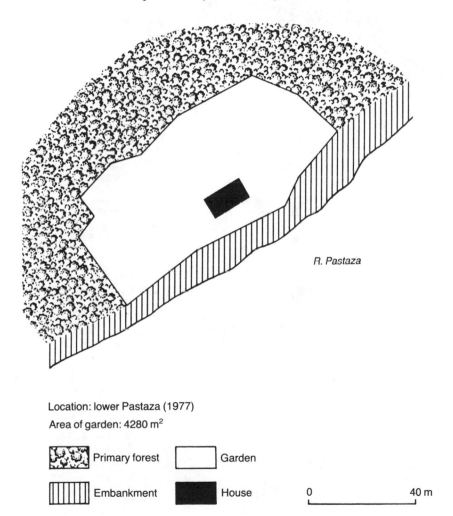

R. Pastaza

Location: lower Pastaza (1977)
Area of garden: 4280 m²

Primary forest   Garden

Embankment   House   0 ⸺ 40 m

19. Typical settlement pattern for a monogamous residential unit (1 wife = 1 garden patch)

entails abandoning the garden near the house and having to make a new one.

When a new co-wife joins the domestic unit, it is not customary to give her an area already planted by one of the other women, since a woman is supposed to be personally responsible for all phases of gardening. Similarly, when a young woman of the house marries, thereby achieving the

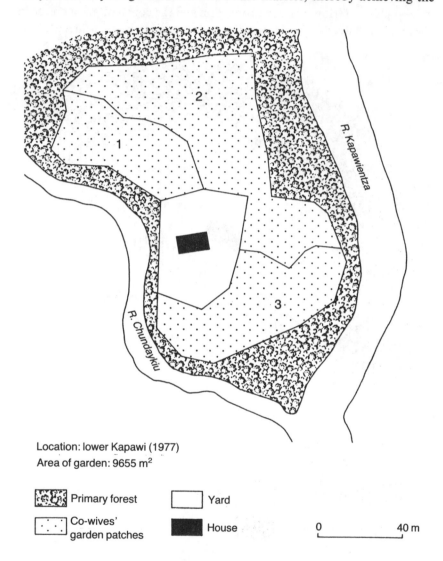

Location: lower Kapawi (1977)
Area of garden: 9655 m²

	Primary forest		Yard
	Co-wives' garden patches		House

0   40 m

20. Typical settlement pattern for a polygynous residential unit (3 co-wives = 3 garden patches)

status of independent "gardener," she may stop working in her mother's garden and be given one of her own. In both cases, as in that of a widow who attaches herself to the household, a new clearing must be made. If there are no limiting factors – swamp, steep hill, or stream – trees will be felled and the clearing made next to the old garden. When they clear a new adjoining space to replace the insufficient production of an old garden, the Achuar usually specialize the patches, keeping slowly maturing cultigens in the old garden (chonta palms, guava, star apple, sugar cane, and banana trees) and planting the new garden in manioc, staple root crops, and cultigens that demand nutrient-rich soils (beans and peanuts).

In order better to grasp the strategy used in the horticultural occupation of various soils, it is perhaps useful to examine a specific example of the evolution of a settlement site. The garden (see lay-out drawn to scale, Fig. 21) is located in a highly fertile riverine milieu (black alluvial soil) and is worked by a domestic unit comprised of fifteen persons. At the time of our study (Nov. 1977), garden n° 1 had been in production for six years, that is since the site was first occupied. When the land was cleared, the head of the family, Yankuam, had only two wives, Yamanoch and Ramun, who received relatively unequal portions (3985 m² and 2418 m²) of the new swidden. Three years later, a second clearing, n° 2, was made below the alluvial terrace where the first stood. A four meter difference in elevation introduces considerable difference between the respective kinds of vegetation, as the lower level contains only smaller, more easily cut species (bamboos, *Inga*, balsa, *Cecropia*). It was because of the easier clearing and because he was anxious to increase the household garden production that Yankuam chose this edaphological level. The new clearing was also divided into two plots, attributed to his two co-wives. Shortly thereafter, Yankuam married off one of his pre-adolescent daughters, and his new son-in-law came to live with him. Inasmuch as the young wife was only seven or eight and still unable to fulfill any of the duties attaching to her new status, the son-in-law's mother, who had been left by her husband, also came to live with Yankuam. This woman, Puar, stepped in and took over, with respect to her son, the economic tasks that her daughter-in-law was unable to carry out because of her youth. As a full-fledged member of the household, the son-in-law felled trees and cleared a garden (n° 3) for his mother, just as he would have done for his wife had she been able to cultivate it. Two years later, Yankuam, the family head, took a very young third wife, Ishkui, and cleared a garden for her (n° 4).

A year later, at the time of our study, the original garden (n° 1) was still producing and was kept up by the first two co-wives, Ramun and

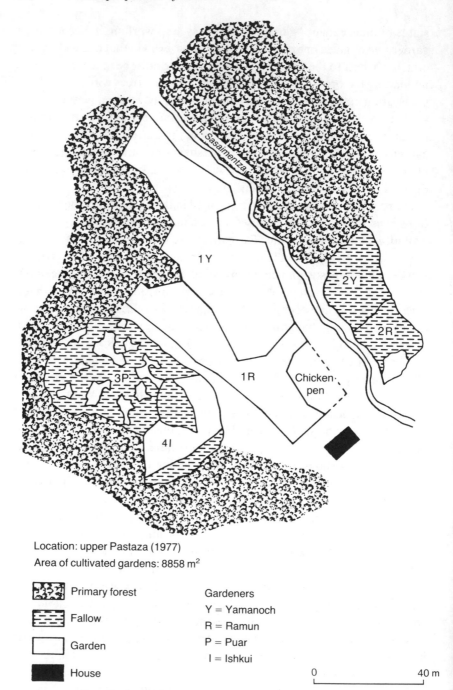

Location: upper Pastaza (1977)
Area of cultivated gardens: 8858 m^2

	Primary forest	Gardeners
	Fallow	Y = Yamanoch
	Garden	R = Ramun
	House	P = Puar
		I = Ishkui

0   40 m

21. Typical settlement pattern for a polygynous residential unit (3 co-wives + 1 female refugee = 6 garden patches)

Yamanoch. The second plot had been abandoned for four months except for a 215 m² patch planted almost exclusively in manioc and which lay in Ramun's part. The ease with which this edaphological level is cleared, according to the Achuar, is counteracted by the extremely rapid proliferation of weeds in the second year of cultivation; in the end weeding demands such an investment of time that it becomes counterproductive to go on cultivating the garden. Puar's garden (n° 3), which dates from the same period, had also partially reverted to fallow, and only a few patches (approximately 1300 m²) were still exploited. The gradual abandoning of this garden was due to the declining strength of the old woman who worked it and who no longer made any more than a very symbolic contribution to the feeding of her son and the household in general. The last garden (n° 4), which was only a year old at the time of the study, had also partially reverted to fallow, and only a patch of some 910 m² was still cultivated. The reason given was the inexperience and "laziness" of the very young Ishkui, of whom the two other co-wives disapproved rather harshly. Their jealousy was fed by Yankuam's patent sexual preference for the girl and exacerbated by his benevolent tolerance of her incompetence as a gardener. The fact is that the contribution of garden products to the household's subsistence rested almost exclusively on the shoulders of Ramun and Yamanoch.

As a rule, when limiting factors prevent the clearing of a new adjacent plot – which is relatively unusual, since the original clearing is always made on a site that allows for later expansion or substitution – the Achuar clear a new garden some distance from the house. In all events, the new plot will always be near a stream so that harvested roots and tubers can be washed *in situ*.

Of some one hundred Achuar houses we visited, we observed only one case in which the household head had been so shortsighted that he built his house and made his first garden on a site where no further clearing was possible because of the very rugged terrain. To complement the insufficient production of his main garden, he had been obliged to clear two new plots for his two wives, one 500 m and the other 800 m from the house. Moreover, both wives had been obliged to enclose their gardens entirely with a picket fence 60 cm high and 300 m long, in one case, and 180 m long, in the other. This is the only instance of fenced gardens that we encountered, their exceptional distance from the house making it necessary permanently to protect the crops from marauding mammals (especially paca and agouti). Ordinarily there is no need for fencing, since the gardens are close enough to watch, and any predator that comes along is quickly spotted. Aside from this altogether exceptional case, a complementary or a substitute garden is never made more than 300 m from the house.

When a site is occupied for the first time, the approximate size of the clearing is determined by negotiation between the household head and his wives, which often entails the confrontation of divergent if not actually contentious points of view. Naturally enough, the head of the family wants his gardens to be as big as possible in order to have a plentiful supply of manioc beer on hand with which to entertain in style. Now, while a woman also makes it a point of honor to cultivate a big garden, she is better able to assess the labor power (hers and that of her unmarried daughters) that she will be able to muster for weeding, that is, for the most time- and energy-consuming of all garden tasks. Whatever its size, a felled clearing is always completely planted; when a discrepancy arises between the area under cultivation and the weeding capacity, either because too much land was cleared initially or because the female workforce finds itself suddenly reduced, the readjustment is made by letting part of the garden go to weeds (as in the case of Yankuam's plot). Besides illness and temporary or permanent incapacitation, several circumstances can alter the work capacity of a married woman, obliging her to reduce the area she cultivates. The most common is the marriage or death of one or more of her daughters, events which amputate an important contribution to the work done by the micro-production cell comprised of a woman and her female offspring. Another less frequent case is the reorganization of the division of tasks caused by chronic illness (especially tuberculosis) in one of the two co-wives in a polygynous domestic unit. The sick woman is physically unable regularly to accompany her husband on hunting trips and distant visits; the other co-wife is therefore obliged to spend a large portion of her time in the forest or on the trail – since the two women can no longer alternate – and necessarily comes to neglect her garden.

It is regarded as disgraceful for a woman to let the weeds in her garden get out of hand, and, except for circumstances beyond her control, she makes every effort to keep it as clean as possible. That is why the initial agreement between the head of the household and his wives on the size of the garden is so important, for the disgrace of a garden full of weeds – because it is too big to be cultivated and weeded with care – falls in part on the head of the house. In effect, it is preferable for the prestige of a domestic unit to have a small, well-tended garden than a huge half-neglected one.

The size of the future garden is assessed on site using a subtle blend of the capacities and the ambitions of each of the co-wives, the social rank of the head of house, and the local ecological constraints. The decision to clear a plot is always taken by a woman's husband; in the case of a widow, it is her closest real or classificatory kinsman in the domestic unit (usually her brother or son) who takes the initiative. The boundaries of the future garden are first stepped out, and at this time certain characteristic trees are designated as boundary markers. There is no preferred geometric shape, and mapping of thirty swidden sites shows that nearly all of them are irregular. As there is no true dry season, there is no prescribed season for felling trees and burning the clearing, although the month of January and the period from September to November, usually marked by a relative decline in precipitation, are generally considered the most favorable. But in no case does anyone purposely wait for these two micro dry seasons to begin felling.

Clearing and burning

Clearing is done in two separate stages: clearing the low vegetation and then felling the trees. The undergrowth is cleared with a machete, cutting all bushes and saplings, the slashings being left on the ground. Some two days to a week later, felling begins: this is done with a metal ax following an apparently very old method, since it is already attested by Up de Graff in his description of clearing with stone axes, in 1899, among the Antipa Jivaro (Up de Graff n.d.: 203–4). The method, designed to save time and energy, consists of deeply notching all the small trees about 40 cm above the ground, then felling the big trees, which bring the surrounding mass of vegetation down with them as they fall. This notching technique is quite common among forest-dwelling agriculturalists; in the Amazon region it is attested in particular among the Amahuaca (Carneiro 1964: 11) and the Campa (Denevan 1974: 98).

Certain trees with flaring plank buttresses cannot be felled at man-height, and must be surrounded with a rudimentary scaffolding to afford access to the smooth part of the trunk. The last stage of clearing consists of trimming the felled trees.

Not all trees are systematically felled, and most fruit trees will usually be left standing. The most common of these are a type of wild mango, *apai*, a variety of breadfruit, *pitiu* (*Batocarpus orinocensis*), a sapote (*pau*), *tauch*, the *achu* palm, and the *sampi* tree (*Inga* sp.) (see complete list of protected species, Fig. 26). Certain non-edible species are spared for practical reasons: the balsa *wawa*, because its broad leaves are used as lids, *yakuch* trees (*Hyeronima alchorneoides*) and *chinchak* trees, because birds, and particularly toucans, are very fond of their fruits. These fruits are not good for human consumption but serve as bait, which enables young boys to practice shooting birds with their blowguns in the garden. The use of bait-trees for learning to hunt is mentioned in mythology, with reference to teaching Etsa–Sun to hunt.

Clearing land, in general, and felling trees, in particular, are dangerous, tiring activities which are the sole purview of grown men and from which not only women but adolescent boys are excluded. When clearing brush, the man bends forward, making regular sweeps through the undergrowth, about 10 cm from the ground, with a big machete which has been whetted on a large moistened river stone. He works more or less continuously for several hours and does not stop until after noon for a well-earned rest, during which the women serve him refreshing manioc beer. The main danger in brush clearing is the risk of disturbing a poisonous snake or a wasp nest (*ete*) hanging in the branches. One of the reasons the men paint their face with achiote is to ward off snakebite; all members of a clearing party therefore make sure to decorate their faces carefully to this end. When the clearing is part of a communal project, the working day always starts with generous libations of manioc beer provided by the head of the household who organized the clearing. The brush cutting is thus most often done in a slightly drunken state, spiced with jokes or ironic remarks not particularly conducive to keeping an eye out for harmful snakes and insects. Despite frequent cries of *"napi anearta!"* ("look out for the snake"), which punctuate the work, it is no accident that most men who have been bitten by a snake and survived were struck while clearing brush.

The danger is less during the felling, for the snakes have already left. On the other hand, the stand of trees now free of undergrowth is carpeted with a thick layer of brush which conceals the big *Grandiponera* ants (*yutui*) and *titink* scorpions which cause the barefooted Indians to proceed with particular caution. When the felling is done by a party, the men generally advance abreast, notching the medium-sized trees. When all the secondary trees have been deeply notched, the men divide up the large ones to be felled, sometimes taking turns in pairs for the biggest. This is the most spectacular stage and also potentially the most dangerous, although accidents are very rare. The trees are usually felled from the center of the clearing towards the edge, which rapidly becomes ringed with an impenetrable wreath of boughs lying every which way. As the tree begins to pop, the man wielding the ax springs back, shouting *"numi anearta!"* ("look out for the tree!"), and his companions scatter, joyously acclaiming the fall of the giant along with its contingent of subordinate plant life. The felling of a big tree in some ways resembles a kill, and the Achuar draw an explicit parallel between clearing and hunting, two physically demanding activities, both of which end in the satisfaction of uncontested victory.

Despite the huge progress brought by metal tools, tree felling is still hard work. For instance, a man working alone takes nearly three solid hours to bring down a tree 1.1 m in diameter. Obviously this is a far cry from the several days, or even weeks (Up de Graff n.d.: 203) it used to take with a stone ax; nevertheless, each time he can, the head of the family will try to invite kinsmen and allies to help him with at least part of the clearing. If continuous cooperation is not possible, he usually invites the kin for the felling, once he has cleared the brush by himself. The time and effort saved by collective clearing is considerable: we watched a team of eight men take five hours to cut down the trees in a clearing 3560 m², while a single man working solidly took ten days to clear a garden 4230 m².

The relative amount of time needed to clear a plot is conditioned in part by the types of vegetation. The Achuar state unanimously that the riverine alluvial terraces have fewer tall, hardwood species than the interfluvial forest. This claim is founded on a two-category system of classifying trees: hard trees (*pisu numi*) and soft trees (*miniar numi*). The distinction is the direct result of the woodsman's empirical experience, measuring the density of the tree by the yardstick of his effort. This proposition seems to be confirmed by a tree-count conducted with the help of Achuar informants on six samples of potentially cultivable climax forest three in the interfluve and three in the riverine biotope. In 100 m² of primary forest, the average density of trees of more than 20 cm in diameter varies between seventeen and twenty-one, in the interfluvial biotope, and between seven and fifteen, along the rivers. Using the same samples, hardwood species (according to indigenous criteria) make up more than half of the total in the interfluve compared to 20% in the riverine habitat.

The results would seem to indicate that, area for area, clearing could not help but be longer and harder in the interfluvial habitat than in the riverine habitat. A later check confirmed this hypothesis: we made a systematic comparison of the number of stumps that remained in the different types of garden after they had been planted (Fig. 22). This table calls for a few restrictions. In the first place, it is only an indication, for it is based on a limited number of small samples: the stump-count was made on sampling units of 100 square meters, that is, depending on the case, from one tenth to one one-hundredth of the area of the gardens sampled. Moreover, to make things easier, the counts were made in parts of the garden containing no logs of more than one meter in diameter.

Despite these restrictions, the trends revealed in this comparative table yield a wealth of information. After only two years of cultivation, there are no stumps over 30 cm in diameter in the two riverine gardens. This means, then, either that there were no large trees in these plots when they were cleared, or that these were soft woods which rotted easily and have therefore since disappeared. Likewise, there were no logs in these two sampling units; in this respect, the sample accurately reflects overall reality, for it is exceptional to encounter large logs in riverine gardens after the second year of cultivation. Moreover, the difference in age between the two riverine gardens does not introduce a difference in the number of stumps left, which would seem to imply that all softwood stumps disappear before the end of the first year of cultivation. Finally, the small portion of the riverine samples occupied by remains of stumps and logs (0.2% and 0.3%) – even if we take the statistical precaution of multiplying by five – is clear evidence that nearly the whole surface cleared can be cultivated.

These results contrast sharply on every point with the data from the interfluvial habitat. The latter samples are characterized by a high proportion of stumps over 30 cm in diameter and of slow-rotting logs. The most spectacular difference is in the percentage of the surface occupied by unmovable plant debris (between 17 and 20%) and which is therefore unfit for cultivation. Although these are rough estimates, the data appear to confirm the Achuar point of view on the marked difference in the vegetation of the two biotopes. It would also seem to indicate that, proportionately, more area needs to be cleared in the interfluve than in the riverine biotope in order to take into account the parts that cannot be cultivated because of debris.

	Interfluvial habitat (3 gardens)			Riverine habitat (2 gardens)	
Relief	Terrace	Hillside	Hillside	Terrace	Terrace
Grade	0%	40%	25%	0%	0%
Age of garden	2 years	2 years	1 year	2 years	6 years
Stumps under 30 cm	76%	63%	71%	100%	100%
Stumps under 65 cm but over 30 cm	8%	27%	18%	0%	0%
Stumps over 65 cm	16% (of which 2 over 80 cm)	10%	11%	0%	0%
Total stumps	13	11	28	4	4
Total whole logs	9	8	13	0	0
% surface occupied by stumps and logs	17%	16%	20%	0.2%	0.3%

22. Stump density in different types of garden (sampling unit = 10 × 10 m)

The Achuar leave from three weeks to two months, depending on weather conditions, between clearing and burning. Burning and cleaning up slashings are the only horticultural tasks done by men and women working in conjunction; it is the only time in the whole process of making a garden when the complementarity of the sexes is manifested by their joint presence in the garden. Burning is generally done in two separate stages. First, and preferably on a day when there is a light breeze, women armed with flaming bundles of kindling set fire directly to the brush piled around the clearing. As they work, they take care not to light any fires near the various trees that have been left standing.

When this first fire has burned itself out, that is, the next day or the day after, the men start clearing up the half-burned remains. They carefully gather all the slashings incompletely consumed by the first burning. In the center of each part of the clearing that has been picked over rises a big stack of blackened branches, which the women again set alight. Then, keeping one eye on the burning pile, they set about loosening the nearby soil with their *wayi*, a heavy, hard digging stick fashioned by the men from the wood of the *uwi* palm.

At this stage it is not necessary to clear the future garden of all dead wood except in the very circumscribed zones where peanuts are to be planted. Cleaning up and burning small slashings left by the clearing party is one of the ongoing tasks performed by the women throughout the first year of the garden's productive life. Every day as she weeds, each woman gathers the plants she has just pulled together with the bits of branches left over from the burning, piles them at the base of a stump and lights them. The softwood stumps are slowly consumed by the fire and rapidly form large concentrations of ash. This will be the favorite spot for planting *kenke* yams, a plant that is particularly fond of light, potassium-rich soils.

After a year of this meticulous cleaning up, the ground resembles a well-tended formal garden; emerging from the highly controlled tangle of vegetation, a few large unrotted logs are a reminder of the original setting underlying this transmutation. But these logs are themselves perfectly socialized, as they serve as elevated walkways linking one part of the garden to another. A few notches at either end provide an easy step up onto these slippery giants, which advantageously replace ground paths. In any event, the area occupied by the logs cannot be cultivated, unlike paths, and because they lie above the manioc stems, these catwalks spare the passerby the cascade of droplets invariably received when walking through the garden after a shower. But avoiding the touch of manioc plants is more than a simple question of comfort, particularly for children, since, as we shall soon see, this plant has literal vampirical tendencies. These fallen logs are also socialized by their function as dividers, most often between plots attributed to different co-wives within the same garden.

Although the common practice is to burn after clearing, in very rare cases this is dispensed with, in particular when it is urgent to bridge the gap between the production of two gardens and there is no time to wait until the vegetation is dry enough to burn. In this case, after a few days, when the brush and weeds are dry on top, they are gathered into bundles and piled around the edge of the garden. The only example we observed of an unburned garden was in a riverine site on a terrace of highly fertile black alluvial soil. This garden was three years old and had an area of 8150 m²; its productivity, estimated from the analysis of a 10×10 m sampling unit of cultigens, was absolutely equivalent to that of gardens of the same age and pedology that had been burned.

The Achuar themselves are of the opinion that a layer of ashes has no effect on the lifetime and productivity of a garden, at least of those on rich riverine soils. Furthermore, the fire does only superficial damage to non-woody plants and leaves the roots and seeds of grasses intact. As a consequence, burning in no way arrests the subsequent development of weeds, and it is entirely possible that it does not even retard their appearance. Thus fire is used to save time in the fastidious process of clearing up brush rather than to increase soil fertility noticeably. This indigenous opinion is shared by specialists on the subject (in particular Phillips 1974: 460 and Schnell 1972, v. 2, Chap. 4), who agree that any increase in soil fertility linked with fire is superficial and of short duration. Only the most acidic interfluvial soils seem to derive any benefit from the very temporary enrichment in mineral salts produced by burning.[3]

There is another method of cultivation that does not call for burning; it is systematically used for gardens planted in maize. Unlike the other cultigens which are planted together in the same garden, maize is usually grown in a garden of its own. This type of monoculture – which is also sometimes practiced in the case of plantain – employs a technique that is fairly rare in the Amazon Basin: slash–mulch cultivation (*utsank*: "to broadcast"). The brush is cleared rapidly, only a small portion of the trees are felled and the seed is immediately broadcast by the men on top of the slashings. These gardens are definitively abandoned after the harvest, which takes place from twelve to fourteen weeks after sowing. Maize gardens rarely attain more than 1500 m² and can be cleared in fairly recent secondary growth, which facilitates felling. With the humidity and the heat, the mulch is rapidly transformed into a rich compost, thus improving the soil and compensating for any original deficiencies.[4]

This technique is costly in terms of seed, since only some will germinate; it is, however, very economical in terms of labor, owing to the rudimentary character of the clearing. Moreover, leaving part of the vegetation provides the young plants with increased protection against sudden gusts of wind which might blow them over. Lastly, as maize has a very short growth cycle, the young plants do not have time to be choked out by weeds, which becomes inevitable in the absence of initial clearing and regular weeding. There can be no doubt that this method of cultivation is particularly advantageous for plants like maize, which the Achuar use as only a secondary food source. Indeed, even if a high percentage of the plants never reaches maturity (around 40%), labor input is still minimal when compared with that required by traditional polyculture.

The time needed to clear and burn depends, as we have seen, on many parameters, such as the nature of the vegetation according to habitat, size of the garden, number of men doing the clearing, and drying time left before burning. And yet, we recorded the times taken for the entire clearing operation in four gardens and found very similar results despite the diversity of the areas (Fig. 23).

With the exception of garden *c*, which highlights by comparison just how little work time is required to clear a maize garden, Figure 23 shows that, when the time inputs for clearing are compared using the same unit of measure, variations are nearly insignificant: they range from 232 hours/ha for clearing and burning garden *a* to 250 hours/ha for garden *d*. The overall average for the interfluvial habitat is 242 hours/ha. We had no opportunity to observe garden clearing in the riverine habitat, and so this sample contains only interfluvial gardens. We therefore have no data to validate our earlier hypothesis (advanced on the basis of stump counts) that less time was needed for clearing in the riverine habitat.[5]

	Garden *a* 3560 m²	Garden *b* 4970 m²	Garden *c** 2100 m²	Garden *d* 4230 m²
Clearing (hours)	63	91	18	80
Burning (hours)	20	30		25
Total	83	121		105
Average (hrs/ha)	232	244		250

*Rapid clearing in secondary growth for a maize garden.

23. Clearing and burning times

Gardening

The first act of socialization is performed on the still-virgin space freshly cleared in the forest by the men, since it is they who are going to bound and divide the plot by planting rows of banana trees, which will act as a border. Although the bulk of the work with the cultivated plants is done by women, it is not insignificant that, through planting the banana trees, thus symbolically inaugurating the garden's productive existence and social appropriation, it is the men who trace out the space in which the women will come to work. Only when each co-wife's patch has been materially marked out under male authority does the garden finally become the closed area of a purely female praxis. It nevertheless does occur that the man eschews his task of refereeing and lets the women of the house share out the patches among themselves. This is particularly the case when the women have close enough consanguineal ties to preclude quarrels of precedence: mother and daughter, or sisters, for example.

The Achuar are no newcomers to gardening; of the many signs that attest to the antiquity of their familiarity with horticulture, the most conclusive is no doubt the high number of stable clones recognized by indigenous taxonomy and cultivated intensively.[6] An Achuar garden commonly contains some one hundred different species, divided into many varieties, and however systematic we tried to be in our inventories, our list surely does not exhaust the number of plants cultivated.

Among the plants grown in gardens, we have made a distinction between truly domesticated species (the cultigens in Figs. 24 and 25) and wild species customarily acclimated in gardens or spared during clearing (Fig. 26). This categorial distinction is not clear in Achuar taxonomy, which tends to subsume into the category *aramu* ("that which is planted by man") all plants effectively present in a garden with the exception of weeds. The term *aramu* designates the possibility of human manipulation and therefore applies equally to semi-cultivated forest species, which are notwithstanding clearly defined as wild (*ikiamia*: "from the forest") when encountered outside the garden setting. This ethnocategory thus denotes not so much an intrinsic characteristic of cultivated plants as the way they relate to a specific human activity: the possibility of their artificial reproduction in the garden.

The sixty-two cultigens we inventoried are grown in nearly every garden, since the highly dispersed pattern of settlement makes it necessary to have on hand at all times the broadest possible range of those garden products required in daily life. It is especially necessary that households be self-sufficient in matters of non-food plants, of which many are used on a daily basis. While for instance yams can perfectly replace sweet potatoes in the diet, cotton cannot be used when achiote is specifically called for. These sixty or so cultigens – some of which, like the tree gourd, are only one to a garden – are divided into over 150 varieties, all of which are named and clearly identified in indigenous systematics. The species with the most

Frequency of use	Vernacular name	Common name	Botanical name	Number of cultivars
C	*ajach*	—	*Dioscorea* sp.	1
C	*chiki*	arrowroot	*Maranta ruiziana*	1
A	*inchi*	sweet potato	*Ipomoea batatas*	22
A	*jimia*	chili pepper	*Capsicum* sp.	8
C	*kai*	avocado	*Persea* sp.	1
B	*keach*	sweetsop	*Annona squamosa*	1
A	*kenke*	yam	*Dioscorea trifida*	12
C	*kirimp*	guava	*Psidium guajava*	1
B	*kukuch*	cocona	*Solanum coconilla*	4
C	*kumpia*	achira	*Renealmia alpina*	1
B	*kuish*	pineapple	*Ananas comosus*	1
A	*mama*	sweet manioc	*Manihot esculenta*	17
B	*miik*	beans	*Phaseolus* sp.	12
C	*namau*	jicama	*Pachyrrhizus tuberosus*	1
C	*namuk*	secana squash	*Sicana odorifera*	1
B	*nuse*	peanuts	*Arachis hypogoea*	7
C	*pinia*	—	*Calathea* aff. *Exscapa* Marantac.	1
A	*paantam*	plantain	*Musa balbisiana*	4
A	*mejench*	banana	Musaccae	15
B	*paat*	sugar cane	*Saccharum officinarum*	3
A	*papachnia*	taro (papa china)	*Colocasia* sp.	1
A	*sanku*	cocoyam	*Xanthosoma* sp.	2
C	*sepui*	onion	*Allium cepa*	2
B	*shaa*	maize	*Zea mays*	2
C	*tente*	squash	Cucurbitaceae	1
C	*tuka*	taro	*Colocasia esculenta*	1
B	*uwi*	chonta (peach palm)	*Guilielma gasipaes*	6
B	*wakamp*	cacao	*Theobroma subincanum*	2
B	*kuchi wakamp*	macambillo	*Theobroma bicolor*	1
C	*wanchup*	cocoyam	*Xanthosoma* sp. (?)	1
C	*wampushik*	inga	*Inga nobilis*	1
B	*wapai*	papaya	*Carica papaya*	3
B	*yaas*	star apple	*Chrysophyllum cainito*	3
C	*yuwi*	squash	*Cucurbita maxima*	3

A = staple; B = Used frequently; C = Used sporadically or in season

24. Food cultigens

varieties are naturally the predominant foods (twenty-two varieties of sweet potato, seventeen maniocs, fifteen bananas, twelve yams) or those invested with considerable symbolic importance (hallucinogenic and medicinal plants).[7]

For making taxonomic distinctions between varieties, the Achuar generally use a basic common name coupled with a series of qualifiers or metonymical images connoting some morphological feature. In most cases the basic vernacular name of a cultigen corresponds to a species in Western scientific botanical nomenclature. Among the numerous varieties of *kenke* (yam, *Dioscorea trifida*), for instance, there are: *kai kenke* ("avocado-yam," because the color of the tuber resembles that of a ripe avocado skin), *mama kenke* ("manioc-yam," for the similarity between the shape of the tuber and manioc roots), *pama kenke* ("tapir-yam," because the tuber is as plump as a tapir), *susu kenke* ("beard-yam," because the tuber has long bristles), *uranchi kenke* ("pubic-hair-yam," because the tuber is hairy), and so on.

Not all varieties of food plants are distributed equally among the different biotopes of the territory, the interfluvial gardens having on the whole fewer cultivars than those in the riverine milieu. The varieties of the most important species, like manioc, bananas, peanuts, or chili peppers, are twice as numerous in the riverine habitat as in the interfluve. Nevertheless, each ecological milieu has developed its own varieties, adapted to the different soils and which generally do not do well when taken out of their original setting. Such parallel development of distinct cultivars (against a common backdrop of species) would seem to indicate that Achuar occupation of the two clearly differentiated biotopes is far from recent.

Sometimes it is difficult for the inexperienced eye to see what distinguishes the varieties of a species, especially when it is some morphological quirk of the root or rhizome. Men, for instance, are usually incapable of telling the difference between the closest varieties of certain plants grown by women. It sometimes even happens that the women themselves are unable to recognize certain varieties – even though they planted them – on the basis of morphological features alone. This is especially the case with certain medicinal plants (in particular *piripiri*, *Cyperus* sp., and ginger), most varieties of which seem to be botanically identical. Nevertheless, each of these varieties has its own therapeutic use, and it is this use that appears in the terminological modifier used to qualify the species (e.g.: *napi piripiri*, "snake-piripiri"; *numpa ijiat piripiri*, "bloody feces-piripiri"; or *uchi takutai piripiri*, "piripiri for having children"). When a women acquires one of these medicinal plants, she therefore asks the woman who supplied it about its particular therapeutic properties; she will choose a spot for it so that she

Use	Vernacular name	Common name	Botanical name	Remarks
Cultivated dyes	*ipiak*	achiote	*Bixa orellana*	
	sua	genipa	*Genipa americana*	
	tai	—	*Warscewzcia chordata*	Red textile dye; mixed with achiote to make *karaur* powder
Textiles and recipients	*uruch*	cotton	*Gossypium barbadense*	
	katsuint	gourd	*Crescentia cujete*	Fruit split in two, hollowed out, and used as bowl
	mati	tree gourd	—	Fruit hollowed out and attached to quiver as a kapok holder
	takum yuwi	sponge-gourd	*Luffa cylindrica*	Dried fruit pulp used for wadding in muzzle-loading guns
	tsapa	tree gourd	*Crescentia cujete*	Fruit, split in two, hollowed out, and used as bowl and serving dish
	tserem	gourd	—	Fruit hollowed out and used to store liquids
	unkuship	tree gourd	*Crescentia cujete*	Fruit split in two, hollowed out, and used to make an oblong bowl for drinking *wayus* (*Ilex* sp.) infusion
	yumi	bottle gourd	*Lagenaria siceraria*	Used to carry and store water (*yumi*: celestial water, for drinking and cooking)
	chiiyumi	gourd	*Lagenaria* sp.	Small, pear-shaped fruit, hollowed out and used to carry *karaur* powder (face paint)
Cultivated fish poisons	*masu*	—	*Clibadium* sp.	Compositae family
	timiu	barbasco	*Lonchocarpus* sp.	A leguminous plant
	payaash	—	*Piscidia carthagenensis* (?)	Papilionaceae family
Cultivated narcotics	*maikiua*	angel's trumpet	*Brugmansia* sp. & *Datura* sp.	Three varieties cultivated
	natem	—	*Banisteriopsis* sp.	
	yaji	—	*idem*	
	parapra	—	—	Unidentified
	tsaank	tobacco	*Nicotiania* sp.	
Cultivated medicinal plants	*ajej*	ginger	*Zinziber officinale*	
	chirichiri	—	—	Different graminaceous plants
	kantse	—	—	Amaranthaceae family
	piripiri	sedge	*Cyperus* sp. & *Cares* sp.	Four varieties commonly cultivated
	pirisuk	—	*Altheranthera lanceolata*	
	tampuk	—	—	Erythroxylaceae family
	wayus	—	*Ilex* sp.	

25. Cultigens for technological, medicinal, and narcotic use

Vernacular name	Common name	Botanical name
achu	aguaje palm	*Mauritia flexuosa*
apai	wild mango	*Grias tessmannii*
chaapi	Ilarina palm	*Phytelephas* sp.
chinchak	tree with inedible fruits used as bird bait	*Miconia* sp., *Leandra* sp.
chirikiasip	narcotic, unidentified shrub	
kuchikiam	wild cacao	*Herrania mariae*
kunapip	edible fruit	*Bonafousia sananho*, Apocynaceae family
kunchai	edible fruit	*Dacryodes* aff. *peruviana*, Burseraceae family
kunkuk	palm	*Jessenia weberbaueri*
mata	chambira palm	*Astrocaryum chambira*
mayu	fish poison	unidentified tree vine
mirikiu	edible fruit	*Helicostylis scabra*, Moraceae family
munchij	granadilla	*Passiflora* sp.
naampi	edible fruit	*Caryodendron orinocensis*, Euphorbiaceae family
naara	nettle	*Urera* sp.
pau	sapote	*Pouteria* sp.
pitiu	type of bread-fruit	*Batocarpus orinocensis*
sampi	inga	*Inga* sp.
chuu sampi	inga	*Inga* sp.
imiu sampi	inga	*Inga tarapotensis*
miik sampi	inga	*Inga* sp.
nakar sampi	inga	*Inga* sp.
tuish sampi	inga	*Inga* sp.
yakum sampi	inga	*Inga pruriens*
sekemur	vegetal soap	unidentified
sekut	vanilla	Vanilla
sesa	medicinal plant	Malvaceae family (?)
shawi	edible fruit	*Psidium* sp. Myrtaceae family
shimpishi	edible fruit	*Solanum americanum*, Solanaceae family
shinki-shinki	bush used to make the rattle of the same name used in shamanic cures	*Piper* sp. (?)
sunkash	edible fruit	*Perebea guianensis*, Moraceae family
tanish naek	edible fruit	Bignonaceae family
tauch	edible fruit	*Lacmella peruviana*, Apocynaceae family
terunch	edible fruit	Myrtaceae family (?)
tserempush	inga	*Inga marginata*
wampushik	inga	*Inga nobilis*
wawa	balsa, leaves used as pot cover	*Ochroma pyramidale*
wishiwish	edible fruit	*Protium* sp., Burseraceae family
yakuch	tree with inedible fruit used as bird bait	*Hyeronima alchorneoides*, Euphorbiaceae family
yapaipa	medicinal plant	*Verbena* sp.
yurankmis	edible fruits	*Physalis* sp., Solanaceae family
yuwikiam	edible fruits	unidentified

26. Forest species acclimated in gardens or spared during clearing, and tolerated weeds

will later be able to identify the plant without risk of confusing it with another variety.[8]

If it is only logical that a garden contain the maximum number possible of medicinal plants specially suited to different therapeutic treatments, this does not explain why it is necessary to multiply the varieties of food plants. The diversity of food species normally cultivated in itself ensures a varied diet, and from a purely gastronomic point of view the multiplication of varieties only marginally increases the range of tastes. Men – whose attitude openly encourages their wives' agronomic capacities – recognize by taste alone only a very low proportion of the varieties of manioc, yams, or sweet potatoes.

Nor does the diversification of varieties seem to be a response to some techno-agronomic imperative, lowering the overall risk of species-specific diseases by the empirical selection of new clones in order to obtain varieties resistant to new pathogenetic agents. At first glance, Achuar gardens do indeed look extremely healthy, and the Indians claim that the cultivated plants are not subject to epidemics. While agronomists list two viruses and some forty cryptogramic diseases that affect tropical American manioc (Wellman 1977: 239), the Achuar recognize only one serious manioc disease. This is a fairly rare malady they call *wantsa* (a generic term denoting sterility), which is probably of bacterial origin; when it is present in a garden, it affects only a small number of plants. The absence of epidemic diseases in cultivated plants is probably due to the Achuar's geographic isolation, which has protected their gardens from outside contamination. The same highly favorable phytosanitary situation can be found in other

Predator	Species attacked	Frequency of predation	Effect on production
Blue-headed parrot	chonta palm (peach palm)	sporadic	little
Agouti	tubers,	frequent	moderate
Paca	roots and	frequent	moderate
Field mouse	peanuts	frequent	moderate
Peccary		rare	serious
Tayra	bananas and papayas	sporadic	little
Tapir	tramples maize	rare	serious
Beetles	pineapple	frequent	moderate
Caterpillars (*màa*)	manioc and bananas	sporadic	little
Cockchafer grubs	maize	frequent	moderate
Locusts	peanuts and beans	sporadic	little

27. Principal garden predators

very remote Amerindian societies like the Barafiri Yanoama, for example (Smole 1976: 138).

The main enemies of the garden are not viruses or cryptogramic diseases, however, but vertebrates: either birds – in particular the blue-headed parrot, *tuish* (*Pionus menstruus*) – or mammals (agoutis, pacas, and field mice attack tubers and peanuts, while the tayra, an excellent climber, prefers papayas and bananas). Nor do gardens lack for parasitic insects: there is the tiny caterpillar (*shuki*) that eats the young shoots of the banana tree, a large black beetle (*shipiak*) that devours pineapples, and a kind of locust (*manchir*) that is fond of the leaves of peanuts and bean plants.

As a rule, the gravity of the attacks is inversely proportional to their frequency; it is altogether exceptional that a tapir tramples a field of corn, but when one does happen to get in just as the corn is coming up, the bulk of the crop is destroyed. On the other hand, the damage caused by rodents is of no real consequence, and if the Achuar take active measures to catch them, it is because they find their meat tasty. It is therefore rare that an agouti or a paca digs up the manioc for any length of time and gets away with it. As soon as one is spotted, the head of the household finds where the animal got in and lays a trap (*chinia*). If he is the happy owner of a shotgun and a flashlight that works, he will lie in wait for the animal at night, thus increasing his chances of success. Producing and recently abandoned gardens are privileged hunting grounds, as they form highly particular micro-ecosystems that usually attract many of the animal species utilized by humans (see next chapter). Inasmuch as these garden predators themselves fall prey to humans, they pose no major threat. It could even be said that the whole garden functions to some extent as one big lure.

The Achuar tendency to grow a considerable number of varieties and species in their gardens is therefore not a result of technical constraints; rather, it shows the very special relationships the women entertain with the plants they cultivate. A woman who successfully grows a rich pallet of plants thereby demonstrates her competence as a gardener and fully assumes the main social role ascribed to women by proving her agronomic virtuosity. Some varieties grown in very limited quantities are cultivated in an almost experimental manner in order to test the limits of the symbolic power potential that underpins all horticultural activity. This "innovative" attitude was especially evident in the women's constant requests that we bring them plants "from our country" so they could try to grow them.

The almost esthetic pleasure that Achuar women get from making an opulent, diversified garden is a good indication that every new plant that comes their way is immediately adopted, even if it never comprises more than an infinitesimal part of the diet. Such is the case, for instance, of the onion[9] and of citrus fruits, still very rare and not particularly valued for their gastronomic virtues, but prestigious because they come from outside. Nevertheless, given the Achuar's isolation, the input of foreign cultigens remains very limited. With the exception of the banana, introduced long ago, the only alien species to have acquired a certain importance is a *Colocasia* (called *papachnia*, a deformation of the Spanish term, *papa china*), that the Achuar acquired from their Shuar neighbors some fifteen years ago. This is a type of delicately flavored Asiatic taro and is regarded as a delicacy to be served to guests.

In contrast to the taxonomic care with which cultivars are designated, suprageneric categories are extremely limited, as though the indigenous mind were concerned more to distinguish similars clearly, often by means of minute details, than to classify into broad categories resemblances that are hard to see. Likewise, among the plants grown in the garden, no categorial distinction is made between wild and domestic species, nor are cultigens formally divided into classes. At best, in speaking of cultivated plants, the Achuar use suprageneric categories applicable to plants in general: *numi* (tree), *nere* (fruit), *shinki* (palm tree), or *nupa* (grass).

There are nevertheless some discernible latent categories which implicitly embrace plants that are botanically closely related, although they go by different basic vernacular names; for instance, the many species of the leguminous *Inga*, which are seen as members of the same class, despite their many different denominations (*wampa, tserempush, wampushik, imiu sampi, yakum sampi* . . .). Another example comprises several squashes, even though they are used for very different purposes: *yuwi (Cucurbita maxima)* and *namuk (Sicana odorifera)* are eaten, while *takum yuwi (Luffa cylindrica)* and *yumi (Lagenaria siceraria)* have a technological function. Their inclusion in a single but unnamed category rests on the indigenous view that these plants are "alike" (*metek*).[10] Nevertheless, this implicit taxonomy remains on a purely conceptual level and never invests the realm of everyday gardening practices.

It is perhaps by the quantity of semi-cultivated forest species – these can be anywhere from half a dozen to more than thirty – that one can really recognize the agronomic completeness of a garden. When not found growing naturally (because they have been spared during clearing), the wild plants most commonly sown are those that bear fruit: *achu, apai, chaapi, mata, pau, pitiu,* and *sampi*. The Achuar palate, like our own, appreciates the agreeable diversity of different fruits as they come into season. The novelty of these treats contrasts with the eternal bland papaya and provides a powerful motive for growing within easy reach that which can ordinarily be obtained only after a trek into the forest. Moreover, to a large extent these fruit trees are domesticated for the benefit of the children (and, secondarily, the women), since the adults deem it their duty to provide their offspring with permanent access to "sweets" (*yumin*). The men, for their part, feign utter disregard for these delicacies of nature, but it would be an exaggeration to say that they are entirely indifferent.

The order of planting is all but invariable. Once the men have put in the banana trees around the edges of the garden and along the internal boundaries, the women take over and begin planting manioc uniformly throughout the garden, leaving only a few spaces for peanuts and beans. The manioc cuttings (*tsanimp*) are grouped in bundles of two or three, for an overall density of around one plant per square meter. The women then plant peanuts and beans in separate plots reserved for these crops. These patches were chosen for their rich, loose soil and concentration of ash. In among the small forest of manioc cuttings that now fills the garden, the women will plant, in no particular order, tubers (yams, taros, sweet potatoes), squashes, papayas, and other food cultigens; the men will plant their fish poisons. Apart from manioc, which, because of its ubiquity, is necessarily mixed with all the cultigens, there are no special plant associations.[11]

When a garden is located on a fairly steep slope, there will be a tendency to favor one type of cultigen in each altitudinal micro-niche. This is not a common situation, since the Achuar prefer level gardens, but it can arise in the interfluvial habitat when the only way to increase the size of a valley-floor garden is to begin clearing the sides. In this case, the banana trees will be planted on the flat, together with the maize and sweet potatoes, while the manioc will be placed preferably on the steepest and best-drained part of the slope. Manioc does not like too wet a soil, whereas it will do very well in the mediocre lateritic soils that prevail on the slopes. An identical differential usage of terrains in accordance with the different cultigens has been observed in Amazonia among the Campa (Denevan 1974: 99) and the Yanoama (Smole 1976: 116), who, unlike the Achuar, systematically make their gardens on steep gradients.

Certain species are rarely planted in the garden proper, but rather around the edges of the house yard. This is a favorite spot for chonta palms, fruit trees (avocado, sweetsop, guava, star apples, cocona), peppers, tobacco, medicinal and hallucinogenic plants, cotton, vegetal dyes, and gourd plants. Surrounding the house like a small kitchen garden, these plants are, in a manner of speaking, banned from the main garden, far too female a space, where men rarely venture. A closer look at those plants handled by men (Fig. 28) reveals that, aside from the fish poisons, the cultigens planted and/or harvested by men are grown outside the main garden. They are planted close to the house, or placed around the perimeter of the garden (banana trees), or grown in a completely separate garden, as in the case of maize and sometimes bananas.

Men rarely help in the garden and sometimes even get their wives to plant the banana trees and the maize, or to make the forked sticks used to prop up fruit-laden banana trees. As we see in Figure 28, the only plants that must imperatively be planted and harvested by men are the fish poisons, for if these were to be handled by women, they would lose their effectiveness. Fish poisons aside, then, no harmful consequences are anticipated when women plant cultigens that should normally be planted by men. Male work in the garden could be likened more to a pleasant pastime than a continuous effort. Plucking a few tobacco leaves from time to time or picking a couple of achiote pods for body paint are often the only forms of gardening the occasional visitor will see Achuar men engage in.

Some fifteen months after it has been planted, the garden has acquired its definitive physiognomy, with its three-story trophic structure, a miniature

Task	Men	Women
Selecting the site	+	
Clearing brush	+	
Felling trees	+	
Piling slashings	+	
Burning		+
Loosening the soil		+
Fencing (exceptional)		+
Making traps	+	
Planting fish poisons and hallucinogens, tobacco, maize, banana trees, and *wayus*	+	
Planting achiote, genip, gourds, chonta palms, cocona, and fruit trees	+	+
Planting rest of cultigens		+
Harvesting fish poisons	+	
Harvesting hallucinogenic plants, tobacco, achiote, genipa, gourds, maize, chonta palms, *wayus*, and fruit trees	+	+
Harvesting rest of cultigens		+
Weeding and upkeep		+

28. Sexual division of swidden horticulture

replica of the surrounding climax forest. On the upper level, here and there the broad banana and papaya leaves provide a first barrier to the destructive action of the rains and the sun; while, in the middle story, manioc, cocona, and *Lonchocarpus* form a relatively dense and nearly uniform layer of vegetation which also protects the soil against leaching. The ground itself is carpeted with patches of intertwining taros, squashes, yams, and sweet potatoes. This cultural imitation of natural vegetation compensates remarkably for the destructive effects of the climate and makes the best use of the mediocre potential of interfluvial soils. Although much less dense and stratified than the climax forest, the layered vegetation of the garden still helps slow the inevitable soil erosion, especially on hillsides. Monoculture, on the other hand, affords little protection to the fragile interfluvial soils, and if the Achuar sometimes resort to this practice – in the case of maize – it is for a very short space of time (three months) and they keep part of the natural tree cover. Furthermore, mixing species with different nutritional needs reduces competition among plants and makes the best possible use of the range of available nutrients.[12] But as B. Meggers rightly points out: "An imitation is never as good as the real thing, and in spite of its adaptive features, slash-and-burn cultivation is no match for the natural vegetation in offsetting the potentially destructive effects of the climate" (1971: 21). While the climax forest is a perfectly balanced system, the swidden garden can only temporarily stave off the moment when the loss of soil fertility becomes an obstacle for cultivation.

Of the one hundred or so species grown in Achuar gardens, only a dozen are used on a regular basis, with sweet manioc well in the lead as the staple cultigen. Several methods can be used to estimate relative importance of the various species of cultigen, depending on whether one is looking at potential use (distribution of the plants in the garden) or effective use (relative quantities actually harvested). Here we will restrict ourselves to the quantitative analysis of the distribution of the species, saving for Chapter Nine the study of the actual use of the cultigens as it appears in daily consumption patterns. The potential use can be established from a series of sampling units in different gardens; they reveal the predominance of manioc and, secondarily, the importance of fish poisons (Fig. 29). The typical unit of 100 m² has the disadvantage of minimizing the importance of certain cultigens which are always planted in particular spots (e.g. bananas at the edge of the garden), but it does demonstrate conclusively the ubiquity of manioc: in six sampling squares taken at random in separate gardens, there will always be at least sixty manioc plants per 100 m².

The sampling units also show the important proportion of space, especially in the interfluvial habitat, occupied by plants used to make fish poisons (*Clibadium* sp. and *Lonchocarpus* sp.). Moreover, this result was predictable, since each fish-poisoning party (see Chapter Seven) uses considerable quantities of plants. The amount of Asiatic taro (*Colocasia* sp.) planted in interfluvial gardens (35.6% of the cultigens) reflects the present infatuation of the Indians with this exotic tuber. The phenomenon shows just how fast eating habits can change, for in the space of a few years the foreign taro (*Colocasia*) – considered to have more flavor – has nearly supplanted the indigenous taro (*Xanthosoma*) in the daily diet.

If the plant density per 100 m² is converted into a per-hectare estimate, one obtains a fairly accurate idea of the gardens' productive capacity. Retaining only the dominant cultigens usually planted throughout the garden (manioc, *Colocasia*, yams, and sweet potatoes), the numbers are as shown in Fig. 30.

For the sake of comparison, densities on the order of 10,000 plants/ha are considered optimal for industrial-type monoculture of both manioc and *Colocasia* (Ministère de la Coopération 1974: 490, 551). Manioc densities in Achuar gardens are altogether comparable to those calculated in the gardens of other indigenous slash-and-burn cultivators practicing polycul-

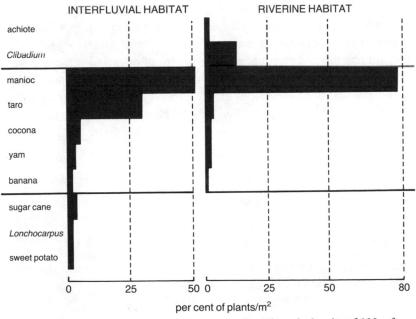

29. Average density of plants according to species (plants in 3 units of 100 m², measured in 3 gardens)

ture: 6,800 plants/ha for the Secoya of Peru (calculated on the basis of sampling units in Hödl and Gasche 1981: 90) and 9,711 plants/ha for the Campa, who associate manioc with maize (Denevan 1974: 102). It should also be noted that manioc densities are around 30% lower in Achuar interfluvial gardens than in riverine sites, which is easily explained by the fact that some 20% of the area of interfluvial gardens cannot be cultivated because of the remains of natural vegetation (unrotted stumps and logs).

With the exception of the digging stick, *wayi*, which the women use to loosen the soil, all garden operations are performed with the same simple all-purpose tool: a small, broad-bladed machete (*uchich machit*). Nearly identical to the old hardwood broadsword made of palm wood, the metal machete gives equal satisfaction as a knife, hoe, scraper, pruning hook, or trowel. Almost all cultivated plants are reproduced vegetatively from stalk cuttings (manioc, taro, sweet potato), sprouts from the parent plant (bananas), or pieces of tuber (yams). Gardening is thus reduced to a few simple actions: planting, digging up, weeding, and making stalk cuttings are the main tasks, repeated tirelessly day in, day out.

Barring exceptional circumstances, an Achuar woman goes to her garden every day; even if she does not work continuously, she spends a large portion of her day there. Towards 9 a.m., while the sun is not yet too hot, a small troop can be seen making their way to the garden. Equipped with her carrying basket (*chankin*), a machete, and a firebrand, carrying her latest baby on one hip and surrounded by a swarm of dogs and small children, each woman transfers her familiar world to the garden for the space of a few hours. The first thing she does is kindle a fire at the base of a stump in the patch where she has elected to spend the day. Next she plants two stakes and

Cultigen	Plants/ha	
	Riverine garden	Interfluvial garden
Manioc	8800	6200
Yams	350	700
Colocasia	450	7000
Bananas	412*	387**
Sweet potatoes	—	1000

*on the basis of 484 plants counted in a garden of 11 749 m²
**on the basis of 494 plants counted in a garden of 12 760 m²

30. Density of dominant cultigens

hangs up the little hammock (*tampura*) where her baby can lie in the shade of a bush. In most cases, the bulk of her work will be weeding and cleaning up the garden. Squatting with feet well apart for balance, the woman will spend a large portion of the day working out in concentric circles from her fire, hunting down every last clump of grass. The machete blade, held parallel and close to the ground, breaks up the hardened dirt at the base of the clump and makes it easier to pull.

Grasses are the most common weed; the most prevalent species, characteristic of interfluvial gardens, is called *chiri-chiri* (*Orthoclada laxa*), while riverine gardens are invaded mainly by *saar nupa* ("whitish grass"). *Jeep* (of the Araceae family) is rarer, but provides a sort of occasional treat: when boiled, the leaves have a pleasant taste much appreciated by the women and children. The clumps of grass are thrown onto the fire with the rest of the debris the woman has encountered on her hunkered rounds. Every day somewhere between 150 and 200 square meters of garden are thus carefully cleared of all naturally occurring plants. Weeding is indispensable, since it eliminates the voracious rivals of the cultivated plants, especially on poor hillside soils where the nutritional elements are rapidly exhausted. But the fanatical perfectionism goes well beyond a simple gardening technique. A well-kept garden is characterized essentially by the degree of mastery shown in the destruction of all that is natural. Its smooth, slightly sandy soil, dotted here and there with manioc stalks, looks like the impeccably raked path of a formal French garden. No sprig or clump of grass must be allowed to spoil this orderly space which asserts itself, no doubt even more than the house, as the anti-forest.

Once the first crop of manioc has been planted, around two thirds of the woman's daily garden time is devoted to fighting off weeds. When illness interrupts the upkeep for any length of time, it often happens that the weeds become so irremediably established that it is necessary to abandon the garden to the grip of the natural vegetation. The effort it would take to clear a garden completely once it has been taken over by weeds is such that it seems easier to fell a new clearing. Even working at it regularly, one manages, at the cost of considerable effort, only to postpone the fatal moment. Achuar women thus readily declare that they are forced to abandon their interfluve gardens after a mere three years, for, given the gradual decline in yield, the fight against weeds ultimately demands more work than it is worth in terms of the results.

The weeding stops only when the sun begins to go down; then the women hastily harvest enough to fill their *chankin* carrying basket. Generally in the freshly weeded area they dig up the roots of a number of manioc plants, from five to twenty, depending on the variety. Some cultivars have very small roots that rarely weigh more than two or three kilos, while others produce enormous roots exceeding ten kilos. When it is the first harvest, lengths of the freshly dug manioc stems are cut and immediately replanted. In the interfluve these slips will produce a second harvest and sometimes even a third and a fourth, but each new set of cuttings yields ever scrawnier roots in an increasingly impoverished soil. In riverine gardens, on the other hand, no decrease is observed in the size of the manioc tubers over the course of the successive cycles of cuttings.

To the daily load of manioc are sometimes added a few sweet potatoes, some yams, a squash, or a hand of bananas. Maize, peanuts, and beans are not picked throughout the growth cycle, but harvested all at one time when they are ripe. By the stream that runs along the garden, the women still have to peel and wash the roots and tubers before they can go back to the house and finally put down their heavy carrying baskets. Then, faces and bodies streaked with sweat, dirt, and ash, they make their way once again down to the water; a relaxed bath, punctuated with playful splashing and games with the children, concludes the day of gardening.

Although gardening is obviously time consuming and hard work, it looks as though it could be decomposed into a series of simple technical operations that require no particular skill or competence. But the impression is misleading, for, if the operations to be carried out on the cultivated plants are simple and few, managing the growing and harvesting of over a hundred different species divided among several thousand plants represents a highly complex undertaking. And it is all the more complicated as each species – and sometimes each cultivar – ripens at its own rate, and certain species are cultivated in continuous cycles while being rotated within the garden. The first plants to ripen, some three months after the new garden has been planted, are the taros, peanuts, and maize. A month or two later, the squash and beans begin to produce; the sweet potatoes reach maturity at six months. But all of these plants are only a minor part of the diet, and the garden only really comes into production in its eighth month, when the yams, manioc (between 8 and 10 months, depending on the variety), and bananas (1 year) begin to ripen. The fruit and palm trees take several years to mature, and often they begin to produce after the garden has been abandoned. That is one of the reasons why they are planted preferably near the house, somewhere that is easily accessible when the garden has reverted to fallow.

Since the Achuar are on the whole indifferent to abstract lunar measures of time, they tell that a plant is ripe by the botanical signs peculiar to each species and not by abstract computations. Moreover, ripening can be slowed down or speeded up by the amount of sunlight, a factor that plays a leading role in the way the Achuar see the process of plant growth. It is for this reason that they say of a plant that has reached maturity that "it has gotten its sunshine" (*etsarkayi*). Water, on the other hand, is not considered crucial for growth; in 1979 no one worried about the gardens during an absolutely unheard-of dry spell that lasted ten straight weeks.

Certain cultigens, like maize, beans, or peanuts, require new, fertile soils, and these are never re-sown after the first harvest.[13] Others propagate themselves by shoots from the parent plant (bananas). Still others, such as manioc and yams, are immediately replanted from cuttings, thereby producing in a continuous cycle. As the harvesting is done a little at a time, there are always manioc and yam plants in the garden that need gathering. These two species can be left in the ground for several months, until they are needed. Plants like the sweet potato, on the other hand, do not tolerate any negligence in harvest dates, and will sprout or spoil if not dug when ripe.

Gardening implies, then, not only the ability to master these complex combinations of crop rotation and succession, but also an intimate knowledge of the garden one is working and of its components from the day it is first planted. It is now easy to understand why each garden is almost physically associated with the woman who created and nurtures it. It is like a public projection of the personality and qualities of its keeper. When a woman dies, her garden usually follows suit, for, with the possible exception of her unmarried daughters, no other woman would dare step into such a relationship that she had not herself initiated. The men, whose knowledge of the garden is confined to the few species that they need regularly (tobacco, hallucinogens) or that they must harvest themselves (fish poisons), by and large know nothing of the private lives of their spouse's plants. They are therefore totally incapable of replacing their wives if the need arises, and moreover have no desire to do so. When a man no longer has any woman (mother, wife, sister, or daughter) to cultivate his garden and prepare his food, he has no choice but to kill himself.

A garden is abandoned selectively and by stages, since there are considerable differences in the time it takes different species to mature and the degree to which they resist takeover by the natural vegetation. The first sign of abandonment is the cessation of weeding, which rapidly leaves the garden looking like a fallow plot. The fast-growing weeds rapidly choke out the smaller plants (yams, taros, squashes. . .), but still allow the occasional harvesting of manioc and bananas for another year or two. Some species, as we have seen, hold out for a fairly long time against the natural competitors (tobacco, *Ilex*, fish poisons), while others do not seem to be affected at all (palm and fruit trees). These will be used for as long as access is not too difficult. In short, a garden is not definitively abandoned until the entire household moves to a new site several hours' walk from the old garden.

Yankuam's gardens showed that the horticultural cycle can take very different forms depending on the individual case and the biotope. In the interfluve region, each domestic unit usually clears a multi-crop garden every two years, the manioc production of the new garden replacing that of the old at the end of the first year. As the length of time a site is occupied depends largely on the lifetime of the house, a household often makes selective use of the three or four gardens cleared in succession and representing different stages of abandonment. The oldest is used only for harvesting gourds or chonta palm fruit; the next still produces papayas and bananas; the most recently abandoned still provides a little manioc, fish poisons, and some tobacco. When the household moves to a new site, bridging the gap between the new and the old is always somewhat difficult if the old gardens are located at any distance. While a household does not take up final residence in a new location until the new garden begins producing manioc, many of the cultigens planted at the same time will not mature until two or three years later. It will become necessary to choose between temporarily doing without certain plants and organizing time-consuming expeditions to harvest them in the old abandoned gardens. The second solution is generally the one adopted as, in most cases, a new garden is rarely made more than a day's walk or canoe trip from the old house. Beyond that distance, it becomes difficult to carry conveniently the large bundles of cuttings needed for the new garden.

By contrast, in the riverine habitat, the cycle of continual clearing is manifestly not determined by agronomic factors. The fertility of these alluvial soils is such that the gardens could be nearly permanent, and they are abandoned well before their production can begin to decline. On one alluvial terrace along the Rio Pastaza, a garden under continuous cultivation for some ten years was producing the same amount of manioc as nearby two-year-old gardens, that is to say around 200 kg/100 m^2. These results fit the data published by Lima, which show an absolutely constant level of sweet manioc production over six years on *varzea* fields in the Amazon estuary (Lima 1956: 113). Moreover, all Achuar maintain that a garden on black alluvial soil (*shuwin nunka*) does not need to lie fallow and can produce "until the man who cleared it dies." Unfortunately we could not verify this claim in practice, since we were never able to examine a garden that had been continuously cultivated for more than fifteen years.

In short, a garden in the riverine biotope is left only when the house site itself is abandoned or when too long an interruption (for example in the case of illness) makes it preferable to clear new land. It seems that the Achuar riverine habitat has the potential to support permanent multi-crop gardens without damage to the soil. If it is carefully weeded and well drained, a garden on river silt probably does not need to rest. Even were a period of fallow to prove necessary, there is so much cultivable land along the alluvial terraces – as we have already shown elsewhere when calculating carrying capacities (Descola 1981a: 617) – that a closed rotation cycle would make it possible to maintain a permanent dwelling on the same site. If, in spite of everything, the longtime inhabitants of this riverine biotope have not seen fit to establish sedentary settlements, it is certainly not because of their horticultural techniques.

Ecological constraints and technical efficiency

The type of swidden horticulture practiced by the Achuar raises a number of questions the theoretical interest of which goes well beyond the framework of Jivaro ethnography. In the first place, the Achuar are exceptional among the indigenous societies of the Amazon Basin in exploiting simultaneously two contrasting biotopes using nearly identical cultivating techniques. The only similar cases described in the ethnographic literature are the Campa of Peru, who occupy both the highlands of the *Gran Pajonal* and the alluvial plains of the Ucayali and Tambo rivers (Denevan 1974: 93–4; Varese 1966: 35–7), and the Yanomami, whose territory now embraces both the Sierra de Parima and the peneplains of the Orinoco and Mavaca (Smole 1976: 39; Lizot 1977: 118). But in both places it turns out that occupation of the riverine milieu is a very recent phenomenon, even though Lizot is of the opinion that, for the Yanomami, it was a case of returning to a formerly occupied region from which they had been expelled by Arawak warriors (Lizot 1977: 116).

In contrast, the Achuar seem to have occupied the hills of the interfluve as well as the alluvial plain of the Rio Pastaza without interruption for at least four centuries (Taylor 1993, Chaps. 3, 5; Descola and Taylor 1981); in this time, they would have had more than enough opportunity to diversify their adaptive strategies to suit the two types of habitat. And yet the only noticeable differences, from the standpoint of distinctive uses of cultivated plants, are the development of certain cultivars specifically adapted to each biotope, the use of two different species of plant as fish poison (*Clibadium* sp. and *Lonchocarpus* sp.), and a greater extension in the riverine habitat of maize, beans, and peanuts, all of which are easier to grow on highly fertile soil.

The differentiation among manioc cultivars is important, since, of the seventeen varieties we counted, only two – both originally from the riverine habitat – are cultivated in both biotopes. This broad range of cultivars attests to the technical refinement in adapting the growing of manioc to the specific constraints of different soil types. Cours' work in Madagascar has shown that manioc does remarkably well on nutrient-poor, acidic soils, whereas, paradoxically, rich, humid soils with a high nitrogen content are less propitious. In the latter type of soil, manioc tends to develop its superstructure to the detriment of its roots (Cours 1951: 296). It is therefore quite probable that the cultivars used in the riverine habitat have been adapted to a soil type that does not normally favor the production of large manioc roots.

There is no maize or peanut counterpart of this specialization of manioc cultivars according to habitat. In effect, plants such as maize, beans, and peanuts are very demanding: they require a high pH and high nitrogen, phosphorus, and potassium contents. They are ill adapted to the poor interfluvial soils and are grown there only as minor crops. There exist bean and peanut cultivars specific to hillside gardens, but not many: one original variety of peanut out of the seven we counted and three original bean varieties (*Phaseolus vulgaris*) of the twelve normally grown. In addition, these two cultigens are planted in minimal quantities in interfluvial gardens; and only a few spindly maize stalks can be glimpsed in one garden in ten.

On the other hand, one might expect maize, beans, and peanuts to be grown intensively in the riverine habitat, where the soil suits them perfectly. It would seem only logical that, given the high nutritional value of these plants compared to manioc, the latter would become a minor crop in alluvial terrace gardens. As an indication, manioc provides an average energy value of 148 calories per 100 g (Wu Leung and Flores 1961: 25), whereas equivalent quantities of maize and beans provide 361 and 337 calories, respectively, (13–66). The difference in protein content is even more striking: 0.8 g per 100 g for manioc (25), compared to 9.4 g for maize (13) and 22 g for beans (66). And yet, despite the enormous adaptive advantage they have in occupying an ecological milieu suited to the intensive growing of maize, peanuts, and beans, the riverine Achuar relegate these plants to secondary crop status. In alluvial zones no less than in the interfluve, manioc remains the predominant cultigen. Although maize is grown by many households in the riverine habitat, it is used almost exclusively as chicken feed; we cannot remember ever having eaten any in the course of our entire eighteen-month stay, during which our gastronomic experiences did not want for variety. As for peanuts and beans, people tend to regard them as occasional treats rather than as a staple that might be used in place of manioc.

Here we find a first type of problem. The riverine Achuar's evident lack of interest in intensifying the growing of maize – something that would be perfectly feasible in view of the optimal soil conditions – seems to contradict a theory defended by certain specialists on cultural adaptation in the Amazon Basin. According to their theory, in Amazonia, manioc and plants that are propagated vegetatively – high in starch but low in protein – are grown in preference to plants with a higher nutritional value, like maize, essentially for ecological reasons.

The very nature of these ecological limitations varies with the author. D. Harris, for example, maintains, after a rapid survey of the upper Orinoco, that regions nearest the equator are not suited to maize because they lack a distinct dry season. In the geographic area that comprises the Achuar territory, it would therefore be impossible to burn a garden efficiently; and in gardens not thoroughly cleared of their natural vegetation, maize would produce pitiful yields (Harris 1971: 495). First of all, one might question the correlation between climate and burning, since Achuar multi-crop gardens are testimony enough to the fact that regular rainfall in no way prevents meticulous weeding. In the second place, the relation between maize yield and presence of weeds depends largely on the technique of cultivation. Agronomists agree that the productivity of a maize field depends to a great extent to the care taken in weeding, as this cultigen does not compete well with weeds in the initial stages of its growth (Aldrich 1970: 56; Miracle 1966: 13). These are optimal growing conditions in a permanent field. But in the slash-mulching technique used by the riverine Achuar, the adverse effect of weeds is considerably lessened, for they generally grow more slowly than the maize plants. Consequently, the maize has plenty of time to mature before it is in danger of being choked by the weeds. Also, the mulch and what remains of the tree cover protect the soil from the deleterious effects of the sun and rain while the plants are growing and thus prevent nutrient leaching. When a maize field is carefully weeded, however, leaching is rapid and intense. It is clear that slash-mulch cultivation makes for the best possible balance between the demands of maize and local ecological conditions.

In his study of Peruvian Achuar populations, E. Ross contends, however, that the obstacles to developing maize cultivation are, on the one hand, poor soil – which is true for the interfluve but false for riverine zones – and, on the other hand, the high labor input (Ross 1976: 3). And yet slash-mulch cultivation demands much less labor than traditional manioc intercropping. In the riverine habitat, we saw that it took only twenty hours (eighteen for rough clearing and two for broadcasting) to sow a maize field 2,100 meters square. A few days before the harvest, this garden had 3,450 viable maize stalks with an average of two ears per stalk. In other words, this technique yielded around 345 ears of maize per hour of labor, not counting harvest time. It seems beyond doubt that, far from demanding a lot of work, the slash-mulch technique of growing maize is well on the way to setting a new record for agricultural productivity.

The Achuar's obvious reluctance to intensify maize production seems also factually to contradict A. Roosevelt's hypothesis. She contends that the prehistoric indigenous populations of the Amazon flood plain were quick to replace manioc with maize as soon as the latter became available, probably during the millenium before Christ (Roosevelt 1980: 159–66). This substitution would then have increased the carrying capacity of the Amazon and Orinoco flood plains, which could have supported important concentrations of population, thereby opening the way for the emergence of complex, stratified societies.

In many ways, this is a highly plausible and even attractive hypothesis; and in any case, it seems to be confirmed by Roosevelt's own archeological research in the Orinoco region (1980: 253). Nevertheless her determinism gives the impression of being a bit too automatic. We have seen that the Achuar have long occupied the Pastaza flood plain; the ethnonym itself, "people of the *achu* palm," is indication enough of their long association with the inundated portions of the lowlands, where this palm tree predominates. Furthermore, maize is a far from recent crop in this zone, and sporadic finds as well as archeological surveys have uncovered the presence of many *metate*-type mortars (Athens 1976).

Even if maize may at one time have been intensively cropped by the occupants of this region, it remains certain that the Achuar never gave it more than very secondary importance in comparison with manioc. Several elements seem to point in this direction: first of all, only two varieties of maize are cultivated; next, the Achuar never drink maize beer, even though they know how to make it; last, maize appears only exceptionally in the list of cultigens mentioned in the myth of the origin of cultivated plants (for a more detailed analysis of the status of maize in Jivaro groups, see Taylor 1993, Chap. 1). Apparently the Achuar did not react to growing maize in the terms set out by Roosevelt. Faced with this *deus ex machina* in their early history (Roosevelt 1980: 253), they failed to seize their historic opportunity. By declining to take up the intensive cultivation of maize, they deprived themselves of the means of increasing their population density, thereby letting a unique opportunity slip by, the chance to elevate themselves from *communitas* to *civitas*. It is true that, in order to support a chieftainry and a clergy, they would no doubt have had to give up their lackadaisical way of growing corn and busy themselves with turning their alluvial terraces into a close-packed checkerboard of permanent fields.

In short, if the riverine Achuar have never felt the need to intensify their production of high-protein plants to the detriment of manioc, it is because cultural models of consumption have as large a hand in determining how the milieu is to be exploited as does the abstract logic of maximization postulated by strictly ecological explanations.[14] Of course, the Asiatic taro example shows that the Achuar are willing rapidly to intensify the production of a new cultigen if they particularly like the taste; but then, the indigenous taro it is gradually replacing had only a secondary role in the diet. The same cannot be said of manioc, regarded as *the* food (*mama*, manioc, is often used as a synonym for *yurumak*, food in general). And manioc beer is so intrinsic a component of social and domestic life that it is hard to imagine the daily routine of an Achuar without *nijiamanch*.

Finally, concentration and sedentarization of a population based on intensified production of vegetable protein would imply giving up not only the growing of manioc, but also the daily intake of animal protein, which would be replaced by a combination of maize and beans. If it has come to be accepted that this combination is as nutritionally balanced as animal protein (Davidson *et al.* 1975: 218), the same cannot be said of its gastronomic value. From personal experience, I heartily approve the Achuars' wisdom in preferring a daily diet of manioc beer, smoked fish, and leg of peccary to dreary bean gruel with heavy tortillas.[15]

The continuous exploitation of two very distinct biotopes by local Achuar groups who could, simply by moving several kilometers further along, change habitats completely, raises another type of problem that we will merely outline at this time (it will be dealt with in more detail in Chapter Nine). At first glance, the riverine Achuar's horticultural use of the flood plains – a use that is deliberate and not imposed by outside constraints – seems to contradict the popular idea that high forest is better suited to slash-and-burn horticulture than is low forest. This interpretation maintains that, as altitude increases, and provided that the rainfall is not too high nor the slopes too steep, these soils deteriorate less quickly and recuperate more rapidly; this is supposed to be due to the relative drop in heat, which causes the humus to decompose more slowly and the levels of nitrogen to fall less rapidly. E. Ross, in particular, advances this thesis to explain why the Achuar of Peru apparently prefer to make their gardens in the hills of the interfluve (1976: 35); Ross rests his claims on the authority of two geographers: Denevan and Smole (Denevan 1970: 73; Smole 1976: 42). But, while Denevan does indeed point out that the conditions of slash-and-burn horticulture improve with altitude, the contrast, he stresses, lies between the rain forest of the foothills (above 800 m) and non-alluvial low forest, or in other words, between two ecological regions that are indeed distinguished by altitude and weather conditions, but not by the nature of the soil. On the other hand, if one compares high forest and the alluvial terraces of low forest, there can be no doubt that the latter have a much more remarkable agricultural potential than the mediocre lateritic soils of the foothills forest.

Smole adopts a different line of argument in support of the horticultural potential of high forest. In an attempt to justify the Barafiri Yanoama's preference for making their gardens on the steep slopes of the Sierra de Parima he, like Denevan, advances the lower rate of leaching compared with the lowlands, but also the less rapid invasion of the gardens by weeds (Smole 1976: 42). The second point seems justified, even though its universal validity is far from being proven by Smole, who is content with citing as a correlate the Chimbu of New Guinea. Moreover, weed proliferation is not in itself an obstacle to slash-and-burn horticulture; it becomes a true limiting factor only if no weeding is done, and the weeds compete for nutrients with the cultivated plants. In any event, the Achuar are effectively aware that the more fertile lowland soils are quickly overrun with weeds. And they take this into account when selecting a site, as we saw in Yankuam's case, where a garden had been cleared on a low-lying terrace and for all intents and purposes abandoned after three years of production because of the weeds. He had struck a balance in the labor input between the facility of making a garden in easily cleared natural vegetation (bamboos, *Cecropia*, balsa. . .) and the difficulty of controlling the weeds after the third year. It should be noted, too, that the Achuar themselves say there is about as much difference in the rate of weed growth between gardens in the interfluve hills and those on non-floodable alluvial terraces (*paka*) as between the latter and low-lying terraces over recent silt (*pakui*), and yet these lie less than five meters below the former. These mini-ecological differences, whose repercussions are perfectly perceived by the Achuar, generally go unmentioned in the hasty generalizing of the "adaptive strategy" specialists.

Does this established difference in the degree of weed proliferation engender significant consequences for slash-and-burn cultivation in either habitat? In order to answer this question, we must first resituate it in the broader context of the reasons for abandoning swidden gardens in the Amazon Basin. Carneiro believes that weeds, more than decline in soil fertility and yields, are responsible for indigenous gardeners abandoning a plot still in production (1961: 57). The same idea is reiterated by Denevan, in nearly identical terms, in his analysis of the agricultural potential of the upper Amazon (1970: 80), and is commonly expressed in ethnographic monographs (e.g. Smole 1976: 155 for the Yanoama; Ross 1976: 177 for the Achuar of Peru).

Carneiro's assertion is based on pedological and agronomical studies of the consequences of swidden horticulture carried out in various parts of the Tropics: in particular in Fiji (Cassidy and Pahalad 1953: 84) and the Yucatan (Morley 1956: 135–6 citing Hester's work, 1953). Carneiro's claim is then entirely an extrapolation from analyses conducted outside the Amazon Basin. Furthermore, none of the monographs that have adopted the weed-proliferation thesis to explain why Amazon swidden horticultura-lists abandon their gardens produces comparative soil analyses in support of the assertion. And yet, as A. Roosevelt has so well established, Carneiro's data was collected in parts of the Tropics whose geomorphology and pedology are completely different from those of the Amazon Basin (for details, see Roosevelt 1980: 24–39). In other words, while B. Meggers most certainly overestimated the role of soil depletion as a limiting factor in the Amazon Basin (Meggers 1957), it seems that, in his eagerness to refute Meggers, Carneiro seriously overestimated the potential fertility of the same soils.

Since Carneiro's 1961 study, a considerable mass of agronomic and pedological data has been gathered on the agricultural potential of the Amazon Basin (in particular, Beek and Bramao 1969 and Bennema *et al.* 1962, for general information; and Falesi 1974, Sombroek 1966 and Sioli 1964 and 1973 for Brazilian Amazonia; Tyler 1975 for Peruvian Amazonia; and Sourdat and Custode 1980a and b for Ecuadorian Amazonia). There is overwhelming evidence that Carneiro's thesis must be moderated and revised; it is impossible to generalize the proposition that it is the prolife-ration of weeds that forces Amazonian slash-and-burn horticulturalists to abandon their gardens. In highly acidic soils with toxic levels of aluminum compounds and low levels of exchangeable bases, like Ultisols and Oxisols, which prevail over most of the Amazon Basin and in particular in the Achuar interfluve, the suppression of natural vegetation generates serious leaching which rapidly lowers nutrient levels. By the end of the first year of cultivation, the drop has become drastic, and crop yields begin to decline badly eighteen months after the first planting. If no weeding is done, the weeds obviously contribute to the decline in yield, but the fall is to be imputed above all to nutrient leaching. The Achuar are perfectly aware of the problem, moreover; they do not have to know that the agricultural productivity of the soil declines proportionately as the pH decreases to see that, in their impeccably weeded interfluvial gardens, the size of the manioc roots decreases regularly with each harvest.

Inversely, the recent alluvial soils of volcanic origin cultivated by the riverine Achuar have low levels of aluminum toxicity, and even when they lack humus, they have a high cation exchange capacity and high levels of exchangeable bases; in other words, these soils are naturally fertile and produce constant yields over a long period. Here weeds become the limiting factor in maintaining a garden, since sustained productivity is possible only provided the garden is kept weeded. In short, it is now commonly acknowledged by tropical soils specialists that, while the reason for abandoning gardens on high base-status soils is the problem of weed control, decreasing fertility is the major reason for abandoning low base-status soils (see in particular Sanchez 1976: 405).

A rapid survey of indigenous gardening techniques in the Amazon Basin proves the rule. In effect, many indigenous societies in the interfluve do practically no weeding at all: this is true of the Amahuaca (Carneiro 1964: 15), the Barafiri Yanoama (Smole 1976: 139), and the *Gran Pajonal* Campa (Denevan 1974: 100). As a result, the gardens can never be cultivated for more than four years before being completely overrun by natural vegetation; now we know that, in any event, their crop productivity would decline nearly as fast if they were weeded regularly. The rotation cycle here is extremely short, then, but the added work of frequent clearing is compensated by the labor saved by not tending the gardens.

Inversely, the riverine populations seem to attach much greater importance to meticulous weeding; this is true, for instance, of the riverine Achuar, the lowland Yanomami (Smole 1976: 139) and the Ucayali Shipibo. In any event, the high fertility of alluvial soils makes it worthwhile to keep up the systematic and ongoing fight against those plants competing with cultivated species. It is therefore logical that the Achuar cultivate and weed their riverine gardens much longer than they do those in the interfluvial hills, even if, as a corollary, the fertile gardens are more vulnerable to the proliferation of weeds.

One last factor, which becomes quite obvious when the observer turns true participant, helps make the job of weeding riverine gardens over a long span of time less gigantic than it appears. This is the highly differentiated botanical nature of the weeds in the two habitats. The dominant weed in interfluvial gardens is a grass, *chiri-chiri*, which has a long tap root that makes it very hard to pull. The malignant character of *chiri-chiri* grass is attested in mythology: as we will see in Chapter Eight, this weed comes from the down of the hummingbird, who deliberately scattered it in gardens as a punishment to make the task of gardening more difficult. By contrast, the dominant weed in riverine gardens is *saar nupa* ("whitish grass"), which has surface roots and is easy to pull. Add to this that the weeding in interfluvial gardens is done in hard, heavy clay which clings to the roots, while it is done in light, sandy soil on alluvial terraces, and it becomes simple to understand why weeding is an incomparably easier matter in the riverine biotope. Despite the heavier infestation of weeds, gardens in the riverine habitat are less trouble to maintain and therefore can be exploited longer than interfluvial gardens, where fighting *chiri-chiri* becomes a superhuman task by the third year of cultivation. And as the high fertility of the black alluvial soils ensures constant yields for at least ten years running, it becomes profitable in the riverine habitat to continue careful weeding as long as possible.

But the choice between continuing to weed and felling a new clearing does not boil down to an abstract calculation of marginal utility, since it is the women who weed and the men who clear. This means that, in the riverine habitat, the decision to make a new clearing is reached by conciliating often conflicting interests. In most cases, a man will begrudge the effort of opening a new clearing if a riverine garden in full production has been engulfed in weeds due to negligence on the part of the wife who works it. This used to be the case in the interfluve as well: the Achuar claim that the introduction of metal axes shortened the lifetime of the interfluvial garden by making it easier to fell new clearings. The generalization of metal tools some fifty years ago completely transformed the conditions of male labor, while they had little effect on that of women. Whereas clearing is incomparably easier with a steel ax (*jacha*) than with one of stone (*kanamp*), a metal machete is not that much more effective for weeding than a sharp wooden broadsword.

Figures on the time saved by clearing with metal axes instead of stone tools vary a good deal with the part of the world in which they were collected and the method used (measuring or estimation). In a watershed monograph, Salisbury showed that the Siane of New Guinea had divided by a factor of 3–3.5 the time spent felling trees by adopting the metal ax (see

Salisbury 1962: 112–22 and Godelier's commentary 1964). A few years later, again in New Guinea, Godelier showed that, when the Baruya replaced stone adzes with steel axes, productivity increased fourfold (Godelier and Garanger 1973: 218). Finally, Carneiro estimates that the time the Amahuaca of Peru now spend felling trees would have to be multiplied by six (1970: 247) to obtain the time it would take with stone tools. According to the Achuar's own very rough estimates, it indeed seems that the time they save by using steel axes is of the magnitude advanced by Salisbury and Godelier. Multiplying the average time it presently takes to clear land in the interfluve (242 hrs/ha) by four, we obtain a total of 968 hours needed to clear a hectare using stone tools, or over four months of absolutely uninterrupted labor for a man working alone. Clearing must have taken even longer in real time, since the biggest trees were not actually cut but slowly burned down. For several weeks a slow fire would be kept burning in a hole at the base of the tree, which would gradually be eaten away from the inside. The procedure saved the worker's time, of course, but it drew out the operations considerably.

It is understandable that, if it took so long to clear an interfluve garden with a stone ax, even taking into account that help with clearing was more widespread then than now, the men strongly pressured their wives to weed as well as possible in order to space out the laborious clearings to a maximum; all the more so because, we are told, both interfluvial and riverine gardens used to be bigger than they are today (Harner claims that this is true for the Shuar as well; 1972: 198).

In short, the Achuar are a living testimony to the fact that the proliferation of weeds, long presented as an absolute limiting factor to the lifetime of a clearing, is actually relatively controllable when weeding is a systematic and socially valued activity. By making it a point of honor to present the critical eye of her sisters with a weed-free garden, the Achuar woman most certainly extends the useful life of her garden. In the interfluve, the extension is relatively marginal and probably prolongs the productive life of a garden no more than a year beyond its normal unweeded span. Nevertheless, in terms of the effort the men engage in clearing, there is a big difference between creating a new garden every three years, as the Achuar do in the interfluve, and clearing every year, like the *Gran Pajonal* Campa (Denevan 1974: 102) or the Amahuaca (Carneiro 1964: 15). In the riverine habitat, on the other hand, the Achuar offer proof that the life of a forest garden on fertile soil depends to a large extent on the care it receives.

The adaptation of Achuar horticulture to the ecological conditions of two distinct biotopes raises one last type of problem, that of differential yields in the two habitats. This question will be dealt with at length in Chapter Nine; here we will be examining it solely from the point of view of the areas under cultivation. In effect, if the differences observed in potential soil fertility and dominant weeds lead to a notable disproportion in garden lifetimes, adaptation to the specific characteristics of the natural vegetation of the two biotopes should also engender a disproportion in garden sizes. We have seen that the area that needed to be cleared in the interfluve should, in principle, be proportionately greater than that in the riverine habitat, to compensate for the zones that cannot be cultivated because of stumps and logs. Analyses of stump and planting densities showed that, in order to accommodate the same total number of manioc plants, an interfluvial garden, in theory, needs to have 20–30% more area than a garden in the riverine habitat. However, when the ratio of cultivated area to number of consumers, according to habitat, is examined, it appears that the nature of the biotope is not a determining factor for deciding how much land to cultivate (Fig. 31).

Of the eleven domestic units sampled, seven lie in a riverine habitat and four in the interfluve. But a close scrutiny of the average areas cultivated per consumer does not substantiate the claim that areas cultivated in the interfluve arc proportionately larger than those in the riverine habitat. Quite the contrary: of the five highest averages (from 1,415 m² to 3,535 m² per consumer), only one is for an interfluvial domestic unit. It is true that the greatest difference is between an interfluvial domestic unit (Wisum) and a riverine one (Paantam). But the disproportion is such (1:13 for the overall cultivated surface and 1:7 for the average area cultivated per consumer) that no ecological explanation is possible, and all the more as there is nearly as great a disparity between Wisum and another domestic unit, Jusi, both of which are located in the interfluve. Moreover, if we automatically subtract 20% of the cultivated area in the interfluve to adjust for the portion unfit for cultivation, the overall ranking of average area cultivated per consumer remains the same, with the (non-significant) exception of Sumpaish (corrected area: 603 m²/consumer), who drops back one slot, changing places with Yankuam (681 m²/consumer). Nor does the ratio of gardeners to consumers seem to explain these disparities, since, again in the case of Wisum and Jusi, it is 3:9 for the first and 3:5 for the second. It will perhaps be said that the sample is not large enough to draw any general conclusions, but the households covered are quite far from each other, and the population (including young children) represents around one twentieth of the entire number of Achuar living in Ecuador. Most National Accounts economic tables are far from being as exhaustive.

The huge disproportion between the areas cultivated by the different domestic units hints that garden size is not really dictated by adaptation to local ecological conditions or the size of the consumer unit. More exactly, as we will see in Chapter Nine, the variations that can be observed in garden size range from a minimal situation, which is tailored strictly to fit the environmental constraints, the capacity of the work force, and consumption needs, to a maximal situation, in which the only real limit is imposed by how much the domestic unit can intensify its work force. In the latter case, the women work more efficiently and the land under cultivation is considerably in excess of the area required for the demands of mere domestic consumption.

To assess whether the Achuar situation is exceptional in this respect, let us attempt a parallel between the average areas cultivated in our sample and those for other Amazonian swidden cultivators. It should be noted that, unlike other parts of the world (Africa and Oceania, in particular), the comparative data available in the ethnographic literature on Amazonia is both incomplete and inaccurate because it is based on estimates and not on measurements, and is presented as global averages, with no mention of the minima and maxima or the size of the sample. Now it is particularly difficult

Household	Total garden area* (m²)	Habitat	Number of consumers (adults + children over 5)	Number of gardeners**	Average area cultivated/ consumer (m²)
Paantam	2437	R	5	1	487
Jusi	3225	I	5	3	645
Yankuam	8858	R	13	4	681
Sumpaish	3016	I	4	2	754
Naychap	10281	R	11	4	935
Chumpi	9729	I	7	2	1390
Mashiant	22642	R	16	5	1415
Sumpa	4280	R	3	1	1427
Kayuye	9655	R	6	3	1609
Nayash	15409	R	7	5	2201
Wisum	31820	I	9	3	3353

R = riverine   I = interfluvial
*areas calculated with a surface integrator from survey drawings done on a portable plane table.
**The number of gardeners can be more than the number of married women or widows since we have included all unmarried girls over the age of 15 who do the same work as an adult.

31. Ratio of cultivated area to number of consumers

to estimate the area of forest gardens, for their shape is irregular and their boundaries erratic. As for averages not based on several samples, these are highly deceptive. It is easy to see how biased our data could have been had we arbitrarily chosen as a single check-sample the Paantam household plots, whose total area is thirteen times less than that cultivated by the Wisum household. Lastly, in their estimates of the average area cultivated per consumer, the authors listed below count the entire population including very young children. Since, in the interests of more probable figures, we do not count children under five as consumers, it must be considered that the average area cultivated per consumer by the Achuar is slightly overestimated with respect to the comparative averages in the following table (Fig. 32).

Of course, average area cultivated per consumer is only a very general indication of the efficiency of an agricultural system; this can be evaluated conclusively only in combination with other data on garden productivity; such information will be presented and discussed in detail in Chapter Nine. Nevertheless, it is clear from this table, that the Achuar are at least average or above for Amazonian swidden cultivators and well ahead of the Cubeo and Yanomami. Finally, if we compare the Achuar with New Guinea slash-and-burn gardeners, renowned for their productivity, we find that the latter cultivate a slightly smaller average area per consumer: 1,142 m^2/consumer for the Kapauku (Pospisil 1972: 183) and 1,012 m^2/consumer for the Chimbu (Brown and Brookfield 1963: 117).

The considerable variation observed in the area cultivated by the different Achuar households is paralleled by the wide disparities that appear when analyzing the areas cultivated per adult woman. Figure 33 breaks down into five groups, ranked by size, the areas cultivated individually by each of the twenty-nine adult women living in the eleven domestic units in the previous sample. This case, too, confirms that differences in biotope do not play a significant part, nor does the relative proportion of

Population	m^2/consumer	Source
Yanoama (Niyayoba-Teri)	405	Smole 1976: 136
Yanoama (Jorocoba-Teri)	607	Smole 1976: 136
Cubeo	810	Goldman 1963: 35
Central Yanomami	900	Lizot 1977: 127
Achuar	1 317	Descola, this volume
Siona-Secoya	1 970	Vickers 1976: 127–28
Kuikuru	2 632	Carneiro 1961: 47

32. Average area cultivated per consumer in seven Amazonian populations

adult women per residential unit. In fact, the three monogamous women cultivate relatively modest gardens (from 1,500 to 5,500 m²), while the three patches of more than a hectare are cultivated by women from domestic units in which adult women abound (3 co-wives in two cases and 4 co-wives in the other). In other words, the increased number of adult women in a residential unit in no way implies a reduction of the areas each cultivates, but quite the contrary.

The largest difference between two areas cultivated by one married woman in polygynous domestic units in the riverine habitat is 1:11 or 10,600 m² for an experienced *tarimiat* (first wife) helped by her sturdy adolescent daughter, compared to 940 m² (out of a clearing initially some 1,500 m²) for a young co-wife in good health, but lacking skill. Certainly technical knowledge and the size of the available auxiliary work force (young daughters) are not factors to be neglected in determining the area a woman can cultivate. But, once again, the disproportions are such that one must inevitably consider motivations from outside the sphere of practical reason.

	Riverine habitat number: 21			Interfluvial habitat number: 8			Total number: 29	
	Number and status			Number and status				
Area of gardens (m²)*	P	M	%	P	M	%	Number	%
500–1,500	3	—	14.0	1	—	12.5	4	14.0
1,500–2,500	5	1	29.0	1	—	12.5	7	24.0
2,500–5,500	7	1	38.0	1	1	25.0	10	34.5
5,500–9,000	3	—	14.0	2	—	25.0	5	17.0
9,000–13,000	1	—	5.0	2	—	25.0	3	10.5
Total	19	2	100.0	7	1	100.0	29	100.0

P: polygamous (several co-wives in the same domestic unit cultivate separate plots)
M: monogamous (one married woman cultivates the domestic unit's entire garden)
*areas calculated with a surface integrator from survey drawings done on a portable plane-table

33. Size of plots individually cultivated by 29 married women in 11 separate domestic units

The sumptuous picture of an immense garden crowned at the center with the smoke-festooned thatch of a spacious house always impresses the traveler as he emerges from the forest. Even the ethnologist, who is sometimes clumsy at interpreting minute signs of status cannot help, upon suddenly stepping into the orderly grounds of a big garden, seeing writ large the social prestige of the man who cleared it. But it would be a mistake to think that men's prestige is built on the enslavement of women, for in order to socialize a piece of nature, their complicity is absolutely necessary. And if a woman works herself to the bone to transform a corner of forest into an immense gardenbed, it is because she shares with her husband both his ambition for preeminence and the fruits of the prestige attaching to his house.

Gardening magic

Achuar gardens are an exemplary testimonial to the degree of technical sophistication attained by slash-and-burn cultivation in certain indigenous societies of the Amazon Basin. Highly productive, demanding relatively little labor in comparison with its productivity, providing an extensive variety of products, perfectly adapted to soil and climate variations, free from epidemics and parasites, Achuar horticulture eschews all contingencies. It also contrasts sharply with certain intertropical agrarian economies that are plunged into famine by the slightest natural calamity which actualizes the passage from structural but latent underproductivity to effective underproduction (see Sahlins 1972: 69). One cannot help being surprised, then, that in spite of everything, the Achuar see the daily gardening routine as a risky endeavor fraught with dangers.

Unlike the very great majority of Amazonian societies, the Achuar consider that the growing of manioc must be surrounded by a tight web of ritual precautions. Gardening in general, that is the manipulation and treatment of the main cultivated plants, therefore demands a definite set of symbolic preconditions in order to be effective. The idea that horticulture cannot be a wholly profane activity has some objective grounds, moreover; not because the outcome of gardening is regarded as a matter of chance, but because the plants cultivated by the Achuar enjoy a very special status. Manioc and most other cultigens are propagated vegetatively. This means that the survival and the descendants of these plants depend to a large extent on humans, who enable them to reproduce and multiply while protecting them from weeds. These close ties of mutual dependence that grow up between the cultivated plants and those who enable them to exist in order to consume them explain why the garden is something more, something other than just somewhere one goes to eke out a daily living. But this still does not explain why the other cultivators in the Amazon Basin who propagate plants from cuttings do in fact regard their gardens as "just somewhere one goes."[16]

And the situation of tuber-growers in Oceania is not very different; they, too, with no objective technical reason, are divided into those who believe in gardening magic – Trobrianders (Malinowsky 1965), Tikopia (Firth 1965:168–86) and Baruya (Godelier 1973: 356–66) for example – and those who – like the Kapauku (Pospisil 1972: 158) – do not. Although there is no functionalist justification for the symbolic overdetermination of Achuar horticulture, it is nonetheless possible to try to understand how the indigenous theory of magical causality informs the representation of gardening tasks.

Nunkui's domain

The necessary condition for effective gardening depends on direct, harmonious, and constant commerce with Nunkui, the tutelary spirit of gardens. Nunkui is a female being whose favorite dwelling place is the topsoil of a cultivated garden. She is the creator and mother of all cultivated plants. As such, her deeds are chronicled in a myth the structure of which is the same in all Jivaroan dialect groups. If the social importance of a myth to a culture were judged by the number of people able to tell the story, there is no doubt that the myth of Nunkui would be the Jivaro Creed. In Achuar society, in particular, where the majority of the population seems to take little interest in *yaunchu aujmatsamu* (myths, literally: "talk of ancient times"), the story of Nunkui is the only myth known by absolutely everyone, if only in an abbreviated version. There is some risk involved in using an esoteric myth to draw up the empirical table of the "system of representations" common to an entire society. Inversely, the Jivaro myth of the origin of cultivated plants is certainly a reference shared by all; that is why we did not hesitate to use one fragment for constructing our paradigm of the concept of the house.

The myth of Nunkui sports a considerable number of variants throughout the Jivaro cultural area; if we have chosen from our corpus the following version, it is because it appears highly original with respect to the usual variants already collected among the Shuar and Aguaruna.[17]

The myth of Nunkui

In olden times, women did not know how to make gardens and they were very unhappy; they got by on picking produce in Uyush's (the sloth's) garden, as she was the only woman who had manioc plants. One day they came upon Uyush in a garden and said to her: "Little Grandmother, take pity and give us a bit of manioc." "Very well," replied Uyush, "but first, tell me what these are." The women answered, "your claws are *wampushik*, your fur is the *kuyu*'s (piping guan) tail and your teeth are *tsapikiuch* (*tsapakush* fish?)." "Well spoken," said Uyush, "and now you may harvest your manioc!" The women filled their *chankin* carrying baskets to the brim. Another day the same women were getting ready to go to Uyush's garden when a foolish woman asked to go along; the others replied: "No, stay here, you make fun of the little grandmother." Ignoring their words, the foolish woman followed them, keeping well back. When the women got to Uyush's garden, she asked them the same riddles; having passed the test, the women were allowed to fill their *chankin* with manioc. Just then, the foolish woman arrived. Uyush asked her: "What is this?" The foolish woman replied contemptuously, "It's the claw of a sloth." Furious, Uyush spat back, "Was that all you came for, to tell me that? Is that any way to talk!" Uyush was angry and retired to the *patach* (perch-like foot rest) at the foot of her bed; Uyush also balanced all the manioc roots carefully on the *patach*. Then Uyush said to the foolish woman, "If that is all you came to tell me, you will get no manioc." The foolish woman decided to go ahead and pick manioc and she took home a whole *chankin* full. She placed the manioc in a pot to boil; but when she took out the roots, she saw that they had turned into pieces of balsa wood, too hard to eat. The foolish woman was continually tormented with hunger. One day she decided to go down to the stream to catch *marunch* (fresh-water shrimp); as she stood on the bank, she saw some manioc peelings drift by; she followed the stream and came to a woman carrying an infant, she was washing and peeling manioc. This woman was called Uyush. Uyush also had along a lot of manioc beer and she served it unstintingly to the foolish woman; the woman said, "Little Grandmother, let's go harvest your manioc." But the other replied, "Take this child with you instead; but I advise you to treat her well and not vex her; when you get home, you will tell the child: 'Drink the manioc beer,' and your *muits* (manioc-beer jars) will fill with manioc beer and you will give her all she wants to drink." The woman did as Uyush had said, and the child grew fatter and fatter; but as she spent all of her time feeding Uyush baby, she did not serve her husband any manioc beer, only the rinse-water from the *muits*; the poor man went all day on an empty stomach and when he came home, all his wife gave him to drink was rinse-water. One day, seeing that all the *muits* were full, some with manioc beer, others with plantain beer, and still others with sweet-potato beer, the husband ordered his wife to bring him some real manioc beer; it was then that she explained that the *muits* filled only when she told Uyush baby to drink. The husband demanded that his wife make the baby pronounce the name of all the cultivated plants; and so the baby spoke the words for manioc, plantain, sweet potatoes, and all the other cultivated plants; and this was how cultivated plants came authentically (*tarimiat*) to exist in gardens. They were all living amid this abundance when the husband decided to take a second wife; the first wife became terribly jealous and resolved to abandon her husband and Uyush baby; so she left the house, telling [the second wife] to take good care of the gardens. In an attempt to imitate the first wife, the second made Uyush baby name all the cultivated plants, and each time she named a plant, a great number appeared; then, for fun, the second wife asked her to name the *iwianch* (evil spirits) and fierce-looking *iwianch* filled the house. In retaliation, the second wife threw a handful of hot ashes in Uyush baby's eyes; the furious baby fled to the roof of the house, which was surrounded by stands of *kenku* bamboo; Uyush baby called one of the *kenku*, chanting: "*Kenku, kenku*, come and get me, let's go eat some peanuts; *kenku, kenku*, come and get me, let's go eat some peanuts." Just then the husband arrived and said: "The baby is saying that because she was mistreated," and he tried to catch her, but he couldn't. Suddenly a gust of wind blew one of the *kenku* over onto the roof and Uyush baby climbed onto it; the *kenku* sprang back and the baby, clinging to the top, amused herself by swaying and chanting: "*Kenku, kenku*, come and get me, let's go eat some peanuts; *kenku, kenku*, come and get me, let's go eat some peanuts." The baby crawled down inside the *kenku*, defecating at regular intervals as she went, thus forming the joints of the bamboo; when she was nearly under the ground, Uyush baby stopped to fix her hair; at that point the members of the household managed to lay hold of her before she had completely disappeared. They begged her to call up manioc beer, but the baby refused; instead, she spoke a curse on each one of the cultivated plants, and these began to shrivel, until they were tiny. At the sight of the plants, one of the men took out his spite by kicking at one of the tiny manioc roots; but the root dodged the blow and entered his anus; once inside his belly, the root rotted and gave off foul-smelling gas. Then Uyush baby entered the ground where she now dwells under the name of Nunkui. This is what I was told a long time ago.

Given the importance of the Nunkui myth in the Jivaro cultural area, it would perhaps be helpful rapidly to point out the main differences between the Achuar variant and the published variants of other dialect groups. In the first place, and like the other Achuar variants we collected, this version establishes an equivalence between Nunkui and Uyush, the two-toed sloth (a forbidden food). But this equivalence apparently holds only for the myth, and, in the indigenous commentaries on Nunkui as tutelary garden spirit, the sloth is never suggested as a possible substitute. Furthermore, the episode of Uyush's riddles is not found in any other known variant of the myth of the Origin of Cultivated Plants. Lastly, while the final episode of Nunkui's flight into the *kenku* bamboo is common to all published variants – including the literality of the *kenku*-call – the fate of the cultivated plants following Nunkui–Uyush's curse diverges to an extent depending on the version. In the Shuar variant collected by Harner, the cultivated plants are swallowed up by the earth, along with the forest trails (1972: 74). In other Shuar and Aguaruna variants, however (Pellizzaro 1978c: 47–8; Berlin 1977), the cultivated plants turn into wild varieties; one Aguaruna variant collected and analyzed by B. Berlin is altogether remarkable from this viewpoint, as it gives a very precise enumeration of the sylvan counterparts of twenty-two cultigens (Berlin 1977). And finally, in the

Achuar variants, the cultivated plants shrink by stages. But whether their fate is to vanish completely, to revert to the wild, or to shrivel, the plants cultivated by the Jivaro are constantly under the threat of Nunkui's curse. In effect, the way in which these plants reappear after the initial catastrophe is on the whole ambiguous. Few of the variants actually mention the process by which humans finally recovered the use of cultivated plants. Achuar commentaries allude to the compassion shown by Nunkui, who changes her mind and gives humans a few seeds and cuttings so that they can plant new gardens. But there is a corollary to this act of kindness; from now on, people will have to labor to keep up the vegetal inheritance carefully handed down from one generation to the next. Attested in mythology, the disappearance of all cultivated plants is a scene which, according to the Achuar, could be replayed in the theater of daily life. The experience of abandoned gardens gives it some empirical basis, which, far from contradicting the lessons of the myth, only reinforces belief in Nunkui's powers.

In one Achuar variant, as well as in one Shuar version (Pellizzaro 1978c: 39), over and above the cultivated plants, Nunkui calls into existence meat (*namank*). *Namank* is the generic name the Achuar give to the flesh of game, and, as the existence of live game (*kuntin*) is never attributed to Nunkui, it seems permissible to regard her as the creator of a category much broader than that of cultivated plants: this is the category of the socially edible. Confirmation of this can be found in the fact that, according to our Achuar variant, Nunkui–Uyush gives humans manioc beer even before giving them the cultivated plants that would enable them to make it. More confirmation is provided by a Shuar variant which tells how Nunkui also brought into being domestic animals, chickens, and pigs (Pellizzaro 1978c: 37).

Furthermore, although we were unable to collect an Achuar myth on the origin of the cooking fire, the Shuar have a short myth that tells how Jempe, the hummingbird, stole fire from Takea and taught humans to use it (Pellizzaro n.d. [1]: 7–15; Karsten 1935: 516–18). This myth clearly presents Jempe's exploit as having given humans a purely virtual instrument and not a corpus of precepts for putting it to good use. In other words, Hummingbird transmitted the cooking fire, but not the art of cooking. The passage from nature to culture made possible by Nunkui is not accomplished so much by graduating from the raw to the cooked as by drawing a clear line between, on the one hand, accidental food resulting from gathering in the forest and, on the other hand, socially sanctioned food resulting from a process of production and culinary transformation.

In one short Achuar variant, Nunkui is also presented as having taught women the art of making pots. The same role devolves to her in Shuar mythology (Pellizzaro 1978c: 80–123; Harner 1972: 74–5). As a rule, in Jivaro groups as well as among their Canelos neighbors (Whitten 1976: 90), Nunkui is closely identified with the techniques of manufacturing and decorating earthen vessels. Here again Nunkui shows how to transform a raw material which she neither created nor supplies. The white clay (*nuwe*) used in making household dishware comes, as we saw earlier, from the excrement of Auju (the potoo bird). Remember that Auju, in an attempt to follow her husband Nantu (Moon) up to the sky, climbed after him along the vine that used to join the earth and the heavens. Incensed, Nantu cut the vine, and Auju fell to earth, where, in her fright, she defecated all about her; each of her excrements became a deposit of white clay. So Nunkui is much more than the creator of cultivated plants; she is a sort of "civilizing heroine" who brings women the domestic skills paradigmatic of the feminine condition: gardening, cooking, potting. The Achuar do not perceive these techniques for the cultural transformation of nature as original acts of creation, but as the daily re-enactment of Nunkui's initial precepts. It is now easy to understand why the proper accomplishment of these precepts demands of every woman who practices them an affectionate complicity with their founder.

I would like to conclude this brief analysis of the myth of the origin of cultivated plants with two incidental comments. First of all, the Achuar see the association between Nunkui–Uyush and the *kenku* bamboo as the mythic confirmation that the presence of stands of *kenku* is an indication of highly fertile soil. The correlation is altogether justified, since this is a typically riverine plant and it normally grows on the lowest part of alluvial terraces on silt deposited by flooding. Second, while all Jivaro specialists are unanimous in affirming that Nunkui is a female being, their opinion diverges as to the nature of her incarnation. Harner, for the Shuar, and Brown and Van Bolt, for the Aguaruna, are of the mind that Nunkui is a family of spirits rather than a single individual (Harner 1972: 70; Brown and Van Bolt 1980: 173). On the other hand, the Achuar tend to think of Nunkui as a single being, but endowed with the gift of ubiquity which allows her to multiply her appearances and to be present in all gardens in which her services are explicitly called upon. This apparent contradiction between unity of being and multiplicity of concrete manifestations is entirely characteristic of the way the Achuar see the existence of mythic beings.

Created through the magic of Nunkui's word, cultivated plants are also thought of as her offspring. As their mother, Nunkui exercises her undisputed maternal authority over them, something women must keep in mind as they go about their gardening. But she is not the parent of inert objects, for many a cultivated plant has a *wakan* (a soul or its own special essence) and therefore an autonomous existence. These plant people entertain the same relations of sociability as humans. Although this aspect of the social life of cultigens is the object of widely divergent interpretations, it seems to be accepted that garden plants can be grouped into four categories: those whose essence is exclusively female, those whose essence is exclusively male, those who are of both genders and live with their offspring as a family, and those lacking any particular gender or essence.

Even though the exact status of certain minor plants depends on highly idiosyncratic commentaries, a consensus can still be gathered as to the main plants that comprise the four classes. In the first category, the Achuar places *wayus, sua* (genipa) and *ipiak* (achiote), three young women reduced by mythological events to their present circumstances; also female are the sweet potato and the squash. In the second category we find *masu* and *timiu* (the fish poisons), as well as *tsaank*, young men formerly notorious for their sexual prowess; the banana tree, too, is male, although it lacks a mythic past. The third category includes primarily manioc and peanuts, plants whose family life is modeled on that of the Achuar, but whose present state is not a sign of a former human existence.[18] Finally, a good many plants do not have a soul at all and exist simply as plants. When asked about the gender of the papaya, one woman retorted: "How in the world could a papaya have a *wakan*?" It should be noted in passing that the set of plants endowed with an essence is not restricted to those with a human past attested in myths. A *wakan* seems to be attributed to a cultivated plant regardless of its effective use, while it seems that such economically important plants as the taro and yam have no soul. Finally, there is no automatic correspondence between the gender of a plant and the gender of its handler, since female *wayus,* achiote, and genipa are successfully planted and harvested by men.

The harmony that reigns among cultivated plants is ensured by Nunkui's invisible presence in the garden; it is reflected concretely by the size of the tubers and roots, the abundance of the harvests, the vigor of the plants, and the length of their productive life. It is therefore imperative that a woman secure Nunkui's constant presence in the garden and that she take every precaution not to offend her, in order to avoid the terrifying risk of a new mythological catastrophe. Nunkui, whose name derives from *nunka* ("earth"), is also conceived as in a way amplifying the potential fertility of the various types of soil in which she dwells. The Achuar are accomplished pedologists and readily admit that Nunkui will not perform as effectively in notoriously mediocre lateritic soil as in rich alluvial ground. Nevertheless, even though the Indians take into account differential soil fertility, they also maintain that a garden's life span and productivity depend as much on the magical skills of the woman who works it as on local ecological constraints. These skills are designated by the term *anentin*, which, applied to an individual, denotes at once the scope of magical knowledge, the capacity to manipulate the symbolic fields specific to his or her sex, and the particularly fruitful relations entertained with the guardian spirits that govern the spheres of activity in which the individual engages. Given identical soils, an *anentin* woman is reputed to obtain better yields than one who is not, even if the latter is a hard worker. But in fact this disjunction is rare: on the whole, *anentin* women are also the hardest workers, the two qualities being intrinsically linked.

To be *anentin* one needs to know a great number of *anent*, magical songs, since it is basically by means of these incantations that a woman can hope to communicate with Nunkui and with the plants in her garden. To be *anentin*, then, is to possess a rich repertory of *anent*, or in other words to be inspired in one's work by the ability to act effectively upon entities that are invisible but attentive to one's supplications. The term *anent* comes from the same root as *inintai*, "heart," the organ esteemed by the Achuar to be the seat of thought, memory, and feeling (e.g.: *enentaimjai*, "I think"; *enentaimprajai*, "I remember"; *aneajai*, "I feel tenderness for. . ."; or "I miss so and so. . ."). *Anent* incantations, then, are words that come from the heart, private supplications designed to influence the course of events.

All *anent* have roughly the same melodic structure (Belzner 1981: 737) and differ only in their verbal content. But, as they proceed directly from the heart, they do not necessarily need vocal mediation to reach their destination; they are usually sung mentally or *sotto voce*, rather than aloud. Instead of singing, men sometimes prefer to interpret their *anent* on the musical instrument of their choice: this can be a two-stringed violin-shaped instrument (*arawir*), a type of mouth bow (*tsayandar*), or a flute (*peém* or *pinkiui*). The instrument plays the melody, while the words are sung mentally by the interpreter. The *anent* repertory is immense, since there are series for every imaginable circumstance of public and private life. These supplications are addressed to all manner of beings which the Achuar postulate as being endowed with a receptive sensibility, that is likely to be convinced, seduced, or charmed by the highly allegorical content of the *anent*. These incantations can thus be directed not only at humans, but also at supernatural beings like Nunkui, and at certain categories of animals, plants, and meteors. *Anent* are relatively short and highly specialized; there are *anent* to ensure the successful outcome of different phases of war, hunting, gardening, to improve a dog's sense of smell and fighting spirit, to be sung when making curare or pottery, to make someone fall in love or to strengthen a couple's bonds, to improve relations with the affines or mend a quarrel between brothers-in-law, and so on.

Inasmuch as *anent* are a privileged medium of the symbolic control exercised by men and women, possession of a rich and varied repertory is one of the aims of all Achuar, who strive to increase their mastery over the invisible constraints impinging upon their practice. But this is difficult to do, for *anent* are precious possessions jealously hoarded and transmitted only by close kin of the same sex (usually from father to son, mother to daughter, father-in-law to son-in-law). Sometimes *anent* can be acquired from a spirit in the course of a "soul journey," for instance while dreaming or in a drug-induced trance. The secret ceremony for transferring an *anent* is called *tsankakmamu* ("the granting"); the person desiring to learn the magical song first drinks tobacco juice to clear his or her mental faculties, then he or she inhales the steam from a decoction of *tsankup* (unidentified plant); meanwhile the *anent* owner stands beside the person repeating the song over and over until it has been thoroughly memorized. Later, and whenever the person wants to endow the *anent* with special strength, he or she can again drink tobacco juice and fast before singing.

Anent are secret, then, and never sung in public, only in the privacy of the garden or forest. There can be no doubt at all that the Achuar represent *anent* as powerful and effective magical instruments the owning of which is an asset. An indication of the value attached to *anent* is the extreme reluctance of so many men and women to record them on tape, thereby dispossessing themselves in public (the same observation has been made in the case of the Aguaruna, see Brown and Van Bolt 1980: 176). Correlatively, we were constantly being asked to play the *anent* we had recorded in other households, the greatest interest being shown for songs collected in remote areas that our hosts had never personally visited. Our corpus of some one hundred recorded *anent* contains for the most part songs designed to influence human beings (spouses, lovers, affines) or domestic animals (mainly dogs). Such *anent* are less esoteric and easier to understand than those highly valued songs enabling the owner to communicate with game, cultivated plants, or the guardian spirits that govern the strategic spheres of praxis (hunting, warfare, gardening, shamanism). *Anent* of this type are particularly hard to obtain, and ours were collected only from men and women with whom we had established special ties of friendship and trust.

Anent are possessed of certain remarkable properties which place them at the fore of the Achuar arsenal of magical weapons capable of acting on the invisible world. In the first place, as A-C. Taylor has already pointed out in her annotated translation of love *anent*, the category of "sung things" functions in certain cases as a metalinguistic mechanism used to qualify the special nature of an utterance (Taylor 1983b). In effect, while magical songs are highly metaphorical and their content often difficult to interpret, even for the Achuar listener, they are not set apart linguistically from ordinary discourse. There are a few idiomatic expressions that belong to the *anent* style, but these stem more from the prosody than from a desire to make the song esoteric. The "sung" mode is a way of clearly designating the profound otherness of an utterance with respect to ordinary discourse; it is therefore used to overdetermine normal language in those circumstances where the latter is not an adequate vehicle, that is when the words must reach the heart of a spatially or ontologically remote target. The singer is attempting to communicate with either a human being not physically present or a being who is non-human but which has certain human attributes.

Furthermore, *anent* are a mode of expression that simultaneously authorizes and reveals the free interpretation of a common symbolic field. It is true that magical songs are supposed to be effective only on the strict condition that they are repeated exactly as they were taught, without ornamentation or additions. But even though they are transmitted in a canonical form, each *anent* was originally composed by an anonymous author as a sort of private gloss on a stereotyped mythological or sociological theme. In this sense, the *anent* entertains very special relations with mythology, for which it acts as a sort of user's guide. In this society, where mythological knowledge does not play a preponderant role, individual commentary is carried out not so much in glosses or variants as in the recomposition and rearrangement of certain mythic components within *anent*. Myths are the original source of a sort of general lexicon of the properties of the supernatural; everyone is familiar with this lexicon, even though only a few are acquainted with the mythological corpus from which it derives. And it is on this lexicon, oblivious of its origins, that people draw freely to give meaning to the events of their daily life, to interpret the world, and to attempt to act upon it. To the alert observer, the field of representation that unfolds in the *anent* reveals the deeply internalized components that organize everyday belief, elements rooted in mythology but which myths, only a few of which are well known, present in a normative, discursive form.

There is a series of *anent* for every phase of gardening, from the initial clearing to the washing of roots and tubers after harvest. Women sing these *anent* to Nunkui as well as to the cultivated staples, asking the former to look with favor on them and urging the latter to grow and multiply. The highly allegorical nature of these incantations can be judged from the following examples.

Being a Nunkui woman, I go along calling edibles into being,
The *sekemur* roots, there where they are supported, there where they stand, I
        made them like that, well apart
Being of the same species, when I have gone, they go on being born (*repeat*)
The *sekemur* roots have "speciated"
They are coming to me
Being a Nunkui woman, I go along calling edibles into being (*repeat*)
Behind me, answering my call, it goes on being born.

> *(Sung by Yapan, a Rio Kapawientza woman)*

Here, as in a great many horticultural *anent*, reference is made to Nunkui by way of a postulated identification ("Being a Nunkui woman, I go. . ."); likewise, gardening appears as a daily repetition of Nunkui's act of creation ("I go along calling edibles into being"). The song does not mention the cultivated plants by name, but speaks of edibles in general (*yurumak*) or *sekemur* roots (probably a member of the Rhamnaceae family). These voluminous roots are ordinarily used as a vegetal soap and share a certain likeness with manioc roots, which are never called by their real name (*mama*) in *anent*, but always by the figurative *sekemur* (a similar metaphorical use of *sekemur* is found in Aguaruna *anent*, see Brown and Van Bolt 1980: 175).

Being a Nunkui woman, going alone to where my babies are
I go along calling edibles into being (*repeat*)
All of them, right here, I call them the same way (*repeat*)
Nunkui woman's adopted children came to be one by one
One by one, they came to rest on the ground (*repeat*)
Being a Nunkui woman, I go along calling edibles into being in my own garden
In this very way, I go (*repeat*)

> *(Sung by Puar, a Rio Kapawientza woman)*

This *anent* confirms the identification between Nunkui and the gardener, since the cultivated plants are presented as the singer's children and by derivation as Nunkui's adoptive children. Nunkui's maternal relationship with the cultigens is transferred to the woman gardener, and then partially retroceded to Nunkui in the form of adoptive kinship; the plant children are thus placed under a twofold complementary, non-competitive protection.

My little sweet potatoes are going to get like big-river papayas
My little sweet potatoes have gotten like big-river papayas
How can I learn to plant gardens like Nunkui woman's?

(Sung by Puar, a Rio Kapawientza woman)

In this *anent*, the woman sings directly to her sweet potatoes and urges them to become as voluminous as a variety of large papaya that grows on the alluvial terraces of big rivers (*kanus*: "wide river"). And in fact, in many *anent* the term *kanus* is used as the archetypal synonym of fertile land. Far from identifying herself with Nunkui here, the singer humbly compares their respective gardening skills, attempting to awaken Nunkui's compassion by this expression of modesty.

Little Nunkui woman, right here, right here, in my own little garden, right here I
    go along harvesting plant by plant
Like Nunkui woman I go along digging edibles *(repeat)*
I go along digging, digging up each one, popping them out of the ground
In my own little garden, I set aside the biggest plants
Harvesting the plants, they have piled up on the ground *(repeat twice)*
Experienced Nunkui woman, it's you speaking *(repeat)*
"You have the experience of a *wea*," that's what you tell me
In your own garden, calling the edibles into being *(repeat)*
Right here *(repeat twice)*.

(Sung by Puar, a Rio Kapawientza woman)

This *anent* is addressed directly to Nunkui in the vocative, but unlike the preceding song, it equates the skills of Nunkui and those of the singer. The equivalence is authenticated by Nunkui in person, who publicly testifies to the woman's talents by saying to her "*weaturuame*" ("You have the experience of a *wea*"). *Wea* is a generic term designating certain men and women on the threshold of old age who are particularly renowned for both their great practical experience and their theoretical and experimental knowledge of the supernatural world.

If the garden, a female space by its destination, is Nunkui woman's favorite spot, there is nevertheless a brief time in its history when it belongs exclusively to men. When it is still only a pure virtuality, a tract of forest to socialize by clearing, the future garden is not yet under the benevolent protection of Nunkui. She takes up residence in her domain only with the arrival of the women and their first plantings. Preceding Nunkui in this place where she is to reside comes a spirit of modest stature responsible for guiding the men in felling the trees. To this male figure, named Shakaim, the men address *anent* suited to the task of clearing. Shakaim is presented alternately as Nunkui's husband or her brother, and it is said that he oversees the fates of wild plants. As guardian of the forest-plant populations, Shakaim visits men as they dream and shows them the best places to clear new gardens. In effect, the forest is sometimes seen by the Achuar as an immense garden in which Shakaim deploys his skills as a somewhat untidy gardener. He is therefore in the best position to know where the most fertile land is, where his wild children will thrive. When the men paint their faces with achiote before clearing a plot, it is as much in homage to Shakaim as to ward off snakes.

In the pantheon of tutelary spirits, Shakaim occupies a very obscure position, which cannot compare with that of his accomplice, Nunkui. He seems absent from Achuar mythology; or at least he does not appear in any of the myths we have collected.[19] Shakaim seems to exist in everyday belief only in this derivative form, oblivious of its origins, which is characteristic of the system of representations operating in the *anent*. Shakaim's peripheral position can probably be attributed to his highly ambiguous status. As master of all wild plants, he is not articulated with a clearly assigned sphere of practice, but partakes of several domains, dominating none. Although he is indeed a forest spirit, he does not have charge of hunting, a paradigmatic male activity; while he is also a garden spirit, he does not have charge of gardening either, a paradigmatic female activity. Despite the huge number of his plant subjects, Shakaim is master of an almost vacant world, for humans have little to do with it; his appearances on the stage of mankind can only be episodic and of no real import.

Shakaim is sometimes mentioned in women's gardening *anent* and that is where we initially surprised him, for we were unable to find any men's *anent* addressed to him, even though the men were quite forthcoming about his attributes. The very special relation women entertain with Shakaim can be seen in the following two *anent*.

My little father, you are like Shakaim (*repeat*)
Right here (*repeat twice*), Nunkui woman's brother, how could you fall ill?
Right here (*repeat*), my little brother went away, having cut the brush from
    Shakaim's plantation (*repeat*).

                           (*Sung by Puar, a Rio Kapawientza woman*)

This *anent* is addressed to the singer's husband, called first "little father" and then "little brother," according to the conventions of magical songs, which require a female Ego always to use a term of consanguinity when speaking of her husband. Here the woman establishes a twofold equivalence: between Shakaim and her husband, on the one hand, and between Nunkui and herself, on the other, the postulated blood tie between the two spirits taking the place of the real marriage tie between the man and the woman, according to the logic of the rules of translation. This is both the singer's homage to her husband for having made her a clearing in the forest (metaphorically termed "Shakaim's plantation") and the expression of a wish that he, who is as brave and healthy as Shakaim, should long have the strength to fell her new gardens.

Being a Nunkui woman, going only to my own little garden
Going by the big river (*repeat*)
I go along filling to the brim (*repeat*)
What might you be?
Wherever Nunkui woman is, what would there not be?
Come all my edibles, into my little garden! (*repeat*)
Shakaim man (*repeat*), little Nunkui woman, who says "I am the edibles
    woman"
"There, you will plant," they say (*repeat*)
Being a Nunkui woman, I go by the big river (*repeat*).

(Sung by Puar, a Rio Kapawientza woman)

Again this is an *anent* in which the singer indicates that she wants to be identified with Nunkui; but the identification is combined with a splitting, since Nunkui also appears, in the guise of an autonomous entity, alongside Shakaim, to show the woman the best places for planting. When a woman takes the role of Nunkui in an *anent,* she is putting on a little play with a view to capturing the attributes of the tutelary spirit; but at the same time, she knows pertinently that their two essences remain separate and that Nunkui does not really enter her body.

By identifying themselves with Nunkui, thereby tapping part of the maternal authority she wields over cultivated plants, women represent the garden as a world ruled by the complicity of consanguinity. The manioc people become the paradigmatic child and, even though they are never named, it is to them that the Achuar woman devotes the bulk of her incantations to cultivated plants. As is only fitting when speaking to children, the tone of the manioc *anent* is fairly imperative; the woman seeks to guide and correct rather than to charm. But consanguinity is not without its dangers, for by a logical enough transfer, plant children thrive at the expense of human offspring. In effect, manioc has the reputation for sucking human blood, and in particular that of infants, blood it needs for its initial growth and which it stealthily draws from its rivals. That is why very young children are not allowed to wander around unsupervised in the garden.

As the heart is the seat of intellectual and emotive activity, the blood is the medium by which life and thoughts are conveyed to the different parts of the body. The Achuar believe that each person has a finite quantity of blood and that lost blood cannot be replaced. Each loss, then, is a step closer to anemia (*putsumar*), a general state of physical and mental weakness which, in the elderly and infants, inevitably leads to death. The threat of anemia is taken very seriously by the Achuar, who are familiar with the regular night-time visits of vampire bats (*penke jeencham*) and who know just how fast these can debilitate a young child. Women sometimes harvest manioc roots that have reddish streaks, which they assimilate to traces of human blood the plant has sucked. Such a discovery is a bad sign and announces an approaching death in the circle of kin closely enough related to walk regularly through the bloodsucking garden.

The wise mother will use the appropriate *anent* to maintain contact with the manioc plants, those unnatural and unpredictable children who threaten her life and that of her human progeny. A particularly *anentin* woman may even attempt to use the vampirical propensities of manioc to keep undesirable persons out of her garden. With the help of specific *anent*, she will attempt to deflect the plants' aggression onto an acceptable object so that, sated, they will no longer attack her children. The following *anent* is an example:

My child's mouth is dripping with blood, he is Shakaim's son
Now run him through for me (*repeat*)
Speaking thus, I heard them multiplying (*repeat twice*)
I saw a vision of the little rockfall
It is us, yes, it is us, coming to harvest
I heard them multiplying, I saw them in my vision (*repeat*)
I heard the rockfall multiplying
I made it fall (*repeat*)
As my little garden was multiplying, I saw it in my vision (*repeat*)
The rockslide, I saw it in my vision

(Sung by Mari, a Rio Kunampentza woman)

This is an *anent* rich in polyvalent symbols, for its register embraces several areas of horticultural practice at once. It begins by placing the human babies in the same position as the plant babies ("my [human] child's mouth is dripping with blood"); the postulated vampirical faculties protect the human child from the dangerous plants, since it is the real children who, in return, are changed into manioc. On the basis of this same identity, the singer commends both sets of children to "run through" undesirable visitors. The expression "*ajintiurata*" denotes putting the victim to death with a war spear and perhaps connotes a puncture wound like that made by the vampire bat. Leaving this theme, the magical song turns to more strictly horticultural concerns, invoking the classic figure of the rockfall (*muuch*). The singer uses this image to transfer to the garden plants the attributes of the big rocks scattered chaotically about, in other words: eternity and volume. Finally the theme of clairvoyance ("I saw it in my vision") must be linked to visions that have come to the singer in her sleep or in a trance induced by the drug *maikiua*.

Despite its peaceful, sleepy appearance, the homely garden is as menacing as the forest that surrounds it, and to subdue and harness it takes a great number of skills. Raising one's leafy children turns out to be all the more dangerous as complete success requires the use of gardening charms which also have vampirical properties. These charms, called *nantar*, are stones, sometimes bezoars, but more often small reddish pebbles that women find in their gardens in places communicated to them by Nunkui in a dream. The fecundating power of "Nunkui's stones," *nantar*, is proportional to their potential for harm, and, in principle, there is a type of stone for each of the main species cultivated by women. But there seem to be no *nantar* for the few species cultivated by men, the use of these charms being the exclusive privilege of women. Nevertheless, a man may receive a dream message from Nunkui, revealing exactly where his wife must look for a *nantar*.

Gardening charms amplify the vitality of their corresponding plants, thereby ensuring abundant harvests over a long time. If these *nantar* are to be truly effective, they must be activated by the appropriate *anent*; in response to the song, they are said to glow brightly and give off a high-pitched whine. Endowed with autonomy, *nantar* can move about under their own power; because of the threat they pose to curious toddlers, they must never be kept in the house. In fact it seems that they are able to draw blood at a short distance without having to be touched. Therefore the owner of the *nantar* secures them between two earthen bowls set rim to rim and buries them in her garden, taking care to disguise the hiding place as well as possible. Even in their underground hiding place *nantar* are still dangerous for the small children who accompany their mother to the garden. She must therefore sing *anent* entreating the *nantar* to spare her offspring.

Ownership of *nantar* is exclusive and a closely guarded secret; women are extremely reticent about speaking of these matters to outsiders and laugh off direct questions uneasily or protest ignorance. It seems that it is exceptional even for co-wives to show each other their *nantar*; but speculation on the strength of other women's *nantar* is a favorite subject of discussion, and women can compare the efficacy of the different charms by the results they produce, that is, by the appearance of the respective gardens. These calculations are not entirely disinterested, since the most powerful *nantar* are also the most dangerous, and an especially fine garden threatens *ipso facto* to be a deadly spot for all but the woman who manages it. One may well understand why our stubborn insistence on measuring gardens, even though we were protected by their legitimate mistresses, could be regarded by certain Achuar as foolhardy.

Like gardening *anent*, *nantar* are inherited through the female line and are probably the most precious possession a mother can transmit to her daughter. Most of the *nantar* a woman owns have been acquired this way, for finding one of "Nunkui's stones" in the garden is not a frequent occurrence in the life of an Achuar woman. For a woman to acquire a *nantar* by means of a commercial transaction from someone who is not her kinswoman is almost unheard of, particularly as she would be exposing herself to grave danger. *Nantar* benefit only the woman who knows how to control them, that is who has received either directly from Nunkui or through her own mother the ability to make use of the magic powers of a particular *nantar*. This ability basically translates into the knowledge of those *anent* which enable one to influence the *nantar* and to activate it for beneficial purposes. Without this knowledge, the *nantar*'s activity is more or less uncontrollable, and it becomes very dangerous to handle. Perhaps even more than homicidal manioc, *nantar* are a device that permits every woman not only to maintain the individualized autonomy of her symbolic practice, but also to control concretely the very access to the exclusive domain where this symbolic practice is exercised and reproduced.

Certain animals are considered to be helpers or avatars of Nunkui; their constant presence in the garden has the same beneficial effect as the *nantar*, but without the disadvantages of the latter. This is the case of a bird with reddish feathers, *mama ikianchim* (literally: "manioc cuckoo"), which corresponds to two closely related species: *Coccyzus melacoryphos* and *C. lansbergi*. It is possible to communicate with this bird by means of *anent* like the following, which enjoins it to use its magical capacities for the benefit of the singer:

Sing for me "*chikiua, chikiua!*"
Call the edibles clearly into being by singing on my behalf "*chikiua, chikiua*"
(*repeat several times*).

(*Sung by Mari, a Rio Kunampentza woman*)

The most valued animal, because it is seen as a direct incarnation of Nunkui, is the *wapau* snake (*Trachyboa boulengerii*), a small, harmless reddish-orange boa. There are special *anent* for coaxing a *wapau* to take up residence in the garden, and this type of snake is itself supposed to sing *anent* that have no equal for making manioc grow and flourish. The sole purpose of certain *anent* is to "call up" a dream in which the nesting place of a *wapau* will be revealed; then all the dreamer has to do is to flush it out and install it in a shallow pit in the garden. In this case, too, the dream can come to a man, though the *anent* that is supposed to bring it on is always sung by his wife. In passing, it may be noted that practical reason is also satisfied here with the permanent presence in the garden of a predator of small rodents.

The proper use of *anent*, charms, and Nunkui's helpers comprises a system of general preconditions for effective gardening, different women's accomplishments being measured by the range of magical instruments each can bring to bear on cultivated plants. No woman can afford to remain totally ignorant of the means of ensuring Nunkui's positive influence over her garden and of warding off the potential dangers that it harbors. Individual variations in symbolic control over gardening are therefore differences of degree rather than of nature. A woman who is not really *anentin* will still know a modest number of magical songs and always own one or two weak *nantar*. But over and above this system of general, unequally mastered preconditions, there is a set of individual precautions that must be observed in exactly the same way by one and all, whatever the state of each individual's expertise in magical means of action. The practice of gardening requires the obligatory performance of certain rituals and the observance of numerous dietary taboos, the fulfillment and respect of which are considered indispensable for success in sowing and planting. The Achuar see these two operations as the crucial phases of gardening, since the subsequent development of a plant, they say, depends upon the care with which it was initially placed in the ground.

The ritual manipulations performed at the time of planting are so unobtrusive and discrete that it seems almost incongruous to regard them as propitiatory conditions. Compared to the elaborate, meticulous rituals that punctuate the agricultural calendar of many indigenous Andean communities, Achuar horticultural rituals seem laughable indeed. They do not even have the big collective ceremony for the fruiting of the *uwi* palm, which is of fundamental importance for their Shuar neighbors (Pellizzaro 1978b). Moreover, like the rest of the relations the Achuar have established with the supernatural, their planting rituals are individual and domestic, carried out discretely in the privacy of the garden.

Given the symbolic importance of manioc, it is logical that it be given special attention when a new garden is planted. Before placing the cuttings in the ground, each woman prepares a gourd full of water and pounded achiote, sometimes extended with grated *keaku cesa* bulb ("red flower"), a wild plant with attractive red flowers. She dips the manioc *nantar* into the solution to "superactivate" it; the water, dyed red by the achiote, is explicitly assimilated to blood, a substance manioc needs in order to grow. Then the woman pours this metaphorical blood over the bundle of cuttings as she exhorts the manioc to drink its fill. The Achuar see this rite as an exercise in substitution, which allows them both to satisfy the manioc's perverse needs and to protect themselves from its vampirical penchants by supplying it with a generous ration of blood in advance. When a young bride is planting her first garden, the achiote is poured over the manioc by an old woman who is particularly *anentin* and experienced in gardening techniques.[20] As a rule, old *anentin* women are supposed to have better luck than young women with techniques that are reputed difficult, such as planting peanuts. As they are *wea*, these elderly women have extensive experience with ritual manipulations and a profound intimacy with Nunkui, which ensure them success with these difficult and purportedly chancy seeds; therefore a young woman will usually ask her mother to sow the peanuts in her stead. But as the system of magic is never univocal and most often answers to competing and apparently contradictory logics, there are also crops that prosper only when planted by children or adolescents. In this case, the skill acquired with age counts less than the vital energy characteristic of youth, which, it is hoped, will rub off on the plants. Similarly, elderly men whose strength is on the wane will ask young boys to plant their gourd plants, their *wayus*, or their *maikiua*.

If youth is the symbol of vitality, so is blood, and, on these grounds, the color red is associated with all symbolic practices involved in gardening. Therefore the ingredients of the solution poured over the manioc are red, of which color achiote is the archetype. When women set out to sow, plant, or handle their *nantar*, they decorate their face with achiote to make themselves pleasing to Nunkui, who is supposed to be particularly partial to red. Beyond paying homage to Nunkui, achiote face paint also unmistakably identifies the woman as being like the helping spirits of the garden, which are, for the most part, red in color (*nantar, wapau,* and *ikianchim*). By assimilating herself to these tutelary spirits on the chromatic level, the mistress of the garden forestalls misunderstandings and creates the possibility of immediate recognition by mimicry. Although it is performed primarily for manioc, the blood-transfer ceremony may also be done when planting other cultigens such as yams, taros, sweet potatoes, or peanuts. The need is not as pressing as in the case of manioc, however, since these plants have no vampirical tendencies and do not threaten to slake their thirst with human blood. On the whole, then, planting rites are not very spectacular, and it seems that we may classify them in that category for which the *anent* is the model, and which embraces all means of direct control and influence over the anthropomorphized existence of nature's beings.

The dietary prohibitions to be respected when planting obey a logic inversely symmetrical to that governing *anent* and all forms of ritual action on nature. The aim here is no longer to arouse positive qualities in the cultivated plants, but, on the contrary, to prevent, by fasting and abstinence, the accidental transmission of negative characteristics. These taboos are based on the extremely classic idea that eating an animal that has certain original attributes will cause these to be transmitted to any plant sown or planted concomitantly. And so, when planting banana trees, one must not eat *kanka* fish or *muntish* palm grubs, or the plants will rot as fast as this fish and be full of worms. The *kanka* is a toothless, rather insipid white fish that is fond of mud. It is said to be geophage, like the earthworm of which it is a sort of aquatic counterpart; the *kanka* is thus often used as a metaphorical support for the idea of putrefaction.[21] The prohibition on *muntish* grubs applies also, and for the same reason, to sowing maize, and is accompanied in this case by an interdiction on eating monkey, so that the plants will not be spindly and bent as though monkeys had been swinging on them, and on peccary, so that herds of these animals will not break into the gardens, inevitably trampling the crops. When sowing peanuts, one must abstain from eating peppers or any meat that has been in contact with smoke or fire so that the seeds will not burn. This prohibition covers a fairly broad category, since, besides roasted and smoked meats, it actually includes all mammals whose fur is singed off before they are boiled (monkey, agouti, paca, rodents. . .).

In addition to these categorial dietary prohibitions, which must be respected during the few days of planting, it is recommended to do the actual planting on an empty stomach, and therefore not to eat until evening, when the garden work is done. As we have seen, fasting (*ijiarmatin*) and frugality are cardinal virtues for the Achuar, who consider it unseemly to undertake delicate activities on a full stomach. Fullness produces bodily and mental torpor, and engenders uncontrollable internal fermentation, all of which are incompatible with the alertness required for the mobilization of the physical and spiritual faculties. Lastly, all sexual relations should, in principle, cease at planting time. This abstinence has to do in part with the fact that sexual intercourse is supposed to occasion the temporary loss of vital energy which should be husbanded for planting. But this prohibition is founded above all on the idea that nocturnal love play is incompatible with dreaming and therefore prevents dream communication with the tutelary spirits of the garden. It is particularly important to establish close contact with Nunkui and her helpers during this crucial phase of gardening; couples are therefore willing to sacrifice the pleasures of sexual commerce for visionary commerce with the spirits.

The dietary prohibitions the Achuar impose on themselves at the time of planting could be articulated according to a logic of the perceptible qualities hypostasized in physiological processes and emblematic animals. Each specific prohibition functions as a sign pointing to one of the three categories of attributes detrimental to plants' harmonious growth: things that rot, signified by the *kanka* fish, the *muntish* grub, and by digestion in general; things that burn, signified by peppers and meat exposed to direct contact with fire; things that are slender, signified by monkeys swinging on flexible branches. Certain animal or plant species are better suited than others to the role of symbolic signifier because they possess striking distinctive features that invite the indigenous observer to exercise what Lévi-Strauss has called a *droit de suite* ("right of continuity"), that is to postulate that their visible qualities are the sign of invisible properties (Lévi-Strauss 1962: 25). Dietary taboos are thus a passageway between the system of qualities and the system of properties, a compulsory intersection connecting praxis and knowledge. The proscription of peccary, on the other hand, seems to rest on a different logic, since it is explicitly presented as a direct act of exorcism. Contrary to the preceding taboos in which the forbidden species is not the one threatening the plants (*muntish* grubs do not attack banana trees and monkeys do not swing on maize stalks), the peccary in question is quite capable of producing the unfortunate results that one seeks to prevent by not eating it. In this case there is an attempt to reach an agreement with the animal, by which its life will be spared for the time being so that it will spare the plants. Although killing and eating seem to be automatically linked in dietary prohibitions, here they are disjoined by indigenous logic. The first category of taboos has more to do with the direct incorporation of perceptible qualities, in other words with forbidding the intake of certain foods, while the taboo on peccary refers less to the fact that it must not be eaten than to the fact that it must not be killed.

The originality of these dietary interdictions, from the standpoint of the Achuar theory of the division of labor, is that they apply not only to the individuals actually doing the planting, but to the entire domestic cell, including children. Success in sowing and planting is thus regarded as highly dependent on the family's self-discipline, as the slightest violation – even accidental – by a member of the domestic unit is reputed to have disastrous consequences. This is an important point which provides a glimpse of one constant in the Achuar representation of the symbolic processes that ensure that all goes well in a labor process: no one individual can personally control all of the symbolic conditions alleged to be necessary for the success of the activity in which he is engaged. As we will see in more detail when we analyze the representations of work (Chapter Eight), relations with the tutelary spirits who govern the respective effectiveness of the various productive activities are clearly individualized and divided between the two genders, but some of the means of keeping up this relation (taboos, dream omens, and so on) are controlled by the voluntary or involuntary action of others.

The most extreme form of this uncontrollable incidence of others on the conditions for successfully carrying out a labor process is expressed in the evil spells jealous women may cast on prosperous gardens. These spells (*yuminkramu*) are conveyed by *anent* sung for the purpose – which no female Achuar informant has ever admitted knowing – and are supposed to cause certain cultivated plants, particularly manioc and banana trees, to rot and/or dry up. The woman whose plants have been thus stricken identifies the author of the spell by an exercise in anamnesis, the purpose of which is to recall the past behavior of all women who have visited her garden. The one who has exclaimed most enthusiastically over the aspect and vigor of the plants has every chance of being the guilty party, because she will have openly shown her jealousy by the very excess of her praises. There are *anent* to conjure spells and send them back to the garden of the attacker without her becoming immediately aware of it. This system of automatic return-to-sender of harmful principles or substances is at the root of Achuar shamanic activity, which provides the conceptual model for the – very limited – practice of "witchcraft" (see Descola and Lory 1982).

Having concluded this overview of the magical techniques used in cultivating plants, we may now re-examine the object of our initial question, which was raised by the fact that the Achuar – and in general all Jivaro – are one of the very rare indigenous societies of the Amazon Basin to practice gardening magic. Why is it that they feel the need to reinforce an objectively effective technical practice with an apparently superfluous magical practice? Why do they represent the task of gardening as a chancy and hazardous undertaking, while at the same time taking all the necessary technical measures to eliminate danger and chance? First of all, the two questions must be separated: the first addresses the general conditions of the practice of magic, while the second concerns the specific content of the Achuar's representations of gardening magic.

The first question is badly phrased intentionally; this formulation nevertheless has the advantage of immediately showing up the vacuity of functionalist interpretations of magic by highlighting the absence of practical effects of Achuar gardening magic. From Malinowski's first articles down to the most recent theses of ecological pseudo-materialism, utilitarian rationality has always argued that, in the final analysis, symbolic practices produce materially objective results. Magic becomes a sort of optimizing mechanism, which ensures the complete success of an operation on nature. This brand of optimization is supposed to work in two ways: in an objective manner because it fulfills in some non-apparent way an indispensable economic, ecological, or biological function and in a subjective manner because it constitutes a sort of institutional tranquilizer that tempers the feelings of uncertainty engendered by precarious conditions of production. In either case, the functionalist interpretation of magic would demonstrate – with laudable intentions – that a priori outlandish, extravagant customs have in reality an eminently practical, positive function. The Achuar case is a dazzling demonstration *a contrario* of the inadequacy of this type of functionalist causality, which argues that only aleatory activities require a compensating apparatus of ritual and symbol (e.g. White 1959: 272). This general axiom has sometimes been used to explain the abundance of hunting ceremonies and the correlative absence of gardening rites in Amazonia (see Carneiro 1974: 129). But Achuar gardening is objectively neither fraught with perils nor subject to chance, and the gardeners are in perfect control of all the technical conditions for obtaining optimal yields. The unpredictability allegedly involved in handling cultivated plants has therefore been induced by a cultural complex that tends to introduce chance and danger there where initially none is involved. The symbolic and ritual conditions posited as necessary to the success of the garden are indubitably functional responses, but their purpose is to mitigate objectively imaginary risks.

Rather than taking a utilitarian view of the practical results of gardening magic, one might look into its logical results, that is its capacity to produce meaning in a given context. Or to put it another way, if one admits that the Achuar do effectively accept nature as a world of anthropomorphic powers, is it conceivable that they should forego the means of acting with or upon these powers? If one considers that the existence of cultivated plants and their tutelary spirits is governed by the same social laws as humankind, is it not normal that these same humans think of their relations with the garden world as a continuum and not as something separate? There where no distinction is made between natural and supernatural, there where the law of universal sociability annexes the plant and animal kingdoms, can one possibly imagine that the Achuar are so schizophrenic as to think of themselves simultaneously as *homo faber*, exploiting a mute environment, and as one species of nature's beings sharing a fellow feeling with all others? As Lévi-Strauss noted, religion (in the sense of anthropomorphism of nature) and magic (in the sense of physiomorphism of man) are always found together, though their respective proportions may vary (1962: 293). If it is impossible to affirm that religion genetically precedes magic or vice versa, it is consequently impossible to affirm that the will to do engenders the will to know, or vice versa, since both occur simultaneously. If the Achuar feel they can influence the fate of plants by the use of magic, it is because their knowledge of nature is so structured that it places technical logic and "religious" logic on the same plane. When one postulates that cultivated plants are beings with souls, it is obviously normal to attempt to keep up harmonious relations with them, using for this magical songs (*anent*) which are employed to the same end in human relations. It is not the presence of horticultural magic in the absence of precarious techniques that is the problem, but rather the possible absence of such magic in societies which represent the agricultural process as depending upon supernatural forces.

Having come this far, we may now query the very content of representations of gardening practice, that is, no longer, why magic?, but, why religious images? Why is the garden seen, most implausibly, as a dangerous place full of lurking vampire-plants? Why is gardening represented as a triangle of consanguinity (Nunkui–woman–cultivated plants)? Why is the successful manipulation of cultivated plants conditioned by unequal access to certain types of magical knowledge? These problems go beyond the field of horticultural representations in the narrow sense to fall into the more general category of Achuar conceptions of the sexual division of labor. Here we will simply indicate the heads of several trails that will be explored at greater length in Chapter Eight.

When the Achuar represent gardening as an eminently dangerous and uncertain activity, it is as though they were seeking to establish that the paradigmatic field of female practices and that of male practices presented equivalent risks. To transform an obviously routine and typically domestic task into a hazardous undertaking in which one risks life and limb is also to preclude that hunting be given any preeminence in a system where status could be founded on ranking productive functions according to the risks entailed. If, to have prestige, a task must require meeting danger head on and mastering uncertainty, then gardening – as conceived by the Achuar – is an activity deserving of every bit as much consideration as the exploits of the great hunters. As she squats day after day at her obscure task of weeding, the Achuar woman does not think of her work as inferior or her economic function as subordinate.

The second original feature of gardening representations is the humanization of relations with cultivated plants, according to the axis of motherhood. One might of course see the figure of Nunkui as marginally illustrating the theme of the fertile, nurturing earth-mother, as figured more particularly by the Andean Pacha Mama. In fact, though, this representation of the earth-mother is almost unknown in Amazonia outside the zones influenced by the Quichua culture and may point to a distant seat of Jivaro culture in the southern Ecuadorian Andes (see Taylor 1993, Chap. 3). But the chthonian motherhood theme is of less interest here for the indications it might provide on cultural diffusion or for the touches it might enable us to add to an already well-analyzed archetype than for the model it provides for female operations on nature. By identifying with Nunkui, the Achuar woman purportedly takes upon herself Nunkui's own maternal relationship with cultivated plants. Nunkui is therefore not an earth-mother from whom one must beg fruits, but the model for a social relation which makes the garden into a world of consanguinity. And so it is not so much the theme of motherhood that seems important here as the idea that the domestic sphere controlled by women can be subsumed by consanguinity. The idea of consanguinity takes on its full meaning naturally only when placed opposite its symmetrical pole; good structural logic should allow us coolly to accept the notion that hunting is thought by the Achuar as an affinal relationship (see Chapter Six).

The domestic space

If the garden is the locus of purported relations of consanguinity, it is also the daily setting of effective maternal relations and an extension beyond the *ekent* of the space of sociality devolved upon the little cell comprised by the mother and her children. The reader will recall that the matrix of spatial organization revealed by the topological analysis of the house centers on the principles of conjunction and disjunction, which divide the areas of sociability into symmetrical, interchangeable pairs. And we saw that, in both topographical (concentric) and schematic (tangential) representations of these areas of sociability (Fig. 15), the garden is the only circumscribed space that keeps its affectation whatever the use assigned it: it is always a place of disjunction, whether the disjunction be between the men and women of the household or between the domestic group and outsiders.

As a place of disjunction between the sexes, the garden operates both a diachronic and a synchronic separation. In the chronological process of its creation, the garden is first a clearing, the exclusive territory of men and Shakaim, before becoming a planted area, the exclusive territory of women and Nunkui. Only during the very short interval when it is being burned, when the *aja* becomes a liminal space that is no longer altogether forest and not yet garden, are the sexes temporarily conjoined within the enclosure. This diachronic disjunction, which is reproduced every time a garden is produced, then lays the ground for the synchronic disjunction which makes the garden into a typically female space. Of course this is the ideal model; in everyday life, men make sporadic incursions into their wives' gardens to pick tobacco leaves or a few pods of achiote. But their visits are always brief and conjunctural, even on those exceptional occasions when their wife receives them in the garden to have intercourse. But this exemplary instance of sexual conjunction rarely takes place in the garden, for reasons of convenience rather than explicit taboo. In a polygynous household in particular, it is more or less excluded that erotic revels take place in a garden setting, since each co-wife's plot usually borders on the others, and there is absolutely no guarantee of privacy.

Sometimes men occupy the garden in a more systematic fashion, when making traps, for example, or lying in wait at night for a marauding agouti or paca. But in such cases they not only use the garden outside of "working hours," when the women are not present, but they transform it into a hunting ground, which they temporarily assimilate to the forest. When waiting for game, the men are acting as predators and not as gardeners, they temporarily reclassify the garden, shifting it from its status as extension of the house to that of extension of the forest. It is therefore permissible to advance that the garden is the only absolutely female space in the Achuar social topography, the only place where women truly exercise a material and symbolic hegemony.

Even more than a space out of bounds to men, the garden is a space out of bounds to all others: a woman's domain it is, but the exclusive purview of a single woman. From this standpoint, the garden differs from the *ekent*, for not only does the *ekent* allow the nocturnal conjunction of the sexes, in a polygamous household it also harbors within a restricted perimeter several matricentric cells whose only individual anchor is a bed, *peak*. In this sense, each plot a co-wife cultivates is like a projection beyond the house walls of her own little territory, her *peak*. When a young girl marries, her new autonomy is symbolized by her right to both her own *peak* and a garden. The *peak* and the garden, then, are, for the married woman, what the *chimpui* stool is for grown men: that which stakes out personal territory within the collective space, denoting as much a status as a place of one's own.

The *peak* is private, but not enclosed, and the loosely joined slats that sometimes screen it are not going to hide what goes on there from the other co-wives. By contrast, each cultivated plot, hedged about with stands of banana trees, provides a retreat, which, while not isolated enough for physical intimacy, at least ensures relative protection from the eyes of others. The garden is a privileged space, then, where the Achuar woman can take refuge without being disturbed. That is where she will go after a serious marital crisis, if she has been insulted or beaten by her husband. That is where she will give vent to her grief after the death of a child or a close relative, crooning the same poignant mournful tune hour after hour. In the days following a death, the gardens continuously sound with these women's voices, hoarse with crying and fatigue. This is because it is unseemly to show strong feelings inside the house; while it is fitting to let one's grief be heard, it is not fitting to let it be seen. The garden is thus the private refuge where one can give free voice to one's feelings, safe from prying eyes.

The garden is where women give birth, periodically bringing forth new human beings there where daily they reproduce vegetal beings. At the first signs of labor, a small frame is hastily erected, comprised of two posts planted upright in the ground, across which is laid a pole. During the last stage of labor – which is usually short – the parturient squats over a banana leaf, clinging to the horizontal bar overhead. Childbirth is the affair of women, it takes place in a female domain and no man is allowed in the garden during the labor and birth, not even the father of the child. The parturient is attended by one or two other women, preferably her mother if she is still living, her sisters, or her husband's other wives. They build the frame, oversee the delivery, cut the umbilical cord and bathe the newborn child. It is evident that, from this standpoint, the garden is clearly opposed to the forest, since the jungle is the normal place for the conjunction of sexes that takes place in copulation, while the garden attests the strict exclusion of men, symbolized by childbirth, the paradigm of the female condition. The right of putative motherhood over cultivated plants is thus concretely rooted in the very place where real motherhood is realized.

The character of the garden as private space obviously corresponds to an ideal norm; just as the men of the house sometimes enter this female space without altering its nature, so women are admitted to gardens that do not belong to them without throwing into question the exclusive right of use. It is not only on the occasion of the birth of a child that women from the same household pay visits to each others' gardens. The practice is common between close kinswomen (sisters, mothers, and daughters), but less frequent between unrelated co-wives, where seeds of jealousy are just waiting to sprout. It can be purely a pleasure visit, the occasion for a long, leisurely chat; it sometimes turns into a few hours of work in common, an excellent pretext for continuing the conversation. It is at these times that secrets are shared and certain pieces of technical information transmitted, on the behavior and needs of a new cultigen or cultivar, for example.

It also happens that outside women, who are visiting for a few days in the company of their husband, may be invited to work in the household garden. The Achuar representation of women's roles and the rules of hospitality demand that a female visitor who spends some time in a house contribute, by helping in the garden, to the collective production of food. Whereas her husband will be fed by the women of the house and eat with the family head, from the second or third day of her stay, she will have to go out to harvest manioc in her hostess' garden. She will be given a fireplace in the *ekent* so that she can cook for herself and her children and so that she can make a contribution, however symbolic, to the meals her husband and the master of the house take together. In the highly codified context of a visit, then, an outside woman enjoys a sort of temporary right of access to someone else's garden. This right flows from the idea that a healthy woman cannot allow herself systematically to be fed by others without losing face and therefore she must be given the means of providing her own meals.

And yet the foregoing seems to contradict the previous claim that the garden is the place of strict disjunction between the domestic group and outsiders. Here it must be stressed that the usufructory right to a garden is not automatic, and it takes effect only upon the formal invitation of the woman who ordinarily cultivates it. It is with her and on her instructions that the visitor will harvest what she needs and it is under her protection that the visitor will explicitly place herself so that she will be safe from the vampirical manioc and *nantar*. There is then a clear rule by which no one from outside the household may enter a garden without express permission from its legitimate user. The disjunction here is one of principle, in that it attests to a norm that is not invalidated by the occasional presence of female visitors in the garden. The same holds for the *ekent*, the place of strict disjunction between the domestic group and outsiders, but where a shaman may always enter to treat a bedridden patient. In either case, the exception does not disprove the rule.

The ban on outsiders in the garden must be taken broadly, particularly because visitors are obliged to cross a garden clearing to reach the house, since the house is always surrounded by a cultivated space. But they are always careful to keep to the well-trodden path, never venturing into the planted areas where the bloodthirsty manioc lurks. In many gardens the path is replaced, as we have seen, by big log catwalks that enable the visitors to advance above the nefarious reach of the manioc. The imaginary perils of the garden are reinforced by the altogether real danger which effectively precludes stealing into a clearing when a woman is present. Watch-dogs run loose in the garden, where they accompany their mistress at all times. These particularly ferocious animals are trained to attack in packs, immobilizing the intruder within a threatening circle; they are an efficient dissuasion to intruders. But secretly entering a temporarily vacant garden is just as dangerous, for if the visitor's passage is detected, from footprints, the alarm may be raised on the spot. Signs of such an intrusion – immediately signaled by the woman, with repeated shouts of "*shuar nawe!*" ("a man's tracks") – can mean only one thing: an enemy spy has come to reconnoiter before an attack on the house. A visitor whose intentions are ostensibly friendly announces his arrival from afar by giving a typical yodeling call or blowing several blasts on a hollow *kunku* snail shell. Any man prowling around a garden can be motivated only by bad intentions and the men of the house lose no time setting out on his trail to kill him.

There is another prowler, though, that a wife will be sure to keep from her husband, for his discovery would bode ill for her. Achuar women receive their lovers in the garden, since it is the only accessible spot where they are more or less assured of privacy. In the house a woman is almost always with others and she can never be alone in the forest since she is always accompanied either by her husband, on hunting trips or visits, or by a band of women and children, on gathering walks. Of necessity, the garden is the only place where assignations can be concluded. These are arranged by leaving messages bitten into the leaves of trees in agreed spots on the edge of the garden. The code is pre-established, and a few simple figures provide for all foreseeable situations. This is an extremely risky exercise, however, for the garden is an illusory haven, sufficiently illusory in any case to be considered unsuitable for marital sexuality. In addition, the men are remarkable trackers, constantly on the lookout for the slightest sign of human or animal presence. It is therefore rare that a secret liaison can go on for any time without arousing the husband's suspicions; he will then take the necessary steps to surprise the guilty parties. If he succeeds, the penalty is the immediate death of the lovers, killed on the spot by the offended husband.

At first glance, these adulterous adventures seem to cast doubt on the principle of the disjunction of the sexes within the garden, since, although this spot is only rarely the site of marital sexual relations, it is the sole theater for illicit copulation. Furthermore, adultery is a sort of absolute paradox to the process of making the garden into a place of consanguine relations, since it is the consummation of a possible but non-authorized marriage alliance. The lovers' sexual activity in the garden leads to a complete break with the social norm, since they join the sexes there where they are supposed to be separated and they establish a secret affinity there where mothering consanguinity should be the rule. But the Achuar do not make a habit of illegitimate affairs, and, as the punishment testifies, these meet with severe reprobation on principle. It therefore seems that the sporadic use of the garden for adulterous purposes produces such a symmetrical reversal of the normal ways in which such a place is used that, far from being contradicted, they are reinforced by antithesis. By working this spectacular inversion of ordinary practices, the occasional violation merely reaffirms the norm.

A place of disjunction and exclusion, the location of an exclusive brand of motherhood that annexes cultivated plants, the garden is also a space where man seems to fashion nature without being its passive subject. In this sense, the clearing would be globally opposed to the surrounding forest, of which it would be the well-ordered scale model, symbol of an ephemeral victory of culture over nature. But certain elements in the Achuar representation of the horticultural process suggest a few corrections to this image, which has become classic in the ethnographical literature. For instance, the dichotomy between wild space and cultivated space does not necessarily reflect a dichotomy between nature and culture, if one adheres literally to the idea that the forest is Shakaim's plantation. To be sure, as the tutelary spirit of wild plants, Shakaim is not an ordinary mortal. But, though he lives in a world misqualified by the West as supernatural, he is nevertheless endowed with all the cultural attributes of mankind. This great forest gardener looks human, communicates with men, and entertains with Nunkui a kinship relation which, even though its nature (affinity or siblingship) is uncertain, is nevertheless obvious to everyone. By representing the jungle as an immense field planted and managed by an anthropomorphic spirit, the Achuar make their own gardens into a conceptual model of a nature untouched by man. In other words, for them the garden is not so much the cultural transformation of a portion of wild space as the cultural homology in the human order of a cultural reality of the same standing in the superhuman order. As co-socializers of the world, Nunkui and Shakaim found the principle of a cultural continuum in which each clearing domesticated by man temporarily realizes the virtualities of a homely wilderness, an enviable arrangement which enables the Achuar to partake of domestic life in the society of nature.

6

The world of the forest

Surrounding the garden, a high wall of vegetation bounds the space unfashioned by human hands. While the garden gracefully bows to the will of its creators, the forest maintains its stubborn independence with respect to those who forage there. It dispenses its wealth now liberally, now parsimoniously, and obliges the Achuar to play by rules they do not always control. The forest behaves in extreme ways: either it effaces itself entirely to make way for the garden, or it conserves its integrity, yielding up only superficial portions of its stores. Though hunting and gathering are the official forms of sporadic foraging, the status of the two are far from identical for the Achuar. Inasmuch as neither hunting nor gathering implies any deliberate transformation of nature, they may be regarded as homologous modes of forest resource procurement; the fact that they are juxtaposed in this chapter devoted to the world of the forest reflects the observer's analytical point of view as well as the needs of a certain economy of exposition. But the Achuar themselves do not situate the two activities on the same plane: gathering wild fruits, snails, or palm fronds for thatching only taps the surface of the environment and requires no compensation; hunting, on the other hand, is predatory behavior, and neither its material conditions of practice nor its possible consequences depend entirely on the hunter's own skills. Fishing is closely related to hunting in that it is a technique of resource procurement that entails killing. Water, however, is another world again, and its denizens are the antithesis of forest-dwelling creatures. The river is not an extension of the forest, then, but a separate world deserving of its own chapter (see Chapter Seven).

Foraging techniques

If the forest is a great wild garden, it is also the place of conjunction *par excellence*, in which the sexes mingle and enemies clash. These activities are not something the Achuar take lightly, and the forest is therefore neither simply a nice place for a walk nor the children's playground. One sets out into the forest for a definite reason and with a definite goal in mind. In this space where the other and death are confronted in a privileged way, there reside beings that command respect. Like a woman, they are coaxed and wooed, like an enemy they are stalked and killed; relations with the animals of the forest demand the entire range of conciliatory and bellicose capacities in the human repertory. Together with lovemaking and warfare, hunting is the third pole of those conjunctive relations set in the forest. It resembles the first two in both the pleasures it affords and the technical and magical skills it requires.

Hunting

We will continue with the provisional distinction adopted in our treatment of the labor process of gardening and deal first of all with the technical procedures involved in hunting. As in any cynegetic undertaking, these are based on the mastery of a combination of death-dealing implements and techniques of tracking and stalking. We will therefore look briefly at the Achuar's weaponry and at their means of positioning themselves to use it.

   The main weapon is the blowgun (*uum*), a thin, straight tube of some three meters in length, with which small, sharp darts are projected. This magnificent, shiny black weapon is particularly difficult to make. Contrary to what its elegant simplicity might suggest, the Achuar blowgun is in fact made of two symmetrical halves of a palm-wood tube cut lengthwise and fashioned to fit tightly together. These hollow halves are bound together with vine fibers and coated with a black substance made from beeswax. The types of palm used – principally chonta, *chuchuk* (*Syagrus tessmanni*), and *tuntuam* – are very hard and warp resistant, as the wood fibers are long and compact. Furthermore the makers take the precaution of waiting nearly a year between felling the palm tree and beginning the planing, so that the wood has time to dry perfectly.

Because of its density, this type of wood is hard to plane and polish, especially when it comes to hollowing out the bore, which must be perfectly round and straight. Once the two hollow halves are joined, the bore must be sanded for several days with a sort of ramrod. The outside of the blowgun is also carefully planed to a perfect cylinder. For all tasks involved in the manufacture of a blowgun, the Achuar use, besides the polyvalent machete, two purpose-made tools fashioned from old machete blades hafted into wooden handles. The first consists of a triangular blade, the sharpened tip of which is used for grooving the bore. The other is a scraper with a semi-circular cutting edge used for smoothing. The wrapping must be done with extreme precision, as the slightest play would render the blowgun useless. Once the blowgun has been bound, it must still be coated with a layer of hot wax (*sekat*), and then fitted with a mouthpiece made from a segment of jaguar or peccary femur.[1] Including the time spent collecting materials in the forest and setting up the three-legged workstand, it takes between fifty and sixty hours to produce a good blowgun.

All Achuar men know how to make blowguns, but all do not enjoy equal success. An excellent blowgun must satisfy requirements that are hard to reconcile: it must be thin and light, and at the same time perfectly rigid. A few men are particularly reputed for their skill in this area, thereby acquiring one of the rare forms of craft specialization known in this society. Rather than using a mediocre blowgun of his own manufacture, a man will come to these experts for a quality weapon. These craftsmen are also sought out to restore an old weapon that is no longer true, since the slightest bowing deflects the dart from its intended path of flight. All hunters are naturally extremely careful that their weapon is not subjected to the slightest warping. When not in use, a blowgun is always lashed upright to one of the houseposts; out of doors it must be kept out of direct sunlight, which distorts the wood. But in spite of such precautions, a blowgun will warp in the end, obliging the hunter to correct his aim at each shot.

The most expert blowgun makers can produce up to ten a year, thus converting their skill into a source of commodities. But even though this commodity circulates within the Achuar group because of individual differences in the quality of blowguns made, its production is intended principally for intertribal trade. The Achuar's indigenous neighbors (the Shuar and Canelos) also use blowguns, although for a variety of reasons they have ceased manufacturing them themselves. Achuar blowguns have an excellent reputation and are particularly valued by the adjacent ethnic groups, who consume a great number of them. North of the Rio Pastaza, they are the principal medium of payment used by the Achuar to acquire manufactured goods from the Canelos. This specialization ascribed to the Achuar in the regional division of labor is founded on factors of a socio-economic more than a technical nature. As is often the case in Amazonian intertribal trade, the scarcity of an item is artificially created in order to bring about the need for exchange. Neither the Shuar nor the Canelos lack the materials or the skills needed to make blowguns; they simply find it more convenient to obtain from their neighbors a handmade product of excellent quality at a very low cost, since they are the inescapable intermediaries between the Achuar and the centers selling manufactured goods.

The projectiles used in blowguns are very sharp, thin darts some 30 centimeters long called *tsentsak*. They are made from the center vein of the *kinchuk* and *iniayua* palm fronds. Once the raw material is gathered, making *tsentsak* is a simple operation; forty can be cut in a matter of two hours. This means that darts are particularly economical to use and a hunter does not need to be sparing with his projectiles. As the diameter of the *tsentsak* is smaller than the bore of the blowgun, a wad of kapok is wound around the tail of the dart to form an elongated plug that completely blocks the conduit when the dart is placed in firing position. These darts are carried in a small quiver (*tunta*) which the hunter wears slung over his shoulder. The quiver is made from a segment of bamboo (*Guadua angustifolia*) into which has been placed a bundle (*chipiat*) of *kinchuk* fronds that have been cut into slices and bound together. This bundle is fairly compact, and the darts stuck into it remain upright and do not rattle around as the hunter walks. A round gourd, *mati* (*Crescentia cujete*) is attached to the quiver; hollowed out with a hole in the side, it is used to store a small supply of kapok for making plugs. Around the place where the gourd is attached to the quiver is wound a long piece of vine, *japik*, which is used as a cleaning rod to swab out the bore of the blowgun. The last *tunta* accessory is half of the lower mandible of a piranha on a cotton string. The teeth of this fish are razor sharp and are used to notch the dart just below the point. This is an ingenious trick, for when a monkey is hit by a curare dart, its first reaction is to tear out the projectile; if the dart has been notched, it will break and the tip will remain embedded in the animal long enough for the poison to act.

Like most Achuar implements, the blowgun and quiver are elegant in their simplicity, their clean lines the product of a perfect fit between function and form. These works of art are particularly adapted to their use, and the blowgun's ballistic qualities make it a highly efficient hunting weapon. The aim can be very accurate since the blowgun is equipped with a small bump about 30 centimeters in front of the mouthpiece that serves as a sight. We conducted a series of experiments with the help of reputed hunters to measure the efficacy of the blowgun. When fired from a horizontal position, the useful range of the projectile is around fifty meters. This is ample for hunting, since, in the luxuriant vegetation of the jungle, it is rare to be able to shoot such a distance without encountering some obstacle. The accuracy of the blowgun is also quite satisfactory, since most hunters can hit a target 20 centimeters in diameter from a distance of 30 meters. Silent, accurate, and economical to use, the blowgun is no doubt the best traditional weapon for hunting small game in the rain forest.

Despite its intrinsic qualities, though, the blowgun would no doubt be less employed were its effectiveness not increased by the use of curare, into which the darts are commonly dipped. Curare is a generic term for the hunting poisons used in Amerindian societies; it covers a number of toxic preparations, usually made from the plants of the genus *Strychnos*. Achuar curare (*tseas*) is always made from the same two basic ingredients: the *machapi* vine (*Phoebe* sp.) and the fruit of the *painkish* tree (*Strychnos jobertiana*). To augment the potency of the poison, some hunters add other elements derived from a half dozen unidentified plants: *yarir, tsaweimiar, nakapur, tsururpatin, kayaipi,* and *tsunkanka iniai.* Every hunter has his own recipe, usually handed down from father to son, and those who make the most potent curare are secretive about its composition. In any event, the active component of *tseas* is always strychnine, which provokes violent tetanization and then overall paralysis resulting in a more or less rapid death.

Making curare is an exclusively male task, performed in the forest in a small hut constructed for the purpose at some distance from the house. For the duration of the preparation, women and children are strictly forbidden to go near the hut. The various ingredients are gathered and placed in an earthenware vessel (*ichinkian*) to cook over a low fire; the brew must simmer for a day in order to reach the sticky consistency and dark black color characteristic of *tseas*. As it cooks, the men sing special *anent* to make the curare strong. The incantations are addressed directly to the *tseas*, in the vocative, enjoining it to "drink the blood" of the animals on which it will be used, each type of game being mentioned in turn. In addition, the man preparing the poison must keep a strict fast and abstain completely from sexual relations, not only while gathering the ingredients, but during the cooking process proper. These precautions are normal for all reputedly difficult undertakings, as we have seen in the case of sowing crops.

As in certain phases of gardening, the effectiveness of the curare is linked to the respect of certain dietary prohibitions, imposed not only on the poison-maker but on all members of his family. While the *tseas* is being made and for at least a week thereafter, the entire household is forbidden to consume anything sweet, and particularly sugar cane and papayas. The logic of opposites is clearly at work here, since these fruits are known antidotes for curare, and must be taken in great quantities to counter its effects in the case of accidental injury. Although the prohibition on sweets is relaxed somewhat once the official time has expired, it remains partially in effect for the person using the curare. Indeed, hunters almost never eat sweet foods and they abstain from consuming honey, the taste of this nectar thereby being reserved for women and children. Honey is supposed to weaken the hunting poison and clog the lungs, the ensuing loss of breath making it impossible to use a blowgun.

At the other end of the taste spectrum, everyone is also forbidden to eat salt on game killed with curare so that the poison will not lose its strength. The same prohibition applies to using chili peppers while making *tseas*. It seems that these condiments, symbols *par excellence* of the cultural aspect of cooking, are irremediably antithetical to curare. The logic of this particular taboo may well lie in the reciprocal cancellation of the effects produced by the conjunction of structurally isomorphic substances. As Lévi-Strauss points out, Amerindian cultures think hunting poison as a case of nature intruding into culture, in that it is a natural product that makes a cultural activity possible (1964: 281–2). From this point of view, seasonings have the same properties, and it seems consistent that salt and chili peppers would cancel the natural effect of curare. Like the blowgun, *tseas* is considered by the Achuar to be an autonomous being whose behavior is unpredictable and whose feelings must be pampered. When a hunting poison loses its potency, usually, people say, because some taboo has been broken, it must be sung *anent* to revive its thirst for animal blood. Moreover, as *tseas* feeds on the blood of game, it must not be used on animals that are not eaten, for the ingestion of "sickening" blood would make it ill and consequently unusable.

Perhaps because it is impossible to ensure that all members of the household have kept the dietary prohibitions connected with making curare, the Achuar consider Peruvian hunting poison to be more effective than their homemade brand. The most common practice is to obtain some Peruvian curare and mix it in equal proportions with their own *tseas*. Together with salt, curare has long been the object of an active interregional trade throughout upper Amazonia, and the Achuar occupy a strategic position on the supply line to the Shuar, who make none of their own (Taylor 1993: Chaps. 2 and 3). According to the Achuar, the best curare at the moment is made by the Lamistas of the Rio Mayo, and in the Iquitos regions, where it is manufactured on a large scale by specialized craftsmen. The product is then relayed via various circuits to the Achuar of Peru, where it is distributed along chains of trading partners among the Achuar of Ecuador. The latter in turn supply the Shuar, providing them with a mixture of Peruvian curare and a local brand. Parallel to the indigenous exchange networks, curare is also sold by traveling mestizo traders (*regatones*) who have agreements on either side of the border. Peruvian curare is very expensive and has become even more dear since the *regatones* managed to secure a major portion of the commercial trade. North of the Pastaza, the exchange rate set by the *regatones* from Montalvo is one tablespoon of Peruvian curare for twenty peccary hides. It is true that this quantity is enough to coat around sixty darts, and many more if mixed with local *tseas*.

Until the 1930s, the only weapon the Achuar used for war or hunting big game was the palm-wood spear, *nanki*. In effect, the blowgun is never used to kill humans nor does it seem that it was in the past. Around two meters in length, the spear was used in close combat, for thrusting and for throwing. Its sharp point was carved into a triangle or diamond (*patu nanki*) or made from a piece of metal. Specially forged for indigenous use, spearheads were the object of intense trading in upper Amazonia. The throwing spear was used for hunting and generally had a barbed point and a slight swelling at the other end of the shaft to provide a better grip. Since World War Two, the spear has been replaced by firearms, which fulfill the same function and are much more efficient.

At present, the Achuar find themselves at the intersection of two areas of diffusion of two distinct types of firearm. The more archaic model is the muzzle-loading shotgun (*akaru*, from the Spanish *arcabuz*), manufactured by craftsmen in the Sierra of Ecuador. This small-gauge muzzleloader is obtained from the Shuar in exchange for blowguns or curare. In the 1950s, on the other hand, single-shot (16–calibre) breechloaders began arriving, brought into Ecuador via Peruvian Achuar who were in contact with the Whites. With a few exceptions, all Achuar men own some type of gun. As a rule, the muzzleloader (*shuar akaru*) is used in the western part of the territory, where regular exchanges with the Shuar have been kept up, while the breechloader (*mayn akaru*, "Maynas shotgun") is the preferred weapon of the eastern Achuar, who maintain contacts with Peru. The Achuar rightly regard the breechloader as more trustworthy and efficient than the muzzleloader, for the latter is often capricious. In a downpour, the muzzleloader may well fail at the crucial moment if either the primer or the powder has gotten wet. It also takes a long time to reload, which is a serious handicap under enemy fire or when the first shot has dispersed a troop of monkeys or a horde of peccary. But, if the shot is suited to the game, there is little difference between the impact of the two weapons, since, in hunting as in warfare, the weapon is always fired at close range.

The main drawback of firearms is that ammunition is obviously hard to come by when one is far from a commercial center and entirely dependent on unreliable circuits of exchange. The *regatones* trade one 16–calibre cartridge manufactured in Ecuador for one peccary hide, that is to say that the cartridge just pays for itself, and then only providing it is not used on game that is smaller or devoid of commercial value. The muzzleloading shotgun turns out to be more economical to use, even though there, too, one must make sure of a dependable supply of shot, powder, and primer through a Shuar trading partner living close to the frontier of colonization. Given this state of affairs, the Achuar prefer to use their shotguns for warfare and to economize on ammunition so that they will not be wanting for firepower if their house is attacked. Furthermore the preferential use of shotguns for fighting entails an unexpected counterreaction to their use in hunting. The consumption of all game shot with a gun previously used to kill a human is prohibited by a taboo called *kinchimiartin*. Violation of this dietary prohibition is supposed to result in extremely painful abdominal pains and diarrhea. In other words, once a man has assassinated an enemy, he can no longer use his shotgun for hunting; he must therefore try to exchange it for another, preferably through a middleman who will pass it along to some remote area where the reasons for the transfer are not known. Any murder thereby puts a gun temporarily out of circulation (or several guns when a volley of shots has been fired) and deprives the murderer of the use of his firearm for hunting.

The consequences of this suspension are not dramatic, for, while the Achuar immediately grasped the immense superiority of shotguns over spears in warfare, the advantage they afforded in hunting was not conclusive. The blowgun is well suited to hunting in dense forest: few animals cannot be easily killed with poisoned darts. Some informants mention the use, in a dim past, of bows and arrows for both hunting and warfare. Although the Achuar have a term for bow, *tashimiuk*, its use among the Jivaro in general must have been extremely marginal, for chroniclers and ethnographers rarely refer to its presence. The Achuar say that the bow fell into disuse as a result of the increasing numbers of blowguns, which were reputed to be more efficient and easier to handle. This is plausible, contrary to some claims (e.g. Ross 1978: 12); the blowgun is a multi-purpose weapon that can be used to equally good effect on large ground-dwelling mammals (except tapirs) and small arboreal game. The critical factor here is the toxicity of the poison and not the range of the weapon or its impact. If they are coated with good-quality curare, two darts embedded in a peccary's side are enough to cause death within five or ten minutes. Now an experienced hunter can blow half a dozen darts in a few seconds, thus riddling the animal before it can escape.

The density of the vegetation and the reduced range of the muzzleloader also impose the same close range as the blowgun. A shotgun is of no real advantage then unless the curare on hand is of poor quality or when actually pursuing the animal. In effect the blowgun is unwieldy when coursing game through tangled underbrush. In the first place, it is so long that it is difficult to extend rapidly for firing when needed. In the second place, it is quite heavy and must be grasped with both hands, close to the mouthpiece; when firing from a horizontal position, the entire weight of the weapon rests on the hunter's arms. The blowgun is much easier to use in a vertical position, that is, for shooting game in a tree directly overhead; by tilting his head back the hunter shifts the weight of the weapon to his whole body. The other obvious advantage of the blowgun for shooting arboreal game – especially troops of monkeys – is its absolute silence, which enables the hunter to wound several subjects fatally before they become alarmed, which is obviously not the case with a firearm, as the first shot sends the animals scattering. Comparing the respective merits of the two weapons, and bearing in mind the endemic scarcity of ammunition, it appears that one of the only decisive advantages of the shotgun over the blowgun is its greater ease of handling when taking aim in the course of pursuit. But that is precisely one of the situations that the Achuar try to avoid, the whole art of hunting being precisely in the silent approach which brings the hunter within firing range of the still animal. Clumsy hunters startle the game and therefore do not have time to take careful aim; a gun then becomes indispensable if one is regularly obliged to shoot on the run.

Besides their active weapons, Achuar also employ passive weapons, traps. These are not used frequently, however, and are reserved particularly for exterminating the rodents that get into the gardens. For killing agoutis there is an ingenious device called a *chinia*, that is placed on the animals' regular run. Two low rows of pickets form a narrow passage covered by a heavy log suspended from a vine. When the animal enters the trap, it runs into a stick laid across the path, which releases the vine, letting the log fall on the animal. A different trap (*washimp*) is used to catch armadillos as they emerge from their hole. Over the exit, the Achuar place a cone made of wooden slats and stuffed with liana and leaves. The animal becomes entangled in the stuffing and all its efforts to free itself only block the entrance to the den, thus cutting off any retreat.[2] Lastly, in order to bring down jaguars and ocelots at point-blank range without damaging their pelts – to obtain the best price – some Achuar build covered enclosures fitted with a sort of drop-gate. Then a dead chicken is dragged along the ground to lay a trail, after which it is left in the enclosure as bait; when the cat enters the cage, it springs the trap, and the gate drops. With the exception of the *washimp*, traps take time to set, and the Achuar justify their lack of interest for such devices by saying they prefer the pleasures of the hunt to the tedious job of trap-building.

The Achuar hunter's preferred sidearm is the dog, and dogs can be rightly included in the same category as weapons, for they are trained to kill certain animals that they hunt. But in Achuar society, as in all Jivaro groups, dogs enjoy a special status which is not reducible to their instrumental hunting function. On the one hand, the dog is the epitome of the domesticated animal (*tanku*) and forms an integral part of the social world of the house in which it lives. The dog contrasts with poultry in that it is not raised for eating, and with pets in that its socialization is part of its essence and not the product of chance. On the other hand, the dog is taxonomically classified with felines and certain other carnivorous mammals whose natural ferociousness and taste for raw meat it is supposed to share. Situated at the crossroads of nature and culture, the ambiguous status of the dog makes it a vehicle for a type of savagery that humans have redirected to social ends. But the dog stands at another intersection as well, since it is one of the points of articulation between male and female praxis.

The first paradox of the domestic socialization of the dog is that this animal, whose main function is to collaborate with hunters in capturing game, is placed entirely in the care of women. Dogs are valuable possessions, the enjoyment of which is an exclusively female prerogative, even though men are sometimes allowed to use them, with their wives' permission, as a medium of exchange in some transaction. In this event, the woman expects her husband to procure her a replacement in the course of a later transaction; in no case may a man make use of a dog without the explicit consent of its mistress. Dogs are transmitted from mother to daughter and may be exchanged among women, particularly at the birth of a litter. There is no scarcity of dogs, and each Achuar woman has anywhere up to a half dozen; but despite their numbers, they are highly valued and can fetch a very high price. It is not unusual for a very good hunting dog to be exchanged for a large dug-out canoe or a breechloading shotgun. As is the case of many other of the Achuar's material or symbolic possessions, a dog's value is measured in terms of the distance of its place of origin, regardless of its visible physical qualities. As a result, the Achuar value Shuar dogs highly and vice versa, while both the Achuar and Shuar set great store by Canelos dogs. As for the inaccessible purebreds that the Achuar have on occasion glimpsed in the company of missionaries or soldiers, these are regarded as miraculous animals that enable the Whites to perform all sorts of wonders.

Dogs are valued as much for their intrinsic qualities (looks, fecundity, intelligence, nose, fight. . .) as for their actual hunting abilities. We were surprised to note that sometimes dogs that never went hunting – because they belonged to a widow, for instance – were still highly praised by other women. This is because each dog has its own personality that can be corrected and shaped by the training it is given. The personalization of dogs can be seen first of all in the fact that, of all domesticated and pet animals, it alone receives a proper name, just like humans. It will usually be named for its color, for a physical trait, or for a quality it either possesses or that one would like it to acquire: for instance: *wampuash* (kapok) if the dog is white, or *makanch* (fer-de-lance) if it is aggressive and fast on the attack.

Dogs sleep on a slat bed beside their mistress' *peak*, they are raised, fed, and disciplined by her with the same care as she takes with her children. When indoors, the dogs are tied to their bed with leashes made from *shuwat* bark or chambira palm fibers so that the different co-wives' packs do not fight. If the pups are taken from the mother, they are breastfed and later handfed pieces of chewed manioc (*namik*), and everyone shows them a great deal of affection. And yet young dogs must be housebroken and taught to obey, an endeavor usually crowned with success; it is unusual for a grown dog to steal food or make a mistake in the house. They must also be toughened for their future tasks; to this end pups are thrown into the cold river at dawn and made to swim until they are on the verge of exhaustion.

Dogs are fed a cultural diet, that is one resulting from an elaborated culinary preparation. They are rarely given raw meat; when they receive part of the prey they have hunted, it is most often the legs roasted over the fire. As a rule, the Achuar feel it is preferable to deprive a dog of meat in order to make it a more aggressive hunter. Their staple diet, served in tortoise shells, is comprised of mashed manioc and sweet potatoes, sometimes accompanied by papayas. When a household has twenty or so dogs, as is often the case, not a negligible part of the garden's daily production goes for their feed. That is one factor that tends to be neglected in most input–output studies devoted to Amazonian societies, but it must be taken into account when analyzing the productivity of an economic system (see Chapter Nine). And finally, like humans, dogs must observe dietary taboos; some of the animals forbidden them may not be eaten by humans either, like the opossum – which is reputed to transmit mange – while others are fatal only to dogs, like *ayachui*, whose flesh is much appreciated by the Achuar.

When a dog falls ill, it is a serious matter, and the indigenous pharmacopeia contains several remedies for the different ailments that can affect canines. In the garden itself, the Achuar usually grow a variety of *piripiri* and one *maikiua* especially for making canine drugs. The first medicinal plant is a sort of all-purpose panacea, while the second is a powerful hallucinogen with the same properties as the *Datura* decoctions used by the men. This narcotic enables the dog to enter into contact with the disembodied twin world and to develop the knowledge and skills that will make it a good hunter. Although the shaman is not called to attend dogs, magical healing techniques are employed that are analogous to those used on humans for benign ailments not attributed to shamanic action. In both cases, the Achuar postulate that physiological disorders may be caused by deliberate curses or by fortuitous combinations of unfortunate circumstances. In these cases, certain conjuring techniques may be used; these are stereotyped and known by everyone, but their effectiveness increases when they are performed by men and women whose control of the symbolic conditions of praxis is universally recognized. It is the hunted animals that are responsible for the spells affecting dogs, and to undo the spell one must ask a woman with experience in raising dogs. She blows over some rainwater held in a cupped leaf and tells the sick dog: "I sweep away the peccary's spell"; this formula should be repeated using the name of each type of game that might be at fault.

Like most sectors of Achuar daily life, raising dogs requires not only technical learning, but a very sophisticated knowledge of magic as well. Here again *anent* incantations play a fundamental role, and a woman whose thriving garden attests to her *anentin* faculties will also quite certainly own a pack of dogs that is the envy of all around. There are *anent* for every critical situation in the life of a dog, with particular emphasis on the birth of a litter. When the litter is large, it is important for the mother to be able to suckle them all, and many *anent* are designed to increase the milk supply. These *anent* metaphorically assimilate the bitch to animals reputed for their nursing capacities, like the tapir. As in gardening, these *anent* are addressed either directly to the interested subject, in this case the dog, or to a tutelary spirit called *yampani nua*, "Yampani woman." Yampani is the mistress of dogs and she allows women to use them; therefore the fate of her wards depends to a large extent on the relations one entertains with her.

Yampani is a very secondary spirit, but she has one original characteristic which throws some light on the ambiguous status of the dog in Achuar society. In mythology, Yampani is a man who was changed into a woman by his *sai* (sister's husband and bilateral cross-cousin for a male Ego) in order to satisfy a sexual drive that had no other outlet; in effect, in those times women did not yet exist. In the myth, then, affinity exists before the object that actualizes it; the exchange is posited as a virtuality even before women were engendered by the copulation of two affines. The first woman was a trans-sexual man, then, and it is doubtless no accident that she presides over the fate of the canine race. Owned, raised, fed, and handled by women, the dog is used by men in a death-dealing activity from which women are excluded, but in which they are nevertheless present through the agency of these domesticated creatures they have delegated to their husbands. The qualities of the dog are closely linked with the skills of its mistress; the woman therefore plays a fundamental, albeit indirect, role in the hunting process. Because of the deviation of his original gender, Yampani is perfectly suited to symbolize the compenetration of male and female roles that characterizes the use of the dog in Achuar society.

Dogs are ranked according to the completeness of their hunting skills, that is by the type of ground game they are capable of pursuing and eventually killing. The lowest – at least in terms of exchange value – are those that hunt only small rodents such as agoutis (*kayuk*) or acuchis (*shaak*). Next come dogs that will also attack armadillos and medium-sized rodents, such as pacas (*kashai*). Much more valued are dogs that do not hesitate to course peccaries, to cut an animal out of the horde, and especially to go for the throat. The white-lipped peccary is in effect extremely dangerous because, when attacked, it fights with its back to a tree. In order to get at the throat, the dog must avoid the sharp tusks which inflict wounds that are usually fatal. At the summit of the canine hierarchy, the Achuar place those stouthearted dogs that tackle ocelots and even jaguars, treeing the cat for the hunter to shoot. To increase the fighting spirit of this elite corps, they are given the entire carcass of the cat they have helped hunt. As they do not usually get meat, they see this feast as a reward and thereby become extremely ferocious when they spot a feline.

Each of these categories can be regarded as a stage in the dog's training, although very few possess the natural qualities to reach the level of ocelot dog. A young novice is broken in by letting it run with the existing pack, where it learns by imitation to follow a trail and to stalk prey. Both men and women have a hand in the training, for, if the latter do not bear arms and are never in on the kill, they nonetheless continue to handle their dogs until they are unleashed on the prey. When a man decides to go hunting with the dogs

– which is not always the case – he invites one of his co-wives, usually the one with whom he has just spent the night, to follow him into the forest with her pack. The dogs are kept leashed by their mistress until her husband begins looking for tracks. The pack is then unleashed, and when a dog picks up a scent, it begins to bay; its mistress urges it on, calling its name and repeating "*sik, sik, sik*," the standard formula for setting a hound on a trail. As soon as the dog has struck off, however, the woman's role ceases; she remains where she is, and it is the man who takes over the task of tracking, running after the pack. In hunting terms, one could no doubt say that the man plays the role of the huntsman while to the woman falls the task of whipper-in.

And yet male–female complementarity continues up to the moment the animal is brought to bay, by the pooling of their respective symbolic masteries. During the entire chase, husband and wife each sing *anent* to stimulate the dogs and to protect them from being attacked by the hunted animal. The following examples illustrate the two respective registers.

Woman's *anent*:

My *patukmai* dog (*repeat 3 times*), now that dawn is breaking, I set you on the
    game (*repeat*)
Now I make you bay (*repeat*)
Having unleashed you, I make you follow your prey (*repeat twice*)
Having taken you along this way, my *patukmai* dog, I saw the dawn when I
    unleashed you (*repeat*)
My little black person, I have taken you along with me (*repeat*)
                      (Sung by Mamays, a Rio Kapawientza woman)

Man's *anent*:

My *patukmai* dog (*repeat 3 times*), being just this way (*repeat*), Why now?
    (*repeat*), why do you come here? tell me now (*repeat*)
While going along (*repeat*), I go and no one can beat me
My *patukmai* dog (*repeat*), while going along (*repeat*), I go terrifying the animals
My little dog (*repeat*), you too being wildly brave, you who know how to take
    risks, you are going to follow the scent, crying "*jau, jau, jau*"
While going along (*repeat*), you tell me, "when I go this way, you steal my wife."
                      (Sung by Taish, a Rio Kapawientza man)

In these two cases, as in the majority of *anent* designed to encourage dogs set upon game, the hound is metaphorically assimilated to a "*patukmai* dog," that is a bush dog (*Speothos venaticus*). These carnivores are reputed to hunt in packs, to be pugnacious and to display tactical intelligence; despite being small, they rarely fail to kill peccaries or even small tapirs.

The Achuar maintain that the *Speothos* is practically untamable and that its wild qualities can be domesticated only by their purported transfer to the hound. The hound hunts for its masters, while the bush dog always hunts for itself. Like all *anent*, without exception, these, too, are addressed directly to one particular individual, in this case the leader of the pack. The complementarity of the gender roles is clearly marked here: the woman sings of the initial impulse that sets the dog on the scent of game, while the man elaborates on the parallel between the daring of the pack leader and himself, which founds their complicity.

Bringing ground game (peccary and large rodents) to bay is the only hunting technique in which the pack is useful, though not indispensable. The Achuar do not always hunt with dogs, then, and there was a time, before the arrival of the Spanish, when they did not even know such things existed. Moreover, we have seen that a started animal is hard to hit with a blowgun and that it is better to use a spear or a shotgun to bring it down before it runs to ground. When a hunter sets out with a pack, he therefore almost always takes along a shotgun to hunt peccaries whose tracks he has seen some time before. Achuar dogs are not pointers; so, while they are good for cutting a peccary out of the horde, they are a drawback when it comes to arboreal game, as their barking alarms the monkeys or birds. If he does not want to use his gun – to save ammunition – and if he has seen no recent signs of ground game, a man will leave his wife and his pack at home and go off on his own with his blowgun. Predictably enough for a dispersed residential pattern, the Achuar do not engage in battues or collective hunts, and each man scours the forest on his own behalf and that of his household.

When they do not take their dogs, the Achuar either lie in wait for game or stalk it. In both cases, the best times of the day are early morning and late afternoon, when both the diurnal and nocturnal animals are all either just waking up or just settling down. When hunting far from the house, it is imperative to start at the crack of dawn in order to be on site at the opportune moment. The hunter leaves at first light and usually stays out the whole day, unless he is fortunate enough to kill a peccary early in the day; if he kills only a monkey, a bird, or an armadillo in the course of the morning, he will continue hunting in the afternoon in order to complete his bag. Any hunting at dusk, on the other hand, is done in the vicinity of the house and is more pre-bedtime entertainment than an efficient hunting technique. The presence of a dwelling usually frightens off big game (peccaries and monkeys), and so it is rare to kill anything larger than the small birds the Achuar call *chinki*. This is almost a game of skill, a chance to practice with unpoisoned darts which sometimes provides a few morsels of meat for dinner if there is no game in the house.

The hunter usually chooses to lie in wait for game near the house or in the garden, particularly when he wants to kill nocturnal rodents – especially agoutis and acuchis – that prey on the crops. In the preceding chapter we saw that the garden works something like a giant lure and that certain trees are even left standing when the swidden is cleared because their fruits, although not eaten by humans, attract birds. The little huts where the chickens are shut up at night are also regularly visited by carnivorous predators such as ocelots or tayras. But the animals taken on these nocturnal raids are counterbalanced by the chance of killing an ocelot, the pelt of which brings a good price – equivalent, for instance, to forty 16-calibre cartridges. In a way, the chickens act as bait in the same way as the garden, but to different ends. Lastly, even though lying in the garden waiting for birds contributes little to the daily diet, it has a very important pedagogical function. In effect, as they practice shooting the sparrows that come into the garden, boys still too young to accompany their father into the forest learn the rudiments of the art of hunting. Waiting for hours on end by the same tree, they gradually learn several cardinal virtues: to stalk noiselessly, to observe animal behavior, to be quick and accurate with a blowgun.

Sometimes a hunter will lie up in the forest near places he knows to be frequented by game, by saltlicks for instance, of which there are few and the locations are well known by the Achuar. They say that each species uses a different lick and thus the salt holes are distinguished according to the game that uses them. The most commonly watched are peccary licks (*paki weeri*, "peccary salt"), those frequented by howler monkeys, and by piping guans. But watching a saltlick yields highly unpredictable results, and the Achuar would rather stake out places where they have spotted signs of recent animal activity: peccary wallows, deposits of howler-monkey dung at the foot of a tree, a recently disturbed water hole, freshly dug agouti holes. To flush out agoutis, the Achuar do a perfect imitation of their cry ("*kru, kru, kuru, kru*"), sometimes using a triangular game call made of balsa wood or *pitiu* bark. As a rule, lying in wait for game is not considered very exciting, and if we may hazard a metaphorical analogy with our own cultural world, we would say that the Achuar do not regard it as much sport.

The most difficult type of hunting, the one that requires perfect mastery of the art and affords the most pleasure in return, is tracking or stalking. Indispensable for shooting arboreal game, in the absence of dogs stalking is an absolute necessity for killing ground game as well. Tracking is generally a prelude to stalking large ground game, for it is rare to stumble upon an animal without having previously seen prints. Each type of ground game leaves a characteristic spoor: peccaries, for example, almost always use the same runs. When a hunter comes upon one of these trails or some forest that has been furrowed by feeding peccaries, he must interpret the signs accurately if he is to identify which way they went, how much time has elapsed, and how many animals there were. Armadillos, agoutis, deer, and pacas also leave characteristic signs, but these are harder to spot since these animals do not move in bands. The hunter must therefore be on the alert for the slightest clue: a few prints barely visible in the dead leaves, a broken branch, fresh dung. Arboreal game do not produce tracks to be followed, but they still leave signs of their passage here and there on the ground. Howler and woolly monkeys, for instance, eliminate strong-smelling urine which impregnates the foot of trees they have visited.

In most cases, however, tree game is located by ear: either by the sound signal characteristic of the species, or, in the case of monkeys, the noise they make moving through the treetops. Auditory location is therefore fundamental to this type of hunting, and a hunter always keeps his ears open and moves as noiselessly as possible. This is why the Achuar almost never go hunting if it looks like rain, since the noise of the raindrops on the leaves is loud enough to drown out all other sounds. When the game has been located by ear, either fortuitously or after a period of tracking, the stalking begins. This is the most delicate phase, when experienced hunters show their superiority. Not only must the hunter make no sound in order to get as close to the game as possible – keeping downwind if he is stalking ground game – but he must also foresee every reaction if the game is startled.

The essence of the art of hunting, in Achuar society as in many other groups (Laughlin 1968), lies not so much in a man's skill at arms as in his knowledge of the ways of the animals he hunts. What distinguishes an old hand from a clumsy novice is not that the former is a better shot with the blowgun – even the anthropologist eventually learns to shoot – but that he has had the time to become a remarkable ethologist; and he will put his knowledge to good use when tracking and stalking. He can do a perfect imitation of the distress calls of young or of a female in heat of any species to draw the parents or males within range of the blowgun. He can instantly pick out the dominant male from a troop of howler monkeys and kill it first; in this event, the females stay "to mourn him," as people say, and are easily slain. He takes care not to shoot wild sows that are pregnant or accompanied by young, in order to preserve the reproductive potential of a peccary horde. As curare is not instantaneous, he also foresees the likely reactions of a wounded animal: the white-lipped peccary will turn and can charge, the collared peccary goes to ground in a hole or hollow tree, the paca makes for water, the woolly and capuchin monkeys tear out the dart and flee, while the howler freezes onto a branch.

It is not always possible to retrieve an animal shot with curare: birds can summon their last resources to fly off only to drop into some impenetrable thicket, monkeys remain clutching their branch, rodents go off to die in some inaccessible burrow, pacas sink straight to the bottom of the river. The Achuar say that a wounded animal that has not been retrieved goes to see its species shaman to be doctored. When a fresh kill bears the signs of an old wound, they discuss – in great detail – the way the scar has healed, the probable gravity of the internal lesions and the consequences on the subject's activity.

When the slain animal has finally been retrieved, it must still be taken home. If the hunter is alone and the animal large (a peccary or large monkey), he will pack out the whole carcass after having summarily gutted it, tying it onto his back with a chest band. Each species of mammal is secured with liana according to the portage technique that best suits its morphology. Birds are immediately plucked and slung over the shoulder, generally tied with a slipknot around the neck. When a woman is present, she will put the catch in her *chankin* carrying basket to give the hunter full freedom of movement. In the case of big game, the wife will begin dismembering it on site so that it will be easier to carry in the basket, each piece being wrapped separately in leaves. As a rule, both men and women possess extraordinary physical stamina; it is not unusual to see a hunter return with two white-lipped peccaries weighing some 30 kg apiece on his back, accompanied by his wife with a third in her basket. When the kill is too heavy for one man to bring back alone, he will hang some of the game and return for it later.

When a polygamous man goes hunting with one of his wives, she will share the game upon their return and distribute equitable portions of the meat to the other co-wives; if she is young, she will generally save the best morsels for the *tarimiat* ("first wed") as a sign of respect. When a man has gone hunting by himself, he lays the game without a word by the fire of the *tarimiat*, or sometimes the wife with whom he spent the preceding night. It is she who will distribute the meat and then immediately grill a few pieces, if it is a big animal, for her husband when he returns from the bath that concludes the hunt.

As mastery of hunting techniques comes essentially from knowing the ways of game, a boy's cynegetic education consists first and foremost of getting to know the animal kingdom. From the time they are very young, boys learn to recognize the various animal behaviors from listening attentively to the interminable hunting stories that make up the bulk of men's conversation. When game is brought home, the children gather round the animal and thoroughly examine its internal and external anatomical features, guided in their observation by the adult commentaries. In addition, nearly every Achuar home has wild animals that are kept as pets, and the children certainly learn a lot about their reactions by playing with them. Finally, when boys reach the age of ten, they occasionally go hunting with their father, thus receiving irreplaceable practical lessons. And so even before they begin to handle weapons, boys are already familiar with the animals they will be hunting. When we were identifying birds from colored plates, we were amazed to see that ten-year-old boys were able to recognize and name hundreds of species, imitate the calls and describe their behavior and habitat.

At first target practice is a kind of game usually played with a small pea-shooter. Boys use this toy, called a *papaisnanku*, or miniature blowguns, made by hollowing out bamboo stalks, to practice on tiny living targets: butterflies, beetles, frogs. Later, under the supervision of an adult male, they are allowed to shoot at a fixed target with an old blowgun. Towards the age of twelve, the father makes his son a genuine blowgun, a smaller version of the adult model. This is the already very effective weapon the young boy uses when he goes hunting with his father or practices alone on birds in the garden. Learning to manage a shotgun comes later, though the fascinated, distant observation of its workings begins at an early age. We never heard of a child having been accidently killed or wounded by playing with a loaded firearm left within reach. Lastly, although a young man rarely takes part in a raiding party before he marries, his apprenticeship as a hunter surely prepares him to become a good warrior. From tracking to dealing with a gun, all the techniques he learns from his father for hunting animals will one day be used to kill men and to avoid being killed by them.

In the center of its garden, each house assumes the right to make use of the forest around it, the exclusiveness of this right diminishing as the distance from the house increases. As a rule, the foraging territory of an isolated residential unit forms a concentric space around the clearing. Each household "assigns" rough boundaries – materialized by streams and rivers – around the territory it exploits for its own use and which its head has marked with a network of hunting trails (*charuk*). Given the highly dispersed pattern of settlement, there is no competition for hunting grounds among Achuar domestic units, and it is very unusual that any one household's exclusive foraging zone be less than forty square kilometers.[3] The techniques of exploiting the forest space vary with distance from the house. The area of intensive gathering, used by all members of the domestic unit, extends for a kilometer or two around the garden. This is still a highly socialized space only a short walk from the house; everyone knows each leaf and blade and is free to roam without constraint. Beyond this familiar circle, into which big game rarely ventures, begins the hunting zone proper. It stretches for a radius of some five kilometers around each house and remains the privileged domain of the men. Women never venture into this zone without their husband, and children are not allowed to enter without adult supervision. Whereas the perimeter of the forest adjacent to the garden is still a domestic space in which ordinary home life continues, the hunting space is a strictly male world.

Beyond the forty or fifty square kilometers to which a hunter normally confines his activities begins a sort of no-man's land, extending a variable distance depending on the density of settlement. Hunting territories rarely touch; in the interfluvial biotope, where the houses are widely dispersed, intervening forest zones are often vast. This is especially true when they act as a buffer zone between the territories of two endogamous nexus that are actively feuding (see Descola 1981a: 626–34; 1982b). These several hundred square kilometers go unexploited and constitute temporary refuges for migratory fauna having at one time come under serious cynegetic pressure. Crossing these no-man's lands, one is immediately struck by the abundance of game, which has become so unaccustomed to human presence that it has lost its fear of people. These interstitial regions act a bit like game reserves, allowing the animals to reproduce in optimal conditions in a milieu free of human predators. However much pressure hunters may put on local game, the presence of such natural reserves ensures, in the middle term, throughout the whole of the Achuar territory a dynamic equilibrium between the animal populations and those who hunt them.

As we will see when we look at hunting returns, it seems that forty or fifty square kilometers are quite enough to guarantee a steady supply of food for one household with one or two hunters. Ross (1976: 231) suggests a figure of 100 kg per square mile for the annual amount that can be harvested from the Amazonian bird and mammal populations without endangering the animals' rate of reproduction; an average Achuar hunting territory would thus tolerate an annual take of at least 6,000 kg of potentially edible animal biomass, or roughly 15 kg of game per house per day. It is true that this is a fairly arbitrary way of estimating a territory's carrying capacity, since it is the end result of a series of rough approximations, beginning with the initial estimate of the composition of the Amazonian animal biomass advanced by Fittkau and Klinge (1973: 2, 8), on which Ross bases his calculations. But these data do suggest a very general order of magnitude, which gives an idea of the relation between the size of a single-family hunting zone and its theoretical returns in terms of game.

In the course of a day's hunting a man covers, on the average, between thirty and forty-five kilometers, some ten of which are used to cross the intensive gathering space going and coming. Because the terrain is rugged, the true distances covered are two or three times the distance as the crow flies, and a man generally takes over an hour to get from the house to the hunting zone proper. When the house stands at the center of the foraging territory, the hunting trails, *charuk*, spread out in a multi-directional network that has the ramified appearance of a snowflake (Fig. 34). In the morning, the hunter sets out in a specific direction, taking the main trail that leads to where he has decided to hunt. He then explores the area, making a wide loop that brings him back to the trail. He does not work to a grid, then, but follows a series of curves, scouring three or four square kilometers of terrain during the day, or around a tenth of his total territory. Although much less productive than a collective battue, the technique of the fragmented individual rounds has the advantage of spreading the take evenly over the entire hunting grounds. Moreover, given the mobility of most kinds of animal, the chances of encountering game are statistically identical each time a hunter strikes out in a different direction.

Often a house is not in the center of its hunting territory, and to get there the hunter must go a certain distance. This happens, for instance, when an isolated domestic unit has remained in a locality for twenty years or so, building two or three successive dwellings; the immediate surroundings have been intensively exploited during this time and, since the house has not moved, the foraging space has had to. It also occurs when two or three households form a small residential cluster, and each foraging zone must be clearly separated from the others (Fig. 34). Since, in this case, the time needed to reach the hunting grounds is much greater, the Achuar build a small hunting cabin inside the territory, which allows them to spend a night or two away from the main house. The hunting cabin is much more than a temporary shelter (*panka jea*) such as are thrown up in a few minutes when it becomes necessary to spend the night in the forest. It is a veritable miniature house, equipped with a few cooking utensils and sometimes surrounded by a small manioc garden to ensure minimal rations. Located between five and twelve kilometers from the main house, this cabin is called

34. Spatial organization of hunting grounds

an *etenkamamu* (literally: "that which is in the center"); the name is a good indication of its function: in effect, the cabin puts the hunter on location, at the very heart of the game zone.

In areas of traditional scattered settlement, approximately one household in four has a permanent hunting cabin used on a regular basis. Our informants told us that this was an old institution that had nothing to do with the dual-residence system adopted by the Peruvian Achuar in order to spend part of the year in the forest cutting exotic woods for mestizo logging concerns (Ross 1976: 96). Karsten already mentions the Jivaro's use of hunting cabins in the 1930s, that is before they had come under any neocolonial pressure (Karsten 1935: 79). The Canelos Indians have a somewhat analogous institution, but it was widely adopted no doubt in response to social and ecological constraints stemming from the proximity of the colonization frontier. The Quichua, who live in sometimes very populous villages, practice the system of *purina* (literally: "long walk"), which means moving for periods of several weeks to another house sometimes located a great distance from their habitual settlement (Whitten 1976: 17 and passim). As nearly all the game has vanished from around the original villages, these forest houses enable the Canelos to hunt and to gorge on meat for at least part of the year. *Purina* is typical of the seasonal double-residence model, since the entire household usually moves *en masse* from one site to the other.

Unlike the Quichua, the Achuar use their hunting cabins only for short stays, the living conditions being less comfortable than the nearby main house. The *etenkamamu* is never more than a day's walk from the house; there is therefore no real discontinuity between the familiar forest space immediately surrounding the house and the territory where the cabin stands (Fig. 34). An ordinary stay at the *etenkamamu* usually lasts two or three days; the hunter is accompanied by one of his wives, who carries the food and baggage. In a polygynous household, the hunting cabin provides the couple with the private space for intimacy so lacking in the large communal house. Moreover, just as a man takes care to rotate his favors equitably among the beds of his various wives, so he invites them in turn to accompany him hunting. By spending the night in the heart of the game zone, a hunter can devote more time to beating the bush than if he had to spend several hours reaching the hunting grounds. Thus, if he comes upon some peccaries the first day and manages to kill a couple, he still has the next day to relocate the horde and bring down a few more before they have drifted too far.

When the head of a household decides to give a drinking party, for instance to ask kinsmen to help him make a clearing, he must plan not only for an abundant supply of manioc beer, but also a lot of meat so that he can give his guests a lavish reception. If he has an *etenkamamu*, he will go out just before the party for four or five days of intensive hunting. Every day the game he brings back is smoke-cured by his wife on a green-wood platform built over the fire. When properly cured, the smoked meat will keep for ten days, especially the haunches of venison and the loins. Beyond that time it begins to be infested with maggots, which are gotten rid of by a thorough boiling. But the Achuar do not like their meat gamy, and it rarely comes to that.

Sometimes the cabin also enables the hunter to exploit an ecological niche different from that of his usual residence. This is the case in the border zones between an interfluvial and a riverine biotope. An Achuar from the interfluve hills will have an *etenkamamu* close to an *aguajal* or a stretch of river, and will thus be able to catch large fish, gather turtle eggs, or hunt the peccary attracted each year by the fruits of the *Mauritia flexuosa*. Inversely, a household living in a swampy, mosquito-infested region will sometimes build a cabin in the nearby hills in order to take occasional advantage of a healthier climate; their stay will also provide an opportunity for intensive monkey hunting, since the Achuar claim that these animals prefer interfluvial forest to riverbanks. This mutual complementarity is not restricted to natural resources: if the hunting cabin has an adjacent garden, the pedological differentiation will be used to sow crops that grow badly in the soil by the main house. For instance, a riverine household will plant *timiu* fish poison around its *etenkamamu* in the hills, while inversely an interfluve household will plant *masu* fish poison in the alluvial soil of its riverine cabin.

Lastly, the *etenkamamu* often serves as an advance post in the search for a new house site. As he ranges the furthest corners of his hunting territory, sometimes as far as two days from the main house, the hunter is always on the lookout for potential new locations for the household. If he decides to concretize his plans, the family head uses the hunting cabin as temporary housing while establishing a pioneer garden (*jakenta*), the first stage in moving house. The *etenkamamu* palpably increases the ordinary radius of residential relocation by extending it to more than one day's walk from the old house. Here the hunting cabin becomes a stopover facilitating the transport of cuttings and the surveillance of the newly planted crops in a particularly distant pioneer garden.

A fine-grained analysis of the ecological and technical constraints weighing on hunting returns is no simple task. Given its highly uncertain character, this activity lends itself less well than gardening to statistical generalizations. All hunters are not equally skilled, the availability of game may fluctuate according to slight changes in the weather, or differences between the ecological niches being exploited; lastly, the rate of hunting is very irregular, for it can be lowered by a number of contingencies (illness, war, visits, house construction, clearing . . .). The only way to analyze the potential efficiency of hunting, keeping in mind all the possible variables, is to study a sample of the bag taken by a group of representative men. Our sample was comprised of all animals killed by 21 hunters, distributed among fourteen different domestic units, in the course of 84 individual hunting trips that break down into 74 whole-day outings (average duration: 8 hr 30 min) and 10 half-day trips (average duration: 4 hr). We eliminated all animals not killed while actually hunting, that is birds and small rodents shot occasionally in the garden. These 84 individual trips were studied in a systematic survey covering 181 days, split into 14 periods of 12 days and spread over all of 1977 and part of 1978 in order to encompass the whole range of climatic and seasonal fluctuations. The domestic units sampled were located in a variety of distinct ecological niches (eight households in the interfluvial habitat and six in the riverine habitat) and included hunters whose skills varied widely. We were unable to balance perfectly the number of trips made for each habitat and so, in this sample, the interfluve households are better represented than those in the riverine biotope (58 trips to 26).

Figure 35 details the global take, thus showing the overall average of hunting returns in the two biotopes. One fact is immediately obvious: the limited number of game species actually killed on a regular basis. Whereas the Achuar regard some 150 distinct species of mammals and birds as edible, only 25 are represented in this table of 106 game items. And even then one of these (the tapir) is normally taboo and others (5 species of small bird) contribute very little mass to the overall take. The daily meat intake therefore comes from a very limited group of game. This table only confirms the observer's subjective impression when, day after day, he saw the same animals turn up on his plate: peccary, toucan, curassow, trumpeter, woolly and capuchin monkey, and agouti.

Inasmuch as the Achuar do not specialize in any one type of game and seek to kill all reputedly edible animals (*kuntin*) without distinction, it would seem that the species most commonly killed are also those most commonly encountered on each forest trip. It should be noted in passing that these species are in the main diurnal, while the mainly nocturnal animals seem to be much better protected from hunting. Obviously no

general conclusions can be drawn from this table concerning the proportional composition of the animal biomass in the Achuar region, but it
does indicate that there is no scarcity of peccary, woolly and capuchin
monkey, toucan, and curassow. The Achuar are particularly fond of the
flesh of these animals, and, despite the heavy hunting to which they are
subjected, there is no sign of their becoming rare. The Achuar case is not
unique, moreover; in the home range of the Siona-Secoya of Ecuadorian
Amazonia, woolly monkey and curassow, in that order, also comprise the
bulk of game captured (Vickers 1976: 140).

In terms of numbers taken, birds are the game item most frequently killed
on a hunting trip (43.5% of total take), with the two species of peccary far
behind in second place (25.5%). But analysis of the bag in terms of the
quantity of meat brought back clearly shows peccary well ahead of all other
species, for they alone account for more than half the total weight of the 106
kills shown in the table. Furthermore, bearing in mind that the tapir is
taboo and is therefore an abnormal game item, and that the black caiman is

Order of frequency	Game type	Bag	Kills	Total kg/ game type	% of total kill/ game type
1	Birds	15 toucans 15 misc. curassows 7 trumpeters 7 misc. birds (weighing less than 500 g) 2 tinamous	46	64	43.5
2	Peccary	14 white-lipped 13 collared	27	626	25.5
3	Primates	11 woolly monkeys 6 capuchins 1 white-headed saki 1 moustached tamarin	19	141	18.0
4	Agouti		5	35	4.7
5	Squirrel		4	3	3.7
6	Armadillo		2	22	1.9
7	Tapir		1	242	0.9
8	Gray brocket deer		1	18	0.9
9	Black caiman		1	49	0.9
Total			106	1200	100.00

35. Order of frequency of kills per game type

rarely killed and when it is only the tail is eaten, it seems that we may subtract the 291 kg of these two kills from the total game weight, thereby bringing our data more in line with a series of normal kills. In the adjusted table, then, peccary represents over two thirds of the meat procured by hunting. Once again the observer's subjective impressions are confirmed by the figures, for in the vast majority of the Achuar households where we spent at least a week, we had the pleasure of dining on peccary.

The Achuar's exploitation of two differentiated ecological niches raises the problem of differential hunting returns as a function of biotope. The first approximation, as we see in Fig. 36, shows no difference in the average number of kills per trip between the interfluvial habitat (1.27 kills) and the riverine biotope (1.23 kills). But the list of game killed in the two cases is not the same. The proportion of peccary with respect to total take is equivalent (25.6% and 25%), which is fairly predictable given that these animals range over vast areas and do not stick to one specialized habitat. Peccaries may be more concentrated in one place at one time of the year, particularly when stands of *Mauritia flexuosa* are in fruit, but no part of the Achuar territory suffers from their absence. It may be, nevertheless, that riverine zones see more peccaries than do interfluvial areas, as some Achuar claim, but our sample was probably not broad enough to show this. In any event, the key factor in hunting peccary is much more the skill of the hunter and his dogs than the nature of the biotope, since it was always the same men who brought back peccary, regardless of the ecological conditions obtaining in their hunting grounds.

The disproportion in monkey kills is greater, with a percentage over twice as high in the interfluvial biotope as in the riverine habitat. The contrast is

	Interfluve	Riverine
Number of kills/trip		
trips	58	26
kills	74	32
kills/trip	1.27	1.23
Main species killed (% of total)		
peccary	25.6	25
primates	21.6	3
birds 1 kg and over	31	50
Probability of encounter/trip for main species (%)		
peccary	32	30
primates	27.5	11.5
birds 1 kg and over	39.5	61

36. Differential hunting returns per biotope

even more striking in reality, for all the monkeys killed by riverine inhabitants were brought down on hunting trips to the neighboring interfluve hills, which would seem to confirm the Achuar's general view that there are many more monkeys in the rugged interfluvial forest than in the alluvial plains.

The disproportion changes camps in the case of birds, since they are clearly the predominant game killed by riverine households (50%), especially the different species of curassow. Once again the data confirm indigenous observation, in the event that guans and tinamous are particularly fond of the terraces along big rivers.

One important conclusion can be drawn from these results: households in the riverine biotope do not enjoy greater access to *socially edible* game than do interfluvial households. In effect, all species of mammals that are well adapted to the riverine habitat but scarcer and sometimes invisible in the interfluve (tapirs, capybara, sloth, red brocket deer) are under a permanent dietary taboo. This prohibition is sometimes violated in the case of tapir, but the practice is not systematic enough to be significant; moreover, occasional transgressions are just as likely in the interfluve, where the tapir is not unknown (that is even where the one on our list was killed), as in riverine areas. The only legitimately edible animals that are typically riverine are the gray brocket deer (*suu japa*: *Mazama simplicornis*); these shy, fleetfooted nocturnal animals are rarely encountered and weigh less than a white-lipped peccary. The black caiman is hard to hunt: it too is nocturnal and has to be shot with a gun, preferably from a canoe, and tends to sink straight to the bottom when hit. In short, the potential adaptive advantage the riverine Achuar derive from the presence of a specific fauna of riparian mammals goes practically unexploited. This observation already provides the beginnings of an answer – as far as hunting returns go, at least – to the question of why the whole Achuar population is not concentrated in the riverine habitat: from the standpoint of the availability of animals defined as game, there is practically no difference between the two biotopes.

Seasonal and climatic fluctuations certainly have more effect on hunting returns than do differences between the biotopes. The "woolly-monkey-fat season," which extends from March to July, does not entail a manifest increase in the numbers killed, but appears only in a very relative rise in the mean weight of certain animals taken. Alternatively, long periods of heavy rain have a nefarious effect on hunting, for they keep the men at home and drive the peccary hordes away. It is during such periods, which can last two or three weeks, that a family may run out of meat, especially since the rivers are in flood, which usually makes fishing impossible. But these calamities are the exception and rarely occur more than once a year. Inversely, low-water season (*kuyuktin*), from November to January, causes a sharp drop and even a halt, in hunting in the riverine habitat. The reason is not that game is any less available, but that fish are more available, making for such abundant catches (by line or spear) that the Achuar find it much easier to fish than to hunt.

Of the eighty-four trips listed in our Figure 36, nine (10.7%) were complete failures, while thirty-four (40.5%) resulted in at least two game items. But, to place this success rate in context, it must be said that, within the sample, it was almost always the same hunters who came home empty-handed – youths for the most part – and the same who brought back a peccary each time out. But the discrepancy in skills has less incidence on the domestic economy than one might think, for the poor hunters were usually young sons-in-law living with their fathers-in-law. It was the latter exper-ienced, mature hunters who provided the bulk of the game for the household. Moreover, all those who returned empty-handed were armed with blowguns, and they justified their failure by saying that the animals they had shot managed to get away because their curare was no good. We never heard a hunter state that he had not encountered any game on his trip; our own modest experience confirms that it is hard to spend a whole day in the forest without the opportunity to fire a single shot. One may therefore legitimately suppose that all the empty-handed hunters could have brought back at least one animal had they had good curare or a shotgun. In short, there is no doubt that the Achuar region still abounds in game and that, when the population density is less than one inhabitant per square kilometer, both the interfluve and the riverine zones of the Amazonian rain forest harbor important game potentials. We are far from the situation of generalized scarcity of game that certain authors present as the norm for the whole Amazon Basin (see especially Gross 1975; Ross 1978).

Average hunting returns for the overall sample are quite honorable: 14.2 kg live weight per individual trip, of which 65% is effectively edible (according to Nietschmann's method of calculation, 1972: 74), making 9.2 kg of meat. If we subtract the tapir (taboo) from the total mass in order to obtain a list of game that is closer to real life, we still have 11.4 kg (live weight) of game per individual trip, or 7.9 kg of edible meat. And this total does not include small birds and rodents shot regularly in the vicinity of the house. In comparison, the average return of Achuar hunters is twice that of Yanomami hunters, who bring back between 3.5 and 5.5 kg of game per individual day-long trip (Lizot 1977: 130). If one accepts the figure of 15 kg live weight of game per household per day as a very rough estimate of the carrying capacity of an average-sized territory, it is evident that, with a dozen kilograms per trip, the Achuar take only a fraction of the game potentially available, since they do not go hunting every day.

The rate of hunting is in effect very erratic and depends on a number of factors. The principle motivation for a man to go hunting is the lack of meat or fish in the house. The main meal, eaten in the late afternoon, is not regarded as complete without meat (*namank*) or fish (*namak*); garden produce is thought of more as a side dish (*apatuk*, literally: "accompaniment") than a main dish. And yet manioc is the paradigmatic food; when the head of the house urges a guest to eat, he generally says "eat some manioc" (*mama yuata*), even if the plate set before him is heaped with venison. The Achuar's pronounced taste for meat is censured in both speech and table manners. Moreover, it is unseemly to give one's guest to understand he is being served a choice morsel, since, for the Achuar, to stress the value of a gift is tactless in the extreme. But institutionalized understatement must not be allowed to conceal the difference of status between manioc and meat: the former is the staple of biological survival, while the latter is the major contribution to well-being. The Achuar maintain that without meat life is hardly worth living, and their vocabulary – like that of many other Amazonian societies – makes a clear distinction between "I'm hungry" (*tsukamajai*) and "I'm hungry for meat" (*ushumajai*). As women are supposed to have little control over their drives, they are the ones who feel this desire most keenly; and venison, in particular, is what they "crave" when they are pregnant. In this light it is easy to see that it is a man's imperative duty never to leave his wives and children without meat or, for want of meat, fish.

Task	Men	Women
Manufacturing and handling weapons, traps, and calls	+	
Training and handling dogs		+
Tracking, stalking, and killing	+	
Carrying the kill	+	+
Butchering game with fur		+
Plucking birds	+	+
Washing internal organs		+
Skinning and curing hides	+	
Distributing the meat		+

37. Sexual division of labor in hunting

Following a very good hunt, a man may go a week without hunting, or even more if the fishing is good; alternatively, if he comes home empty-handed, he will go back out the next day. When a hunter returns with a meagre catch (e.g. a small fowl), he will usually go out again the next day or the day after in order not to leave his wives without meat for more than a day or two. And finally, in preparation for a party, a man may hunt on four or five consecutive days in order to lay in a supply of smoked meat. The decision to go hunting is taken individually and apparently free of all outside pressure, but behind their air of indifference, the men keep an ear tuned to the women's quarters; no man wants to run the risk of displeasing his wives for too long by depriving them of the game they so love.

If men claim they go hunting to satisfy their wives, the women also beat the forest with their husbands. In roughly two out of three cases, a man goes hunting with one of his wives, and they play what is far from a negligible role in this activity. The table of the division of hunting tasks (Fig. 37) clearly shows that women are directly involved at all points of the operational sequence, with the exception of tracking and the actual kill. Moreover, their material and symbolic control over the pack is a key element of this labor process, something that the Achuar explicitly perceive as such. The women's knowledge of zoology and animal ethology is almost as extensive as the men's, and we feel justified in saying that the complementarity of the genders in Achuar society is just as much a part of hunting as it is of gardening. The fact should be stressed, for the role women play here is exceptional for hunter societies, whether in Amazonia or in other parts of the world. It is of little importance here that this female collaboration was probably not aboriginal, since it is linked to the arrival of the dog, for there is, in any event, no technical necessity that the packs should be handled by the women. In other words, the presence of Achuar women in hunting is not the product of a material constraint, but an illustration of the very special kind of relations the genders entertain in their practice of nature.

Gathering

The area of intensive gathering, that is the five or six square kilometers of familiar forest immediately adjacent to the garden, is covered throughout the year by the women and children who go there to collect a wide range of natural resources. Because there is such a huge diversity of cultigens and an abundance of fish and game, gathering wild foods is primarily a topping-up activity designed more to vary the daily fare than to replace it. Nevertheless it is hard to subscribe to Karsten's claim that gathering produces insignificant returns for the Jivaro because of the small numbers of fruit-bearing forest plants in this part of upper Amazonia (1935: 116). One could even easily become convinced of the opposite by consulting Figure 38 (probably incomplete), which lists fifty-two wild species of trees and palms whose fruit or heart are consumed on a regular basis by the Achuar.

Most of the above species fruit only in *neretin* season, which runs from December to May; but during this time there is no Achuar household that does not eat some gathered fruits every day. A dozen species head the list because they are the ones most often encountered in the forest and most appreciated for their taste: *achu, apai, chimi, iniaku, kunkuk, mata, mirikiu, naampi, pau, pitiu, tauch,* and the various *Ingas*. Although many of these gathered fruits are eaten boiled or roasted rather than raw, they enjoy the same status as garden fruits, that is they are not served with the meal but are regarded as special treats, something like candy in our culture. As such, wild fruit is consumed mainly by women; the men like to feel that having a sweet tooth is below their dignity. Nevertheless, they are not above tasting, and are particularly fond of *kunkuk* palm fruits, the extremely oily flesh of which appeals to the Achuar's pronounced taste for animal and vegetable fats. The entire household is familiar with every leaf and blade of the intensive gathering zone, and the exact location of every fruit or palm tree is well known. It is unusual to find an area of five to six square kilometers with less than a dozen different species, and so the near forest serves as a sort of orchard-annex to the garden.

Throughout the fruit season, the women and children pay regular visits to the main trees and palms in their domain, a good excuse for a little walk to break the monotony of everyday chores. They usually set out in the early afternoon, when the gardening is done, in the direction of a particular tree or clump of trees. The Achuar keep a close eye on the time each plant comes into fruit and on the ripening fruits; gathering walks are therefore organized so as to make regular rounds of all the species, of the individuals within a single species, and of the different moments in the productive life of a single subject. The fruit is either beaten out of the tree with a long pole or picked off the ground; if the tree is climbable, the small boys swarm up to shake the big branches and pick what they can reach. The harvest remains modest, though, and it is unusual to bring back more than two or three kilograms of fruit.

The forest species exploited for food do not all grow in the intensive gathering zone, particularly as some must be destroyed in order to be eaten. This is true of all palm trees, of which the food part is the heart: they are

Vernacular name	Botanical name	Edible part
achu	*Mauritia flexuosa* palm	fruit and heart
apai	*Grias tessmannii* (Lecythidaceae family)	fruit
awan	*Astrocaryum huicungo* palm	juice of fruit
chaapi	*Phytelephas* sp. palm	fruit
chimi	*Pseudolmedia laevigata* (Moraceae family)	fruit
iniaku	*Gustavia* sp. (Lecythidaceae family)	fruit
iniayua	*Maximiliana regia* palm	heart
ishpink	*Nectandra cinnamonoides* (Lauraceae family)	dried flowers
kamancha	*Aiphanes* sp. palm	fruit
katiri	unidentified palm	heart
kawarunch	*Theobroma* sp. (Sterculiaceae family)	fruit
kinchuk	*Phytelephas* sp. palm	fruit
kinkiwi	*Euterpe* sp. palm	fruit
kuchikiam	*Herrania mariae* (Sterculiaceae family)	fruit
kunapip	*Bonafousia sananho* (Apocynaceae family)	fruit
kunchai	*Dacryodes* aff. *peruviana* (Burseraceae family)	fruit
kunkuk	*Jessenia weberbaueri* palm	heart and fruit
kupat	*Iriartea exorrhiza* (?) palm	fruit
kuyuuwa	unidentified palm	heart
mata	*Astrocaryum chambira* palm	fruit
mirikiu	*Helicostylis scabra* (Moraceae family)	fruit
munchij	*Passiflora* sp.	fruit
naampi	*Caryodendron orinocensis* (Euphorbiaceae family)	fruit
pau	*Pouteria* sp. (Sapotaceae family)	fruit
penka	*Rheedia macrophylla* (Guttiferaceae)	fruit
pitiu	*Batocarpus orinocensis* (Moraceae family)	fruit
sake	*Euterpe* sp. palm	fruit
sampi	*Inga* sp. (legume): 6 separate species	fruit
sekut	*Vanilla* sp. (Orchidae family)	fruit
sharimkuit	*Marilea* sp. (Guttiferaceae family)	fruit
shawi	*Psidium* sp. (Myrtaceae family)	fruit
shimpi	*Oenocarpus* sp. palm	fruit
shimpishi	*Solanum americanum* (Solanaceae family)	fruit
shuwinia	*Pourouma tessmannii* (Moraceae family)	fruit
suach	unidentified tree	fruit
sunkash	*Perebea guianensis* (Moraceae family)	fruit
taishnumi	unidentified tree	fruit
takitki	*Cupania americana* (Sapindaceae family)	fruit
tanish naek	*Paragonia pyramidata* (Bignonaceae family)	fruit
tauch	*Lacmella peruviana* (Apocynaceae family)	fruit
terunch	unidentified tree	fruit
tserempush	*Inga marginata* (legume)	fruit
tuntuam	*Iriartea* sp. palm	heart and fruit
uwis	unidentified tree	fruit
wampushik	*Inga nobilis* (legume)	fruit
wayampi	unidentified tree	fruit
wishiwish	*Protium* sp. (Burseraceae family)	fruit
yaasnumi	*Pouteria camito* (Sapotaceae family)	fruit
yantunma	unidentified tree	fruit
yurankmis	*Physalis* sp. (Solanaceae family)	fruit
yutuimias	*Sabacea* sp. (Rubiaceae family)	fruit
yuwikiam	unidentified tree	fruit

38. Forest plants used for food

chopped down with an ax to get at the edible part at the base of the fronds. When these palm trees also bear fruit and grow fairly close to the house, the Achuar tend to spare them so they can be beaten regularly. Extracting palm hearts is a sideline, as it were, something done in the course of hunting or fishing expeditions, or trips into the forest for other specific operations (gathering thatching fronds, cutting house timbers, making a canoe. . .). Sometimes, though, an expedition is organized especially to cut palm hearts, when the palm trees grow in thick enough stands, as in the case of the *achu* and *tuntuam*. The Achuar are very fond of this food, which they eat raw or made into soup, sometimes enriched with the palm grubs that make their home there. While the tract of forest immediately around the house is the site of systematic programmed gathering by women and children, they do not limit themselves to this familiar space. When the circumstances are favorable, time out is taken anywhere to stop and pick up fruits or cut down a palm tree.

Natural plant resources have many uses. Certain wild fruits are employed in making special delicacies, particularly those of the *shimpishi*, the *apai*, the *achu*, and the *kamancha*, which make tasty fermented drinks when mixed with manioc beer. Other species, such as the *taishnumi* and the *yaasnumi* are explicitly thought of as "survival trees" because they are fairly plentiful and their fruit can be eaten if one is lost in the forest. These are the first trees that children and the greenhorn ethnologist learn to recognize. Furthermore, the Achuar regard a half dozen mushrooms as edible; women and children eat them boiled. These rather insipid cryptogams are a metaphor for the female sexual organ, and men are not supposed to ingest them. It must also be pointed out that forest fruits are not only destined to be eaten, since at least thirty species are used in preparing, for example, medications, cosmetics, poisons, and pottery glazes. In terms of edible plant output, the forest is a complementary economic space of very secondary importance compared to the garden. But the variety of forest products added to the variety of cultivated products no doubt makes all the difference to the Achuar between simply having enough to eat because food is abundant and the rare luxury of being able to enjoy a broad range of tastes and dishes.

Gathering is not limited to plants, and several types of animal and animal product fall within the scope of this activity. Under the heading of edibles come some thirty species of small amphibians (mainly frogs), six species of shellfish (five crabs and one crayfish), three species of snail, three species of coleopter larva, two species of bee larva and one of termite larva, two species of ant, one species of beetle, four species of annelid, the honey from three species of bee, and this does not include the eggs of several species of bird and four species of turtle. Catching frogs, shellfish, snails, and worms is left primarily to young boys and is more a game than a systematic subsistence activity. This is their chance to play the hunter, which they do particularly well when they swagger home and hand over their catch for little sister to cook. When she has boiled up the frog or the handful of crayfish, the young siblings gravely take their meal, mimicking the table manners of the adults. Adults strongly encourage this behavior, which is a prelude to the roles the little boy and girl will play in the future.

Although the children take part in the mass frog hunts during *puachtin* season, these are organized by the adults; the same holds for the collection of honey and various kinds of grubs. The three types of Achuar honeybee have no sting and they nest in hollow trees; it therefore suffices to smoke them out and then collect their strong full-flavored honey (*mishik*). Custom dictates that a tuft of hair should be left in the hollow so that the insects will rebuild their hive in the same place. Bee and termite larvae are collected by cutting the nests into slices to make a cross section of the cells; each slice is held up to the fire and then shaken over a banana leaf so that the larvae fall out; these are eaten boiled. But the Achuar treat *par excellence*, the delicacy offered to special guests, are the three species of beetle grubs (*muntish, charancham*, and *puntish*) that live in the heart of palm trees. These thumb-sized larvae are eaten boiled with a soup of palm hearts, or raw and still alive. In the latter case, it is good form to bite off the head and then slowly suck out the gelatinous fat of which they are almost entirely composed.

Several seasons are named after the type of animal product harvested at that time; this temporal coding is a fair indication of the symbolic importance the Achuar attribute to certain natural resources. The most significant of these are *weektin*, "flying-ant season," in August, and *charapa nujintri*, "water-turtle-egg season," from August to December. These two resources are not of the same order of importance, for the flying ants are all caught at one time and thus provide only a fleeting treat, whereas *charap* turtle eggs are available over several months. Inversely, *week* ants are found throughout the whole Achuar territory, while *charap* turtles are confined to the lower stretches of the Pastaza. With the exception of the few households established on the banks of the lower Pastaza, going to gather turtle eggs entails a canoe trip of at least ten days, an expedition that can rarely be made more than once a season. In fact though, only the riverine Achuar with direct access to the Pastaza flood plain use this resource in a systematic fashion. To reach the sand bars where the turtles lay, the interfluve Achuar would have to travel long distances through remote, hostile territories, something few are disposed to do. Still, for those who are able to exploit them, the deposits of turtle eggs guarantee an abundant and durable supply of animal protein. With a little luck and skill, a one-week trip can yield between two and three thousand eggs; these are then boiled and smoked, which preserves them for up to ten weeks.

The capture of the two species of edible land tortoise (*kunkuim*: *Geochelone denticulata* and *tseertum*) may also be included within the definition of animal gathering, for these slow, awkward beasts are not classified as "game" (*kuntin*). It is therefore permissible for the women to catch them and club them to death with a machete, just as they would a crab or a domestic fowl. What differentiates game hunted by men from animals picked up by women is, in effect, the inability of the latter to defend themselves or to run away. Tortoises rarely weigh over 5 kg, and their rather tough meat does not make them a particularly sought-after resource. Alternately, the big water turtles, *charap* and *pua charap* (*Podocnemis unifilis*), are regarded as genuine game; they may be killed only by men, who hunt them from a canoe using either a shotgun or spear. The meat is particularly delicate, and individuals may weigh up to 70 kg. But water turtles can be hard to kill, and it is somewhat easier to catch them on land than in the water.

If we except *charap* turtles and their eggs, which concern only a few riverine households, the contribution of gathering to the daily diet must be defined in terms of quality rather than quantity. Sometimes, however, gathered products may play a larger-than-normal role if they are sought out systematically. This is what happens notably in households in which there is no hunter, either because the head of the house is away on a visit or because he is seriously ill or wounded. In these cases, the women must find some way to procure game substitutes on their own, by the intensive exploitation of all available animal resources. Under these conditions, the gathering of grubs, shellfish, and frogs becomes a highly productive daily activity. It is important to know that a single palm tree may harbor up to 80 palm-beetle grubs, which provide 700 or 800 g of edible material containing more protein than most game. The exploitation of palm-beetle grubs may at times take on the appearance of veritable grub farming; all one has to do is to chop down a large number of palm trees and then wait for the *tsampa* to lay their eggs in the decomposing hearts. One then makes the rounds of the various palms in order to keep an eye on the grubs and collect them when they reach the right size.

The women's ability to replace, in certain circumstances, the product of hunting with that of gathering or line fishing entails one important consequence. While a man temporarily without a wife has no alimentary autonomy, for it would be unthinkable for him to work the garden and to make his own meals, a woman temporarily without a husband can manage quite well on the produce of her garden and the small animals she and her children collect. The exclusive mastery of the forest space on which the men pride themselves is, in the end, fragile; if the women venture into the jungle only to perform apparently subordinate tasks such as gathering, handling the dogs, and carrying game, once they are there, they are still less dependent upon their spouse than he on them.

Affinal nature

Gathering is an easy-going, totally profane activity: a good excuse for having some fun or taking a pleasant walk, its outcome at the end of the day is of little matter. There is no shame in returning from a gathering trip with meagre spoils. Hunting in the depths of the rain forest is a far more risky undertaking in which no man can be sure of success. Sometimes the game stubbornly eludes the hunter, sometimes the trail that was so fresh inexplicably vanishes, sometimes the well-aimed dart misses its mark. Skill is necessary, but skill alone is not enough to neutralize chance, and know-how is effective only when combined with the fulfillment of two series of conditions. Some of these conditions constitute the mandatory prerequisite for hunting in general, while others, of a more contingent nature, are indispensable to the individual success of each trip.

If he is to be an effective hunter, a man must live in good intelligence with the game and with its guardian spirits, following a principle of complicity more or less openly at work in all Amerindian hunting societies. These spirits are called *kuntiniu nukuri* (literally: "game mothers"), and they are seen as exercising the same kind of control over game as the Achuar exercise over their children and their domestic animals. The tutelary consortium of "game mothers" is made up of several categories of spirits quite distinct in both morphology and their behavior towards humans. The three main varieties of game protectors are Shaam, Amasank, and Jurijri. The Shaam look like ordinary men and women, but they carry their heart slung across their chest (*hectopia cordis*); they live in the most impenetrable reaches of the forest and in the big swamps. Amasank is usually represented as a lone man hunting toucans with a blowgun; his favorite dwelling is the forest canopy or hollow trees. Jurijri is a bearded white man, a maneater and polyglot who lives with his family under ground. His clothes are reminiscent of the conquistadores' costume – morion, corselet, boots, and rapier –

and his all-consuming mouth is in the back of his neck, concealed by his hair.

Despite their apparent dissimilarity, these spirits share one basic ambiguity: they are at once the hunters and the guardians of the animals they hunt. They behave towards wild game as humans do towards their domestic animals. Like the Achuar, who kill and eat their domestic fowl while protecting them from animal predators, the spirits kill and eat game while protecting it from human predators. If men are to hunt, a *modus vivendi* with these "game mothers" must be found and a tacit accord agreed.[4]

An Achuar may harvest game from the multifaceted herd controlled by its tutelary spirits only provided he obeys two rules: first, he must take with moderation – that is, never kill more animals than he needs – and second, neither he nor his family must show disrespect for the animals he has killed. While a close examination of the anatomical features of the game taken is an integral part of hunting pedagogy, children must not be allowed to play with the remains. Likewise, the hunter must not throw the skull of big game to the dogs, it must be kept in the house, stuck into the thatch of the roof. The skulls festooning the roofing strips under the eaves attest of course to the skill of the head of the house, but their function goes well beyond that of simple trophy. By sparing game the desecration of being thrown to the hounds and by reverently keeping part of its skeleton, the hunter is not far from paying the hunted animal a form of last respects.

The duty to respect the slain animal becomes clearly emphatic in the case of the woolly monkey, which stands out as the paradigmatic game animal. Hunters unable to control themselves, because they are too boisterous or too eager, run the risk of seeing the roles reversed, that is of themselves being devoured by the Jurijri, the cannibal spirits especially responsible for watching over monkeys. The game master's fury at men who make a laughing stock of his subjects is a classic figure of Amerindian hunting lore, which the Achuar relate in the form of a cautionary myth.

The myth of Amasank and the Jurijri

Once several hunters from an Achuar household returned from a hunting trip with many woolly monkeys they had shot with their blowguns. As the women smoked the monkey meat, they made fun of the animals. They were young and foolish and amused themselves by bombarding each other with the dung they cleaned from the intestines. Amasank came upon the scene; he took one of the women aside and remonstrated with her: "Why are you making all this fun of my sons instead of eating them normally? This is not a game and one mustn't be disrespectful of woolly monkeys." Then Amasank announced to the woman that that very night the Jurijri would come to punish the women for their shameless behavior towards the monkeys: "If you would escape their wrath, hide in a hole and stop up the opening with a termite nest." The woman told the others of the threat to the household, but no one believed her and they all made fun of her. When night fell and everyone was asleep, the woman heard the voices of the Jurijri in the distance. She tried to wake the others by making a racket, pinching them, burning them with a firebrand, but to no avail. So she ran and hid herself in her hole, which she plugged with the termite nest as she had been advised. The Jurijri devoured all the members of the household. The next day, having been spared, the woman went to tell their kinfolk what had happened and they decided to organize a party to exterminate the Jurijri. Following the trail of blood the Jurijri had left, they came to a big hollow tree which obviously served as their dwelling place. But the men became terrified and returned without having struck a blow. The most powerful shamans were then called, and in particular *unturu* (the fasciated tiger-heron) (*Tigrisoma fasciatum*), to put an end to the problem. When they had come to the Jurijri tree, the shamans built a fire into which they threw chili peppers to smoke out the cannibal spirits. One by one, as the Jurijri left their lair, they were exterminated by the Achuar, intoxicated with rage. Amasank too was in the tree, but he left through the top and gained the neighboring tree, using his blowgun as a bridge, and by this ploy gradually made away. The Achuar saw him and wanted to kill him as well, but he called out that they should spare him, relating his role as messenger before the Jurijri massacre. And they let him go.

We see then that killing and eating monkeys are not bad in themselves, but making fun of their remains is a serious fault, sanctioned by a terrifying punishment. Certain hunters express doubt that such a punishment could occur nowadays. Nevertheless, all Achuar concur that the "game mothers" have numerous less spectacular means of retaliation, the most commonly cited being snakebite. The condemnation of overzealousness and excess are leitmotifs of the moral teachings transmitted in myth, and we see them here. Hunting is certainly permitted, but the "game mothers" are there as a continual reminder that it must not be a thoughtless act.

In principle, the "game mothers" can be seen only by shamans, whose helpers they are, and in the company of several other kinds of spirits who have no effect on animals. And yet it is generally felt – by shamans and laymen alike – that familiarity with the "game mothers" is of no advantage to shamans in hunting. In the cynegetic sphere it seems that direct shamanic intervention has more to do with amplifying the hunter's technical skills than with charming animals and their tutelary spirits. To this end, shamans have the ability to enhance the drawing power of certain hunting charms, a capacity they employ on behalf of those who request it. Likewise, they can blow magic darts into a hunter's mouth and larynx to strengthen his wind for the blowgun. In both instances, the shaman's intervention is assimilated to a normal cure, and should be remunerated accordingly. In one case that we witnessed personally, a reputed shaman who had done a healing session to restore a hunter's "wind" did not hesitate to demand a feather crown, *tawaspa*, in payment for his services. Now this prestigious ornament – which he was indeed given – is an Achuar's most valuable possession, and its exchange value far exceeds that of a shotgun.

Shamans are also supposed to exercise over animals an indirect influence of a purely negative order. It is claimed, in effect, that they are able to use their magic to make traditional peccary runs disappear from enemy territory, which in turn drives the hordes out of the area. And so, as is often the case in Amerindian cultures, the Achuar shaman controls certain magical components of hunting, but such privileged access is never converted into personal advantage. As a matter of fact, the best hunters are rarely shamans, and all the more because the shaman's practice often causes him to lead a life that is incompatible with intense hunting activity.

If shamans derive no hunting benefits from their familiarity with the "game mothers," it is no doubt also because direct complicity with hunted animals is deemed more important than the invocation of their tutelary spirits. From the standpoint of the symbolic conditions of practice, the situation is the inverse of that found in gardening, since it is Nunkui's intercession that permits friendly relations with her plant children. Hunting is a never-ending effort to charm animals, and the outcome is never sure. The hunter must establish with each game type a personal bond of unity that he must cultivate throughout his lifetime. For instance, a man must never eat the representative of a game type he has killed for the very first time. The relationship between the hunter and the individuals of that species is still tenuous, and were he to eat the slain animal, it might endanger future complicity. This type of game, disgusted by such behavior, would do its utmost in the future to avoid the paths of the tactless hunter.

Each game species can be represented as a collection of interdependent individuals, for each has a leader who, *primum inter pares*, watches over the fates of the others. This animal, called *amana*, is slightly larger than the rest and is so adept at concealing himself in the forest that it is exceptional to see him. It is the "game *amana*" (*kuntiniu amanari*) much more than the "game mothers" that are the hunters' privileged interlocutors. Although ordinary humans cannot see them, the tutelary spirits and the game *amana* can be contacted by means of *anent*. There are series of *anent* for every situation encountered in the course of hunting, from the songs that help pick up a broken trail to those that make a dead monkey frozen onto a high limb relax its grip and fall at the hunter's feet. As the following examples show, these hunting *anent* are even more esoteric than the gardening songs.

Little brother-in-law (*repeat 3 times*), let's see now where I am going to blow you
    to pieces
Little brother-in-law (*repeat*), little *shuni* man is on your trail, little brother-in-
    law (*repeat*), wherever am I going to shoot you
Brother-in-law of mine, I am going to kill you in some far-off land
Wherever am I going to shoot you (*repeat 3 times*), little woolly monkey, let's see
    now where (*repeat*) I'm going to shoot you (*repeat 4 times*).

This *anent*, addressed to the woolly monkey, presents the animal as a
brother-in-law (*sai*, which, for a male Ego, corresponds to the category:
sister's husband, wife's brother, father's sister's son, mother's brother's
son), according to the convention used in all game incantations. The song is
meant to attract a troop of monkeys, and the hunter compares himself to a
shuni caterpillar to show that he is as determined a tracker as this animal,
which is notorious for clinging.

Little *amana* (*repeat 3 times*), if both of us are *amana*, what are we going to do?
    (*repeat twice*)
I become as dark as the Shaam (*repeat*)
Little *amana*, send me your children (*repeat 3 times*)
On this very plateau, may they go *chururui*, may they go *waanta* as they rustle
    the branches (*repeat twice*)

As in the preceding song, this *anent* asks the woolly-monkey *amana* to cause
a troop of his fellow game to approach the hunter, who presents himself as
an *amana*, too, that is a prominent man. The metaphor evoking the Shaam
refers to the fact that these guardian spirits of game leave their home at
nightfall. *Chururui* evokes the stereotypic fear-cries of the woolly monkey, while *waanta* imitates the sound of the swaying branches.

Little brother-in-law (*repeat twice*), bend down to me the *wachi* bamboo (*repeat*),
    you yourself (*repeat*), I raise you up (*repeat 3 times*)
Of the little hook, of the little dart (*repeat*) how could the flight deviate? (*repeat 3
    times*)

This is another *anent* addressed to a woolly monkey qualified as brother-in-
law; it should be sung mentally as the hunter shoots his blowgun at the
animal so that the dart will go home and not miss. The hook metaphor
evokes the fact that the dart should hook into the monkey's flesh so that he
cannot tear it out.

Little brother-in-law (*repeat twice*), little sharpshooter (*repeat*), your little sisters
    (*repeat*) coming this way (*repeat 3 times*) would go *waanta, waanta*
They come (*repeat 3 times*) upon waking, going *chiankai* (*repeat twice*)

In this *anent*, the alleged affinal relationship is carried to the extreme, since the brother-in-law woolly monkey's sisters are also possible spouses for the hunter. He must therefore convince the animal that it has to hand over its sisters to this man for a necessarily deadly union. In this loaded exchange, there being no counterpart, the alliance assumes the full weight of a tragic wager.

Most hunting *anent* are addressed to two privileged brothers-in-law, the woolly monkey and the toucan, which, as we have seen, are also, after the peccary, the animals most commonly killed by the Achuar. They are also emblematic of family life: it should be recalled that the toucan is the model for married life, while the woolly monkey is reputed to respect scrupulously the prescribed marriage with his bilateral cross-cousin. According to the Achuar, the *Lagothrix* is the only monkey that does not mate *more ferarum*, but face to face, like humans. Generally handed on from father to son or, more rarely, from father-in-law to son-in-law, hunting *anent* are as jealously guarded as gardening *anent*. But the relationship that is established with nature's beings is quite different in the two spheres: the woman keeps her plant children under the illusion of a relationship of consanguinity, while the man keeps up a constant barrage of affinal charm. Hunting *anent* therefore have a cajoling, wheedling tone that is not found in gardening *anent*, the garden being a world of kindred beings devoid of the touchy feelings that the man must take care not to ruffle in dealing with allies.

Above and beyond knowing a vast repertory of *anent*, owning various types of charms is useful but not indispensable for hunting. Some of these charms are used to reinforce the hunters' capacities, while others serve to attract animals. Among the first is the *tsepeje*, a parasite found in the toucan's eye and which, according to the Achuar, considerably improves the bird's visual acuity. It is said that some hunters place this parasite in their own eye so that, by a phenomenon of symmetrical transfer, the toucan will not see them as they approach within shooting range. Drinking a mild drug made from the *chirikiasip* tree increases the hunter's skill with a blowgun and is standard practice before a big hunt.

The nature of animal charms varies greatly. Toucan lice (*temaish*) must be taken from under the wings and tail of the slain bird while it is still warm and placed in little containers then sealed with wax. These charms, which the hunter carries in his sack (*uyun*) when he goes hunting, are supposed to attract all types of game. If the toucan lice are to remain effective, the hunter must observe the same dietary prohibitions as for making curare: all salty or sweet foods are forbidden. This taboo clearly suggests that hunting instruments have a degree of autonomy with respect to their users, whether they be agents of destruction (curare) or of attraction (*tsepeje*). A sweet-water dolphin's tooth is used primarily as a fishing charm, but its inherent effect can be amplified to affect all game if a shaman blows on it using a special procedure. An extremely potent charm, for both hunting and fishing, is made by pounding achiote with the heart and brain of an anaconda, the most versatile predator of the animal kingdom. In order to acquire the intrinsic qualities of their direct rival, men paint their faces with this mixture before setting out to hunt. The use of face paint – with or without anaconda viscera – is an indispensable preparation for any forest trip, for the designs a hunter paints on his face are used to charm animals by disguising his human nakedness.

The most prized charms, which are the hunting equivalent of the *nantar* gardening stones, are bezoars called *namur* (literally: "testicles"). Just as each main cultigen has its own Nunkui stone, so there is an appropriate *namur* for each type of game; these valuable charms are handed down from father to son, just as the *nantar* are transmitted from mother to daughter. One original feature of *namur*, which differentiates them from *nantar*, is that these bezoars operate according to a sort of chiasmus between their origin and their destination. For example, bezoars found in fish are considered to be hunting *namur*, while those found in birds and mammals are considered to be fishing *namur*. All bezoars are not necessarily *namur*, and it is obvious that the gravel found in gizzards is not interpreted as anything out of the way. For a *namur* to be judged to be such, the circumstances in which it will be found and the way it is to be used must be announced in a dream, just as for *nantar*. These *namur*, which the hunter carries on his person, tightly sealed in a small container, are endowed with a life of their own of the same kind as Nunkui's stones, but without the latter's vampirical properties. Like the other charms, the function of *namur* is to attract game and fish and to facilitate their capture.

The ability to charm game, their *amana*, and their tutelary spirits by means of the various techniques examined above is the general condition for being a hunter. Not all men possess equal mastery of this condition, however. Among men, as among women, there are certain individuals who are particularly *anentin*; the Achuar usually explain the success of these individuals by their eminent skill in controlling the symbolic field of hunting. But above and beyond this general prerequisite, each trip has its own conditions, which must be refulfilled time and again. The most important of these special conditions is the premonitory dream. Inasmuch as dreams are journeys, in the course of which the soul comes in contact with the souls of the spirits, nature's beings, and so on, the interpretation of each dream provides a clear outline of the conditions under which a project is feasible or not, using the information gathered in during the soul's wanderings. The Achuar distinguish several types of omen dream, according to the nature of the events announced, but we shall concern ourselves with only one category, the hunting dream or *kuntuknar*.

The *kuntuknar* works on the same principle as the *namur*, that is according to a systematic chiasmus between the representational fields. In this case, however, the distribution of symmetrical inversions is much more complex and covers a broad spectrum. One category of *kuntuknar* faithfully reproduces the chiasmus between content and destination that operates in the bezoar-charms. When a man dreams of fishing with a line or spear, it is a favorable omen for hunting small arboreal game and vice versa. This type of omen dream, which is always dreamed by men, is founded on the symmetrical equivalence of two labor processes that are distinct but which both lie within the field of male practice and are performed on opposing upper and lower levels of the physical world.

A second category of *kuntuknar* plays on the inversion between the human and animal worlds. This is a bipolar system in which animal behaviors are anthropomorphized and human behaviors naturalized, the transformational rule establishing the interpretative principle that founds the dream's premonitory nature. To dream of meeting a band of warriors on the warpath is a good omen for hunting peccary (the Achuar interpretation is based on the behavioral homology and the mortal danger represented by both groups). To dream of a group of crying women and children is a good sign for hunting woolly monkeys (here too is a behavioral homology based on the apparent despair of the females of a monkey troop when a male is slain). To dream of a plump, naked woman willing and ready to have sexual intercourse is taken as a favorable sign for hunting peccary (homology between the picture of a reclining woman exhibiting her vagina and the image of the eviscerated animal). Or to dream of being stared at by a motionless man with a handsome painted face is an omen for encountering and slaying a jaguar or an ocelot (homology between the spotted coat of the big cats and their crouching posture when they are about to spring). Inversely, it is interesting to note that dreams warning of armed conflict (*mesekrampra*) are based on the interpretation of images featuring the animal kingdom. For instance, to dream of encountering a horde of angry peccary is a sign of an impending skirmish with a band of warriors, following a chiasmus that is exactly symmetrical to that found in the hunting *kuntuknar* and based on the same homological interpretation.

And finally there is a third category of *kuntuknar* that differs from the first two in that the omen dreams are exclusively female. This system of omens, too, operates on the basis of inversion, but the chiasmus between content and destination articulates itself within the field of female practices and plays upon a dialectic between independence and dependence. Thus, when a woman dreams of carrying a basket full of manioc tubers, it means that she will soon have to carry the carcass of a peccary killed by her husband. To dream of stringing glass beads announces that she will soon be washing the intestines of a slain animal. To dream of spinning cotton announces she will soon be plucking a piping guan (the *Pipile pipile*'s feathers have white spots). Here, too, interpretation is based on obvious homologies, but the inverted fields clearly oppose, within the area of women's tasks, that which is specific to the women's world (handling and processing manioc, making certain types of necklaces, spinning and weaving cotton) and that which depends on the men's world (carrying and handling animals killed by the men).

This however is not the place for a detailed analysis of the Achuar system of omens, and even further study of the *kuntuknar* complex would be considerably overstepping the boundaries of our present concerns. Nevertheless, perhaps it would not hurt to mention a few remarkable features of hunting omens. In the first place, it must be noted that *kuntuknar* are not solely a male prerogative, since women, dogs, predatory animals (big cats, anacondas, eagles. . .) are also visited by premonitory dreams of the same order. The Achuar do not claim to know the exact content of an anaconda's *kuntuknar*, but they maintain that, as for humans, these dreams are the necessary prerequisite for the animal's capturing its prey. As for dogs' premonitory dreams, they are considered to be of the utmost importance for a successful hunt. If a dog has not had a *kuntuknar*, it will not be able to pick up the scent and track ground game, whatever other intrinsic aptitudes it may have. People say that dogs' *kuntuknar* are characterized by direct premonitions; when they jerk in their sleep and their stomach growls, they are supposed to be dreaming of eating the game they are going to help kill. If a man has had no *kuntuknar* dream, his wife's premonitory dream – although statistically a less frequent occurrence – will be regarded as a sufficiently explicit omen to authorize going hunting.

The practice of the *kuntuknar* is not in itself sufficient for hunting to be designated as a labor process the preconditions for which fall entirely within the male sphere of representations. Alternatively, if one carefully examines the content of women's *kuntuknar*, one notices that they are based on a series of displacements, which oppose pairs of female practices of different orders. It seems then that, in the interpretation of women's *kuntuknar*, one can see at work a logical principle of the differentiation of contents, which metaphorically points to the opposition between independent practice (gardening) and dependent practice (hunting); and we think that this principle is one of the manifestations of the indigenous classification of labor processes.

In the second place, we must stress the fact that the Achuar omen system – or that part of the system which has to do with hunting – is both systematic and automatic: the dream always foretells something, and is also the initial condition for acting. A man will be reluctant to go hunting if he, or his wife, has not had a favorable *kuntuknar* the night before. Although it is not absolutely necessary to have had a premonitory dream in order to go hunting small arboreal game, it is definitely indispensable to have had one in order to kill big game. If not, the hunter may see a horde of peccary, but in the end will be unable to bring down a single animal. Nevertheless, men are not entirely helpless in the face of the extreme determinism of human action introduced by the omen dream; before going to bed, they can always take their *arawir* violin and play a few *anent* specifically designed to "call" a *kuntuknar*. Furthermore, interpretations are highly normalized, and, in principle, for every specific onirical situation there exists a specific *anent*. Following a principle widely found in Amazon cultures,[5] the interpretation of *kuntuknar* is generally based on the inversion or reversal of dichotomized notional poles, either along the fundamental nature–culture axis (humans → animals), or in terms of more discrete oppositions within the sphere of human praxis (hunting → war, hunting → fishing, gardening → hunting, sexuality → hunting).

In his study of Apinayé omens, Da Matta interprets the transformational rule that humanizes nature and naturalizes culture as the means of resolving the abrupt juxtaposition in dreams of features that normally belong to two separate worlds. Da Matta maintains that it is this juxtaposition which engenders the dream's premonitory character, insofar as it is accidental and exceptional, and that the resulting oddity can be interpreted only by projecting into the future the discontinuity experienced in the dream (Da Matta 1970). And yet the Achuar do not seem to perceive inversion between the dream content and its assigned message as a sign of abnormal conjunction introduced by some strange homology. In fact, far from being exceptional, *kuntuknar* are an almost daily occurrence and on the whole announce a positive, desirable result that is not amenable to interpretation as a discontinuity. No doubt Da Matta's hypothesis would work for certain omens, particularly those foretelling a sudden death; nevertheless, the augural systematics at work in the *kuntuknar* is of a more general order.

The symbolic displacements that occur in the interpretations of *kuntuk-nar* can be assigned to the elementary modes (homology, inversion, symmetry) used by the Achuar to bring order into the world; to my mind, therefore, they do not need explaining. These operations of cosmological classification are simply made more visible than usual because they are grounded in dreams and because the general rule that the operations of the unconscious are structured in terms of primary processes implies that the dream typically works on the systems governing a subject's relationship with his physical and social environment and not on the empirical content of these relationships (Bateson 1972: 138–43). It would seem normal, then, that the indigenous stock of stereotyped dream pictures constitutes a privileged matrix for combining the various possible systems of relationships. Furthermore, it should be noted that, by postulating the equivalence between human–human relationships and human–animal relationships in the interpretation of dreams, the Achuar are consistent with their assumption that nature's beings have an anthropocentric sociability.

The only interest that the chiasmus of these representations, in either charms or dreams, holds for us, then, is that it clearly classifies the terms that it inverts and in so doing allows us to identify equivalent homogenous "bundles" of representations. Now as we have already seen in the case of women's *kuntuknar*, these "bundles" of representations are discrete units which define the area covered by specific practices, and these units appear as such only because a relationship is established between them. Hunting, fishing, or manipulating cultivated plants thus emerge on an implicit – not unconscious – level as specific labor processes if one accepts that these practices form cores that are interchangeable within the sphere of the representations of their conditions of possibility.

The last condition, chronologically speaking, that is an indispensable prerequisite for success in hunting is the mystification of the hunter's intentions, which is necessitated by the assumed presence of a fluid reservoir of jealous, depersonalized ill-will which could abruptly crystallize upon the hunter were he to publish his plans. The Achuar also think that if a man announces his hunting trip, he will alarm the animals by the undisguised exposition of his intentions. This explains the absence of a specific term to denote hunting, for its use under any circumstances before setting out would fatally cause the plans to fail. The expressions used to announce a hunting trip are vague and polysemic, of the likes of "I'm going into the forest," "I'm going for a walk," or "I'm going looking." When, upon occasion, two men go hunting together, a father and his adolescent son, for instance, they can exchange information about game only in coded language. If one of the hunters has heard a troop of monkeys, he will simply say: "There are a lot of little birds around." Alternatively, there is a common expression, *shimpiankayi*, which means precisely: "I've come back empty-handed because I showed my intention of going hunting too clearly." Hunting language is rife with double meanings, hidden meanings, and word play, for it would be difficult to charm one's animal affines if one were to announce the fate that awaits them.

I would like to end this chapter on representations of hunting with an incidental remark. Contrary to what one might expect, the ways in which the Achuar represent hunting and warfare are not entirely homothetic. A comparison of the different *anent* incantations used in either circumstance is highly revealing. In both cases, enemies and game are often presented as affines: brothers-in-law, in the case of game, and *nuasuru* (literally: "wife-giver"), for enemies. But, whereas in war the alliance fracture becomes an irreparable breach when affines are killed, in hunting the alliance is maintained despite the killing by the implicit contract, as it were, established with the animals' *amana* and guardian spirits. The difference in the handling of the representations of beings one kills – representation, it must be stressed, of an ideal object, for, in practice, it happens that classificatory kin are killed with the help of affines – is particularly obvious in war *anent*, in which the warrior identifies himself with a big cat about to pounce on its prey, a metaphorical assimilation never encountered in hunting *anent*. The warrior becomes identical with animals hunting, and the normal obligations of alliance are nullified by the savagery of war. Hunting, on the other hand, is founded on a gentleman's agreement and implies the need to charm animal affines; whatever the outcome of the hunt, animals are at least recognized as having a social existence, something that is denied the enemy. This is an obvious inversion of the field of representations, already identifiable in the chiasmus between dreams about hunting and those about war, in which a type of human relationship appears as an animal relationship, while relations between humans and animals appear as relations between humans. Hunting and warfare are predatory activities, but the symbolic protocols for killing make an essential distinction between the two. As an extension of the domestic domain to include game, hunting is experienced as an affectionate form of endocannibalism in which animals are the very special "guests" at human meals. There is no such thing in warfare: by exiling the enemy into the anomy of the world of animal predators, by periodically expelling him into the otherness of nature, warfare is a way of keeping at bay the constraints of alliance and of perpetuating the dream of an unattainable togetherness unhampered by real affines. As a space where men and women come together, and also humans and animals, the forest is an ideally affinal world in which the very principles upon which society rests are constantly being called into question.

7

The world of the river

The closed world of the garden is set, term for term, against the open world of the forest in a series of antithetical pairs, which correspond only in very small part to the usual dualist figures. In effect it is not the classic oppositions between wild and cultivated or male and female that govern the representation of space, since, for the Achuar, the forest is a superhuman garden from which women are not barred (see the role of Shakaim, pp. 202–204). The network of topographical oppositions is organized more by the activities that go on in each place than by the attributes of the places themselves. Opposite the space of sexual disjunction, which is the realm of mothering and consanguinity, stands a space of conjunction devoted to the dangerous interplay of alliance. Opposite the domesticating cultivation of plant children stands the seductive hunting of animal affines. The question now is, between these two places, each defined by its own praxis, is there room for yet a third world, that of the river, which would be a separate term and not simply an extension of the garden or the forest?

The reader will no doubt recall that, at one bend or another of our exposition, the river has shown very different faces. As a topographical and cosmological axis, the river system structures space into upstream and downstream, and regulates time by the aquatic course of the Pleiades, which each year plunge into the water to die and be reborn. When we postulated that an imaginary river flows through the Achuar house, we were thereby positing an equivalence between aquatic and domestic worlds, with each isolated dwelling linked to the others in one great continuum by this invisible flow. Metaphor of the contents of the stomach passing through the house as through the digestive tract, the river is also the site of the cosmic fermentation which causes its waters to rise and fall with the seasonal floods. And so waterways are not so much autonomous spaces, like forests or gardens, as they are instruments of mediation, articulating along their axis, and on the level of each house, all levels of the Achuar cosmology.

This privileged mediator status appears in exemplary fashion in the multitude of combined social uses for which the river is the setting. In effect, the river cannot be reduced to a binary function, for, by the uses to which it is put, it transcends the opposition between conjunction and disjunction that normally governs the spatial definition of relations between the genders within the residential unit as well as those between the household and outsiders. In the latter case, the river can be seen as combining conjunction – by the link it establishes among the houses along its banks – and disjunction – by the private, domestic use of a segment of river. In the context of the household, the river is at once the site of sexual conjunction (husbands and wives bathing together, fish-poisoning parties) and of disjunction (men bathing at dawn and going down alone to defecate, women washing dishes and clothes).

This mediating space is not only a symbolic vehicle for cosmic metaphors, it is also a resource which, for all its abundance, is nonetheless of vital importance. The river is what you navigate on; it is what you wash in – yourself, your clothes, your utensils; the river is what you drink; it is all of these at once by means of the lexical transformation that changes impure terrestrial water, *entza*, into celestial water for cooking, *yumi*, the minute it is drawn. Lastly, the river is the exclusive home of beings that are very special because their daily life is hidden from human eyes. Among these "water beings" (*entsaya aents*), whose nature is as different from that of humans as it is from that of forest beings (*ikiamia aents*), one particular population – *namak* ("big fish") or *tsarur* ("minnows") – is of highly pragmatic interest. The upper Amazon is very rich in fish; here fishing is much more than a simple substitute for hunting, and the Achuar take great pleasure in practicing this art almost daily.

Fishing techniques

The Achuar practice specialized fishing, in the sense that each of their techniques of capture is adapted to a specific type of waterway and to the fish found there. Of the seventy-eight species of fish identified by vernacular name that we have recorded, only two are not considered edible: the electric eel, *tsunkiru*, and the tiny parasite fish *kaniir* (*Vandellia wieneri*). The other seventy-six – plus a few that have certainly escaped our attention – provide a respectable and highly varied source of protein, from the huge *paits* down to the modest hatchet-fish *titim* (*Carnegiella strigata*) via the great catfish family represented by some fifteen species. In other words, there is not a stream or waterhole that, after a few minutes or hours of effort, will not yield up some of its denizens to the determined fisherman. The Achuar also have a varied armory to choose from: fish traps, harpoons, nets, hook and line, fish poisons.

Fish are trapped with a rectangular woven mat or screen some 60 cm high by 150 cm wide, made, like the blowgun darts, from thin strips of the central vein of the *Maximiliana regia* palm frond. This pliable mat, called *washimp*, can be rolled to make a conical fishing device that is open wide at one end and nearly closed at the other. As it is normally used, the *washimp* is placed in small streams (*kisar*) no more than a meter across. The mouth of the trap is placed upstream and the passage on either side of the entrance is dammed with stones so that the fish are driven into the trap. Once they have entered, they are inexorably squeezed into the narrow end of the *washimp*. This trap, which the men set in a stream near the house, allows them to catch only minnows, *tsarur*. This is not a very productive technique, as the catch is comprised mainly of small Cichlids, which rarely measure more than a dozen centimeters.

Harpoon and net fishing, on the other hand, are very productive, but can be practiced only during the three or four months of low waters and in very specific spots along the river. When the waters subside, certain secondary channels of the Pastaza are in effect temporarily cut off from the main branch and form small lakes in which large fish remain trapped and can be easily harpooned. The harpoon, *puya*, has a palm-wood shaft some two meters long, one end of which is equipped with a barbed metal point, which the men usually make from a ten-penny nail obtained by exchange from the Shuar. As with all harpoons, the point is removable; it is wedged into a hole in one end of the shaft and bound in place by a string. Made from chambira fibers, this several-meter-long piece of twine is wound halfway down the shaft. When the fish is harpooned, the point comes away from the shaft and the twine unravels until the fisherman pulls in his wriggling catch. The net, *neka*, is also made from chambira twine. It is a large rectangle of around one meter high by five or six meters long, with a four or five centimeter lozenge-shaped mesh. The bottom of the net is weighted with a row of small pebbles, while the top has a row of balsa-wood floats.

When a man spots a promising channel, easily identified by the large fish jumping all about, he creeps up and strings his net across the section which seems to him to contain the most fish. The net seals off a small stretch of the channel so that the fish cannot escape. All he has to do then is wade into the shallow water to harpoon the trapped fish, while those that try to get away become entangled in the net. When all the fish in the closed-off section have been harpooned, the net is moved to another portion of the channel, and the operation recommences. The technique can also be used in subsiding lakes, when the feeder channel has dried up and the river fish are imprisoned as in a secondary branch.

This form of fishing produces exceptional results for a man working alone, provided he chooses his site well. In effect, given the size of the harpoon and the mesh of the net, this method can be used only on large fish, and so it is necessary to select the favorable sites ahead of time. Most commonly caught by this method are *penke namak* (*Ichthyoelephas humeralis*), a savory, toothless fish that weighs nearly a kilogram. The two occasions on which we observed men fishing with a net and harpoon, the volume of the catch was respectively 35 kg in six hours and 37 kg in five hours. It must be said, however, that only the Achuar living near the Pastaza are in a position to practice this type of fishing and that very few of them own a net, the manufacture of which demands a large investment of labor. Of course it is always possible to use only the harpoon and dispense with the net, but that is a particularly difficult undertaking, for one must either stand completely motionless until a fish swims by or frantically pursue it in all directions as it twists and turns.

Although line fishing is not an aboriginal technique, it was enthusiastically adopted by all Amerindians as soon as they were able to obtain metal fish hooks. Formerly the Achuar made their own hooks (*tsau*) from nails they procured by exchange with neighboring ethnic groups. The lines were plaited from chambira palm fibers. It is only since the end of the 1960s that they have had regular access to manufactured hooks and especially to the nylon fishing line indispensable for landing the heaviest catches. Very heavy line capable of supporting over 80 kg is a highly valued item not yet in wide use. This type of line is the only convenient means the Achuar have of catching *Arapaimas* and the large Pimelodids (*tunkau*). The techniques used in hook-and-line fishing can be distinguished according to the strength of line used and where it is dropped.

Fishing for large fish in streams and rivers is an exclusively male activity that requires a canoe and a strong line. Usually a two-man operation because of handling the canoe, this method often entails a several-day expedition. In effect, the lines must be dropped in the deepest parts of the river, in holes whose depth often exceeds 30 meters and which appear on the surface as slowly turning sworls. But such holes, which are the favorite habitat of the large Pimelodids, are not that common along a river; exploiting a number of these takes several days of navigation. When the canoe has been more or less stabilized in a sworl, the lines are dropped; these are baited with palm grubs or pieces of meat. The hook is attached to a thick piece of wire which is tied on to the line; this system avoids the line being cut by a piranha snapping up the bait. For this kind of fishing, very strong line is necessary, as it is not unusual to hook fish weighing over 50 kg, like the *Aparaima* (*paits*) or the *juunt tunkau* (*Pimelodus ornatus*). To land these monsters, a man needs to be very strong, to be a very good boatman, and to know the reactions of a hooked fish. Some men possess these skills to a high degree and show a marked tendency to forsake hunting in order to specialize in fishing for large specimens. These men are not necessarily riverine Achuar, though, for any large river can be fished all year round, provided it is not in flood and therefore unnavigable because of the eddies.

While canoe fishing is restricted to men, as it implies a veritable combat with the animal, catching minnows from the bank is perceived as a form of gathering that can legitimately be done by women and children. The line used is good for modest-sized fish only, those weighing between 300 g and 2 kg. The lines are set along the river at nightfall and often left overnight. The bait consists mainly of earthworms and insects, or sometimes pieces of meat if one wants to attract piranha. Armed with a short line tied to a pole, adolescents systematically explore the good fishing spots near the house and rarely come home empty-handed. This type of fishing produces fairly low returns per trip (on average less than a kilo per day per house), but with great regularity, since, if the women and the children of a house have line and hooks, they set the lines every day. The daily fish supply of these houses over the year rests, in fact, more on this small-time fishing than on the other halieutic techniques. However there are still many isolated residential units that have no hooks or that have lost them and cannot procure replacements.

Unlike the preceding methods, fish poisoning (*entza nijiatin*, literally: "washing the river") is a collective undertaking in which all members of the household participate. It even happens that several neighboring domestic units join forces in a big fishing party calling for the damming of a large river. The techniques used to poison fish can be distinguished according to the nature of the fish poisons locally available and the waterways in which they are placed. The reader will recall that the plants used for fish poison in the two biotopes are not the same. While the Achuar living in the interfluvial habitat grow only *timiu*, riverine gardens will grow only *masu*. But these two fish poisons are far from having the same effect: *masu* is much less potent than the same dose of *timiu*, and can only be used for minnows. That is why certain riverine Achuar make small isolated *timiu* gardens in the lateritic soil of the hills, several hours' walk from the main house. Nevertheless, the two poisons work alike, by very temporarily modifying the chemical balance of the water, which causes the fish to suffocate.

Masu is a small shrub whose leaves are gathered as needed before each fish-poisoning expedition. Only men are allowed to handle these plants and they are therefore the ones responsible for picking the three or four bushes in order to get enough leaves to fill a *chankin* carrying basket. *Masu* is used when the water level is low, in the secondary channels cut off from the main branch of the Pastaza or in the shallow pools of the riverine habitat. When they arrive at the site, the men pound the leaves to a pulp, using a stone or a piece of wood. Then they take the basket into the shallow water and partially immerse it, vigorously swishing it back and forth until the milky juice of the leaves has been entirely diluted. In a few minutes the fish begin to feel the lack of oxygen and come gasping to the surface; women and children then join the men and splash about collecting the stunned fish. *Masu* can also be used in small streams; while the men poison the water, the women wait downstream and gather up the small fish as they float by.

Masu fishing is done in very shallow water and generally yields only small fry, classified in the ethnocategory *tsarur*: these are mainly *nayump* (Loricariidae), *kantash* (Cichlidae), *kusum*, pencil-fish (Anostomidae), *putu* (Cichlidae), *shuwi* (*Ancistrus* sp.), and large tadpoles, *wampuch*. The returns are low, and rarely are more than four or five kilos of fish brought back per trip. The riverine Achuar consider *masu* fishing more of a pleasant family entertainment than an intensive subsistence technique. It provides a half-day outing for the entire household, a time to have fun and a good laugh. *Masu* can also be used to catch larger fish in the ox-bow lakes (*kucha*). When it is ascertained that one of these subsiding lakes contains a great number of sizeable fish, the feeder channel is closed off with a *washimp* mat, and large quantities of *masu* are tipped into the lake – six to eight basketsful at least. The men then canoe around the lake harpooning the large fish that float to the top. Sometimes these small lakes form veritable breeding ponds, and that is when *masu* fishing really becomes worthwhile.

The most spectacular results, though, are obtained in the interfluvial habitat with the use of the fish poison *timiu*. Like *masu*, *timiu* is a shrub, but its active ingredient, rotenone, is contained in the roots, not the leaves. To obtain the poison, the men pull up the plant, taking care to replace part of the root in the ground to ensure its reproduction. This is why one usually encounters quantities of *timiu* bushes in interfluvial gardens, as each fish-poisoning party requires the destruction of several plants. In the interfluve, *timiu* fishing entails the construction of a temporary weir, since the streams flow too fast to permit the relaxed gathering of the fish that is the practice in the lakes and dead channels of the riverine habitat. The dam, *epeinmiau*, can be any of several shapes, depending on the width and depth of the watercourse, but its basic structure is always the same.

Timiu is used for the most part in small, shallow rivers whose width rarely exceeds four or five meters. The men build the weir across a narrow section, first planting four or five triangular supports in the river bed to serve as pilings. Set parallel to the current, these frames are hooked together by transverse poles, which are in turn attached to the banks. Rows of stakes are then lashed to the poles, forming a vertical barrier leaning slightly upstream. The lower part of the barrier serves to hold back the water, the accumulation of several layers of broad leaves making it relatively water-tight. An opening is left in the center of the weir, occupied by a small platform overhanging the downstream course but on the same level as the upstream portion. The drop between the two levels is around a meter, and the platform functions as a spillway, allowing the evacuation of the overflow. This platform is usually made of a *washimp* mat laid over a light scaffolding; and this kind of weir with spillway is usually called a *washim-piamu*. On one *timiu*-fishing trip in 1976, two men took a whole day to build a *washimpiamu* dam across a river five meters wide.

When the fishing proper begins, the downstream-end of the spillway-platform is blocked off to keep back the fish washed down by the current. The *timiu* roots are crushed by the men, who place baskets of the crushed roots in the water some 600 meters upstream from the dam. The men then make their way slowly downstream, towing the immersed baskets, which release their toxic juices. Halfway down there is usually a small pile of pounded *timiu* roots waiting for the men, who put them into the water as they go by. Soon the whole river has taken on a characteristic milky tint, and the fish poison begins to take effect: the small fish come wriggling to the surface and finally flap their way into the water plants along the banks, while the big fish flop about in a desperate attempt to escape suffocation. At the second pile of *timiu*, everyone enters the water and slowly advances toward the dam; the men harpoon the large fish, and the women use baskets to scoop up the small ones along the banks. When they reach the dam, both men and women post themselves at the foot of the barrage to catch the fish that continue to float down, while one man collects the fish caught on the spillway platform. When it is all over, the weir is dismantled so that it will not obstruct the further circulation of fish.

In this type of fishing, the Achuar catch about as many fish on their way down the river as they do at the foot of the dam. *Timiu* fishing is highly productive: in 1976, seven adults and five children over eight brought in 70 kg of fish by damming a river five meters wide, while, in 1978, four adults and four children took 25 kg from a stream three meters across. Inasmuch as the effect of the fish poison lasts only a short time, the operation can be repeated every year in each of the waterways in the vicinity of a house. During low-water season, the only time *timiu* can be used in conjunction with a weir, a domestic unit in the interfluvial habitat will organize a fish-poisoning party approximately every three weeks. The fish are immediately gutted and then smoked by the women, which allows them to be kept four or five days. And so during the three months of low water, most interfluvial households lay in a total of two or three weeks' worth of fish from the total number of poisoning excursions.

Much less frequent are the truly big collective *timiu* fishing parties on large rivers whose width can exceed 15 meters. Building a weir on such a waterway demands a large male workforce, which can be mustered only by combining the resources of a half-dozen residential units. Technically the only difference between big and little dams is that big ones have no spillway, but they must be built in deep water, which requires the use of canoes and rafts. The size of the river also requires the use of great quantities of *timiu*, and each participating household must therefore contribute an approximately equivalent share. When the poison is placed in the water several kilometers upstream from the weir by the men, there may be as many as forty persons stationed along the river banks. The women and children post themselves in the shallows, where they can use baskets while maintaining their footing; the men harpoon the big fish, letting their canoes and rafts drift towards the dam. On these occasions, as with fish poisoning in general, everyone keeps his catch, and so the members of each domestic unit try to collect as many fish as they can. The overall productivity of this type of fishing seems very high, but is impossible to quantify given the number of participants and the absence of any procedure for sharing the catch. The erection of a large weir is an altogether exceptional event and happened only twice (on the Kapawientza) during our stay among the northern Achuar.

Fish poisoning is an original technique, and its operational sequence seems to break down the same way in nearly all cultures of the Amazon

Basin. In nearly every case, it is the men who handle the fish poison, while the women merely gather the fish that float down on the current. In this labor process, gender complementarity is a technical necessity because of the labor power that must be mustered in order to gather all the stunned fish. Fish poison (commonly called *barbasco* in montaña Spanish) is an instrument which, like the weir, makes it possible to capture fish, but it is not actually a lethal agent in itself. By causing the fish gradually to suffocate, *barbasco* makes them easier to catch without actually killing them; in streams and rivers, the fish that slip by often recuperate once the toxic film has become diluted. Consequently, building the weir and handling the fish poison are conditions for neutralizing the fish and can be assimilated to other forms of male predatory intervention in the natural environment. But if the neutralization is to be complete, the fish must still be harpooned – a killing technique on the same order as those used by men in hunting and warfare – or scooped up in baskets, a female task which resembles a gathering activity. Thus the division of labor present in fish poisoning reproduces the gender roles assigned in the other modes of exploiting nature.

Furthermore, there is no generic term for the whole set of halieutic practices, and fishing, in the Achuar lexicon, is therefore divided among as many individual expressions as there are methods of capturing fish. Taking a synoptic look at the sexual division of labor in fishing (Fig. 39), we see that the opposition hunting/gathering not only governs fish-poisoning, but also provides a general paradigm for the assignment of tasks by gender in the various techniques. Everything involving collecting or gathering (fishing with baskets, line fishing from the bank) is attributed to women, while

Task	Men	Women	Children
Fish poisoning			
a) constructing weirs in rivers or streams and handling fish poison	+		
b) scooping up fish with a basket		+	+
c) harpooning fish	+		
Fishing with a trap (*washimp*)	+		
Fishing with harpoon and net	+		
Fishing with hook and line			
a) catching big fish from a canoe in rivers and streams	+		
b) catching small fish from the bank in still waters		+	+
Scaling, gutting, and smoking the fish		+	

39. Division of labor in fishing

everything involving the construction and use of traps (weirs, fish traps, nets), the use of penetrating weapons (harpoons) and physically dangerous combat (catching large fish in rivers and streams) remains the purview of men.

It should also be noted that the theoretical productivity of fishing in the two biotopes more or less balances out due to the differential efficiency of the techniques used. In effect, the absence of very large fish in the interfluvial habitat is compensated by the very good results obtained with *timiu*, compared with the modest catches possible with *masu* in the riverine habitat. Hook and line can be used to catch big fish all along the large rivers of both biotopes, and the only significant advantage of the riverine habitat is the possibility of using the harpoon–net combination in the dead branches of rivers and in the shallow ox-bow lakes and pools. If the overall ichthyological potential of the riverine habitat is no doubt greater than that of the interfluve, it remains that the different fishing techniques used in each of the two ecotypes more or less compensate for any disparity in the availability of fish.

The marital bed

As in all strategic domains of practice, proper fishing demands the fulfillment of a certain number of propitiatory conditions. Women's line fishing is, as we have seen, assimilated to gathering and is therefore located entirely within the sphere of the profane. Alternatively, the symbolic preconditions for the use of fish poison (a predominantly male collective activity) and for the harpoon, and the hook and line, in rivers and streams (exclusively male activities) appear, in an attenuated form, as structurally identical with the prerequisites for hunting. Magical techniques are alleged to be of much less importance than in hunting, and fish are attracted by means of specific charms, not through direct dialogue. While men can communicate with some "water beings" (otters, anacondas, black jaguars...), who live half on land, half in the water, they cannot establish an interlocutory relationship with fish, which spend their whole lives under water. Therefore the Achuar do not sing *anent* to fish, and rely solely on charms to attract them.

Fishing charms come in a limited selection which partly duplicates the hunting charms. The *namur* bezoars used in fishing are, as we have seen, inversely related to hunting *namur*, since their target (fish) is inversely symmetrical to their origin (the entrails of land animals). They are used by men when fishing alone, are transmitted from father to son, and possess all the properties ascribed to hunting *namur*. A dolphin's tooth is also supposed to exert a magical attraction on fish, and should be carefully rubbed on the line and the hook before dropping them into the stream or river. Each individual fishing trip is subject to the same kinds of contingent conditions as hunting. The fisherman should theoretically have dreamed a *kuntuknar* omen, the content of which announces the outcome by antinomy, since the fishing *kuntuknar* features a hunting scene. But, unlike premonitory hunting dreams, fishing *kuntuknar* do not seem strictly indispensable for success. Lastly, except for fish-poisoning expeditions, which of necessity must be planned in advance, the prohibition on announcing one's intentions is just as strong for fishing as for hunting. If the fisherman does not conceal his plans, he runs the risk of seeing the fish escape his net or of not landing those that bite.

Fish poisoning poses a special analytical problem, for its field of representation is entirely original with respect to that of the other Achuar subsistence techniques. It is aligned on the complementarity of the sexes and not according to the usual individual symbolic competence of the man and the woman. This complementarity, which can be objectively observed in the successive phases of the labor process, is symbolically expressed by constant reference to sexual themes. On the most immediate level, the equivalence between sexual relations and fish poisoning can already be seen in the men's standard play on the vernacular expression that designates this technique, *entza nijiatin* ("to wash the river"), and *entza nijirtin* ("to copulate with the river"). It is obviously not difficult to see an immediate analogy between semen and the milky juice of the fish poison that the men alone tip into the river. Women may not touch the toxic plants, for the contact would make the *timiu* and the *masu* impotent; women are especially forbidden to crush the leaves and roots, an operation that can be assimilated metaphorically to ejaculation. But this analogy is not based on superficial likeness alone, and Achuar mythology quite explicitly establishes an equivalence between fish poisons and the penis.

The myth of Timiu and Masu

Once upon a time there were two young bachelors, Masu and Timiu, who were dipping darts in curare, for they were getting ready to go hunting. As they performed this operation, they heard Kaka (a small brown-colored frog) singing: "*Kakaa...kakaa...,*" quite near the house. They said to each other: "She must really be in heat; how I'd like to hug her to me and copulate with her until she bursts." Kaka was listening and had heard everything. Masu and Timiu picked up their blowguns and set out. On the way, they came upon a plump young woman, lying in their path with her legs apart and her vagina exposed. Timiu looked away quickly and continued on his path, because it was he who was to become the most virulent. Masu was behind him, and, seeing the woman offering herself, became all aroused. He put aside his blowgun and quiver, exclaiming: "I'm going to try her out!" But after having copulated, Kaka took Masu's penis in her mouth to suck it, and then fled into a tree, leaping from branch to branch. Masu's penis stretched and stretched. As she fled, Kaka cried back in scorn: "*Kakaa. . .kakaa. . .*you were going to burst me open. . .*kakaa. . .kakaa. . .*and you couldn't do it. . .*kakaa. . .kakaa.*" Kaka continued to climb until she came to a *wasake* (an epiphytic plant of the Bromeliaceae family). And there she opened her mouth and dropped Masu's penis, which, considerably elongated, fell to the ground in a great heap. Masu coiled his penis up, hoisted it over his shoulder and left the trail, abandoning his blowgun and quiver where they lay. He came at last to a river where many Wankanim lived (giant otters, *Pteronura*). Masu sat down, prostrated, on the sand, surrounded by swarms of flies drawn by the pestilential odor of his huge penis. At that moment, the Wankanim emerged from the water, finely arrayed, and burst out laughing at the spectacle of Masu and his penis. Masu wondered: "Whoever are these people?" Then one of the Wankanim spoke to Masu: "What happened to you?" "It's because I copulated with Kaka." "All right, I'll have a look at it later." Then the Wankanim cooked some fish and served them to Masu, saying: "Eat and stop crying, I'm going to cure you." When they had eaten, Wankanim measured his own penis and then shortened Masu's, cutting it to the same length as his own. Then Wankanim chopped the rest of the penis into pieces of the same length and piled them into baskets. Wankanim set off in his canoe, with his wife, to throw the pieces of Masu's penis into all the waterways, where they immediately turned into anacondas. At one time there were no anacondas, and people say that they all came from Masu's penis, which Wankanim and his wife threw into the lakes and rivers. Because he copulated with Kaka, Masu lost his strength and became *micha* (literally: "cold," "raw," or "limp"). As for Timiu, he is highly virulent (*tara*, used to qualify hot peppers), because he abstained from copulating. That is why, when a man goes fishing after having had sexual relations the poison does not work.

This myth, given here in one of the three versions we collected, raises complex problems of interpretation, especially when placed alongside Lévi-Strauss' analyses of the South American fish-poison theme.[1] There is no question of going into all the variations here, but simply of suggesting a few significant elements peculiar to the Achuar symbolism of fish poisoning. In the first place, the difference in efficacy between *timiu* and *masu* is interpreted in terms of cooking: Masu's sexual incontinence made him "raw," in other words reduced him to a natural state, while Timiu remained virulent, like the hot pepper which enhances the taste of food. The interpretation of the use of fish poison as an allegory of copulation, which has a positive outcome only if it has been preceded by a period of effective abstinence, comes out clearly in the moral of the myth. Respecting this principle is regarded by the Achuar as the condition *sine qua non* for success, and should be compared with the idea that unexplained flooding – making the use of fish poison impossible – is caused by the inappropriate behavior of certain couples who engage in erotic play while bathing. Abstinence thus allows the potential energy stored up by the man who curbs his desires to be metaphorically transferred to the fish poison that is dumped into the river. An erection is usually denoted by the expression "the penis is angry," and so the virulence of the fish poison is proportional to the violence of the contained sexual drive.

The myth also suggests a very special relationship between the sphere of hunting and that of fishing, since all variants stress the preparations for the hunting trip and Masu's abandonment of his weapons after copulating with Kaka. Timiu, on the other hand, continues his quest for game while becoming the strongest of the fish poisons, thanks to his sexual continence. There is therefore no antinomy between hunting with curare and fishing with *timiu*, both being activities in which male skills in handling plant poisons are expressed. Alternatively, the man who foregoes hunting is condemned to a type of fishing that yields little in the way of either fish or prestige, for there is no difference between men and women when it comes to scooping up minnows stunned with *masu*. And lastly, it could be noted that the giant-otter people, *wankanim*, prey directly on fish, inasmuch as these "water people" feed exclusively on the fish they catch. Now the relationship between the *wankanim* and their aquatic game is highly symptomatic of the subordinate status of fish in the Achuar representation of nature's beings and the world of the river.

Although it is not stated in the myth, the *wankanim* are normally a metamorphosis of the water spirits, Tsunki; but while the Tsunki feed on fish, they do not afford them benevolent protection as the tutelary spirits of the garden and the forest do their cultivated plants and game. The aquatic populations can therefore be clearly divided into predators and prey. The predators are the Tsunki and their familiars (anacondas, caimans, black jaguars, crab-eating raccoons . . .) with which humans communicate in their dreams. The prey are fish, an ill-defined mass sometimes called "Tsunki's cockroaches," which everyone can take as they please. It does not seem that the Achuar attribute a soul to fish;[2] fishing therefore does not entail a seduction campaign of the same magnitude as that unleashed on land game. When humans enter into contact with these water beings living among the fish, it is not, as in the case of hunting and gardening, in order to maximize the returns of fishing expeditions by asking them to intercede. More particularly, human relations with the Tsunki are devoid of immediate utilitarian preoccupations and most often take the form of a marriage alliance.

The reader will recall that, in describing the world of the house, we drew a parallel between the domestic sociability of the Tsunki and that of the Achuar, the former providing a sort of normative model for the latter. This analogy is particularly well expressed in an anecdote that we mentioned briefly at the time and which we heard in roughly the same form from different men, in different places, and in different circumstances. Each of the storytellers readily explained how he had met a very beautiful Tsunki maiden, who stepped out of the river and invited him to make love. As the first experience fulfilled his desires, he decided to see her regularly. After a time, the Tsunki maiden asked him underwater to meet her father, a kindly, majestic man seated on a *charap* turtle in a fine house. The Tsunki asked the narrator to stay and take his daughter as his legitimate wife. When the man explained that he already had human wives he could not abandon, the Tsunki gave him leave to return only periodically to carry out his husbandly duties and proposed that he divide his time between his land family and his water family. Each of the storytellers described at length the ensuing double life, naming his water children or boasting of his Tsunki wife's cooking. Sometimes the wife would come to meet her husband on the river bank and converse tenderly with him in the guise of a *wankanim* otter.

If we qualify these tales with their identical storyline as anecdotes, it is because, unlike myths, the events are always presented as something that happened to the teller personally. Yet this recurring anecdote uncomfortably resembles a Shuar myth whose equivalent we have never found in Achuar mythology.[3]

With its sexual and marital connotations, the water world defines itself as that mediating space whose characteristics we have already outlined. If I may emphasize the metaphor with a play on words, one might even say that the river bed is a marital bed, symbol and discrete haven of the marriage with the beautiful Tsunki maiden, just as the house symbolizes and harbors a union with human wives. Even if it is clandestine, domestic life with a Tsunki cannot be assimilated to a passing extramarital affair, since the detailed etiquette governing relations with the aquatic in-laws is scrupulously respected, and the children born of this union are recognized. Now marriage, a mediating operation if ever there was, is, when all is said and done, the social act by which two affines join together to produce consanguines. Situated between the consanguineal world of the garden and the affinal world of the forest, the river can thus be seen as the place where the two are allegorically articulated, an intermediary plane dominated by an ideal domestic peace devoid of pragmatic ambitions.

8

Categories of practice

Whatever may be the setting in which they are accomplished or the forms of the technical procedures, all ways of using nature are mediated by human work. Although this seems self-evident, it is not wholly free of bias and therefore calls for some preliminary clarifications. As Marx already pointed out in the middle of the last century, labor, as something that can be conceived as separate from the worker who performs it, is a relatively new idea. The notion of labor in general acquired its full meaning only with the development of wage labor within a system of production in which labor power became an alienable commodity. Cornerstone of political economy since Adam Smith, the category "labor" is historically determined by a certain stage in the evolution of socio-economic forms. Like many non-market societies, the Achuar do not recognize the concept of "work-in-general," definable as a form of activity distinct from other types of social activity. But is this a reason to bypass this component of the modes of using nature? While no one doubts that all societies have abstract models that dictate the division of labor, some are reluctant to accept that archaic peoples can be fully conscious of the type and amount of effort that should be accorded each task. But is there not, in every society, one sector of the system of representations that more or less explicitly defines the differential allocation of labor, and the intensity and rate of energy expended according to the task at hand or the status it enjoys?

For instance, the Achuar unquestionably have a clear idea of the amount of effort demanded by each of the productive techniques they practice. They obviously do not think of the energy expended in terms of a quantifiable allocation of labor that forms part of the production factors. But that does not mean that the Achuar see the very real physical effort they put into socializing certain portions of nature as a ludic pastime or the means of communing in some vague way with the universe. It is therefore inexact to claim that work is constituted as an objective reality only in societies in which it is perceived as a specific category of activity. Achuar work is non-alienated because its ends and its means are controlled by the person who does it; but that does not mean that it is not work. Now is not a bad time to recall this, in order to rectify the idealized image of these Amerindian societies of which it has sometimes been said that they live out their lives blissfully rejecting work.[1] It is entirely legitimate to criticize the indiscriminate projection of political economic categories onto societies that have none of the institutions these categories were created to analyze. But unless one is to retreat into solipsism, this must not be carried to the extreme of eliminating all of the analytical concepts of the social sciences on the pretext that they are not constructed as such in the vernacular representations.

An examination of Achuar categories of activity poses a twofold problem, then. The problem is one of quantity, first of all, which entails questioning the differential allocation of labor input according to age, sex, function as producer or non-producer, subsistence sphere, the resources of the habitat, and the composition of the workforce in each residential unit. But such a study makes sense only if it is based on the indigenous model of division of labor, which in turn sets the modalities and proportions of this input with respect to cultural imperatives largely independent of material constraints. This indigenous model is consistent with the isolated domestic group's view of itself as a microcosm cultivating its social and economic independence: it is logical that a system of production marked to this degree by deliberate autarky be organized around the sexual division of tasks. The reader will have noticed in the preceding pages how closely the men and women of the domestic group are bound up in a reciprocal relation of dependence and complementarity with respect to their material conditions of reproduction. The whole question is whether the sexual division of labor is an operator which makes it possible to establish a clear-cut dichotomy of labor processes or, on the contrary, whether the necessary complementarity of male and female tasks does not induce a more complex system of representations the logic of which remains to be uncovered.

The quantitative order

With remarkable consistency over four centuries, observers and ethnographers have been unanimous in stressing the industriousness of the Jivaro. Missionaries favorably compare their penchant for work with the purported indolence of surrounding ethnic groups; it fuels their regret that such a naturally hardworking people has the insolence to resist conquest and forced work, unlike their more easy-going, less warlike, indigenous neighbors. It is a fact that a large Achuar house, especially at the end of the day, always gives the impression of a hive buzzing with activity. No lines of hammocks with men, women, and children swaying lazily, after the dreamlike stereotype of the good Amazonian savage. But it is the women, more particularly, who create this impression of bustling home life; around the house, the men are the very picture of leisure. This apparent contrast stems from the differentiated structure of work in the two instances.

Men intervene primarily outside the house; at home, a man spends most of his time in a state of inactivity, drinking manioc beer and talking freely with his wives and children. His only task is handiwork (basketweaving, making blowguns, woodworking. . .) and this is often interrupted. Inversely, nearly all the housework falls to the women (preparing the food, making the manioc beer, sweeping the floor, washing dishes and clothes, carrying water, tending the fire, taking care of the children and animals), plus the manufacture of artefacts, which they do inside (spinning, weaving, potting). Men work at very irregular intervals, but each activity is sustained for long periods, while women's work is parcelled out into a multitude of interrupted, repetitive tasks. When a man goes hunting, makes a clearing, or works on a blowgun, he devotes most of the day to the job, pausing for only short breaks. After a day of such intense activity, he will usually spend a day or two resting, doing nearly nothing; this rest is punctuated by a few secondary tasks such as sharpening darts, fetching big logs for the fire, or repairing a basket. The women, on the contrary, follow a schedule, which is nearly identical, day in day out. They go to the garden on an average of three days out of four always to perform the same tasks; when they get home, they resume the eternal household routine. No wonder, then, that a chance visitor gets the impression that Achuar women lead an extremely laborious life. And yet if work time is examined in detail over a long period, it must be admitted that the Achuar in general do not come off badly as far as leisure goes and that the women, in particular, do not put in much more work than the men.

In order to study the differential allocation of labor, we selected a sample of eight households (four in the interfluvial habitat and four in the riverine) in which daily time allocation was recorded for all adults over the age of sixteen and for a total of eighty-seven observation days. The interfluve sample is based on the analysis of 216 man/woman-days of work put in by five men and thirteen women, compared with 124 man/woman-days put in by six men and thirteen women for the riverine households. Average work times were thus calculated on the basis of a total of 340 man/woman-days spread over the entire year to take into account eventual seasonal variations, however slight. Finally, it should be noted that, in each case, my wife and I were the guests of the households under study; despite our clumsy participation in subsistence activities, the two extra mouths to feed certainly entailed a little more effort. The extra work occasioned by our presence is probably more noticeable in the area of male activities, as Achuar men make it a point of honor never to let their guests go without meat. Our stays therefore certainly increased the frequency of hunting trips. Nevertheless the Achuar often receive visits of several days, and the situation we created is repeated often enough not to be regarded as unusual.

A look at the average time spent daily at each place of work by the men and by the women (Fig. 40) brings empirical confirmation to the sexual connotation of the different areas of praxis. The house indeed turns out to be the privileged space of domestic sociability that we described earlier, since that is where both men and women spend the bulk of their time, between 80–90% of a twenty-four-hour day. Alternatively, the other places are clearly marked by the preponderance of either male or female presence. Men spend five times as long in the forest as women, while women spend four to five times as long in the garden as men. Furthermore, it should be noted that male presence in gardens is amplified in this sample by the fact that we have counted time spent in clearing, that is in an activity that takes place in what is not yet an altogether genuine garden.

Figure 41 lists the average daily times devoted to the different production sectors, the quantitative data thus confirming earlier general indications on the structuring of subsistence activities according to gender and habitat. It must be said, however, that the categories are necessarily arbitrary, particularly in the case of household tasks, where what is or is not work remains highly ambiguous. For instance, it is the women who serve manioc beer to the men and, when their husband receives visitors, the women stand at the edge of the *tankamash* with a serving bowl, listening to the men's conversations and from time to time chiming in, while waiting to be asked to refill the men's *pininkia* drinking bowls. But there are often visitors, and the drinking sometimes goes on for hours. Should this domestic service be regarded as work, then, or should it be assimilated to a form of female sociability, since it is through the manioc-beer offering that women participate in encounters between men of the household and outsiders? Confronted with this typological problem plus the practical impossibility of timing this daily sequence of discontinuous operations that make up women's household chores, we have had to fall back on overall estimates for the heading "housework and cooking." Alternatively, it seemed impossible to measure such activities as "table service" (e.g. offering manioc beer) and childcare (suckling, grooming, delousing. . .); these two headings have therefore been included under "rest and leisure," which corresponds fairly closely to Achuar women's own interpretation.

On the basis of sample measurements, we can estimate that making the fermented manioc mash for beer (on average three times a week), sweeping, doing the washing and the dishes, and fetching water represent a work time of between 130 and 170 minutes per woman per day, it being understood that much of the food preparation time (peeling and washing tubers) is counted as gardening time, since these activities are an extension of harvesting and are performed *in situ*. With this estimate in mind, we may now affirm that Achuar women do not work much more than the men. In effect, the latter devote an average of 284 minutes per day to production tasks, compared with 187 minutes for women. If we add to these 187 minutes the time taken up by household chores, 170 minutes at the maximum, women's work time comes to a global daily mean of 357 minutes. In sum, Achuar men devote an average of around five hours a day to ensuring the daily existence of the household, as compared with around six hours for the women.[2] The rest of the time is free, and the Achuar use it for eating, talking, sleeping, bathing, making visits, dancing, making war, and making love.

	Habitat											
	Interfluvial						Riverine					
	Men			Women			Men			Women		
Place of activity	hr	min	%	hr	min	%	hr	min	%	hr	min	%
House	19	32	81.3	20	46	86.5	20	19	84.7	21	29	89.5
Garden	—	28	2.0	2	22	9.9	—	41	2.8	2	—	8.3
Forest	4	—	16.7	—	52	3.6	3	—	12.5	—	31	2.2
Total	24	—	100	24	—	100	24	—	100	24	—	100

40. Average daily time spent in places of work

Given the different rates of activity for men and women, however, time does not divide between work and leisure in the same way for the two sexes. Men have a tendency to be inactive in a continuous manner, that is all day long, since they work in the same way, eight or ten hours straight. Inversely, women's rest periods are as fragmented as their work sequences, and generally take the form of shorter or longer pauses between the various chores to be done. Men and women share the same leisure for any length of time only when visiting far from home, and particularly during drinking parties, when every activity but cooking ceases for two or even three days.

An examination of labor input by sector and by type of biotope exploited (Fig. 41) reveals the incidence of ecological parameters on the distribution of tasks. It is immediately evident that the proportions of time spent hunting and fishing are inverted in the two habitats: men from the interfluvial forest spend less time fishing than those in riverine regions (0.7% compared with 5.5%), while the latter spend less time hunting than the former (6.4% compared with 15%). Labor input for hunting, however, is slightly overrepresented in the interfluvial sample, for in one of the four houses where we stayed, the head of the house had undertaken a major expedition to lay in stocks of meat for a celebration. Despite this correction, the difference between the respective portions of work devoted to hunting and to fishing in the two biotopes comes as no surprise, in view of the contrast in natural resource availability.

If, as we have seen, returns per hunting trip are roughly equivalent in the two biotopes, the mean duration of each trip, on the other hand, is shorter in the riverine habitat than in the interfluvial zone. In other words, and for

	Habitat											
	Interfluvial						Riverine					
	Men			Women			Men			Women		
Sector	hr	min	%	hr	min	%	hr	min	%	hr	min	%
Gardening	—	28	2.0	2	22	9.9	—	41	2.8	2	—	8.3
Hunting	3	35	15.0	—	38	2.6	1	32	6.4	—	10	0.7
Fishing	—	11	0.7	—	1	0.06	1	20	5.5	—	16	1.1
Gathering	—	8	0.5	—	13	0.9	—	6	0.4	—	5	0.3
Making and repairing artefacts	1	6	4.5	—	12	0.8	—	21	1.5	—	17	1.2
Housework, cooking	—	—	—	2	50	11.8	—	—	—	2	50	11.8
Rest, leisure, sleep	18	32	77.3	17	44	73.8	20		83.4	18	22	76.5

41. Average daily times devoted to each production sector

an identical result, it takes the upstream hunters of the hills more time (on average two or three hours more) to bring back game than it does the downstream hunters of the plains. This systematic disproportion should probably be related to the Achuar's claim that there is a higher concentration of peccaries in the riverine habitat than in the interfluve. The discrepancy could not show up in the quantitative data of our analysis of hunting returns per trip, for, however many peccaries a hunter may encounter, his kill is necessarily limited by the portering capacity he can muster. From the standpoint of the availability of peccaries, the adaptive advantage of the riverine habitat lies in the fact that a man does not need to travel as far, on average, to encounter a horde of peccary, and therefore devotes less time to hunting than his counterparts in the interfluvial habitat. Yet this time saving is of no benefit in terms of a possible reallocation of the labor saved: when a man has finished hunting he does not generally undertake any other major activity until the next day, even if he has returned home in the early afternoon. As for the disproportion between fishing times, it can be perfectly explained by the different techniques used in the two biotopes. The reader will recall that fish poisoning was practiced only sporadically in the interfluvial habitat, during the low-water season, when only a few men devoted the bulk of their time to line fishing in rivers and streams. In the riverine habitat, on the other hand, when the waters are low, all forms of fishing constitute an almost daily activity in all households.

The higher rate of male gardening that appears in the riverine habitat is not significant in this sample, for it is simply the statistical repercussion of a temporary increase due to work begun on a new clearing in one of the riverine households. In the long term it is obvious that it is, on the contrary, the men of the interfluvial habitat who expend the most labor in gardening, since they clear more often and must fell bigger trees than their riverine counterparts. Nevertheless, exactly how much more work they put in is particularly hard to assess, given the number of variables that must be taken into account. If we extrapolate from the average clearing time per hectare and the average productive lifetime of a garden in the two habitats, we can probably advance that it is likely that exploiting a riverine habitat represents a saving of horticultural labor of something like ten minutes per day. On the other hand, the slight decrease in female work time devoted to gardening in the riverine habitat, as compared to the interfluve (22 minutes), reflects a concrete advantage: the greater ease with which weeds are pulled in the gardens on alluvial terraces. Given the same area, it is faster to weed a garden in the riverine habitat than one in the interfluvial habitat.

In the area of hunting, the differential ratio between the two biotopes for male labor input is mirrored in the female times. Women in the riverine habitat spend fewer hours hunting than their counterparts in the interfluvial habitat and more time fishing. In any case, Fig. 41 shows that women's participation in hunting does not involve a great labor investment on their part since generalized polygyny spreads the hunting trips among several co-wives. Even in the case of monogamous domestic units, the increase in workload engendered by the obligation regularly to accompany a husband is relatively slight.

This is what we see in Figure 42, which shows the allocation of labor per woman as a function of the number of co-wives in her residential unit. It is effectively in monogamous homes of the interfluvial habitat that the percentage of female time devoted to non-horticultural production sectors is the highest, which is consistent with the impossibility of dividing the hunting trips and regular manioc beer production among several women. But the extra work thus recorded is fairly slight when compared to the average times allocated to identical tasks in polygynous homes of the same habitat. As for the corresponding work times in the riverine habitat, these show a fairly regular progression as co-wives are added, or at least up to the series of houses with more than three co-wives, when inputs fall below the level of monogamous households. The average work times for agricultural production, on the other hand, have a tendency to rise with the number of wives, whatever the nature of the biotope exploited. This is altogether understand-

	Composition of residential unit							
	1 wife		2 co-wives		3 co-wives		more than 3 co-wives	
	I	R	I	R	I	R	I	R
Sector	h mn	h mn	h mn	h mn	h mn	h mn	h mn	h mn
Gardening	1 25	2 6	2 33	2 24	2 16	1 30	2 52	2 34
Hunting, fishing, gathering, crafts	1 20	– 32	1 15	– 48	– 51	1 7	1 10	– 27
Percentage	I%	R%	I%	R%	I%	R%	I%	R%
Gardening	6.0	8.8	10.7	10.0	9.4	6.3	11.9	10.7
Other sectors	5.5	2.2	5.2	3.3	3.5	4.6	4.9	1.9

I = interfluvial habitat   R = riverine habitat

42. Average daily times devoted by a woman to each production sector according to the number of co-wives

able, since each adult woman constitutes a small independent production cell, and the work she does in her patch of garden is unconnected with that of the other women in their adjacent patches. As a rule, then, it cannot be said that increasing the female workforce in a domestic unit implies as a corollary an overall decline in the workload for each of the women in it.[3]

An apparently more surprising conclusion becomes obvious if one tries to correlate the average quantity of female labor invested in gardening with the size of the plot cultivated. In effect, we have already said that the relative size of the women's individual gardens depends neither on ecological factors nor on the number of consumers in the domestic unit. Great men (*juunt*) generally have many wives, and each wife strives to contribute to the house's renown by cultivating vast plots. It might be thought that such a quest for prestige is costly in terms of labor and that a large garden therefore takes up much more time than a small one. But Figure 43 shows that this is not so. This table correlates the average daily time devoted to gardening by sixteen women in sixteen different-sized plots, divided for convenience into six groups. Each group of approximately same-sized plots is coupled with a work time, obtained by averaging the daily times of each woman cultivating these plots. We see that the daily time spent gardening is roughly the same for all groups, irrespective of the size of the plots. In other words, whereas the size of the gardens varies from one to thirteen, the work time remains steady: a woman does not need to work thirteen times longer, then, to cultivate a garden thirteen times as big.

This paradoxical result naturally needs explaining. In the first place, the help small and adolescent girls give their mothers in the garden is not shown in this table. Their contribution should not be overestimated, however, especially as, in this sample, only two adult women enjoy the permanent help of two small girls apiece. One of these women fell into the 8,000–13,000 m^2 group (with a plot of 10,600 m^2), while the other was in the 4,000–

Plot size (m²)	Daily gardening time h	mn
1,000–2,000	2	39
2,000–3,000	2	10
3,000–4,000	2	14
4,000–6,000	1	45
6,000–8,000	2	11
8,000–13,000	2	30

43. Relation between plot size and average daily gardening time for an adult woman

6,000m² group (with a plot of 5,960 m²). Of the seven women cultivating plots of between 4,000 and 13,000 m², only two had regular additional help with work, then. The key to this apparent anomaly lies elsewhere, in the relation between the area planted and the area effectively exploited for daily tuber production. Only a small portion of the species planted in the very large gardens is actually harvested, the remainder constituting an enormous surplus stored in the ground and never used.

It may be objected that, even if only partially exploited, a large garden still demands more work than a small one to plant, maintain, and weed. And indeed large gardens are meticulously weeded, including the portions that are not intensively cultivated. If planting and weeding great gardens does not entail an increase in work time, it is because, as we have observed many times, the women who exploit these gardens work faster than their fellow gardeners who cultivate small ones. The former are usually middle-aged, experienced gardeners, inured to work, who, in the same amount of time, accomplish much more than young carefree wives cultivating small areas. The differential intensity of work is an important element to be considered when analyzing production factors, especially since it is how hard one works and not how long that is socially sanctioned. For exactly the same amount of time spent daily, one gardener will be accused of being lazy because she cultivates only a small area, while another will be admired because she manages to keep up a very large garden.

One last problem remains to be examined, that of the effect the number of a man's wives has on his work time. As the purveyors of game and fish, the burden of production in this particularly valued sector of the daily diet rests squarely on the men's shoulders; it would therefore seem logical that an increase in the number of mouths to feed would be reflected by an increase in the time that has to be spent hunting and fishing. Figure 44 itemizes the average daily time a man spends in each of these areas of activity as a function of the number of wives in the residential unit. But here again the variations do not seem particularly significant; in the interfluvial habitat we can see a slight increase in male work times which correlates with the increase in the number of wives, while practically no difference is visible in the riverine habitat.

The stability of work times allocated to hunting and fishing can be attributed in part to the inequality in hunters' skills and to the repercussions of this on matrimonial status. It is a fact that hyperpolygamous men are usually the best hunters and that they bring back on average more game per trip than inexperienced young men with only one wife. The phenomenon parallels women's gardening: for the same work time, the cynegetic and halieutic productivity of a great man considerably exceeds that of a recently married young man. This brings us back to the necessary distinction between work time, which is roughly the same for everyone, and the variability of its productive efficiency. Here, unlike the case of gardening, the criterion of rank is not so much the relative intensity of the labor as the inequality of technical skills.

And yet some men with several wives turn out to be poor hunters, and their wives and children eat less game and fish on average than other, more fortunate households. This disparity is clearly perceived by the wives balked of their ration of game; without actually voicing recriminations, they never miss a chance to show their displeasure to their dejected husband. The stormy domestic situation – which can lead to one or more of the wives leaving the home – does not make these unlucky or unskilled men go hunting or fishing any more often to maximize their chances. Here we touch on a crucial point concerning the way the Achuar represent the allocation of labor, which may be stated as a general rule: whatever the individual capacities, there exists for everyone the same ceiling on the average expenditure of labor. In other terms, an individual man's or woman's estimation of the average amount of work he or she should do is independent of the observable, empirical productivity of this work; this assessment is entirely determined by the indigenous norm for the division of time between work and leisure. One cannot help being struck by the fact that all Achuar, male and female, spend approximately the same average

	Composition of residential unit							
	1 wife		2 co-wives		3 co-wives		more than 3 co-wives	
	I	R	I	R	I	R	I	R
Sector	h mn	h mn	h mn	h mn	h mn	h mn	h mn	h mn
Hunting	3 20	– 53	3 53	3 36	4 15	1 7	4 2	2 37
Fishing	– 15	2 46	– –	– 24	– 40	2 10	– –	1 7
Percentage	I%	R%	I%	R%	I%	R%	I%	R%
Daily times spent in hunting and fishing	15	15.2	16.2	16.6	20.4	13.6	16.8	15.5

I = interfluvial habitat   R = riverine habitat

44. Average daily time devoted by a man to hunting and fishing according to the number of co-wives

amount of time per day working, and in no household did we record any notable surplus or deficit of work. The Achuar do not intensify work by extending its duration, but by optimizing its conditions of realization.

The idea that the time invested in work is socially limited naturally entails some interesting theoretical consequences. On the one hand, one is obliged to assume that, in the absence of any other indigenous procedure for quantifying work time and faced with the diversity of individual rates and sequences that can affect the labor input, there must be some relatively accurate conceptual paradigm organizing individual daily lives so that, in the long run, everyone always achieves the same overall balance between work and leisure. On the other hand, and besides the fact that it is now absurd to speak of "rejection of work" in reference to societies that have so clear an intuitive awareness of the quantity of work that it is legitimate to do, one may find that setting a limit on the increase of work times constitutes a determining factor for explaining what is customarily called the homeostasis of productive forces in archaic societies. If the way to the intensification of production historically lies in a gradual increase in the average length of the working day, it is clear that any obstacle society places in the way of this increase will result in either maintaining the productive forces at the same level or directing their development towards progress of the technological system. When, for various reasons, the conditions do not obtain for the emergence of fundamental technological changes within a society, the existing system of production will tend to perpetuate itself without change over very long periods of time, provided that it continues to fulfill the objectives society assigns it.

But to return to the Achuar, it will now be understood why there are no major differences in work times between biotopes, domestic units, and even the genders, since everyone shares the same representation of a limit on the labor that should be expended. Individual adjustments are made in terms of relative intensity of effort and unequal skills, but these do not affect the overall structure of time allocation between work and non-work. It will also be understood why a balance is always struck between the time allocated to the different production sectors depending on the alternative resources of the biotopes and the seasons, since the total quantity of work done must remain the same regardless of the specific operations that comprise it. And so the quantitative analysis of work times yields results that a more impressionistic approach would have left undetected; these run counter to both a naive application of the "law of least effort" and the extension to all societies of the principle of optimizing scarce means.

The qualitative order

For reasons of typological convenience, we have been classifying the sectors of Achuar activity according to our own categories, filing under the heading "work" all activities aimed at food acquisition. The validity of this approach has been empirically confirmed by the fact that all Achuar divide their time in the same way, between two categories, the indigenous definition of which we do not yet know, but which we have chosen to call work and non-work. We still have to see, however, if the Achuar represent the various labor processes as independent areas of activity and if the indigenous model of the division of labor assigns distinct valences to the various sectors, thereby making some tasks more desirable than others depending on whether they are perceived as more or less simple, arduous, pleasant, or prestigious.

This last question arises particularly in the case of hunting and garden-ing, two highly contrasted labor processes, from both material and symbolic points of view, which, because of this, could serve as a paradigma-tic matrix for the division of labor. In effect, the ethnographic literature on upper Amazonia usually presents hunting and gardening as two clearly antinomic elements divided into a sequence of dichotomies distributed along opposite sides of the gender axis: garden and forest; domestic group and outsiders; animal and vegetable; foraging in nature and transformation of nature; imposing death in war and hunting, and producing life in childbirth and gardening; biological reproduction and social reproduction. Within this series of opposing pairs, the hunting–gardening dichotomy usually banishes gardening and the women who do it to a demeaning, profane world of hard labor, while hunting and warfare appear as ludic activities, charged with emotion and danger, the performance of which requires the knowledge and use of esoteric ritual techniques. We have seen, however, that the Achuar make a few unexpected adjustments to this convenient stereotype elevated to the role of model; and these raise questions about some of our assumptions as to the near-geometric similar-ity between sexual dichotomy and division of labor.

First of all we should ask ourselves if the Achuar possess the concept of something that could be analogous to the modern concept of work as we conceive it. Like the majority of precapitalist societies, the Achuar have no term or notion that synthesizes the idea of work in general, that is the idea of a coherent set of technical operations the purpose of which is to produce the material means necessary to existence. Nor does their language have words for labor processes in the broad sense, like hunting, gardening, fishing, or crafts; and so from the outset we are confronted with the problem of the intelligibility of indigenous categories, which divide up labor processes very differently from our own. This non-congruency of areas of meaning calls for a rapid exploration of the notional regions that surround the Achuar's productive activities.

The indigenous lexeme whose meaning most closely corresponds to one of our modern uses of the word "work" is *takat*, the noun form of the verb *taka*, which designates an arduous physical activity involving a technical skill and the mediation of a tool. In performative utterances, *takat* is almost always explicitly associated with such notions as hard labor, physical suffering, and sweat, and it is most often applied to gardening, whether as a male activity (clearing) or a female task (planting, harvesting, or weeding). This meaning of *takat* comes quite close to the Greek *ponos* and the Latin *labor*, as it designates not so much a definite category of activities as a mode of performing certain tasks. In effect, *takat* also means touching, handling, and carries the idea of direct action on nature with the aim of transforming or reorienting its goal. This is very clear in the sexual connotations of the term, since the same expression, *takamchau*, "unworked," is used for both a young virgin and a tract of climax forest that has never been cleared. Here *takat* takes on an additional determination roughly equivalent to the French *besogner*, the idea being that the productive potential of women and the forest are useless unless they have undergone socialization, which enables both to realize their potential. Unlike one of the traditional European denotations of labor since Ancient Greek times, *takat* does not designate the labor of childbirth, but, on the contrary, that of fecundation.

Takat is thus a mode of activity for which gardening provides the model without exhausting all of the meanings; but it is also an unequally shared personal quality, which seems endowed with a certain degree of autonomy. In effect, people say "my work is at work" (*winia takatrun takaawai*), meaning "I am driven to work, I am moved by my capacity as a worker," thereby making it understood that the agent in some way lies outside the realm of one's will. This conception of work as a personal attribute flows naturally from a situation in which work and the worker are conceptually inseparable; work not being an object of commercial transaction can therefore not be conceived as a separate entity. It is interesting to note that, in the few rare cases when Achuar had worked as unskilled labor for petroleum companies, they referred to their paid activity using the Spanish term *trabajo*, rather than the word *takat*, even though its meaning adequately covered the technical operations they performed for these companies (cutting trails with machetes for seismic lines). Nevertheless, they obviously felt that *takat* was an inappropriate notion for designating a task based on a commercial transaction and whose ends they did not control, that is a task which suddenly turned a glaring light on the newly acquired exteriority of their labor power. Those Achuar who had undergone this experience implicitly recognized the coexistence of two contrasting representations of the same type of technical activity: *takat* as work-attribute and *trabajo* as work-commodity, their coexistence being made possible only by the use of two terms belonging to distinct vocabularies and referring to two incompatible types of reality.

The Achuar have no term for being a good worker, but it is possible to circumscribe fairly accurately the content of such a representation by deducing it from its would-be antonym, *naki*, "a lazy person." Laziness is clearly defined as the halfhearted performance of certain duties incumbent on everyone: a man is lazy if he rarely goes hunting and if he makes only small clearings; a woman is lazy if she does not keep up her garden and makes only small amounts of manioc beer. Laziness brings with it inferior social standing, probably even the only explicitly inferior status in what is an otherwise extremely egalitarian society. When one is saddled with a spouse, husband or wife, publicly recognized as lazy, it is perfectly acceptable to abandon him or her, since it is judged that he or she has not fulfilled the normal role in the necessary complementarity of productive tasks.

But laziness is unusual, and, if being lazy is degrading, being a good worker, on the other hand, does not in itself confer status, since this is only the normal performance of the tasks assigned by the sexual division of labor. In other terms, the qualities that are valued in the order of sexual complementarity do not refer to a symmetrical inversion of laziness, that is they do not refer only to the intensity of work or the amount done, but are based on an assessment of aptitudes of which *takat*–work is only a small part. Being a "good wife" includes raising fine hounds or being an expert weaver or potter, but also the duty to provide one's husband with an abundant supply of smooth manioc beer. Seen from the standpoint of the qualities by which she contributes to the reproduction of the household, a "good wife" will be called by her husband *umiu* ("obedient," in the sense of "someone who does not shirk her obligations"). Among the possible spouses, the desirable wife is defined as much by this virtue of tacit acquiescence to the duties of her station as by conformation to the indigenous canon of physical beauty. Symmetrically, for a woman, the *penke aishmank* ("complete man") is one who not only satisfies the biological needs of his wife (by fulfilling his sexual and hunting duties), but who also contributes, by his preeminence in warfare, to establishing the prestige of the entire household.

Takat has an ambiguous status, then: on the one hand, it is not particularly prestigious, since it is synonymous with hard work and suffering, and it is not the exclusive criterion of an individual's positive capacities; but, on the other hand, non-*takat* is very degrading, when it is systematic and takes the socially defined form of laziness. *Takat* appears curiously here as being very similar to a modern representation of work as a necessary evil that no one can avoid without loss of respect. But this necessary evil did not always exist, and mythology teaches us that it was because he brought too much zeal to his work that mankind was cursed with hard *takat*. One sequence from the Hummingbird myth, which we summarize below, is very instructive in this respect:

When Hummingbird had felled a large clearing, the two sisters, Wayus and Mukunt (*Sickingia* sp., a Rubiaceae) decided to plant a garden and so they went to the clearing with bundles of manioc cuttings. Catching sight of them, Hummingbird said: "No need to plant them! Just leave the cuttings in the clearing! All I have to do is blow on them and they'll all be planted in a flash!" Then he left the clearing. Very skeptical as to Hummingbird's ability to keep his promise, Wayus, one of the sisters, took up a digging stick to begin loosening the soil for planting; but at the first stroke, the stake was immediately sucked into the ground, and Wayus, who had not let go, found herself sticking head down in the earth and unable to get free. Whereupon Hummingbird returned to the garden and immediately understood that Wayus had disobeyed him and, carried away by her zeal, had not believed his promise of effortless planting. Hummingbird sentenced Wayus to become her vegetal homonym (a plant cultivated exclusively by men); furious, Hummingbird said: "I wanted it to be the men who planted by blowing on the cuttings and seeds, and I also wanted it to be the men who weeded by blowing on the weeds, but as Wayus has disobeyed me, henceforth clearing will be hard *takat* for men, while planting and weeding will be hard *takat* for women. Men who do not cut down large clearings and women who weed badly will be the object of public disapproval." And to make matters worse, Hummingbird scattered tufts of his down around the gardens, where it immediately turned into *chiri-chiri* weed.

This myth is a remarkable synthesis of Achuar representations of *takat*, providing a sort of basis for both the beginning of garden *takat* and its present division between the sexes, a double event the responsibility for which is attributed to a woman's overweening zeal. This over-eagerness brought about the two hardest chores women now have to contend with, planting and weeding, tasks of which they could have been relieved, since, in the beginning, they were the exclusive province of men. We also see that the collective opprobrium attaching to laziness is correlative with the appearance of hard labor, without which it would have no reason to exist.

The Hummingbird myth is yet one more component of the huge set of Achuar myths based on the theme of overweening zeal, which brings into being an arduous or dangerous activity which, without this excessive behavior, would never have existed. Such is the case notably of building houses and making canoes, two activities which could have happened alone had men not interfered and brought down a curse upon themselves which now forces them to work hard. It is also the case of the threat of being devoured by Jurijri which has hung over mankind ever since he made fun of game.

Likewise the myth relating the origin of cultivated plants introduces a temporal sequence in three parts, distinguished by the presence or absence of garden *takat*. Before there were any gardens and when the diet was based on gathered wild foods, life was harsh, not because it was necessary to work hard, but because people were constantly hungry. Then Nunkui gave humans the use of cultivated plants, and there was a time of rest and plenty, for one had only to call the plants by their name and they would appear. Finally, following the offense people inflicted on Nunkui, she took away the privilege of idleness and sentenced humans to work in order to cultivate their gardens.

Here we see that garden *takat* and the curse that founds it are not unrelated to the Western idea of work, rooted in Christianity and the Old Testament, which regards it as a necessary evil brought about by a transgression. But in the present case, the transgression is of a different order, and the mythic theme of excessive zeal is really the antithesis of the normative rule of moderation and self-restraint which, as we have seen repeatedly, is basic to harmonious relations with nature. Thus, while *takat* undeniably bears the stamp of the garden, it is nevertheless clear that neither *takat* nor gardening is totally on the female side and that, in the indigenous configuration of values, the burden of hard work does not fall exclusively on women. Attested in myth, the sexual division of garden *takat* is adequate proof that, to the Achuar way of thinking, gardening is a fundamentally composite activity that rests on the complementarity of male and female tasks. This complementarity is accomplished diachronically rather than synchronically, but it is nonetheless perceived as necessary to the overall realization of the labor process.

If we now turn to the semantic world of hunting, we see that it is naturally not included in the category of *takat*, since hunting is always designated by vague, polysemic expressions such as "to go into the forest," "to go looking," or "to go for a walk." Which is to say that the Achuar language does not identify hunting by an independent lexeme which would give it unequivocal specificity. The linguistic specificity of hunting comes by default, as it were, inasmuch as, for the reasons we have seen, hunting is the only forest activity that is not explicitly announced beforehand. The very metaphorical expressions used to designate hunting are ample indication that it is not regarded as hard work, even if the ethnographer's own participant observations defy him to imagine what there is about hunting that makes it physically less arduous than clearing. Chasing a peccary through swamps and spinneys is hardly a restful activity, and yet no man returning from the hunt will ever admit to being tired whereas he readily confesses fatigue after a few hours of wielding an ax.

Hunting is a labor process in which women play a not negligible role, and all the more as it traditionally provides the best occasion for licit sexual commerce. It is therefore clear that, if we represent hunting as a unified labor process, roughly definable as the set of those operations by which a domestic group procures wild animals for eating, this labor process, like gardening, involves gender complementarity. And in this case the complementarity is all the more marked in that it is physically reinforced by sexuality.

Fishing, too, poses a problem of vague semantics, for it does not fall into a unified category either, but is lexically atomized into as many expressions as there are techniques for catching fish (harpoon and net, hook and line, poisoning). Of all the techniques, we have seen that the poisoning parties are the clearest demonstration of complementarity. Fishing is never seen as hard *takat*, but rather as a form of entertainment that breaks up the monotony of everyday life. Fish poisoning, in particular, is carried out in a general atmosphere of good humor and competition which contrasts singularly with the formalism that normally presides over public contacts between the sexes.

Gathering is also perceived as entertainment, and in this closely resembles mushroom hunting in our own climes. There is no general term for gathering as a unified activity, and it is therefore always specified according to the particular fruits or insects one plans to collect. Indeed people almost always set out on a gathering walk knowing full well what type of seasonal products they are after, and the action is then stated with respect to the specific, circumscribed goal (e.g. "to go looking for sapote fruit" or "to go looking for palm grubs").

We will end this overview of vernacular categories by analyzing the notional terms for what we ordinarily call craft production. The idea of making is expressed by two suffixes, one which designates everything that is accomplished without the help of outside power, and the other which is used to denote everything that comes about following the action of an outside agent. The Achuar therefore generally use the second suffix, added to the name of an artefact, to express the complete series of operations that results in the object (e.g.: *jea*, "house," becomes *jeamjai*, "I am making a house"). Within the making process, individual moments can be distinguished which are identified in the language by *ad hoc* lexemes: thus "I am plaiting palm fronds for the roof" (*napiarjai*), forms a discrete linguistically specified unit within the overall process of "I am making a house."

Now there is one general term that subsumes a good number of these technical making processes and sheds some light on the way the Achuar think about the production of artefacts. This is the verb *najana*, which means to effect a transformation, that is consciously to change a shape without altering its content or essence. *Najana* is the usual term employed in myths to designate the process by which an apparently human being, having been cursed, changes into a plant or an animal; the essence of this being already present in its name before the transformation is fulfilled in the change of shape without the concomitant loss of any of its spiritual characteristics. This is what happened to Wayus, in the Hummingbird myth, who in her new vegetal aspect still possessed the same soul (*wakan*) as in her human existence.

In the sphere of material production, *najana* is used above all to designate women's pot making and men's wickerwork, two crafts that are paradigmatic in many respects. Indeed, if it is generally accepted that not everyone is equally skilled in the areas of manufacture ascribed to the two sexes, and that consequently some men are more reputed than others for making blowguns or some women are better than others at weaving cotton belts, pottery and wickerwork are considered to be indispensable, basic techniques that everyone must master. Craftwork is not production, then, and even less creation; it is the regular repetition of an unchanging pattern, a repetition that tolerates neither deviation nor decoration. It is significant that the same term, *emesra* ("to spoil") is used when an accident occurs during fabrication – for example when a pot cracks during firing – and in myths, when an error or some excess irremediably upsets the world order.

If we try to summarize what we have learned from this rapid semantic tour, several things become evident. In the first place, it is obvious that the indigenous terms for productive activities do not make a clear distinction between male and female tasks, and that the vocabulary remains vague when it comes to dividing up labor processes, which are either atomized into a host of individual operations or hidden behind very broad terms. Categories like *takat* and *najana* do not designate specific labor processes, but ways of doing work, differentiated forms of human action.

Furthermore, strictly speaking, different production activities are not more or less prestigious according to whether they are performed by men or by women. The only thing condemned by society is non-work, whether male or female. Of course a good hunter builds up prestige, but so does an expert gardener; and their skills are complementary and interdependent within the household unit. It is therefore hard to conceive of a good hunter married to a bad gardener or vice versa. This complementarity manifests itself as much in a sort of rivalry invested in the respective spheres of activity as in the need to combine skills in certain tasks, such as gardening. Of course women sometimes compare their fate with that of men, remarking that men have an easy life, but what they mean is not that gardening is any less prestigious than hunting but that it is, as they see it, harder work.

We are faced with a problem of logical articulation, then. If there is nothing in the overt categories of the Achuar language that permits the differentiation of one or more labor processes and if, furthermore, this absence of lexical reification is empirically confirmed by apparent gender complementarity in certain labor processes, what then allows the Achuar – and the ethnologist observing them – to think the relationship between hunting and gardening in terms of sexual dichotomy? What authorizes us, in sum, to postulate that the Achuar classify their productive activities in terms of clearly differentiated labor processes?

This logical obstacle vanishes if we realize that the Achuar represent differentiation of the labor process almost entirely implicitly, that is, not as a seriation of concrete operational sequences subsumed into singular linguistic categories, but as issuing from the specific sets of preconditions necessary for carrying out these operational sequences. In effect the Achuar do not conceive work in the same way as we do, as taking and transforming the natural entities needed to satisfy material needs; rather they see it as a continual commerce with a world governed by spirits that must be charmed, constrained, or moved to pity by appropriate symbolic techniques. Technical know-how is inseparable from symbolic know-how, and the two domains are not analytically distinguished. Now each of these spirits controls a very specific sphere of human praxis and demands in return personalized treatment befitting their area of influence. This means that a certain number of labor processes not even distinguished as separate activities in everyday speech are nonetheless defined with great precision by the symbolic and ritual manipulations that are the necessary condition for their being effective.

As technical operational sequences have no lexical existence, they emerge as latent categories of representation in the coherent system of their preconditions. But it is only the ethnographer who sees these preconditions as such – i.e. as separate from that which they condition; the Achuar see them as an integral part of that which they make possible. The oneness of the field of representations of a labor process is thus manifested by the oneness of the representations of its conditions of possibility. As we have seen in the foregoing pages, the realization and success of all forms of food production, with the exception of gathering, closely depend on a complex set of propitiatory prerequisites.

We must now try to find a pattern of themes running through the elements that make up the systems of hunting and gardening preconditions if we are to justify our claim that these are two clearly distinguished categories within the indigenous system of representations. The Achuar's idea of hunting is not that different from our own, since they think of it as an activity aimed at finding beings that are hiding, and killing them for food. On the other hand, the goal of cultivating gardens is to ensure the presence of beings who might suddenly disappear, while trying not to be killed by them before they are eaten. This inverted symmetry between the hunter taking the life of animals and manioc taking the life of humans might be deemed artificial, since the overzealous hunter is just as threatened by cannibalism. But having one's blood sucked by manioc is different from being devoured by the "game mothers" in that the former is an unavoidable fact of daily life (the death of infants is often attributed to this), while the Achuar see the latter as altogether hypothetical. There is then no equivalence between the very real danger of anemia (*putsumar*), imputed to touching manioc, and the highly improbable sanction entailed by killing too much game.

Although the nature of their uncertainty is symmetrically inverted around two poles (desired presence of game/feared absence of plants – agent of killing/subject of vampirism), both hunting and gardening are still thought of as risky endeavors the outcome of which is unpredictable. The hazardous character of hunting and gardening therefore makes it necessary to establish permanent personal relations with the tutelary spirits that control their respective conditions of realization. But the modalities of commerce are quite different depending on whether one is dealing with forest spirits or the garden spirit. As the bond postulated between a woman and Nunkui is basically a relation of identification, the relationship that develops between this woman and the plants she grows must be seen as a double of the maternal relationship Nunkui entertains with her plant children. Nothing of this sort occurs in hunting, the effectiveness of which depends on the interaction of three elements: man, go-betweens ("game mothers" and "game *amana*"), and the hunted animals. The relationship of complicity and seduction a hunter entertains with these go-betweens closely resembles that which prevails in his relations with his animal brothers-in-law. Furthermore, inversely to gardening, the threat of cannibalism does not come from the beings that are eaten, but from their protectors, whom it is therefore crucial to appease. Some of these "mothers" have a highly ambiguous attitude towards their flock in that they actually eat them. While the gardening model of sociability is built around two identical relationships of consanguinity with the same object (Nunkui–cultivated plants and woman–cultivated plants), the hunting model is articulated around two identical relationships of affinity with two separate objects (hunter–go-between and hunter–game), which are themselves related by blood. Thus, whereas Nunkui is a paradigm with which one identifies, the go-betweens are beings with whom one must negotiate.

This relatively clearcut opposition between models of the relationship with tutelary spirits is reinforced by differentiation between the symbolic media that make the relationship possible. The hunting dream is the immediate condition of effective practice, but its content is never explicitly the same as the activity it announces. On the other hand, the gardening dream is the direct sign of a condition for the realization of the practice (locating charms), for it explicitly designates the condition of practice without itself being that condition. Although each type of dream is, by preference, assigned to one or the other gender, the assignment is reversible. Hunting and gardening *anent* are necessary conditions of practice, which have the same type of efficacy and the same type of origin; but they are clearly differentiated by both their destination and the sex of their users. Lastly, *nantar* and *namur* are useful conditions of practice, which have the same physical nature, but neither the same type of efficacy, nor the same origin, nor the same destination. The symbolic means of entering into relations with the supernatural are all drawn from the same limited stock. But if all charms are fundamentally alike, if all *anent* are in effect songs that have the same melodic structure and if all dreams are in effect soul journeys, they are nonetheless clearly distinguished by features proper to the symbolic spheres in which they are used.

In sum, the killing of wild animals and gardening are represented as two different processes each distinguished by the particular set of preconditions that makes it possible. Moreover, an analysis of these preconditions allows us to reconstruct the coherent model of the implicit reference behind these preconditions, that is the particular system of interactions with the supernatural that underlies each of the two processes. These interaction models are not canonical representations shared by all subjects; they are totalities only in the eyes of the observer, who pieces them together from the clues gleaned from the system of preconditions. One must thus make a clear distinction between the implicit modalities of commerce with tutelary spirits, which provide a precise definition of the sphere of symbolic interaction assigned to each sex, and the contingent, explicit conditions of the possibility of this commerce, which, even though formally set out by the specific nature of their media, often depend on collaboration between the sexes.

The reader will recall that the symbolic conditions governing the success of a labor process lie in part beyond the grasp of those who carry it out. Although the relationship with the tutelary spirits that control the efficacy of hunting and gardening, respectively, is clearly individualized and dichotomized in the conditions of exercise, some of the media of this relationship are strongly subordinated to cooperation between men and women. This is exemplified by the food taboos that apply to the entire domestic unit when curare is being made or planting being done by men or women, these being operations whose success depends on the self-restraint of each and every person. This is also the case of *namur* hunting and fishing charms, which, because they are bezoars, are of necessity procured for men by women, since it is always the women's task to gut the fish and wash the tripe. It is the case, too, of premonitory dreams, which, as we have seen, have less to do with the gender of the dreamer than with the general conditions of realization of a labor process. Finally, it is possible to think of the malevolence that spoils the hunt and devastates gardens as the extreme form of the uncontrollable incidence of others on the preconditions for realizing a labor process. In a sense this is a model of what non-collaboration can produce when it dons the mask of systematic animosity. Here we have a process by which the material conditions for realizing labor processes are transposed onto the level of conceptual conditions, since the necessary complementarity of the sexes in the fulfillment of certain symbolic preconditions of labor processes merely recalls the complementarity required concretely to realize these processes.

Unlike many other societies, the Achuar sexual division of labor is not based on some discriminatory theory that holds that women are incapable of hunting and that working in the garden is unworthy of a man, but on the idea that each sex reaches its full potential in the sphere befitting its symbolic area of manipulation. Tenuous as the difference may appear, it is one to be reckoned with, for the Achuar representation of the division of labor does not engender any idea of hierarchical disparity between the sexes. Not only is gardening not less prestigious than hunting, but the women's ability to reproduce themselves as gardeners largely eludes the men's control. Separated as they may be by the conceptual configurations of their respective activities, men and women still meet in those complementary spaces in which these activities are carried out: in the forest, in the direct conjunction of a hunt spiked with eroticism; and in the garden, in the successive conjunction of the steps that lead to the domestication of plants.

9

The good life

How effective an economic system is depends not so much on the amount of wealth it generates as on its ability to accomplish the goals it is set. In societies that produce predominately for use, these goals are set culturally and have no alternative. For the Achuar, using nature in a fitting way does not mean accumulating an unending list of consumer items, but arriving at the state of equilibrium they term the "good life" (*shiir waras*). Clearly delineated in the stable context of the household, a sketch of the good life has already been outlined in the foregoing pages. Here and there we have traced the lineaments of a few rustic convictions that could sum up the Achuar philosophy of daily existence. The cornerstone of a harmonious life is without doubt peace in the home, that little something that makes a house a pleasant place that the ethnographer always leaves with a twinge of regret. Contrary to a widespread cliché, marital harmony is not inversely proportionate to the number of wives in the house. The best way to have peace at home is to marry sisters; then the co-wives are bound by ties of true affection, which keeps them from competing for their husband's favors. This homely serenity is confined to a microcosm, but it is all the more precious for the Achuar as this closed world is their only refuge from an outside environment constantly riven by grave social tensions. And in a society in which outside relations are mediated by war, it is vital to one's psychological equilibrium that home be a haven of peace.

The definition of the good life is not solely a question of economy or hedonism, then, since domestic peace is simultaneously one of the conditions for satisfying needs as well as its partial result. Marital harmony is evident when there is an abundant supply of game to keep the wives in good humor and repeated libations of manioc beer to quench the husband's immense thirst. In these circumstances, one must be singularly cranky or suspect adultery for discord to come upon the home. But a household's productivity also depends in part on the spouses' getting along, for this conditions effective collaboration between the sexes in subsistence activities. Such fine intentions do not, however, transform the Achuar into an idyllic society where harmony reigns under every roof. In reality men sometimes exert their domination over women with excessive brutality, particularly when they are under the influence of drink. In some households, the wives are regularly beaten by their husband, and sometimes to death. Female suicide is not exceptional and is the most dramatic means of protesting against chronic ill treatment. In homes torn by the war of the sexes – brute force versus reproachful idleness – the atmosphere is morose, the exact opposite of the good life. These households were held up as helots by sharp-tongued native informants who used them to illustrate the evils of marital strife.

So domestic peace is not universal, nor is it an absolute condition for effective food procurement, for the production system is such that even the worst discord would not disorganize the economic life of a household. In its social dimension, the good life is a sort of normative horizon of domestic life, an optimum which is neither desired not achieved by all Achuar. It can be apprehended only subjectively by the observer from the pleasure or lack of it that he takes in living with his hosts. In its strictly economic dimension, on the other hand, the good life can be defined by easily objectifiable criteria: the productivity of work, the rate of resource exploitation, or the quantitative or qualitative composition of the diet. That is why we will confine ourselves to this far less risky area, leaving the Achuar to decide for themselves whether or not they have a happy home life.

Underexploitation of resources

One of the most practical ways of analyzing the efficiency of an economic system producing primarily for use is to look at the real extent to which it exploits its productive capacity, that is at the safety margin it maintains when fulfilling its goals. There are two intrinsically linked factors to consider here: the potential productivity of the resource system, and its actual returns with respect to the potential productivity of the system of means. It is already clear from the preceding chapter that the Achuar use only a minute fraction of the total work power they could muster. If we take only those activities involved in food procurement (excluding transformation), average daily work time per person comes to three and a half hours (206 minutes); based on a ten-hour work day, then, the Achuar spend only 35% of their time every day in subsistence production. There is no doubt that, in theory, there are still ample possibilities for intensifying work, which are not exploited for reasons of socially imposed limits on the expenditure of labor. If labor is not a scarce resource on the individual level, neither is it on the collective plane, since an entire segment of the potentially productive population remains systematically inactive. Up until they are of an age to marry, adolescent boys spend nearly all their days completely idle; while little girls are put to work in the garden at an early age, no one would think of asking a boy to participate in the household subsistence effort. Here the ways of expending labor as well as the specific composition of the workforce are determined by cultural paradigms and not by physical constraints, since husky young men are excused from production tasks.

The underexploitation of productive capacities can be seen in areas other than that of human labor; it is just as flagrant in the underutilization of certain types of resources. The level of underutilization is easiest to assess in the case of gardening, because of the measurable nature of horticultural productivity. And yet, given the extreme diversity of the cultigens planted by the Achuar, it is nearly impossible to do a statistical analysis on garden productivity for all horticultural products actually exploited. We will therefore confine our demonstration to manioc, since it is the main cultigen in Achuar gardens in terms of numbers of plants (64% of all plants on average). This preponderance of manioc obviously corresponds to its role as a dietary staple. Thus when the main Achuar cultigens are listed by gross daily harvest weight (Fig. 45), manioc jumps well ahead of the others, accounting for 58.5% of total garden production.[1] The rest of the cultivated plants – particularly members of the Musaceae family and sweet potatoes – lag well behind. In addition, the bulk of the daily sweet-potato harvest is used for making dog food and must therefore be subtracted from the volume assigned to human consumption. It should be noted in passing that Figure 45 shows significant differences between the biotopes in the composition of garden production. There is less diversity in the interfluvial habitat than in the riverine (no maize or peanuts) and, as a consequence, manioc plays a much greater role. None of this is surprising in light of the distinct pedological constraints that influence the gardening techniques in the two biotopes.

Whatever the importance of these proportional differences, it remains that in all Achuar houses, manioc represents at least 50% of the vegetable dietary intake, and thus growing manioc occupies a strategic position in the equilibrium of the productive system. It is therefore legitimate to look at the extent to which manioc needs are covered, that is at the relation between garden productive capacity and actual consumption. We have already mentioned, on several occasions, the considerable disparity between the areas different households actually cultivate and weed regularly. The difference in areas exploited by various production units varied from 1 to 13, and this could not be explained by adjustments for size of the consumer unit. We were forced to conclude that certain households underexploited their horticultural productive capacity and we postulated that the large discrepancies between cultivated areas could be attributed in the end to a quest for prestige. Figure 46 shows the extent of this underutilization and reveals that even the smallest gardens still have room for potential intensification of production. For instance, the household whose productive capacities are most closely adapted to its subsistence needs still exploits only 79.9% of its productive potential in manioc. As for the household whose needs are covered to a level of 581%, it only uses 17.2% of its productive capacity.

The data in Figure 46 clarify some distinctive features of Achuar horticulture. In the first place, the amount of manioc planted in each garden clearing is such that there is always an enormous potential surplus amounting, depending on the case, to between 20 and 80% of a garden's productive capacity. It is true however that, unlike bitter manioc, sweet manioc can be "stored" only in the ground, and so part of the garden acts as a sort of "larder" that can be drawn on in an emergency. But one may question the need to set aside such a large surplus inasmuch as there is no

Cultigen	Habitat			
	Interfluvial		Riverine	
	kg	%	kg	%
Manioc	19.5	69.7	22.3	51.2
Musaceae	3.0	10.7	6.8	15.6
Sweet potatoes	2.4	8.6	6.4	14.8
Various tubers	3.1	11.0	7.0	16.1
Maize	0	0	0.9	2.0
Peanuts	0	0	0.04	0.01
Total	28	100	43.44	100

45. Importance of main cultigens according to gross daily harvest weights

conceivable catastrophe capable of gravely reducing the production of a garden. The absence of serious manioc diseases in the Achuar region and the extreme consistency of the weather are obvious guarantees against crop losses; no untoward precedent warrants providing such a safety margin. The only really serious accident that could imperil a garden's production is a large horde of peccary getting in and eating the roots and tubers. But this is inconceivable when the garden is near the house; it can happen only in pioneer gardens located at a great distance and left unattended once they are planted. In this case, which is altogether exceptional, the size of the garden is no insurance, since the peccaries will feed for as long as they are not disturbed.

The explicit purpose of the productive overcapacity of gardens is therefore not to provide an emergency surplus, which, in the event, is never exploited. Once again the principle of prestige must be called upon to account for the disparities in the areas brought under cultivation by each household. But the Achuar do not found prestige on the intensification of horticultural production and its redistribution to a network of clients, as is the case of Melanesian big men, since the largest gardens are exploited, on the contrary, to the minimum of their capacity. As we noted earlier in the chapter on gardening, the simple fact of a house surrounded by large spread

	Riverine habitat				Interfluvial habitat	
	1	2	3	4	5	6
Garden area (m²)	2437	9655	15409	22642	9729	31820
Garden productivity (kg)*	4570	18102	28892	42452	14594	47730
Annual consumption (kg)**	3650	8760	10585	8935	6497	8212
% needs covered	125.0	206.6	273.0	475.0	224.0	581.0
Exploitation of productive potential (%)	79.9	48.4	36.6	21.0	44.5	17.2

*Gross production (unpeeled roots) estimated on the basis of 0.75 manioc plants/m² (an average of 3 sampling units) and an average root weight per plant of 2.5 kg in the riverine habitat as compared with 2 kg in the interfluvial habitat (the roots of riverine cultivars are on average larger than those of the interfluvial habitat).
**Estimated consumption on the basis of each household's average daily supply of unpeeled manioc roots.

46. Exploitation of the productive potential for growing manioc

of garden allows the experienced visitor to gauge at a glance the idea a household has of its own social importance.

Nor do differences between biotopes play a role in manioc production, for, whatever the local constraints imposed by the ecosystem, the area planted is always considerably greater than that actually exploited. Of course riverine gardens are qualitatively richer in species, and yield per plant is generally higher than in the interfluvial habitat. But if one considers that the underexploitation of manioc is a generalized phenomenon, there is no particular quantitative advantage in cultivating the more fertile lands of the alluvial plains. So whether in the area of labor or in the domain of resources management, underexploitation of productive capacities is determined by social and cultural specifications, not by ecological limits. The symbolic gains that flow from oversized gardens cost only a little more effort, with no increase in its duration, since what brings prestige is the visible result and not the means by which it is achieved.

There is one last domain in which underexploitation of productive capacities seems highly likely, but impossible to prove statistically, and that is the area of natural resources. As there are yet no scientific criteria for accurately assessing the carrying capacities for hunting and fishing, one can only presume, on the basis of impressionistic estimates, that the Achuar could capture more game and fish if they wanted to. Despite the high productivity of hunting and fishing (789 g gross weight of game and fish per consumer per day in the riverine habitat compared to 469 g in the interfluvial habitat), it does not seem that the Achuar make excessive demands on their natural resources. All informants are agreed in saying that never in human memory have they seen game dwindle or fish decrease in areas in which there was no competition from neighboring ethnic groups. In sum, one criterion of the good life is the ability to ensure balanced domestic reproduction while exploiting only a small fraction of the production factors available. As far as the institutionalized economy of means goes, the Achuar have manifestly achieved great success; it remains to be seen whether the attainment of their goals measures up to their elegant economy of resources.

Productive efficiency

In the present case productive efficiency can be assessed by analyzing the structure of food consumption, since the strategic use-values are those that supply the energy to keep the physiological machine in good running order. We have already observed that the Achuar diet offered a broad range of tastes and that, despite the preeminence of manioc, their gastronomic life was far from monotonous. From the partial data already presented, the reader will also have gathered that the Achuar are not accustomed to going hungry. But these impressions still need to be confirmed by a nutritional study to ascertain whether the abundance is evenly distributed and if some lack of protein is not causing dietary deficiencies. Figure 47 lists the daily per capita contribution in kilocalories and grams of protein of hunting, fishing, and gardening.

The data for this table come from a sample of six households (two from the interfluvial habitat and four from the riverine habitat); all food products entering the houses were weighed daily for a total of sixty-six observation days. The number of consumers per household was calculated by counting all adults of both sexes as whole consumers (including in each case my wife and I) and all children under ten and over one as half-consumers. The overall total for the six households was 56.5 consumers, with an average of 9.5 consumers per household. Only the food for human consumption was taken into account, the portion reserved for the domestic animals (maize for the chickens and sweet potatoes for the dogs) was deducted from the volume of production. To convert gross weight into edible weight, that is to calculate the average proportion of waste from each type of product, we drew up a table of standard reduction coefficients. For the garden products, the coefficients were obtained by experimentation, while we used White's work (1953) for fish and game. The conversion of edible weight for each food type into energy and protein value is based on the food-composition table compiled by the Institute of Nutrition of Central America and Panama (Wu Leung and Flores 1961).

	Sector,							
	Hunting		Fishing		Gardening		Total	
Habitat	kcal.	protein (g)	kcal.	protein (g)	kcal.	protein (g)	kcal.	protein (g)
Riverine	1047	102.0	106	19.0	3404	30.0	4557	151.0
	666	65.0	98	17.5	2958	26.0	3722	108.5
	0	0.0	196	35.0	2111	19.0	2307	54.0
	988	96.0	227	40.0	3016	26.0	4231	162.0
Interfluvial	498	49.0	71	12.0	2024	18.0	2593	79.0
	429	42.0	43	8.0	2567	23.0	3039	73.0
Overall average	604.5	59	123.5	22	2680	23.5	3408	104.5

47. Daily per capita dietary contribution of each production sector

There is one drawback to this method, which is that the table lists the daily production of edible items and not what is actually eaten by each individual according to age, sex, and weight. A truly scientific nutritional analysis would require that all food about to be eaten by the various household members be weighed at each meal, an obviously impossible task not only on technical grounds but for reasons of simple decency. Now in light of the results obtained, particularly in the area of animal-protein intake, the doubt dawns that the Achuar are capable of consuming, on a daily basis, so much over the normally recommended levels. It must be added, then, that everything that is edible is not actually eaten, especially in the case of game and fish. After a particularly fruitful expedition, the haunches of game and fillets of fish are smoked and stored in a basket exposed to smoke from the cooking fire. Despite such precautions and the incredible quantities of meat the Achuar are capable of putting down in a day, the stores eventually go off, and the spoiled meat or fish must be disposed of. But the fraction of production subtracted in this way does not imply any temporary deficiency in protein supply, since, as soon as the supply of meat is no longer edible, the hunter sets out once more. By reserving part of their food for the garbage heap, the Achuar avail themselves of the same luxury as hyperindustrialized societies, and in so doing provide a signal refutation of the traditional image of the primitive society singlemindedly struggling to survive.

This apparent prodigality becomes convincing when we examine the adequacy of calorie and protein consumption. For lack of any detailed anthropometric study, we were unable to establish the exact calorie and protein needs per sex and per age group. Moreover, the levels recommended by nutritionists vary a good deal and do not sufficiently take into account the energy costs of various activities. We therefore chose to retain, as the safe daily calorie and protein intake for an average individual, Lizot's highest figure for the Yanomami, a population fairly similar to the Achuar in physical make-up and way of life. In a detailed analysis, Lizot (1978: 94–5) calculates that maximum energy needs per capita come to 2,600 kcal. (for a 10–12 year old), while the maximum protein needs are 27.4 g per day (for a grown man). One may thus assume that, if an Achuar's mean intake approaches the maximum Yanomami level, his needs will be adequately covered. Reading Figure 47, it appears that, in all the households of our sample, average consumption is well above both these figures. In other words, the average Achuar consumes many more calories and much more protein than is necessary for the Yanomami in the age groups having the highest needs. With an average of 3,408 kcal. per day, the energy needs of our sample are covered to a level of 131%; average protein intake is 104.5 g, which is 381% of the safe level. In these circumstances, we did not think it necessary to include gathered wild products in our assessment, despite their non-negligible contribution at certain times of the year.

However remarkable these results may seem, they are nothing out of the ordinary and compare favorably with identical data gathered among other Amerindian populations, Jivaro and non-Jivaro alike.

First of all it should be noted that the average dietary composition, in terms of both energy value and protein intake, is similar in the three Jivaro groups studied. These results corroborate our data and attest that the abundance and quality of the diet in our sample households should not be attributed to exceptionally favorable circumstances. The composition of the diet of these five groups also helps cast doubt on the hyperdeterministic interpretations of certain proponents of the ecological materialism school, who see protein availability as the absolute limiting factor for the density of Amazonian aboriginal populations. In the best-argued version of this hypothesis, D. Gross indulges in some mathematical acrobatics to show, on the basis of a sample of six Amerindian societies, that indigenous dietary protein intake is always below or just at the safe level, which he sets at 63 g per person per day (Gross 1975: 531–2). Lizot has already advanced a convincing criticism of the arbitrary character of such a high level (Lizot 1977: 134–5); but even if one were to accept 63 g as a minimum, there are still at least five samples of Amerindian societies for which we have dependable data that consistently exceed this level of protein intake. Alternatively, if we look carefully at how Gross arrives at the protein contribution in each of his ten societies, it becomes apparent that his reasoning is based on shaky extrapolations and not on accurate and extensive measurement. Although there is no doubt that some Amazonian

Population	Average consumption		Source
	Kcal.	Proteins (g)	
Achuar Jivaro of Ecuador	3408	104.5	Descola, this volume
Achuar Jivaro of Peru	3257	107.7	Ross 1976: 149
Aguaruna Jivaro	3356	—	Berlin and Markell 1977: 12
Siona-Secoya	2215	80.9	Vickers 1976: 135
Central Yanomami	1772	67.55	Lizot 1978: 96

48. Average calorie and protein consumption in five Jivaro and non-Jivaro Amazonian populations

societies do experience protein deficiencies in their diet – especially in situations of acute contact or acculturation – one cannot help wondering about the validity of generalizations based on so unreliable a sample.

We happen to share Beckerman's views on this subject when, in a review of Gross' article, he advanced the opposing idea that in all probability protein sources are underexploited by the aboriginal populations of the Amazonian hylea (Beckerman 1979: 533). Our studies on the Achuar, like Lizot's on the Yanomami, show that, when their living conditions have not been perturbed to too great an extent, Amerindian societies exploit only a small fraction of their natural resources, and so these societies cannot be "limited" by the availability of proteins. In fact, any deficiency that exists is more likely to be in the data on which the hyperdeterministic ecological interpretations are based than in the diets of Amazonian populations.

That ecological factors have a far less determining role than is often claimed is exemplified in the small difference between average Achuar protein consumption regardless of the nature of the biotopes they exploit. Early in this volume, we mentioned the favorite thesis of many North American anthropologists and archeologists, who see the greater availability of protein in the Amazonian riverine habitat as a decisive adaptive advantage which may provide a material base for the emergence of complex societies. But in Achuar society at least, the disparity between biotopes does not seem particularly significant: average daily protein intake is 76 g per person in the interfluve houses, compared to 119 g in the riverine households. It is true that 43 grams seems an enormous difference, but only if such a deficit causes the interfluve Achuar to fall below the fatal threshold of 27.45 g, which is not the case. Thus, despite the fact that households in the interfluve take in less protein than those in the alluvial plains, their daily consumption is still nearly three times the recommended level. The interfluvial hills are in no way a "protein desert," and if one had to establish a contrast between the two biotopes from this standpoint, it would have to be more between abundance and overabundance than between deficiency and adequacy.

Inasmuch as they contradict popular theories, these results could seem suspicious or insufficiently documented. But they are perfectly confirmed by the only anthropologist, to our knowledge, who like us has gone to the trouble of carefully measuring the differences in productivity between an interfluvial and a riverine biotope exploited in an identical way by the same Amazonian population. In his article on work and diet among the Yanomami, Lizot remarks in effect that: ". . .the distinction between habitats is not worth keeping for the presentation of the results on the

Central Yanomami, [although] it may be useful for other regions" (Lizot 1978: 96). No doubt it may be, and we must wait for more information on other Amazonian ethnic groups – if there is still time to gather it – before being more categorical. It remains that the objective convergence of two Amazonian societies having so many similar structural features inclines one to the greatest prudence in accepting the theory that sociological variation is engendered by unequal access to proteins.

In concluding our examination of the differences in Achuar population density according to biotope (Chapter Two), we raised a disturbing question: why, given the low population density of the riverine habitat (0.44 persons/km^2), have all the interfluvial Achuar not converged in this alluvial plains zone, where the resources were potentially greater than those to which they had access in the interfluvial habitat? The reply to this riddle is now clear. Besides the fact that the adaptive advantage of the riverine habitat in terms of natural resources goes practically untapped for cultural reasons (taboos on large riparian mammals), the productivity of the economic system in the interfluvial habitat is such that, provided the population density remains stable, there are no major reasons to migrate to the riverine habitat, where malaria is, moreover, endemic. It is true that the present population density in the interfluve may seem exceptionally low (0.08 person/km^2); but this is scarcely lower than the 0.1 person/km^2 Denevan proposes as the most likely level for this type of biotope before the Spanish conquest (Denevan 1976: 228).

The generalized overproduction of Achuar households also invites skepticism as to the universal truth of the conclusions M. Sahlins infers from his analysis of structural constants in what he calls the domestic mode of production (Sahlins 1972: 41–99). Sahlins argues that primitive societies function at the lowest level of their productive capacities, and concludes that underproduction is in the nature of economies organized exclusively around the domestic group and kinship relations between domestic groups. He advances the idea that one inevitable consequence of this systematic underuse of resources is that "a fair percentage of domestic groups persistently fail to produce their own livelihood and therefore must be helped by more successful households" (69–74). This regular failure of at least several production units in any "large enough community" (74) would thus be one of the structural constraints of the domestic mode of production as Sahlins defines it. The three ethnographic examples with which he illustrates this trend (the Iban, Mazulu, and Yakö) are no doubt an insufficient basis upon which to construct a general rule; one of the groups is even a bad example, since an apparently large part of the Iban domestic workforce is used in the production of exchange-values to the detriment of the production of use-values (71–2).

It is obvious that no Achuar domestic unit is safe from the unexpected accident that decimates its workforce. Certain informants' tales of the dramatic consequences of a measles epidemic in the fifties suggest that debilitating diseases that strike down most of a household's producers can have a disastrous effect on the level of food acquisition. Furthermore, the widespread practice of levirate and polygyny, mechanisms which constantly work to readjust the workforce when domestic productive capacity is disorganized by death, is not in itself sufficient to keep certain households from experiencing moments of difficulty. In this sense it is true that the threat of a temporary food shortage due to the illness or death of a strategic member of the domestic unit is always hanging over the Achuar's heads. But that is a universal threat, since, in every historical society, the domestic consumption unit always depends for its material subsistence on the work of its members. If some accident interrupts this work, the group has to fall back on kinship solidarity, in a traditional society, or on government aid, in an advanced industrial society. This kind of temporary economic breakdown is not peculiar to the domestic mode of production as Sahlins defines it, then. Alternatively, if Sahlins means that the inability of certain domestic units to ensure their own subsistence on a regular basis stems from their structural inability to foresee their true consumption needs because of their too systematic underuse of productive resources, it is not certain that this proposition can be generalized. In any event, it does not apply to the Achuar, who, as we have seen, maintain a wide margin of safety while underexploiting their productive potential.

We therefore feel safe in saying that the technical components of certain productive systems – such as those practiced by many indigenous societies in the Amazon Basin – make it nearly impossible for chronic failure to beset some portion of the domestic units when this failure stems from improvidence alone. In the Achuar case, the near-automatic guarantee of success flows not only from the security ensured by extensive manioc cultivation in an environment free of noteworthy climatic fluctuations, but also by the high productivity of labor in all subsistence sectors. In effect, it takes only an average of 1 hour 22 minutes of gardening per person to produce 2,680 kcal. and 23.5 g of protein or 1 hour 28 minutes of hunting to obtain 604.5 kcal. and 59 g of protein (Figs. 41 and 47). In other words, *an average per capita input in hunting and gardening of less than three hours a day produces a return of 3,284 kcal. and 82.5 g of protein.* Compared with such remarkable results, the gross productivity of rural France in the famine-ridden seventeenth century seems modest indeed.

If the labor returns from each subsistence activity are plotted against their energy and protein contribution to the diet (Fig. 49), the symbolic dimension of the prestige attached to each of these labor processes becomes clear. Predictably enough, gardening is the food-procurement technique that produces the most calories per unit of time invested (78.3% of the kcal. for 40% of the daily work), while, more paradoxically, it is fishing that produces the most protein per unit of time expended (21% of the protein for 13% of the daily work time). This can be explained in particular by the fact that setting lines along a bank takes only a few minutes a day while ensuring a small but steady supply of fish. Although hunting represents nearly half of the labor expended per day (43%), it provides just over half the daily protein input (56.4%). Considering that the tandem of fishing and gardening contributes 45.5 g of protein per day, it could be said that hunting productivity is not very high; if the Achuar reasoned in terms of marginal utility, they could almost give up hunting altogether. All they would have to do is grow a little more maize and beans, catch a few more fish, and eat a few more eggs from their hens to maintain a more than adequate protein level. But that would be to forget that hunting is not merely a means of procuring protein, it is first and foremost a source of pleasure, for both the men who hunt and the women who relish the taste of game. The rational allocation of scarce means has no place in a society in which neither needs nor the means of satisfying them proceed from a conscious maximizing choice. It is easy to be convinced of this upon seeing the low returns of wild plant gathering, which supplies only 0.5% of the calories and 2.2% of the protein for 4% of the daily work.[2] Now the Achuar regard gathering as entertainment and not as hard work; it therefore makes no more sense to call this food acquisition technique unproductive than it would to condemn our Sunday mushroom walks as a waste of time.

In a now-famous article, Sahlins developed the idea that Paleolithic hunter-gatherers, far from all living on the verge of starvation, as a common preconception would have it, could legitimately be regarded as the "Original Affluent Society" (Sahlins 1968). He claims that the picture darkened considerably with the social and technico-economical evolution of society, with a gradual increase in individual work time and a correlative decline in productivity. And yet, the Achuar example, like that of other Amazonian "hunter-gardeners," shows that the domestication of plants is not necessarily the first step on the productivist path to inevitable economic

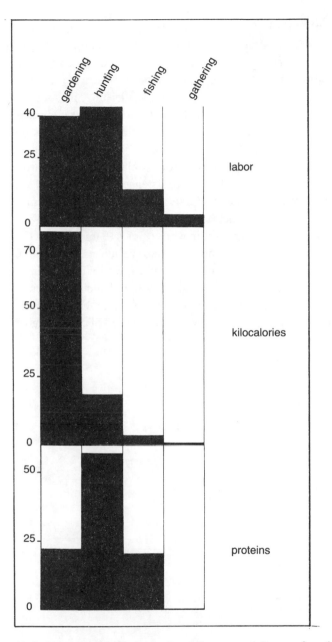

49. Labor productivity for each subsistence activity as a function of its dietary contribution (%)

alienation. The Achuar do not work any more than most of the hunter-gatherer societies Sahlins has looked at, and their diet is visibly better in terms of quality and quantity. In the last four or five millenia since Amazonian populations first chose to grow manioc, this mutation has apparently engendered neither food shortages, nor less leisure time, nor the exploitation of man by man. That this was the best of all possible choices is no doubt illustrated by the nearly unanimous adoption of root crops by South American rain-forest societies. We now know, in effect, that nearly all hunter-gatherer societies attested in the Amazonian hylea were originally swidden horticulturalists, and that subsistence systems based on foraging alone should be regarded as regressive or pseudo-archaic forms.

Sahlins' staunchly heuristic stance is certainly praiseworthy, and we cannot but subscribe to a research program whose aim is to understand the mechanisms behind mankind's social and economic evolution. And yet one must be wary of any single-factor interpretation which would turn agriculture into the *deus ex machina* of exponential growth and social stratification.[3] The sort of political anarchy in which the Achuar live is ample evidence that an efficient agricultural economy has no need of chiefdoms or alienation in order to function adequately.

Conclusion

From the outset, we have accompanied the Achuar on their daily rounds. Having now come to the end of this spiral journey, it remains not so much to recapitulate what has slowly been established as to attempt to draw a few lessons. It is true that the complicity felt by the ethnologist with the familiar world he is writing about sometimes dampens the ambition of his conclusions. Beyond the information it provides, the monographic genre is justified only if it allows the ethnographer to progress inductively from the particular to the general. Each unique society proposes its own solutions to universal problems, and, while proof must no doubt be built on comparative generalizations, it is not unthinkable that each particular illustration offers its own store of lessons to be learned.

Because of the framework chosen for the study and the analyses it has produced, this book is marked with the stamp of the domestic. In choosing the home as the site of social praxis, we were doing no more than adopting the Achuar point of view, with no intention of endowing this sphere with the theoretical status it has enjoyed in one school of thought from Aristotle to the present day. This is not the place to discuss how problematic we consider the typological use to which this configuration has so often been put – called variously the *oikos* stage or the domestic mode of production – except to make it clear that we reject its use as a category of analysis. If Achuar ecology can be termed domestic, it is because each household thinks of itself as a unique, autonomous center and the permanent staging point for all relations with the surroundings. Now this fragmented multiplicity of connections with the natural world is organized around the notion that nature is governed by the same social relations as those set in the house. Nature is therefore neither domesticated, nor domesticable, but simply domestic.

Far from being a wild world of vegetal spontaneity, the forest is perceived as a superhuman garden whose logic follows rules different from those that command ordinary garden life. This spectacular reduction of forest tangle to garden order is ample indication that the relationship between nature and culture manifests itself less as a division than as a continuum. The concentric transition from house to forest does not seem like advancing ever deeper into the wild as long as it is possible to establish with the jungle beings those relations of sociability that ordinarily prevail in the house. The affinal relationship experienced in the *tankamash* is constantly projected onto the forest animals, thereby placing hunting process and alliance relationship on the same level. At first, both appear to fall outside the domestic domain, but that would be to forget that, through the visits it receives, a household is constantly attempting to reappropriate the outside world. Moreover, the distinction between members of the household and others vanishes entirely in the perpetual flow by which each house procures sons-in-law, an assimilation that is the prime example of successful domestication of affines. War caps the inevitable failure of such an intellectual experiment in which the local group attempts to convince itself that extending temporary hospitality to the allies is an adequate substitute for living together. Game animals should know something about this, as day after day they suffer the cruel consequences of the duplicity of such a wager.

And yet the Achuar have not completely subdued nature by the symbolic networks of domesticity. Granted, the cultural sphere is uncommonly encompassing, since in it we find animals, plants and spirits which other Amerindian societies place in the realm of nature. The Achuar do not therefore share this antinomy between two closed and irremediably opposed worlds: the cultural world of human society and the natural world of animal society. And yet there is a certain point at which the continuum of sociability breaks down, yielding to a wild world inexorably foreign to humans. Incomparably smaller than the realm of culture, this little piece of nature includes the set of those things with which communication cannot be established. Opposite beings endowed with language (*aents*), of which humans are the most perfect incarnation, stand those things deprived of speech that inhabit parallel, inaccessible worlds. The inability to communicate is often ascribed to a lack of soul (*wakan*) that affects certain living species: most insects and fish, poultry, and numerous plants, which thus lead a mechanical, inconsequential existence. But the absence of communication is sometimes due to distance; the souls of stars and meteors, infinitely remote and prodigiously mobile, remain deaf to human words.

While for the Achuar language is the discriminating criterion between nature and culture, this does not mean that they place all cultural beings on the same level. Beings endowed with speech are classified in a subtle hierarchy the lower echelons of which are barely distinguishable from the natural state. Nevertheless, the cultural continuum is not marked off by degrees of verbal competence but by degrees of sociability. At the top of the ladder come "complete beings" (*penke aents*), humans in other words. Achuar society is the paradigm of this perfect humanness, and its standards are the rod by which deviation is measured. Neighboring ethnic groups are seen as lesser humans, who do not always follow those principles that govern Achuar social life; even if marriages can sometimes be contracted with these Indians, they are already tainted with otherness. Some beings, although they do not look human, are very close to the Achuar because they follow the same marriage rules. This is the case of those spirits of exemplary sociability, the Tsunki, or several types of game (woolly monkeys, toucans. . .) or cultivated plants (manioc, peanuts. . .).

A decisive step in the direction of nature is taken when we come to those beings that delight in sexual promiscuity and are thus constantly flouting the principle of exogamy. The howler monkey, so human in other aspects of its family life, is the epitome of these incestuous beasts. The dog, too, ranks in the fore of these animals; this highly socialized creature introduces the disorder of bestiality into the very heart of the most domestic area of life. In the case of these shameless beings, incest is perceived less as the violation of a behavioral standard than as its systematic inversion. Their sexuality therefore does not come entirely under the rule of natural law, as it is governed by the symmetrical reversal of the laws of culture.

The lowest rung on the ladder of beings endowed with speech is occupied by the loners; their isolation from social life relegates them to the borderline between culture and nature. Incarnation of the souls of the deceased, *iwianch* spirits are condemned to a life of hopeless solitude, which they seek to fill by abducting children. Alternatively, animal predators appreciate their asociability because it absolves them from any debt to their prey. The most dangerous of these solitary killers are the jaguar and the anaconda, with whom only shamans manage to contrive some agreement. As laymen are unable to contract alliances with these beings who reject the obligations of social life, the fierce war they wage against mankind becomes the best illustration of the effects of anomy. And yet, far though they may be from the laws of ordinary society, jaguars and anacondas are still the shaman's familiars, guarding his house like a watchdog; they still belong to the order of culture, as the masters they serve live within the bounds of society. By way of this subordination of solitary predators to shamans, Achuar thought domesticates the wildest of the jungle animals: their purported harmfulness is in the end socialized to the benefit of a fraction of mankind.

If the perpetual endeavor to domesticate others is set in the forest, the garden and the river, on the other hand, are defined as those sites *par excellence* where the household can at last achieve its completeness. Realm of maternal consanguinity, made possible nonetheless by the efforts of a husband, or metaphoric scene of successful conjugality, these two worlds are the perfect illustration of the domesticity of nature. Why then speak of domestic nature, since by now it is clear that by this we mean that which the Achuar think of as culture? At the risk of being misunderstood, we have used this expression as a rhetorical device in order to emphasize that that portion of materiality which has not been directly engendered by man and which we usually call nature can also be represented in certain societies as a component of culture. Of course there is a whole sector of nature that has been transformed by humans and therefore depends on them for its reproduction: the humanization of domestic plants and animals is thus a predictable result of the biological coercion that subjects the perpetuation of these species to human intervention. But as the Achuar illustrate, the mental domestication of nature can extend well beyond the concrete borders established by man's transformation of his material surroundings. One might even advance the hypothesis that the portion of the natural realm a society is going to socialize in its imagination will be all the larger as the portion of nature that it is actually capable of transforming is small. This phenomenon of transposition cannot be reduced to a sort of ideological compensation for impotence; such an approach would be eminently ethnocentric, since it would be assuming that, like our own, all societies see nature as a kingdom to be conquered. By endowing nature with social properties, humans are doing more than granting her anthropomorphic attributes, they are mentally socializing the relationship they establish with her. This mental socialization is nevertheless not completely imaginary: in order to exploit nature, humans weave a network of social relationships between themselves, and it is most often the form of these relationships that provides the conceptual model for their relationship with nature.

Achuar daily praxis fully confirms the idea of a correspondence between the ways of dealing with nature and the ways of dealing with others (Haudricourt 1962). This correspondence is the result of an overall congruency between the social frameworks for using the environment and the mental forms of sociability into which these uses are translated. For instance, the domestic autonomy characteristic of the Achuar's material intervention in nature is transposed into the autonomy of their control over the conceptual conditions purported to make this intervention possible. The men and women of a household are at once independent of each other in the exercise of their technical and magico-religious specializations, and strictly complementary in the realization of the overall domestic productive process as well as the accomplishment of certain symbolic preconditions which govern the efficacy of their respective practices. This highly peculiar mixture of independence and complementarity between the sexes is restricted to the domestic unit: no supralocal authority or mediation could ever threaten the privilege the members of a household enjoy of reproducing their own symbolic capacities of intervening in nature. In sum, this idea of domestic autonomy so dear to the Achuar is much less the product of a necessarily impossible material autarky than the acknowledgement of the power each household has to control the overall conditions of its symbolic reproduction.

But the symbolic socialization of nature goes well beyond its domestication in the mind, since the Achuar see each of the processes of exploiting the environment as a different mode of social behavior. For instance, the distinction between hunting and gardening is nurtured by an opposition between two types of sociability: the women's consanguine mothering of cultivated plants and the affinal charming of game practiced by the men. But the assignment of male and female modes of dealing with others is not a product of chance. The Achuar have brought an extreme refinement to the property every Dravidian kinship system has of splitting the social world into kin and affines, in that they have this classificatory axis play the additional role of operator of differentiation between male and female behaviors. Of course the referential nomenclature distinguishes clearly, for male and female Egos, between affines and kin of both sexes and at each genealogical level. But a contextual study of the vocative terminology and modes of behavior shows that female affinal relations tend to be consanguinealized, while men treat their distant kin in the way normally befitting affines (for the details of this analysis, see Taylor 1983a). Such recurrent manipulation of the kinship system would seem to indicate that the Achuar associate women with the realm of consanguinity, while they place the dangers and obligations of alliance in the men's camp. No wonder then that hunting and gardening are represented as two separate forms of social relations with non-human beings, homologous with the two prevailing forms of social relations with human beings to which each of the sexes is reputed to confine itself.

The projection of the split between these two modes of dealing with others onto the forms of exploiting nature is not without consequences for women. It is true that their curtailment to the world of consanguinity is reinforced by the maternal role assigned them in the growing of plant children. Isolated in their domestic retreat, the mistresses of manioc are completely cut off from the realm reserved for men: the negotiation of marriages, by which men dispose of women, and the conduct of wars, in which it is not unusual that women are killed. In this society where the husband's dominion over his wives often finds expression in extreme brutality, gardening provides one compensation for women's subjection. Without claiming that the sole function of garden magic is to give women the illusion of enjoying an autonomy that is denied them elsewhere, it is not forbidden to think that their acknowledged command over the lives of cultivated plants helps them forget in part the violence of male domination. (The reader will recall that everyone regards gardening as a difficult and dangerous endeavor, the fruits of which are passed on to the men only because the women so wish it.) Because of the margin of independence they garner from their material and symbolic control over a strategic sphere of practice, women have a refuge in which they reign unrivaled. But then again perhaps this is only a cunning ploy to make them forget to envy men's power.

If it is true that "man has a history because he transforms nature" (Godelier 1984: 10), it remains that some of the ideas he entertains about this transformation have long relegated this history to a side track. For instance, the homeostasis of the productive forces in "cold societies" has often been explained by the idea that needs that are socially limited and perfectly satisfied offer no incitement to engage in the infinite accumulation of wealth. The Achuar are a good illustration of this harmonious self-restraint in which a restrictive definition of goals does not engender frustration. To this must be added the fact that one way of accumulating wealth is to improve the productivity of work by extending its duration; now, we have demonstrated that, contrary to the predictions of the principle of maximization, the Achuar do not automatically adjust the volume of work to their production goals. When all members of an acephalous society implicitly concur on the maximum amount of time each person should normally devote to production functions, it seems that an extension of the work time cannot be obtained without ideological or supralocal political constraint, in other words without disrupting the egalitarian organization of society.

The way the Achuar have of socializing nature in their minds suggests yet a third way, which does not exclude the other two, of interpreting the capacity of certain production systems to continue unchanged over long periods of time. In effect, when a society sees the use of nature as homologous with a type of relationship between humans, any modification or intensification of this use must come through a profound reorganization of the representation of not only nature but the entire social system used metaphorically to think its exploitation. Although this hypothesis, as it is formulated, may seem abstract, it flows directly from our detailed analysis of the Achuar adaptive response to two contrasted biotopes, an analysis that is legitimated a posteriori by the theoretical results to which it gives rise. For when used as an end in itself, the measurement of social phenomena usually serves only to couch self-evidences in a statistical form. The geometrical turn of mind that we invoked at the outset is no doubt not the most natural inclination of ethnological investigation and when it is indulged in out of duty, it is for very precise reasons. If we felt compelled to undertake meticulous quantifications and detailed analyses of the ecosystem, it was in order to take the precise measure of the limits of ecological determinism, something a more relaxed approach would not have allowed us to do. Confronted with the host of limiting factors that certain anthropologists had discovered in Amazonia, it was necessary to establish an accurate framework of the range of possibilities and therefore to assess the margin for an eventual intensification of the exploitation of natural resources.

Our original doubts about cultural ecology's reductionist theses were, on the whole, of an epistemological order; in the event, the results of our analyses of Achuar adaptation to their ecosystem amply confirmed our initial wariness. We now believe we have clearly established that an altogether real difference in the productive potential of the various biotopes exploited by the Achuar does not necessarily engender a difference in the effective actualization of these potentials. In other words, within the broad limits of the undeniable constraints imposed on a society by the ecosystem it exploits, there is no automatic adjustment of productive capacities to virtual resources. Organized by nearly identical techniques and underpinned by nearly identical representations of their relationship with nature, the productivity of the systems used by the Achuar for exploiting their two environments is also roughly equal. And yet, whereas the ecological characteristics of the interfluvial biotope would allow only a limited intensification of food procurement, those of the riverine biotope undeniably would permit considerable development of the material subsistence base.

Without spending too much time speculating on the eventual outcome of historical development, one may nevertheless assume that intensive exploitation of their habitat's demographic carrying capacity would have forced the riverine Achuar to make some drastic choices. The stratified societies of the Amazon alluvial plains, rapidly destroyed by colonial violence, form the historical horizon of this type of choice. We know from the chroniclers and from archeological reports that members of these societies lived in a long string of densely populated villages and that their sophisticated maize-growing techniques allowed them to accumulate large surpluses. We also know that the storage of food was at once the condition and the result of the political dominion of a few supreme chiefs who wielded broad powers. Now it would be hard to think of a type of life more antithetical to that adopted by the Achuar. Not only is the idea of collective life in village communities profoundly repugnant to them, but the loss of symbolic autonomy implied by the political planning of domestic production would be a negation of the good life as they see it. If, in spite of all their ecological assets, the Achuar did not choose to develop their material base, it is perhaps because the symbolic paradigm that organizes their use of nature was not sufficiently flexible to absorb the reorientation of social relationships that such a choice would have engendered. In this case, the homeostasis of the "cold societies" of Amazonia would be less the result of the implicit rejection of political alienation, with which Clastres credited "savages" (1974: 161–86), than the effect of the inertia of a thought system unable to represent the process of socializing nature in any way other than through the categories that dictate the way human society should function. Counter to the over-hasty technical determinism with which evolutionist theories are often imbued, one might postulate that, when a society transforms its material base, this is conditioned by a prior mutation of the forms of social organization that serve as the conceptual framework of the material mode of producing.

The legitimacy of such an induction is of course highly debatable, for nothing predisposes the Achuar to be the unwitting underwriters of a conjectural history. However, the fact remains that even the most scrupulous chronicler, when closely observing an exotic society, always has the insidious feeling of traveling backwards in time. Although they usually deny it, many ethnologists are motivated by an unspoken quest for the very beginnings. Oracular vaticinations and divine decrees no longer rule our destinies, but the illusion of a return to mankind's past crouches, ready to pounce, at some bend in the trail. This illusion is the origin of the metaphysics of nostalgia as well as of the divagations of retrospective evolutionism. But that is perhaps a modest price to pay for the privilege of entering the privacy of certain peoples whose uncertain future still hangs on the ties they have formed with nature's beings.

Achuar woman returning from the garden, Kapawientza

Notes

General Introduction

1 The effectiveness of this type of "bricolage" is illustrated by certain ethnological interpretations of Amazonian societies based on indigenous representations of space, the person, and organic processes; a good synthesis of these views can be found in Seeger *et al.* 1979. I heartily applaud essays of this type which attempt to go beyond the arbitrary nature versus society dichotomy by showing the importance of environment and corporeity in the structuring of indigenous models of social life. Nevertheless, despite their rich heuristic value, analyses of this kind are still akin to what I call symbolic morphology, in that they fail to take into account the effect of material determinations on the concrete processes involved in the socialization of nature.

* Translator's note: The French word is "idéel," a concept extensively developed by Maurice Godelier. Rupert Swyer notes in his translation of Godelier's *The Making of Great Men* (London/Paris, Cambridge University Press/Editions de la Maison des Sciences de l'Homme, 1986): "*idéel* (the translator feels that the near-equivalent most readily comprehensible to the English-speaking reader is 'conceptual', although *idéel* is a neologism in the French). It is a system of ideas, values, beliefs and representations that go to make up a society. It should not be confused with its system of ideals." Martin Thom, in his translation of Godelier's *L'Idéel et le matériel, The Mental and the Material. Thought, Economy and Society* (London/New York, Verso, 1986) has adopted the translation "mental," but the word seems to lack the idea of values expressed in "conceptual."

2 My exclusive use of the synchronic approach in no way means that a history of the constitution of Achuar identity is impossible. It is, in fact, the subject of a vast study that Anne-Christine Taylor has been conducting for a number of years, the aim of which is to show diachronically how the various Jivaroan-dialect groups have constructed the system of their internal differences in a tribal context. The existence within the Jivaroan group of an autonomous cultural entity called "the Achuar" is thus taken for granted in my own work; for an explanation of the forms of their differential specificity and the conditions of its constitution, see Taylor, 1993.

3 The feeling that it was urgent to conduct an ethnographic study of the Achuar

seems to have been shared by several Americanists in the early 1970s. On our first exploratory trip to Ecuador in the summer of 1974, we learned that a couple of American ethnologists had just spent a year with the Achuar of Peru. These two disciples of Marvin Harris seemed concerned primarily with gathering data on energetic flows in order to demonstrate, for a case in point, the validity of their mentor's ecological theses. No doubt because they did not speak the language, the ethnographic content of the work they produced was quite summary, but it does provide figures particularly useful for a comparative study of the Achuar economy; we will make copious use of this information as an element of comparison (Ross 1976, 1978). In the same year in Ecuador, we met two Italian researchers, the linguist Maurizio Gnerre and the ethnologist Antonino Colajanni, who were preparing for a summer of fieldwork among the Achuar in order to complete the data they had already gathered during a short stay in 1972. These two colleagues and friends had worked mainly with the Achuar living along the Rio Huasaga, and they recommended that we concentrate rather on the Pastaza Achuar, who at that time were on hostile terms with the Huasaga communities. Their advice proved precious, and our long episodic discussions on Achuar ethnography over the last ten years with A. Colajanni make it all the more regrettable that he has not yet had the opportunity to publish his material. Finally in 1976, just as we were beginning our long-term investigation among the Pastaza Achuar, we suddenly learned of a North American ethnologist, Pita Kelekna, who had just finished a stay with the Huasaga Achuar, during which she had gathered material for a thesis on the socialization of children (Kelekna 1981).

4 Certain constraints – like the difficulty of access to the Achuar territory and the need to renew the stock of trade goods used to remunerate our hosts – obliged us to divide our total stay into a series of six successive periods lasting from three to five months each and spread over two years (from October 1976 to September 1978). The following year, 1979, was largely spent working in Quito (photo-interpretation, cartography, plotting topographic information, working on our tapes . . .) except for an additional visit of ten weeks to the field. As the Achuar speak no Spanish, the first hurdle was to learn the language, to which we devoted many months. All of the Achuar texts used in this work were recorded in the vernacular, then transcribed and translated by Anne-Christine Taylor or myself, with the help of bilingual Shuar informants. Moreover, as the traditional habitat is widely dispersed and as the hospitality of any one family rarely extends beyond two weeks, we were perpetually on the move. The fragmented living arrangements together with the difficult travel conditions and permanent tensions resulting from feuding sometimes made our work difficult indeed.

1: The territorial space

1 For information on the Canelos and their relations with the colonization frontier, N. Whitten's monograph (1976) is very useful. On the history of Canelos–Achuar relations, see more particularly Taylor 1993, Chaps. 4–5; Whitten 1976: 3–34; Descola and Taylor 1977; Naranjo 1974; and Descola and Taylor 1981.

2 Relations between the Peruvian Achuar and the patrones, the recent changes in the extraction trade, and new forms of small-scale market production in the

region have been studied more closely by Ross (1976: 40–86) and Mader and Gippelhauser (1982).

3 Much ink has flowed over the very old border conflict between Ecuador and Peru, each side bombarding the other with historical erudition in support of its respective territorial claims. An excellent analysis of the changes in Ecuador's boundaries can be found in Deler 1981: 90–5.

4 The economic part of our study focused as much on the *centros* as on the dispersed households, thus providing data for the comparative analysis of the transformations undergone by the aboriginal mode of production in the wake of the nucleation of settlements and, in some cases, the introduction of cattle raising. Within the framework of the present study, however, and for the reasons we have given, we will make almost exclusive use of the data we collected in the sector of dispersed settlement. The quantifications (time allocated to various tasks and food production) were carried out in eleven dispersed households, eight of which are polygamous and three monogamous, a ratio close to that for the population in general. The duration of the time study in each household varied between one and five weeks, our stay sometimes being split into two periods. The extremely difficult working conditions in the dispersed settlements (endemic feuding, tension caused by raids, foot travel without porters, lack of means of procuring our own provisions and food and therefore having to depend on the "good will" of our hosts) made a longer stay in any of the houses out of the question. It should nevertheless be noted that the total time spent measuring the daily input–output data in the eleven households comes to 32 weeks, which constitutes a reliable scientific basis for analysis, considering the exceptional circumstances in which the fieldwork was done. Moreover, the number and variety of domestic units studied – as well as the lack of any marked seasonal cycles in agriculture – should amply compensate the short time spent with each unit. Finally, the essential data on native representations of nature and its uses (myths, magical songs, taxonomy, technical skills...) was collected in the course of a number of studies, each lasting several months, conducted among the Achuar of the various *centros*, where working conditions were appreciably better.

5 For the overall Achuar population of Ecuador and Peru, E. Ross advances estimates that vary slightly from one publication to the next: 0.5 persons/square mile or 0.31 persons/km² (Ross 1976: 18), but 0.4 persons/km² (Ross 1978: 4). In both cases, the global estimate is greater than our figure for the Achuar of Ecuador alone (0.17 persons/km²); but Ross stayed only with the Peruvian Achuar and he grossly underrates the area inhabited by their Ecuadorian counterparts, which inevitably vitiates his estimate.

6 Because of the very high productivity of their ridge cultivation techniques, the Taino and the Chimbu, like all intertropical societies who practice ridge-field agriculture, have no doubt reached the population limit tolerable for a society of forest horticulturalists. The fact remains that the densities typical of many ethnic groups practicing swidden horticulture are far higher than those for the Achuar: e.g. 30 persons/km² for the Philippine Hanunóo (Conklin 1975) and 9–14 persons/km², depending on the habitat, for the Iban of Borneo (Freeman 1955). Within Amazonia itself, which is on the whole less densely populated

than Southeast Asia, the Achuar were at the bottom of the scale: 1 person/km² for the Campa (Denevan 1974: 93); 0.8 person/km² for the Machiguenga (Johnson 1974: 8); 0.5 person/km² for the Barafiri Yanoama (Smole 1976: 3); 0.34 person/km² for the central Yanomami (Lizot 1977: 122). With 0.17 person/km², the Ecuadorian Achuar come close to Steward and Faron's estimate of 0.23 person/km² – judged too low by many – as the average density for Amazonian aboriginal populations before the European conquest (Steward and Faron 1959: 53). On the other hand, the Achuar are situated at the upper end of the density scale for numerous hunter-gatherer societies: 0.01 person/km² for the Algonkian Indians of Great Victoria Lake (Hallowel 1949: 40); 0.18 person/km² at Groote Eylandt; 0.06 person/km² for the Murngin and 0.01 person/km² for the Walbiri (Yengoyan 1968: 190). In the end, swidden cultivators though they may be, the present density of the Achuar population is slightly lower than that of the hunter-gatherers of the Pleistocene era, if, for the latter, we accept the figure advanced by Lee and DeVore of 0.6 person/km² (Lee and DeVore 1968: 11).

2: Landscape and cosmos

1 Our main sources of information for the geomorphological and pedological analyses of the Achuar region are Tschopp 1953; Sourdat and Custode 1980a,b; De Noni 1979. Michel Sourdat and Georges-Laurent De Noni, ORSTOM pedologist and geomorphologist, respectively, serving in Quito, were also kind enough to avail us of their expertise in the earth sciences, spending long hours helping us with maps and aerial photographs of a region which, until then, had been completely unknown to geographers. We would like to express our gratitude at this time.

2 For soil typology we have followed the standard American nomenclature (*United States Department of Agriculture Soil Taxonomy*) widely used in Ecuador by researchers from the Ministerio de Agricultura y Ganaderia and from ORSTOM.

3 Our climatological analysis of the Achuar region is based on personal observation, the annals of Ecuador's Instituto Nacional de Meteorologia e Hidrologia, and on tables published by the Peruvian Servicio Nacional de Meteorologia e Hidrologia; we also had the benefit of the enlightened advice of Michel Sourdat and the hydrology department of the Quito branch of ORSTOM. The region of Ecuador occupied by the Achuar is not directly covered by any meteorological station; but it is bounded on the northwest by an Ecuadorian station (Taisha) and on the southwest and the southeast by two Peruvian stations (Sargento Puno and Soplin). The fact that these stations abut on our territory and the variety of their positions, both in terms of altitude and distance from the eastern Cordillera, give us a fairly clear picture of the climatic variations within the Achuar territory.

4 All botanical identification of wild and cultivated species mentioned in this work was done by us from personal observation and reasoned collation of documentary data. For technical and financial reasons, we were unable to constitute a systematic collection, and the identifications we propose are subject to subsequent validation. In addition to the classics of botanical literature, we used three

sources: (1) the Aguaruna botanical nomenclature collected by the Jesuit missionary Guallart (Guallart 1968, 1975); (2) the computer-coded list of plant species collected by Professor Brent Berlin's expedition to the Aguaruna, of which he was generous enough to lend us a copy; (3) the inventory of tree samples collected on Shuar territory by engineers from the Centre Technique Forestier Tropical and the SCET-International, working for the State of Ecuador. In the last case, the French technicians were kind enough to share their forest experience with us on site, thus giving us an exceptional chance to establish a plant catalogue.

5 The scientific identification of animal species was done from personal observation and by systematic consultation with our native informants using illustrated zoological plates: De Schauensee and Phelps 1978 for birds, Eigenmann and Allen 1942 for fish, Patzelt 1978 for mammals, Klots and Klots 1959 for insects, Cochran 1961 and Schmidt and Inger 1957 for amphibians and reptiles.

6 According to Karsten, for the Jivaro, *yankuam* corresponds to the planet Venus (1935: 504). In the case of the Achuar, this identification is not appropriate, if only because of *yankuam's* regular disappearance every year at the same time and its permanent polar opposition to the Pleiades.

3: Nature's beings

1 When Harner (1972: 2) rejects Karsten's whole monograph on the Jivaro on the grounds that the Finnish ethnographer's data differ from his own, he makes the mistake of elevating his favorite informants' interpretations to the rank of sacrosanct dogma. However the erratic impression the reader gets from Karsten's portrait of Jivaro religious life (1935: 371–510) is in fact more consistent with what we have been able to observe among the Achuar than the normative paradigm to which Harner, in his positivist zeal, would reduce it. Not one readily to appreciate the dynamic virtues of contradiction, Harner has bent his efforts to constructing "canonical" versions of the native system of representations (1972: 5–6). By proposing an outline of the stages of metempsychosis, Harner (1972: 150–1) has frozen into a single dogmatic version one of the many interpretations proposed by the Jivaro.

2 For lack of space, we will deal only marginally with the problem of taboos as one specific example in the more general framework of Achuar taxonomic systems. But, even though we do not wish, for the moment, to go into all the details of this thorny problem, we cannot help but refute E. Ross' assertions on Achuar food taboos. In a 1978 article in *Current Anthropology*, Ross sets out to show that Amazonian prohibitions on eating certain animals should be seen as a way of adapting to the ecological constraints of a particular environment and not as abstract elements of a system for classifying the world. In view of the heated debate sparked by this thesis among Amazonian specialists and inasmuch as the Peruvian Achuar are used as the principal illustration, it is only fitting that I clarify a few ethnographic facts conveniently left unmentioned in the article.

Ross maintains that, if the Achuar and many other Amerindian societies prohibit the eating of such large mammals as the deer and the tapir, this is because these animals are scarce, scattered and hard to capture. They would be in danger of vanishing altogether were not such cultural mechanisms as food taboos to prevent their extinction. To the obvious question of what good it does to protect species that are not used by humans anyway, Ross responds this time not with an ecological argument, but with an economic justification. Briefly, he argues that hunting small animals is more productive in terms of optimizing labor input than hunting big ones. By placing a general taboo on deer and tapir, the Achuar automatically avoid adopting an economic strategy that would prove to be a waste of time. But if these taboos ensure the maximization of labor input, he argues that they also have important side effects on the overall equilibrium of the ecosystem. For example, prohibiting the hunting of deer is an adaptive strategy inasmuch as deer are selective grazers, which favors the growth of certain plants, which in turn provides food for several species of animal that the Achuar do hunt. As for the prohibition on eating sloths, he maintains that this stems from the fact that sloth droppings are a fertilizer which provides the material for the growth of trees, which are in turn exploited by monkeys; now, since the Achuar hunt the latter, it is therefore essential to spare the sloths in order to ensure that the monkeys have an abundant supply of food. It is not our job to judge the cogency of this ecosystemic line of reasoning, but we cannot suppress a few doubts about the scientific validity of so teleological a determinism.

The problem raised by this type of hyperdeterminism is that the interpretation must explain absolutely everything if it is to be valid. If the proposed explanation cannot account for all exceptions, it loses all heuristic value. Now Ross bases his demonstration on abstract food taboos and not on actual practices; this is a strange deviation indeed for someone who claims to be a materialist. An Achuar hunter rarely sets out to hunt a single type of game; so it is absurd to say that it is more efficient to pursue relatively plentiful monkeys than to waste time trying to flush out notoriously scarce tapirs. On a forest expedition, a man will try to bring down all the allegedly edible animals he encounters or of which he sees the tracks, without seeking to specialize in any one species. It even happens upon occasion that the dogs will start an animal that is forbidden food (a great anteater, collared anteater, sloth. . .) and the hunter makes no attempt to restrain them. In most cases the animal is killed by the pack, and the dogs are so famished that they devour part of the kill.

But what about tapirs and deer, the only animals prohibited by the Achuar that seem to interest Ross? The prohibition on eating tapir is often transgressed by the Achuar, and, according to our informants, this is neither new nor engendered by the rarification of "authorized" game, which they feel is, on the contrary, more abundant now than it used to be. On the other hand, the taboo on eating *iwianch japa* (*Mazama americana*) is universally observed. But the brocket deer is not the only Cervidae in the Achuar habitat, and when Ross refers, with no further details, to a taboo on deer, he is no doubt being very rash. When a scientist seeks to explain culture as an epiphenomenon of environmental constraints, the least precaution he should take would be to have a good knowledge of the environment. Of the four species of deer common to the Achuar region, only the red brocket is forbidden as food. The other three can legitimately be eaten and their meat is even regarded as a delicacy: *suu japa*

(*Mazama simplicornis*), *ushpit japa* (*Mazama bricenii*), and *keaku japa* (*Odocoileus gymnotis*). Consequently, if three out of four species of deer are authorized game, without having vanished for all that, if the tapir is occasionally hunted, and if most taboo animals are, at one time or another, thrown to the dogs, it is hard to see what the ecological and economic "gain" from food taboos would be. In the last place, it is surprising indeed that Ross offers no interpretation to justify the ecological cogency of the Achuar prohibition on eating certain small animals like the spider monkey, the *tuich* armadillo (*Dasypus* sp.), the woolly opossum (*Philander* sp.), the collared anteater, or the coati. For his argument to be consistent, not only would all big animals that are scarce and hard to flush have never to be killed by the Achuar, which is not the case, but, too, all small animals with edible flesh would have to be exploited as sources of food, which is far from being the case. By proposing his so-called materialist interpretation of Achuar taboos and basing it on the analysis of abstract norms alone, and not on the observation of concrete behaviors, Ross advances much further along the path of idealism than the structuralist ethnographers he claims to refute.

3   Two Shuar versions of this myth have been published (Pellizzaro 1980a: 167–215, and Karsten 1935: 527–32); they differ from Achuar versions in that they give preeminence to the *tsantsa* ceremony organized by the forest animals to celebrate the massacre of the water animals. Aside from the allusion to the fish-head *tsantsa* made by *unkum*, our version is silent on this subject. This is quite understandable, for the Achuar do not usually shrink heads and therefore do not know the Shuar ritual performed on this occasion. The version collected by Father Pellizzaro is especially rich, for it gives very specific details on the circumstances in the wake of which some twenty different species of forest animal took on their present appearance during the *tsantsa* feast.

4: The world of the house

1   The prevalence of feuding is the reason why the pattern of residence in fortified houses may appear to the chance observer to be the dominant form of human settlement for the Achuar. This probably explains Harner's error in making a clear distinction between the composition of Shuar and Achuar household groups: "The permanent matrilocality [among the Achuar] results in household populations considerably in excess of those normally found among the Jivaro [Shuar]" (Harner 1972: 221). If it is true that the fortified multiple-family house is a relatively common pattern of residence, the fact remains that it is only a derivation of the single-family household. Furthermore, although Achuar matrilocality is of longer duration than that among the Shuar, it is not permanent.

2   *Iwianch jea* refers to the conical form of Sangay (*tunkurua* in Shuar), a high volcano of the Andean cordillera located at the edge of the Shuar territory. According to a belief introduced among the Shuar by Catholic missionaries, the volcano, from which plumes of smoke rise continuously, is hell, i.e. the home of the *wakan* souls of unconverted Indians who, after death, undergo eternal punishment in the fiery crater and change into *iwianch* evil spirits. This syncretic notion probably dates from the beginning of the century (it was noted by Karsten in 1935: 382 and confirmed by Harner in 1973: 203), but it has only

recently reached the Achuar and then in so fragmented a form that it does not upset their traditional systems of beliefs about the changes undergone by the soul after death. As Sangay is much too far from the Achuar's territory to be visible, the notion of a volcano, imperfectly transmitted by the Shuar, comes down to three paradigms: *iwianch* evil spirits, cone, and fire.

3 The Shuar house frame is fairly different from that of the Achuar, even though, once the roof is finished, the outward appearance is quite similar. Furthermore, some terms like *pau* and *makui*, common to the architectural vocabulary of both groups, in fact designate two entirely different pieces of the skeleton. The *pau* has great symbolic significance for the Shuar, since it is the center post of the house and serves as the spatial axis in many rituals. Having no equivalent piece (in Achuar, *pau* designates the main beams), the inside of the Achuar house lacks any such explicit connotations of centrality. Finally, it should be pointed out that variations internal to the Achuar group occur in the naming of house parts, but apparently not in the way they are assembled (Bolla and Rovere 1977, for Achuar architecture along the lower Makuma and the upper Huasaga).

4 The Salesian missionary Siro Pellizzaro (1978a: 12) proposes a different interpretation of the Shuar funeral ceremony. He maintains that the corpse's position with its feet toward the setting sun indicates that the deceased is going to follow Etsa–sun down to the "kingdom of shadows." Elsewhere Pellizzaro's equation between Etsa and God inclines us to suspect this interpretation of unconscious ethnocentrism. At any rate, nothing we have on the Achuar corroborates it. To our knowledge, there is no explanation in the ethnographic literature of the symbolic function of the canoe-coffin among the Jivaro groups; Karsten notes simply that the Canelos, the Achuar's neighbors to the north, justify the use of a canoe as a coffin by saying: "The deceased . . . ought to make his last journey in a canoe" (Karsten 1935: 166).

5 To justify abandoning a house after the death of its owner, the Achuar argue that his *nekas wakan* would haunt the vicinity and keep the survivors from leading a normal life. But this rationalization does not account for the fact that, when a less important member of the household (a wife or a child) dies, the body is merely buried under his or her platform bed. Daily life takes up where it left off, and no one seems concerned about the possible harm that could be done by the wandering *nekas wakan*. In such cases, the only precaution taken is to forbid young children to play on the grave for fear that the deceased's *wakan* might enter their bodies (*imimketin*), seriously upsetting their physiological equilibrium, which would ultimately mean death.

6 Three main types of ritual dialogue are staged in the house: *aujmatin* ("palavers"), for visitors who have come a long way, *yaitias chicham* ("slow talk"), the most common form of greeting dialogue, and *atsanmartin* ("negative talk"), a fairly rare monologue signifying the refusal of a visit.

5: The world of gardens

1 The expression was coined by N. Chagnon to describe Yanomamö techniques of cultivation (1969: 249). It corresponds roughly to what H. Conklin calls the "integral system of pioneer swidden farming," which he defines as the method "where significant portions of climax vegetation [were] customarily cleared each year" (Conklin 1975: 3).

2 The topographical outline map used for mapping site n° 1 was produced by the French company SCET-International (SCET International-PREDESUR 1977). The topographical outline map used for sites n° 2 and 3 was produced by M. Sourdat, from the Quito branch of the French organization ORSTOM. The geomorphological and edaphological interpretations of the sites were made possible by M. Sourdat and G.L. de Noni, and the analysis of soil samples was carried out by the ORSTOM mission in Quito. The phytological description of the sites was the product of a count of dominant species carried out with the help of Achuar informants. Furthermore, the Achuar know perfectly well what dominant plant species are associated with each type of soil and terrain identified in indigenous taxonomy.

3 The Canelos, neighbors of the Achuar to the north, occupy a classic interfluvial habitat and yet never burn their manioc gardens (Whitten 1976: 70–6). It is true that, in their case, the additional work is more equitably divided as, unlike the Achuar, their men take an active part in all horticultural tasks.

4 The Canelos use this method for growing maize and bananas (Whitten 1976: 76), and it is also practiced by the black populations on the Pacific coast of Ecuador (Whitten 1974). The Shuar have also been known to grow maize on mulch (Harner 1972: 49 and Karsten 1935); Karsten, who had the opportunity to observe this method of cultivation during the second decade of our century, believes that it is recent and probably replaced the intercropping of maize, a technique that can sometimes still be seen in Achuar gardens. Lastly, the Aguaruna, too, seem to have adopted the principle of single-crop gardens, not only for maize but for bananas as well (Berlin and Berlin 1977: 11).

5 If we compare them with the meagre data that we have on other Amazonian horticulturalist societies, Achuar time inputs for clearing seem extraordinarily high. Ecuador's Siona-Secoya, for instance, clear a hectare of primary forest in 59 hours, while the Miskito carry out the same operation, in secondary forest, in 138 hours (Vickers 1976: 88). It seems that the differences can be attributed to the methods of measuring used, since we base our quantifications on the true total duration of a sequence of operations, thereby taking into account the differences in intensity of work according to the stage and the individual, while Vickers mathematically reconstructs the total duration by adding up the separate elements of the operational sequence, each element having been timed for one individual. Although this method is no doubt effective for determining the productivity of industrial work stations, it seems hardly reliable when applied to societies in which work is not subjected to machine-like regularity. Carneiro's estimate of 138 hours for clearing a plot of slightly less than a hectare (approximately two acres) among the Amahuaca is extrapolated from information so vague that it does not seem reliable either (Carneiro 1970: 246). On the other hand, B. Meggers' data (unfortunately no sources are cited) for the time taken to clear a tract of *várzea* forest near Belem seem to correspond entirely with the Achuar figures (Meggers 1971: 30–1).

6 Aside from the rich variety of cultivars, the most striking indications of the very old practice of horticulture among Jivaro groups come from both within (detailed knowledge of ethnobotany and agronomy, multiplicity of myths concerning cultivated plants, ritualization of agricultural activities . . .) and

without (archeological analysis of ceramic materials, bio-geographic models of the evolution of the Amazonian forest . . .). This question is treated more particularly in A-C. Taylor's ethno-historical study (1993, Chap. 3).

7 In his ethnobotanical study of Aguaruna horticulture, Brent Berlin also stresses the abundance and diversity of the plants cultivated by this ethnic group, very similar in many respects to the Achuar: fifty-three cultigens (compared to sixty-seven for the Achuar) and twenty-seven semi-cultivated plants (compared to thirty-seven for the Achuar), the lot being divided into 276 varieties. Brent Berlin notes furthermore that, according to the preliminary results of a survey conducted by a botanist on his team, the Aguaruna recognize over 200 manioc cultivars; it is very likely that a systematic ethnobotanical survey of Achuar plants would greatly increase the number of varieties we have recorded (Berlin 1977: 10).

8 In his analysis of the ethnobotany of Aguaruna hallucinogens, Michael Brown makes the same remark about the highly idiosyncratic character of the taxonomy of morphologically identical hallucinogens (Brown 1978: 132–3).

9 The popularity of the onion (*sepui*, from the Spanish *cebolla*), consumed in manioc soup, stems from the protective powers attributed to it. In effect, the Achuar have acquired from their Shuar neighbors the conviction that white men are protected from the indigenous shaman's magic darts by the great quantities of onions they eat.

10 These latent categories are identical to the "covert categories" Brent Berlin finds in Aguaruna horticulture, and which he also illustrates with the *Inga* (Berlin 1977: 8; Berlin and Berlin 1977: 7).

11 Unlike the Aguaruna, who seem to have an indigenous symbolic interpretation which justifies their planting a few cultivated species in specific associations (Brown and Bolt 1980: 182).

12 H. Conklin, who pioneered the modern study of slash-and-burn cultivation, was the first to note that its similarity with the trophic structure of primary forest gave slash-and-burn polyculture an important advantage over monoculture (1954: 133–42).

13 Peanuts and beans fix nitrogen in the soil and thus make an excellent first crop.

14 W. Denevan subscribes to this idea when he concludes his study on the Campa by writing: "The emphasis on protein-poor root crops in Amazonia seems to be culturally determined. . ." (1974: 108).

15 A remarkable article by J. Murra, on the generalization of maize growing in the Andes under the Inca administration, shows how the adoption by a society of a new tool of production does not always proceed automatically according to the logic of marginal utility (Murra 1975). Before the Inca invasion, most Andean communities had grown maize as a very secondary food plant, used mainly for making ritual libations. It was the Inca State that intensified the growing of maize and turned it into a large-scale production through an ambitious empire-wide program of terracing. Here the expansion of the habitat's carrying capacity was engineered by a bureaucracy that needed important surplus production in order to reproduce the machinery of the State. There is, on the other hand, nothing to indicate that a similar process of technological transformation would have been undertaken from within by Andean communities not subjected to the

pressing need to multiply the productive capacity of their habitat. Maize had long been a virtual production factor, but the relations of production that would have made it possible to actualize its strategic importance did not yet exist. This lesson on the dangers of theorizing about technological determinism is surely valid for the Amazon Basin as well.

16 A good example of this indifference to agricultural rituals is related by Carneiro who, when he asked an Amahuaca gardener if he performed a ceremony to help plants grow, was answered in the purest positivist vein: "How could such a ceremony make crops grow, I wonder?" (Carneiro 1964: 10).

17 Among the published Shuar variants, see Wawrin 1941: 52; Harner 1972: 72–5; Karsten 1935: 513–16; and especially Pellizzaro 1978a: 1–80, who provides a large number of variants with facing translation. For the Aguaruna, see Berlin 1977; García-Rendueles 1978; and Ballon and García-Rendueles 1978; the last article proposes an original analysis of the myth of Nunkui inspired by Greimas. The Achuar variant we have chosen was told to us in Achuar by Mirijiar, a widow of around 50 who lives on the lower Rio Kapawi.

18 Karsten maintains that the Jivaro represent the spirit of manioc as having a female essence (1935: 123), but the Achuar and Aguaruna both contradict this assertion (Brown and Van Bolt 1980: 173).

19 Pellizzaro relates a Shuar myth in which Shakaim is presented as having taught men the technique of felling trees with an ax (n.d. [1]: 16–43); according to this scholarly missionary, the word Shakaim means "gust of wind" (from *shaka*, an onomatopoeia denoting the sound of a storm and *yumi*, rain); following this thinking, Shakaim would be a metaphor for the windstorm that creates natural clearings by blowing down big trees (3).

20 The Shuar (Karsten 1935: 127–30) and the Aguaruna (Brown and Van Bolt 1980: 177–9) have the same ceremony.

21 According to Karsten, the Shuar prohibition on *kanka* stems from the fact that this fish is assimilated to a shrunken head, *tsantsa* (Karsten 1935: 192). The Achuar – who, it seems, have never practiced head shrinking – are entirely unaware of this equivalence.

6: The world of the forest

1 For a more detailed description of the manufacture of a blowgun, see C. Bianchi's abundantly illustrated fascicle (1976a: 1–49). His account of the operational sequence refers to the technique used by the Shuar, but it differs from Achuar technique by only a few minute variants.

2 Both of these traps are described in detail and accompanied by numerous illustrations in C. Bianchi's work on Achuar traps (1976b: 2–20). The book also shows a dozen traps presently or formerly used by the Shuar but which we have never seen employed by the Achuar.

3 Analytically speaking, the complex mechanisms regulating territoriality, and thereby the distribution of hunting grounds, fall outside the sphere of productive forces, since they depend on the set of social relations that, intentionally or unintentionally, organize the processes involved in the appropriation of nature. Achuar territoriality therefore lies outside the scope of this study, but will be dealt with in a future work devoted to the analysis of relations of production and reproduction.

4 The northern Achuar almost never associate their actual hunting with the mythological figure of Etsa ("Sun"), in whom the Shuar see the paradigm of the hunter (Pellizzaro n.d. [1]). Etsa does appear in several Achuar myths as a major hunter-figure, but his direct intercession is rarely sought in hunting, over which he seems to have little or no influence compared to that of the *amana* and the "game mothers." Furthermore the set of "game mothers" (the Shaam, Amasank, and Jurijri) seems to be a cultural feature peculiar to the northern Achuar, for it would seem that they are unknown to the Achuar of the Huasaga river basin and the lower Rio Macuma (L. Bolla and A. Colajanni, pers. commun.).

5 On inversion in the interpretation of premonitory dreams, see examples from the Maku (Reid 1978: 15) and the Apinayé (Da Matta 1970: 95) cultures.

7: The world of the river

1 See in particular the analysis of the group of "frog" myths, in which the origin of fish poison is attributed to the physical or moral filth of a woman who is mad about cooking (Lévi-Strauss 1964: 261–87).

2 With the exception of two large catfish, *juunt tunkau* (*Pimelodus ornatus*) and *aakiam* (*Pseudoplatystoma fasciatum*), particularly hard to catch and reserved for fisherman who are brave and experienced. Highly prized by the Achuar, these fish in turn prey voraciously on small fry and because of this enjoy a special status (cf. Conclusion).

3 The Shuar myth of man's marriage with the Tsunki (Pellizzaro 1980a: 9–113) is naturally much richer than the corresponding Achuar anecdote; in particular, it contains a version of the first flood provoked by the ill treatment to which the human wives subjected the aquatic wife.

8: Categories of practice

1 See in particular Clastres, who writes: "Primitive societies are indeed, as J. Lizot writes of the Yanomami, work-rejecting societies" (Clastres 1974: 167).

2 It would be hard to agree with Rivet's claim when, reiterating a common ethnocentric prejudice, he presents Jivaro women as perpetual slaves of their idle husbands (Rivet 1908: 69). Karsten, as the excellent observer he was, had already criticized this simplistic view, remarking on how much independent control Jivaro women had over their own sphere of activity and in particular in assessing the amount of work that they felt they needed to allocate to subsistence activities. Although not based on statistical data, his discussion of the differential assignment of tasks revealed that the sexual division of labor does not penalize women (Karsten 1935: 56).

3 These conclusions would seem to contradict the famous "Chayanov rule" central to Sahlins' definition of the domestic mode of production, which is stated as follows: "intensity of labor in a system of domestic production for use varies inversely with the relative work capacity of the producing unit" (Sahlins 1972: 91) Apart from the fact that Chayanov's prerevolutionary Russian peasantry still devoted part of its labor force to small-scale market production (Chayanov 1966), we cannot help wondering why Sahlins was so willing to adopt a marginalist interpretation completely in contradiction with his own theoretical position. Either, as marginalist logic would have it, the peasant domestic unit optimizes its means of production and economizes its labor as a rare commo-

dity, as Chayanov claims (1966: 75–6); or the composition and expenditure of labor depends on cultural specifications, as Sahlins writes elsewhere (1972: 55), in which case the intensity of labor cannot be automatically adjusted to the size of the production unit, since the product of individual labor is culturally rated on a prestige scale.

9: The good life

1 This table, like all of the data presented in this chapter, is based on a sample of six dispersed households (four from the riverine habitat and two from the interfluve) observed over a total period of 66 days. The shortest stay in a house was eight days and the longest, eighteen. The sample homes were selected for their representativeness from a broader set of observations of fourteen households over a total period of 163 days. In each household daily food production and work times were recorded. The six households retained for the final sample were chosen because the observation periods were evenly spread over the entire seasonal cycle and because the average results were closer to the overall averages.

2 The daily contribution of gathering vegetable products is largely underestimated in this sample because of the short duration of the observation periods and the fact that these were spread over the entire year. On the basis of our more extensive studies, it can be considered that in *neretin* season (i.e. for at least five months of the year), wild fruits contribute between 200 and 300 g per capita to the daily diet, or around 2% of daily calorie intake. But the importance of gathered fruits should not be evaluated in terms of their gross energy contribution, but for certain vitamins they contain (in particular, vitamin A, thiamin, and riboflavin), which are crucial to balanced nutrition. These vitamins are notoriously deficient in the staple cultigens and particularly in manioc.

3 Like the nineteenth-century evolutionists, Sahlins tends to view the agricultural revolution as the source of stable political forms, the condition for social ranking, and the original tool for the unending accumulation of wealth. As he writes: "Agriculture [. . .] allowed neolithic communities to maintain high degrees of social order where the requirements of human existence were absent from the natural order. Enough food could be harvested in some seasons to sustain the people while no food would grow at all; the consequent stability of social life was critical for its material enlargement. Culture went on then from triumph to triumph, in a kind of progressive contravention of the biological law of the minimum [. . .]" (Sahlins 1972: 37).

References

Acosta-Solis, M. 1966. *Los recursos naturales del Ecuador y su conservación*, t. 2. Mexico, Instituto panamericano de geografía e historia

Aldrich, S. 1970. "Corn culture." In G. E. Inglett (ed.), *Corn: culture, processing, products*. Westport (Conn.), AVI Publishing Company

Amadio, M. and L. d'Emilio 1982. "La alianza entre los Candoshi Murato del Alto Amazonas." Paper presented at the 44th International Congress of Americanists, Manchester, September 1982

Arnalot, J. 1978. *Lo que los Achuar me han enseñado*. Sucua (Ecuador), Ediciones Mundo Shuar

Athens, S. 1976. "Reporte preliminar sobre el sitio de Pumpuentza." Unpublished report, University of New Mexico, Albuquerque

Ballon, E. and M. García-Rendueles 1978. "Análisis del mito de Nunkui." *Amazonía peruana* 2: 99–158

Bateson, G. 1972. *Steps to an Ecology of Mind*. New York, Ballantine Books

Beckerman, S. 1978. "Comment on Ross' food taboos, diet and hunting strategy: the adaptation to animals in Amazon cultural ecology." *Current Anthropology* 19(1): 17–19

1979. "The abundance of protein in Amazonia: a reply to Gross." *American Anthropologist* 81(3): 533–60

Beek, K. J. and D. L. Bramao 1969. "Nature and geography of South-American soils." In E. J. Fittkau *et al.* (eds.), *Biogeography and Ecology in South America*. The Hague, Dr. W. Junk Publishers, Monographiae Biologicae 18

Belzner, W. 1981. "Music, modernization and Westernization among the Macuma Shuar." In N. Whitten (ed.), *Cultural Transformation and Ethnicity in Modern Ecuador*. Urbana, University of Illinois Press

345

Bennema, J. M., N. Camargo and A. S. Wright 1962. "Regional contrast in South-American soil formation in relation to soil classification and soil fertility." *International Society of Soil Science Transactions and Communications* 4–5: 493–506

Berlin, B. 1977. *Bases empíricas de la cosmologia aguaruna jíbaro, Amazonas, Perú.* Berkeley, University of California, Studies in Aguaruna Jivaro Ethnobiology, Report 3

Berlin, B. and E. A. Berlin 1977. *Ethnobiology, subsistence and nutrition in a tropical forest society: the Aguaruna Jivaro.* Berkeley, University of California, Studies in Aguaruna Jivaro Ethnobiology, Report 1

Berlin, E. A. and E. Markell 1977. *Parásitos y nutrición: dinámica de la salud entre los Aguaruna Jivaro de Amazonas, Perú.* Berkeley, University of California, Studies in Aguaruna Jivaro Ethnobiology, Report 4

Bianchi, C. 1976a. *Armas.* Sucua (Ecuador), Centro de documentación e investigación cultural shuar, Mundo shuar, Series C, N° 6

1976b. *Trampas.* Sucua (Ecuador), Centro de documentación e investigación cultural shuar, Mundo shuar, Series C, N° 2

Bidou, P. 1972. "Représentation de l'espace dans la mythologie Tatuyo (Indiens Tucano)." *Journal de la Société des américanistes* 61: 45–105

Bolla, L. and F. Rovere 1977. *La casa achuar: estructura y proceso de construcción.* Sucua (Ecuador), Centro de documentación e investigación cultural shuar, Mundo shuar, Series B, N° 9

Bottasso, J. 1980. "Los Salesianos y los Shuar, análisis de una política indigenista." Unpublished thesis for Laurea, Gregorian Pontifical University, Rome

Brown, M. 1978. "From the hero's bones: three Aguaruna hallucinogens and their uses." In R. I. Ford (ed.), *The Nature and Status of Ethnobotany.* Ann Arbor, University of Michigan Press

Brown, M. and M. Van Bolt 1980. "Aguaruna Jivaro gardening magic in the Alto Rio Mayo, Peru." *Ethnology* 19(2): 169–90

Brown, P. and H. C. Brookfield 1963. *Struggle for Land.* Melbourne, Oxford University Press

Buffon, G. L. Leclerc, comte de 1833–34. *Œuvres complètes.* Pourrat Frères

Camargo, F. 1948. "Terra e colonisaçâo no antigo e novo Quaternario na zona da Estrada de Ferro de Bragança, Estado de Pará." *Boletim do Museo Pará. Emilio Goeldi* 10: 123–47

1958. "Report on the Amazon region." In *Problems of Humid Tropical Regions.* Paris, Unesco

Carneiro, R. 1957. "Subsistence and social structure: an ecological study of the Kuikuru Indians." Unpublished doctoral dissertation, University of Michigan. Ann Arbor, Xerox University Microfilms

1960. "Slash-and-burn agriculture: a closer look at its implications for settlement patterns." In A. Wallace (ed.), *Men and Cultures.* Philadelphia, University of Pennsylvania Press

1961. "Slash-and-burn cultivation among the Kuikuru and its implications for cultural development in the Amazon Basin." In J. Wilbert (ed.), *The Evolution of Horticultural Systems in Native South America: causes and consequences.* Caracas, Sociedad de Ciencias naturales La Salle

1964. "Shifting cultivation among the Amahuaca of eastern Peru." *Völkerkundliche Abhandlungen* 1: 1–18

1970. "The transition from hunting to horticulture in the Amazon Basin." *Proceedings of the VIIIth International Congress of Anthropological and Ethnological Sciences*, t. 3. Tokyo, Science Council of Japan

1974. "Hunting and hunting magic among the Amahuaca of the Peruvian montaña." In P. Lyon (ed.), *Native South Americans: ethnology of the least-known continent*. Boston, Little, Brown, and Co.

Cassidy, N. G. and S. Pahalad 1953. "The maintenance of soil fertility in Fiji." *Fiji Agricultural Journal* 24: 82–6

CERM 1970. *Sur les sociétés précapitalistes. Textes choisis de Marx, Engels, Lénine.* Paris, Editions sociales

Chagnon, N. 1969. "Culture-ecology of shifting cultivation among the Yanomamö Indians." *Proceedings of the VIIIth International Congress of Anthropological and Ethnological Sciences.* Tokyo, Science Council of Japan

1974. *Studying the Yanomamö.* New York, Holt, Rinehart, and Winston

Chayanov, A. 1966. *The Theory of Peasant Economy.* Homewood (Illinois), Richard Irwin for the American Economic Association

Clastres, P. 1974. *La société contre l'Etat.* Paris, Editions de Minuit

Cochran, D. 1961. *Living Amphibians of the World.* New York, Doubleday

Conklin, H. 1954–55. "An ethnoecological approach to shifting agriculture." *Transactions of the New York Academy of Science* 2nd series, 17: 133–42.

1975 (first edition 1957). *Hanunóo Agriculture: a report on an integral system of shifting cultivation in the Philippines.* Northford, Elliot's Books Reprints

Cours, G. 1951. *Le manioc à Madagascar.* Tananarive, Institut scientifique de Tananarive, Mémoires de l'Institut scientifique de Madagascar, Series B, t. 3, Fasc. 2

Da Matta, R. 1970. "Les présages Apinayé." In J. Pouillon and P. Maranda (eds.), *Echanges et communications: mélanges offerts à Claude Lévi-Strauss en son soixantième anniversaire*, vol. 1. Paris/The Hague, Mouton

Davidson, S. *et al.* 1975. *Human Nutrition and Dietetics.* Edinburgh, Churchill Livingston

Deler, J-P. 1981. *Genèse de l'espace équatorien: essai sur le territoire et la formation de l'Etat national.* Paris, Institut français d'études andines/Editions ADPF

Denevan, W. 1970. "The aboriginal population of western Amazonia in relation to habitat and subsistence." *Revista geografica* 72: 61–86

1974. "Campa subsistence in the Gran Pajonal, eastern Peru." In P. Lyon (ed.), *Native South Americans: ethnology of the least-known continent.* Boston, Little, Brown, and Co.

1976. "The aboriginal population of Amazonia." In W. Denevan (ed.), *The Native Population of the Americas in 1942.* Madison, University of Wisconsin Press

1978. "The causes and consequences of shifting cultivation in relation to tropical forest survival." In W. Denevan (ed.), *The Role of Geographical Research in Latin America.* Muncie, Association of American Geographers

De Noni, G-L. 1979. "Commentaire de la carte pédo-géomorphologique de la province de Pastaza." A working draft kindly lent by the author. Quito, ORSTOM

De Schauensee, R. and W. Phelps 1978. *A Guide to the Birds of Venezuela.* Princeton, Princeton University Press

Descola, P. 1981a. "From scattered to nucleated settlements: a process of socio-economic change among the Achuar." In N. Whitten (ed.), *Cultural Transformation and Ethnicity in Modern Ecuador.* Urbana, University of Illinois Press.

1981b. "Limitaciones ecológicas y sociales al desarollo de la Amazonía: un estudio de caso en la Amazonía ecuatoriana." Paper presented to the "Primera reunión técnica sobre Asuntos Indígenas de los Paises del Tratado de Cooperación Amazónica," Puyo (Ecuador), 27–30 July 1981. In Oficina Nacional de Asuntos Indígenas (ed.), *Población indígena y desarollo amazónico.* Quito, Abya-Yala, 1984

1982a. "Ethnicité et développement économique: le cas de la Fédération de Centres shuar." In *Indianité, ethnocide, indigénisme en Amérique latine.* Toulouse/Paris, Editions du CNRS

1982b. "Territorial adjustments among the Achuar of Ecuador." *Social Science Information* 21(2): 299–318

Descola, P. and J-L. Lory 1982. "Les guerriers de l'invisible: sociologie comparative de l'agression chamanique en Amazonie (Achuar) et en Nouvelle-Guinée (Baruya)." *L'ethnographie* 87–88: 85–109

Descola, P. and A-C. Taylor 1977. "Contacts interethniques dans l'Oriente équatorien: un exemple d'acculturation médiatisée." In *La forêt dans ses confins andins.* Grenoble, Université de Grenoble/AFERPA

1981. "El conjunto jivaro en los comienzos de la conquista española del Alto Amazonas." Bulletin de l'Institut français d'études andines 10(3–4): 7–54

Dresch, J. 1966. "Les paysages tropicaux humides." In *Géographie générale, Encyclopédie de la Pléiade.* Paris, Gallimard

Dreyfus, S. 1980–81. "Notes sur la chefferie Taino d'Aiti: capacités productrices, ressources alimentaires, pouvoirs dans une société précolombienne de forêt tropicale." *Journal de la Société des américanistes* 67: 229–48

Drown, F. and M. Drown 1961. *Mission Among the Head-Hunters.* New York, Harper and Row

Dumont, L. 1975. *Dravidien et Kariera: l'alliance de mariage dans l'Inde du sud et en Australie.* Paris/The Hague, Mouton

Eigenman, C. and W. Allen 1942. *Fishes of Western South America.* Louisville, University of Kentucky, 2 vols.

Falesi, I. C. 1974. "Soils of the Brazilian Amazon." In C. Wagley (ed.), *Man in the Amazon.* Gainesville, University of Florida Press

Federación de Centros shuar 1976. *Federación de Centros shuar: una solución original a un problema actual.* Sucua (Ecuador), Don Bosco Printers

Fernandez de Navarrete, M. 1825. *Collección de los viajes y descubrimientos que hicieron por mar los españoles desde el siglo XV,* vol. 1. Madrid

Firth, R. 1965 (first edition 1939). *Primitive Polynesian Economy.* London, Routledge and Kegan Paul

Fittkau, E. J. 1969. "The fauna of South America." In E. J. Fittkau *et al.* (eds.), *Biogeography and Ecology in South America,* vol. 2. The Hague, Dr. W. Junk Publishers, Monographiae Biologicae 18

Fittkau, E. J. and H. Klinge 1973. "On biomass and trophic structure in the Central

Amazonian rain forest ecosystem." *Biotropica* 5(1): 2–14

Flornoy, B. 1953. *Jivaro: among the headshrinkers of the Amazon.* London, Elek Publications

Freeman, D. 1955. *Iban Agriculture.* London, Her Majesty's Stationary Office, Colonial Research Studies 18.

García-Rendueles, M. 1978. "Version primera y segunda del mito de Nunkui en aguaruna y español." *Amazonía peruana* 2: 10–52

Gasche, J. 1974. "L'habitat witoto: 'progrès' et tradition." *Journal de la Société des américanistes* 61: 177–214

Godelier, M. 1964. "Economie politique et anthropologie économique: à propos des Siane de Nouvelle-Guinée." *L'Homme* 4(3): 118–32

1973. *Horizons, trajets marxistes en anthropologie.* Paris, Maspero

1984. *L'idéel et le matériel: pensée, économies, sociétés.* Paris, Fayard.

Godelier, M. and J. Garanger 1973. "Outils de pierre, outils d'acier chez les Baruya de Nouvelle-Guinée." *L'Homme* 13(3): 128–39

Goldman, I. 1963. *The Cubeo Indians of the Northwest Amazon.* Urbana, University of Illinois Press

Grenand, F. and C. Haxaire 1977. "Monographie d'un abattis wayâpi." *Journal d'agronomie tropicale et de botanique appliquée* 24(1): 285–310

Gross, D. 1975. "Protein capture and cultural development in the Amazon Basin." *American Anthropologist* 77: 526–49

Grubb, P., J. Lloyd and T. Pennington 1963. "A comparison of montane and lowland rain forest in Ecuador, 1: The forest structure, physiognomy and floristics." *Journal of Ecology* 51(3): 567–601

Grubb, P. and T. Whitmore 1966. "A comparison of montane and lowland rainforest in Ecuador, 2: The climate and its effects on the distribution and physiognomy of the forest." *Journal of Ecology* 54(2): 303–33

Guallart, J-M. 1968. "Nomenclatura jivaro aguaruna de palmeras en el districto de Cenepa." *Biota* 7(57): 230–51

1975. "Contribución al estudio de la etnobotánica jivaro aguaruna." *Biota* 10(83): 336–51

Guyot, M. 1974. "La maison des Indiens Bora et Miraña." *Journal de la Société des américanistes* 61: 177–214

Hallowell, T. 1949. "The size of Algonkian hunting territories: a function of ecological adjustment." *American Anthropologist* 51: 35–45

Harner, M. 1972. *The Jivaro, People of the Sacred Waterfalls.* Garden City (New York), Doubleday/Natural History Press.

Harris, D. 1971. "The ecology of swidden cultivation in the upper Orinoco rain forest, Venezuela." *The Geographical Review* 61(4): 475–95

Harris, M. 1974. *Cows, Pigs, Wars and Witches: the riddles of culture.* New York, Random House

1979. "The Yanomamö and the causes of war in band and village societies." In M. Margolis and W. Carter (eds.), *Brazil, Anthropological Perspectives: essays in honor of Charles Wagley.* New York, Columbia University Press

Haudricourt, G. 1972. "Domestication des animaux, culture des plantes, traitement d'autrui." *L'Homme* 2(1): 40–50

Hegen, E. 1966. *Highways into the Upper Amazon Basin: pioneer lands in southern*

Colombia, Ecuador and northern Peru. Gainesville, University of Florida Press
Hester, W. 1953. "Agriculture, economy and population densities of the Maya."
    Carnegie Institution Yearbook 52: 288–392
Hödl, W. and J. Gasche 1981. "Die Secoya Indianer und deren Landbaumethoden
    (Rio Yubineto, Peru)." *Sitzungberichte der Gesellschaft naturforschender
    Freunde zu Berlin* 20–21: 73–96
Hugh-Jones, C. 1977. "Skin and soul, the round and the straight: social time and
    social space in Pira-Parana society," vol 2. In *Actes du 42ᵉCongrès international
    des américanistes*. Paris, Société des américanistes
Johnson, A. 1974. "Carrying capacity in Amazonia: problems in theory and
    method." Paper presented at the 73rd Annual Meeting of the American
    Anthropological Association, Mexico City
Kaplan, J. 1975. *The Piaroa*. Oxford, Clarendon Press
Karsten, R. 1935. *The Head-Hunters of Western Amazonas: the life and culture of the
    Jibaro Indians of eastern Ecuador and Peru*. Helsinki, Societas Scientarum
    Fennica, Commentationes Humanarum Litterarum 7
Kelekna, P. 1981. "Sex Asymmetry in Jivaroan Achuar Society: a cultural
    mechanism promoting belligerence." Unpublished doctoral dissertation,
    University of New Mexico. Ann Arbor, Xerox University Microfilms
Klots, A. B. and E. Klots 1959. *Living Insects of the World*. London, Hamilton
Lathrap, D. 1968. "The hunting economies of the tropical forest zone of South
    America: an attempt at historical perspective." In R. Lee and I. De Vore (eds.),
    Man the Hunter. Chicago, Aldine
    1970. *The Upper Amazon*. London, Thames and Hudson
Laughlin, W. 1968. "Hunting: an integrating biobehavior system and its evolution-
    ary importance." In R. Lee and I. De Vore (eds.), *Man the Hunter*. Chicago,
    Aldine
Leach, E. 1958. "Magical hair." *Journal of the Royal Anthropological Institute*
    88(2): 147–64
Lee, R. and I. De Vore 1968. "Problems in the study of hunters and gatherers." In R.
    Lee and I. De Vore (eds.), *Man the Hunter*. Chicago, Aldine
Lévi-Strauss, C. 1950. "The use of wild plants in tropical South America." In J.
    Steward (ed.), *Handbook of South-American Indians*, vol. 6. Washington, D.C.,
    Smithsonian Institution, Bureau of American Ethnology
    1962. *La pensée sauvage*. Paris, Plon
    1964. *Mythologiques*, t. 1: *Le cru et le cuit*. Paris, Plon
    1967. *Mythologiques*, t. 2: *Du miel aux cendres*. Paris, Plon
Lima, R. 1956. "A agricultura nas várzeas do estuário do Amazonas." *Boletim
    tecnico do Instituto agronomico* (Belém) 33: 1–164
Lizot, J. 1977. "Population, ressources et guerre chez les Yanomami." *Libre* 2:
    111–45
    1978. "Economie primitive et subsistance: essai sur le travail et l'alimentation
    chez les Yanomami." *Libre* 4: 69–113
Mader, E. and R. Gippelhauser 1982. "New trends in Achuar economy." Paper
    presented at the 44th International Congress of Americanists, Manchester,
    September 1982
Malinowski, B. 1965 (first edition 1935). *Coral Gardens and their Magic*. Bloom-
    ington, University of Indiana Press

Marx, K. 1965. *Pre-capitalist Economic Foundations.* New York, International Publishers

Meggers, B. 1957. "Environment and culture in the Amazon Basin: an appraisal of the theory of environmental determinism." In *Studies in Human Ecology.* Washington, Pan American Union, Social Science Monographs 3

1971. *Amazonia: man and culture in a counterfeit paradise.* Chicago, Aldine

1975. "Application of the biological model of diversification to cultural distribution in tropical lowland South America." *Biotropica* 7(3): 141–61

Ministère de la Coopération 1974. *Memento de l'agronome: techniques rurales en Afrique.* Paris, Ministère de la Coopération

Miracle, M. 1966. *Maize in Tropical Africa.* Madison, University of Wisconsin Press

Morley, S. 1956. *The Ancient Maya.* Stanford, Stanford University Press

Murra, J. 1975. "Maiz, tubérculos y ritos agrícolas." In *Formaciones económicas y políticas del mundo andino.* Lima, Instituto de estudios peruanos

Naranjo, M. 1974. "Etnohistoria de la zona central del Alto Amazonas: siglos 16–17–18." Unpublished master's thesis, University of Illinois

Nietschmann, B. 1972. "Hunting and fishing productivity of the Miskito Indians, eastern Nicaragua." In *Actas y memorias del XXXIX Congreso internacional de americanistas,* vol. 4. Lima, Instituto de Estudios peruanos

Odum, H. 1971. *Environment, Power and Society.* New York, John Wiley and Sons

Patzelt, E. 1978. *Fauna del Ecuador.* Quito, Editorial Las Casas

Pellizzaro, S. 1978a. *La muerte y los entierros.* Sucua (Ecuador), Centro de documentación e investigación cultural shuar, Mundo shuar, Series B, N° 13

1978b. *La celebración de Uwi.* Quito/Guyaquil, Publicación de los Museos del Banco central del Ecuador

1978c. *Nunkui.* Sucua (Ecuador), Centro de documentación e investigación cultural shuar, Mundo shuar, Series F, N° 8

1980a. *Tsunki: mitos y ritos de la pesca.* Sucua (Ecuador), Centro de documentación e investigación cultural shuar, Mundo shuar, Series F, N° 2

1980b. *Ayumpum: mitos de la cabeza cortada.* Centro de documentación e investigación cultural shuar, Mundo shuar, Series F, N° 5

n.d. (1). *Shakaim.* Centro de documentación e investigación cultural shuar, Mundo shuar, Series F, N° 10

n.d. (2). *Etza, defensor del pueblo shuar.* Centro de documentación e investigación cultural shuar, Mundo shuar, Series F, N° 6

Phillips, J. 1974. "Effects of fire in forest and savanna ecosystems of subsaharan Africa." In T. Kozlowski and C. Ahlgren (eds.), *Fire and Ecosystems.* New York, Academic Service

Pierre, F. 1889. *Voyage d'exploration d'un missionnaire dominicain chez les tribus sauvages de l'Equateur.* Paris, Bureaux de l'Année dominicaine

Pospisil, L. 1972 (first edition 1963). *Kapauku Papuan Economy.* New Haven, Human Relations Area Files Press

Reid, H. 1978. "Dreams and their interpretation among the Hupdu Maku Indians of Brazil." *Cambridge Anthropology* 4(3): 2–28

Rivet, P. 1908. "Les Indiens Jivaros: étude géographique, historique et ethnographique." *L'anthropologie* 19(1–3): 69–87

Roosevelt, A. 1980. "*Parmana: prehistoric maize and manioc subsistence along the*

Amazon and Orinoco. New York, Academic Press

Ross, E. 1976. "The Achuara Jivaro: cultural adaptation in the upper Amazon." Unpublished doctoral dissertation, Columbia University. Ann Arbor, Xerox University Microfilms

1978. "Food taboos, diet and hunting strategy: the adaptation to animals in Amazon cultural ecology." *Current Anthropology* 19(1): 1–36

Sahlins, M. 1968. "La première société d'abondance." *Les temps modernes* 268: 641–80

1972. *Stone-Age Economics.* London, Tavistock Publications

Salazar, E. 1977. *An Indian Federation in Lowland Ecuador.* Copenhagen, International Work Group on Indigenous Affairs, IWGIA document 28

Salisbury, R. 1962. *From Stone to Steel.* Cambridge, Cambridge University Press

Sanchez, P. 1976. *Properties and Management of Soils in the Tropics.* New York, John Wiley

Santana, R. 1978. "Le projet shuar et la stratégie de colonisation du Sud-Est équatorien." *Travaux et mémoires de l'Institut des hautes études de l'Amérique latine* 32: 55–66

Sastre, C. 1975. "La végétation du haut et moyen Igara-Parana et les modifications apportées par les cultures sur brûlis." In J. Centlivres, J. Gasche and A. Lourteig (eds.), *Culture sur brûlis et évolution du milieu forestier en Amazonie du nord-ouest.* Genève, Société suisse d'ethnologie

SCET International-PREDESUR 1977. *Mapa de aptitud de los suelos (zona A norte, hoja n° 1).* Quito, Programa regional de desarollo del Sur

Schmidt, K. and R. Inger 1957. *Living Reptiles of the World.* London, Hamilton

Schnell, R. 1972. *Introduction à la phytogéographie des pays tropicaux.* Paris, Gauthier-Villars, 2 volumes

Seeger, A., R. Da Matta and E. B. Viveiros de Castro 1979. "A construçâo da pessoa nas sociedades indigenas brasileiras." *Boletim do Museu nacional* 32: 2–19

Sigaut, F. 1976. "La dynamique des systèmes culturaux traditionnels en Amérique tropicale." In *Actes du 42ᵉ Congrès international des américanistes,* vol. 3. Paris, Société des américanistes

Sioli, H. 1950. "Das Wasser im Amazonasgebiet." *Forschungen und Fortschritte* 26: 274–80

1954. "Beitrage zur regionalen Limnologie des Amazonasgebietes, 2: der Rio Arapiuns." *Archiv für Hydrobiologie* 49: 448–518

1957. "Sedimentation in Amazonasgebiet." *Geologische Rundschau* 45: 508–633

1964. "General features of the limnology of Amazonia." *Verhandlungen des International Verein Limnologie* 15: 1053–8

1973. "Recent human activities in the Brazilian Amazon and their ecological effects." In B. Meggers, E. Ayensu and W. Duckworth (eds.), *Tropical Forest Ecosystems in Africa and South America: a comparative review.* Washington, D.C., Smithsonian Institution

Siskind, J. 1973. *To Hunt in the Morning.* London, Oxford University Press

Smith, N. 1976. "Utilization of game along Brazil's Transamazon Highway." *Acta amazonica* 6(4): 455–66

Smole, W. 1976. *The Yanoama Indians: a cultural geography.* Austin, University of Texas Press

Sombroek, W. 1966. *Amazon Soils: a reconnaissance of the soils of the Brazilian Amazon region*. Wageningen (Netherlands), Center for Agricultural Publication and Documentation

Sourdat M. and E. Custode, 1980a. *Carta pedo-geomorfológica de la provincia de Morona-Santiago: informe provisional*. Quito, ORSTOM-PRONAREG

1980b. *La problemática del manejo integral y el estudio morfo-pedológico de la region amazonica ecuatoriana*. Quito, Ministerio de Agricultura y ganaderia-ORSTOM

Steward, J. 1948. "Culture areas of the tropical forest." In J. Steward (ed.), *Handbook of South-American Indians*, vol. 3: *The Tropical Forest Tribes*. Washington, D.C., Smithsonian Institution, Bureau of American Ethnology

(ed.) 1948. *Handbook of South-American Indians*, vol. 3: *The Tropical Forest Tribes*. Washington, D.C., Smithsonian Institution, Bureau of American Ethnology

Steward J. and L. Faron 1959. *Native Peoples of South America*. New York, McGraw Hill

Stirling, M. 1938. *Historical and Ethnographical Notes on the Jivaro Indians*. Washington, D.C., Smithsonian Institution

Taylor, A-C. 1981. "God-wealth: the Achuar and the missions." In N. Whitten (ed.), *Cultural Transformation and Ethnicity in Modern Ecuador*. Urbana, University of Illinois Press

1983a. "The marriage of alliance and its structural variations in Jivaroan societies." *Information sur les sciences sociales* 22(3): 331–53

1983b. "Jivaroan magical songs: achuar *anent* of connubial love." *Amerindia* 8: 87–127

1993. Unpublished thesis for Doctorat d'Etatès-lettres, to be defended at the Université de Paris X-Nanterre.

Tschopp, H. J. 1953. "Oil explorations in the Oriente of Ecuador." *Bulletin of the American Association of Petroleum Geologists* 37(10): 2303–47

Tyler, E. J. 1975. "Genesis of the Soils with a Detailed Soil Survey in the Upper Amazon Basin, Yurimaguas, Peru." Unpublished doctoral dissertation, Soil Science Department, University of North Carolina

Up de Graff, F. W. n.d. *Head Hunters of the Amazon: seven years of exploration and adventure*. New York, Garden City Publishing

Varese, S. 1966. "Los Indios Campa de la Selva Peruana en los documentos de los siglos 16 y 17." Unpublished thesis for bachillerato en etnologia, Universidad Católica, Lima

Vickers, W. 1976. "Cultural Adaptation to Amazonian Habitats: the Siona-Secoya of eastern Ecuador." Unpublished doctoral dissertation, University of Florida. Ann Arbor, Xerox University Microfilms

Wawrin, Marquis de 1941. *Les Jivaros réducteurs de têtes*. Paris, Payot

Wellman, F. 1977. *Dictionary of Tropical American Crops and their Diseases*. Metuchen (New Jersey), The Scarecrow Press

White, L. 1959. *The Evolution of Culture: the development of civilization to the fall of Rome*. New York, McGraw Hill

White, T. 1953. "A method of calculating the dietary percentage of various food animals utilized by aboriginal peoples." *American Antiquity* 14: 396–8

Whitten, N. 1974. *Black Frontiersmen: a South-American case*. New York, Halsted

1976. *Sacha Runa: ethnicity and adaptation of Ecuadorian jungle Quichua.* Urbana, University of Illinois Press

Wu Leung, W. and M. Flores 1961. *Food Composition Table for Use in Latin America.* Bethesda (Maryland), Interdepartmental Committee on Nutrition for National Defense

Yengoyan, A. 1968. "Demographic and ecological influence on Aboriginal Australian marriage sections." In R. Lee and I. De Vore (eds.), *Man the Hunter.* Chicago, Aldine

Subject index

Names of places and peoples are in small capitals, vernacular terms are in italics.

acculturation 31
adaptation; ecological 33, 177–91; to soil
    types 43; adaptive function 3; adaptive
    responses 5
adultery 126, 219–20, 309
aents 93
affinity, *see* kinship
agronomy 340 n. 6
aguajal 19, 41, 57, 61, 139, 142, 145, 244
AGUARUNA 7, 21, 22, 193; *anent* 199;
    hallucinogens 341 n. 7; manioc spirit
    342 n. 18; Nunkui myth 194, 196, 342
    n. 17; nutrition 316
Aldebaran 67–68
ALGONQUIN 335 n. 6
alluvial plain, *see* flood plain
AMAHUACA 153, 184, 186; agricultural rituals
    341 n. 16; clearing times 340 n. 5
amana 261, 262, 263, 268, 343 n. 4
AMAZON BASIN 17, 19, 177; flood plain 180
AMAZON R. 54, 55
AMBATO 22
ANASU R. 20, 21
ANATICO, LAKE 21, 24
Andoas 26; mission 30, 57
anemartin 94
anent 96, 199–215, 268, 305; affines 199; for
    charms 206; for curare 199, 226; dogs
    199, 232, 234, 235; to call a dream 208,
    266; evil spells 212; fishing 279;
    gardening 198; game 199; hunting 199,
    260–62; love 199, 200; to manioc 204; to
    Nunkui 201–202; pottery 199; war 199
animal calls 82–83, 99
animals; domestic 90, 258; social behavior of
    96–98; taxonomy 82–92, 336 n. 5; *see*
    also game, pets

anomy 9
Antares 68, 70
anthropology, economic xv, 5, 106;
    reductionism 5
APINAYÉ 266, 343 n. 5
ARAWAK 177
architecture 111–18; vocabulary 338 n. 2,
    339 n. 3
army; Ecuadorian 23, 24, 25; Peruvian 25
artefacts, manufacture 289
arutam, see soul
astronomy 67–71, 336 n. 6, *see also* celestial
    bodies, cosmology
autonomy (of households) 105, 109, 135,
    324, 327, 330; social and economic 285
ax, *see* tools

BAÑOS 15, 22
BARAFIRI, *see* YANOAMA
BARUYA xv, 186, 192
bed 113, 129–30, 216, 231, 339 n. 5
beer; manioc 36–37, 49, 50, 94, 114, 127,
    128, 134, 154, 181, 195, 244, 254, 286,
    287, 288, 309; plantain 193; sweet
    potato 193
bezoar, *see* charm
biotope, *see* habitat
birth 121, 217
blood 204–205; of game 226; manioc 204, 205
bloodsucking (manioc) 209
blowgun 128, 153, 222–25, 228, 229, 235,
    236, 249, 257, 261, 262, 280, 281, 286,
    302, 342 n. 1; children's 239;
    manufacture 223–24
BOBONAZA R. 15, 16, 17, 18, 20, 21, 22, 30,
    33, 53, 57, 141, 143; valley 38, 40, 57
bodily control 133–34

Index of plants and animals

English names appear in lower case, Achuar names in capitals and the Latin botanical and zoological classifications in italics. The page references are listed after the botanical or zoological classification when one has been given.

AAKIAM (*Pseudoplatystoma fasciatum*)
Accipitridae 87
ACHAYAT (*Teleonema filicauda*)
achiote (*Bixa orellana*)
achira (*Renealmia alpina*)
ACHU (*Mauritia flexuosa*)
acuchi (*Myoprocta* sp.)
agouti (*Dasyprocta punctata*)
aguaje palm (*Mauritia flexuosa*)
Aiphanes sp. (KAMANCHA) 253, 254
AJACH (*Dioscorea* sp.)
AJEJ (*Zinziber officinale*)
AJINUMI (*Mouriri grandiflora*)
Alcedinidae, or the kingfishers 57, 88
Altheranthera lanceolata (PIRISUK) 163
Amaranthaceae 163
AMICH (*Tayra barbara*)
AMICH YAWA (*Tayra* sp.) 85
AMPAKI (*Iriartea ventricosa*)
AMPUSH (generic term for the owls, Strigidae)
anaconda (*Eunectes murinus*)
Ananas comosus (KUISH), or pineapple 161, 165, 166
Anatidae, or ducks 57, 88, 90
Ancistrus sp. (SHUWI) 275
angel's trumpet (*Brugmansia* sp. and *Datura* sp.)
Annona squamosa (KEACH), or sweetsop 161, 168
Anostomidae 95, 275
ant (WEEK) 74, 82, 94, 95, 154, 254;

Amazon (YARUSH) 84; flying 74, 255; *see also Grandiponera*
antbird, *see* Formicariidae
anteater collared 337 n. 2; great 337 n.2
APAI (*Grias tessmannii*)
APAICH NUMI (*Himathantus sucuuba*)
Apeiba membranacea (SHIMIUT) 124, 145
Apocynacae 119, 164
APUP (*Inia geoffrensis*)
Araceae 173
Arachis hypogoea (NUSE), or peanut 122, 145, 146, 149, 161, 162, 165, 166, 168, 174, 175, 178, 179, 197, 209, 210, 310, 311; nitrogen 341 n. 13
Arapaima gigas (PAITS), or paiche 55, 56, 58, 272, 273, 274
ARARATS (unidentified tree) 80
armadillo (unspecified) 95, 229, 233, 235, 237, 246; *see also Cabassou* sp., *Dasypus* sp. *Dasypus novemcinctus* and *Priodontes giganteus*)
arrowroot (*Maranta ruiziana*)
Aspidosperma album (CHIWIACHIWIA) 116, 119
Aspidosperma megalocarpon (TAUN) 79
Astrocaryum chambira (KUMAI and MATA), or chambira palm 51, 78, 164, 167, 231, 252, 253, 272, 273
Astrocaryum huicungo (AWAN) 51, 52, 253
ATASH (chicken)
ATASHMATAI (*Iryanthera juruensis*)
Ateles belzebuth (WASHI), or spider monkey 87, 92; prohibited 338 n. 2

Atelocinus microtis (KUAP YAWA), or
   bush dog 85
AUJU (*Nyctibius grandis*)
avocado (*Persea* sp.)
AWAN (*Astrocaryum huicungo*)
AYACHUI (*Nothocrax urumutum*)

balsa (*Ochroma pyramidale*)
bamboo (*Bambusa* sp.)
Bambusa sp. (WACHI), or bamboo 51, 53,
   58, 79, 119, 146, 224, 261; giant 18
banana (*Musa* sp.)
Banisteriopsis sp. (NATEM) 100, 163;
   (YAJI) 163
barbasco (*Lonchocarpus* sp.)
bat, *see* Chiroptera
Batocarpus orinocensis (PITIU), a bread-
   fruit 153, 164, 167, 252, 253
beans (*Phaseolus* sp.)
bear, spectacled (*Tremarctos ornatus*)
bee 73; honey 255; larva 254, 255
beetle (SHIPIAK) 165, 166, 239, 254
Bignonaceae 164, 253
Bixa orellana (IPIAK), or achiote 134, 163,
   169, 197, 198, 203, 216, 263, for *nantar*
   208–209; *see also* face paint
Boidae, or constrictors (PANKI) 87, 88, 95,
   111, 124; *see also* anaconda
Bombaceae 124
Bonafousia sananho (KUNAPIP) 164, 253
bread-fruit (*Batocarpus orinocensis*)
Bromeliaceae 281
Brugmansia sp. (MAIKIUA), or angel's
   trumpet 163
Bucconidae, or the puffbirds 84, 88, 94
Bursarellus nigricollis (MAKUA), or black-
   collared hawk 87
Burseraceae 164, 253
bush dog (*Atelocinus microtis*)
butterfly (WAMPISHUK) 92, 239; larvae
   (CHARANCHAM) 255: (PUNTISH) 255

Cabassou sp. (SEMA), an armadillo 89
cacao (*Theobroma subincanum*); wild
   (*Herrania mariae*)
cacique 86, *see also* CHUWI
caiman 97, 119, 282; black (*Paleosuchus
   trigonatus*); spectacled (*Caiman sclerops*)
Caiman sclerops (KANIATS), or spectacled
   caiman 56, 58
Calandra palmarum (TSAMPU, adult;
   MUNTISH, larval stage), or palm grub
   84, 254, 255, 301; prohibited 210, 211
Calathea aff. *exscapa* (PINIA) 161
Calathea altissima (PUMPU) 50, 142
Campephilus melanoleucos (SASERAT), or
   red-crested woodpecker 84

Capsicum sp. (JIMIA), or chili pepper 161,
   162, 168, 259; prohibited 211, 226
capybara (*Hydrochoerus hydrochaeris*)
Cares sp. (PIRIPIRI), or sedge 163
Carica papaya (WAPAI), or papaya 161,
   166, 167, 168, 170, 176, 197, 202, 231;
   prohibited 226
Carnegiella strigata (TITIM), or hatchet fish
   272
Caryodendron orinocensis (NAAMPI) 164,
   252, 253
cat, *see* Felidae
caterpiller (MAA) 165; (SHUKI) 166,
   (SHUNI) 261
catfish (*Pimelodus ornatus* and
   Pseudoplatystoma fasciatum) 272
Cathartidae, or the vultures 84
Cebus capucinus (TSERE), or capuchin
   monkey 87, 238, 245, 246
Cecropia sp. (SUU, SUTIK and TSEEK)
   51, 56, 137, 149
Cecropia sciadophylla (SUU) 137, 142
Cedrela sp., or cedro 25
Cedro (*Cedrela* sp.)
Ceiba pentandra (MENTE) 25, 50, 52, 65,
   142
Ceiba trischistranda (WAMPUASH), or
   kapok 47, 50, 51,52, 53, 58, 142, 231;
   dog's name 237; floods 47–48
Cephalopterus ornatus (UNKUM), or
   umbrella-bird 95, 338 n. 3
Cervidae 86, 88, 337 n. 2; *see also* JAPA
CESA (unidentified plant) 80
CHAAPI (*Phytelephas* sp.)
CHAAPI 73
CHAE (*Tremarctos ornatus*)
chambira (*Astrocaryum chambira*)
Characidae 56
CHARAKAT (Alcedinidae)
CHARANCHAM (butterfly larva)
CHARAP (*Podocnemis expansa*)
chicken 90, 314
CHIIYUMI (*Lagenaria* sp.)
CHIKAINIA (*Talauma* sp.)
CHIKI (*Maranta ruiziana*)
CHIMI (*Pseudolmedia laevigata*)
CHINCHAK (several species of *Miconia*
   and *Leandra*) 79, 145, 153, 164
CHINIMP (generic term for the swallows
   and martins) 88
CHINKI (generic name for small birds,
   "sparrow") 88
CHIRI-CHIRI (*Orthoclada laxa*)
CHIRIKIASIP (narcotic shrub) 164, 262
Chiroptera (JEENCHAM), or the bats 87,
   88; vampire (PENKE JEENCHAM) 205
CHIWIA (generic name for the trumpeters) 94

Iriartea sp. (TUNTUAM) 51, 52, 81, 111, 116, 145, 222, 253, 254
Iriartea exorrhiza (?) (KUPAT) 116, 235, 253
Iriartea ventricosa (AMPAKI) 51, 116
Iryanthera juruensis (ATASHMATAI) 116
ISHPINK (*Nectandra cinnamonoides*)
IWIANCH CHINKI (*Pitylus grossus*)
IWIANCH JAPA (*Mazama americana*)
IWIANCH JII (Shuar, *Mucuna huberi*)

JAAPASH (*Nyctanassa violacea* and *Nycticorax nycticorax*)
Jacaranda copaia (TAKATSA) 137
jaguar (*Pantera onca*); black 85, 279, 282
jaguarundi (*Felis yagouaroundi*)
JAPA (generic name for the Cervidae)
JAPA YAWA (*Felis concolor*)
JEENCHAM (generic term for the Chiroptera)
JEEP (unidentified Aracaea) 173
JEMPE (generic term for the hummingbirds)
Jessenia weberbaueri (KUNKUK) 51, 52, 73, 81, 139, 164, 252, 253
jicama (*Pachyrhizus tuberosus*)
JIISHIMP (*Leucopternis shistacea*)
JIMIA (*Capsicum* sp.)
JINICHAM (generic term for the Tyrannidae)
JUICHAM (*Conepatus* sp.)
JURUKMAN (*Momotu momota*)
JUUNT TUNKAU (*Pimelodus ornatus*)
JUUNT YAWA (*Pantera onca*)

KAAP (*Heteropsis obligonfolia*)
KAASHAP (*Potamotrygon hystrix*)
KAASHNUMI (*Eschweilera* sp.)
KAI (*Persea* sp.)
KAITSAIP (a species of ant) 94, 95
KAKA (*Trema micrantha*)
KAKAU (*Miconia elata*)
KAMANCHA (*Aiphanes* sp.)
KAMPANAK (*Hyospatha* sp.)
KANIATS (*Caiman sclerops*)
KANIIR (*Vandellia wieneri*)
KANKA (*Prochilodus nigricans*)
KANTASH (a Cichlidae) 275
KANTSE (an Amaranthaceae) 163
kapok (*Ceiba trischistranda*)
KASHAI (*Cuniculus paca*)
KASUA (*Coussapoa oligoneura*)
KATIRI (unidentified palm with edible heart) 81, 253
KATSUINT (a type of gourd) 163
KAUTA (*Herpetotheres cachinnans*)
KAWAU (generic term for the macaws)
KAWARUNCH (*Theobroma* sp.)

KAYAIPI (unidentified plant) 225
KAYA YAIS (*Oxandra xylopiodes*)
KAYUK (*Dasyprocta punctata*)
KEACH (*Annona squamosa*)
KEAKU CESA (unidentified plant with red flowers) 208
KEAKU JAPA (*Odocoileus gymnotis*)
KENKE (*Dioscorea trifida*)
KENKU (*Guadua angustifolia*)
KERUA (*Ramphastos culminatus*)
KINCHUK (*Phytelephas* sp.)
kingfishers, *see* Alcedinidae
KINKIWI (*Euterpe* sp.)
KIRIMP (*Psidium guajava*)
kite, hook-billed (*Chondrohierax uncinatus*)
KUAP YAWA (*Atelocinus microtis*)
KUCHIKIAM (*Herrania mariae*)
KUCHI WAKAMP (*Theobroma bicolor*)
KUISH (*Ananas comosus*)
KUKUCH (*Solanum coconilla*)
KUKUKUI (*Micrastur*)
KUMAI (*Astrocaryum chambira*, leaf fibers)
KUMPIA (*Renealmia alpinia*)
KUNAPIP (*Bonafousia sananho*)
KUNCHAI (*Dacryodes* aff. *peruviana*)
KUNKU (a species of snail)
KUNKUIM (*Geochelone denticulata*)
KUNKUK (*Jessenia weberbaueri*)
KUPAT (*Iriartea exorrhiza* ?)
KUSUM (pencil fish)
KUTUKU (generic name for tadpoles)
KUUNT (*Wettinia maynensis*)
KUYU (*Pipile pipile*)
KUYUUWA (unidentified palm with edible heart) 81, 253

Lacmella peruviana (TAUCH) 73, 153, 164, 252, 253
Lagenaria sp. (CHIIYUMI) 163
Lagenaria siceraria (YUMI), or bottle gourd 163, 167
Lagothrix (CHUU), or woolly monkey 262
Lauraceae 253
Leandra sp. (CHINCHAK) 79, 164
Lecythidaceae 253
Lecythishians (YUNKUA) 116
Leguminosae 51, 79
Leucopternis shistacea (JIISHIMP), or slate-colored hawk 76, 87
Licania sp. (NASHIP) 79, 142
locusts (MANCHIR) 165, 166
Lonchocarpus sp. (TIMIU), or barbasco 117, 137, 146, 163, 170, 171, 178, 197, 244, 275, 276, 277, 280–82
Loricariidae (NAYUMP) 88, 275
Luffa cylindrica (TAKUM YUWI), or sponge gourd 163, 167
lupuna (*Ceiba pentandra*)

Nicotiania sp. (TSAANK), or tobacco 119, 137, 163, 168, 169, 175, 176, 197, 199, 216
nightjars (*Steatornis caripensis*)
Nothocrax urumutum (AYACHUI), or nocturnal curassow 91, 232
NUSE (*Arachis hypogaea*)
Nyctanassa violacea (JAAPASH), a nocturnal heron 84
Nyctibius grandis (AUJU), or potoo 69, 83, 196
Nycticorax nycticorax (JAAPASH), a nocturnal heron 84

ocelot (*Felis pardalis* and *Felis wiedii*)
Ochroma pyramidale (WAWA), or balsa 137, 142, 149, 153, 164
Odocoileus gymnotis (KEAKU JAPA) 338 n. 2
Oenocarpus sp. (SHIMPI) 253
Oleacinae 119
onion (*Allium cepa*)
Ophidia 87
opossum 91, 232; woolly (*Philander* sp.), Orchidae 253
oriole; yellow-tailed 79; *see also* CHUWI, Icteridae
oropendola; crested (*Psarocolius decumanus*); green (*Psarocolius viridis*); *see also* CHUWI, Icteridae
Orthoclada laxa (CHIRI-CHIRI) 163, 173, 185, 299
otter (*Lutra annectens*); giant (*Pteronura* sp.)
owls, see Strigidae
Oxandra xylopiodes (KAYA YAIS) 116

PAANTAM (*Musa balbisiana*)
PAAT (*Saccharum officinarum* and *Gynerium sagittatum*)
paca (*Cuniculus paca*)
Pachyrrhizus tuberosus (NAMAU), or jicama 161
PAENI (*Minquartia punctata*)
paiche (*Arapaima gigas*)
PAINKISH (*Strychnos jobertiana*)
PAITS (*Arapaima gigas*)
PAKI (generic term for the Tayassuidae)
Paleosuchus trigonatus (YANTANA), or black caiman 55, 56, 58, 119, 124, 246, 247, 248,
palm grub (*Calandra palmarum*)
palms 51, 52, 80, 111, 116, 139, 252, 254; *see also* aguaje, chambira, chonta
PAMASUKI (a pulse)
PANKI (generic name for the Boidae, and in particular the anaconda, *Eunectes murinus*)
PANKI NAI (anaconda's fang, a pulse) 79

Pantera onca (JUUNT YAWA), or jaguar 85, 97, 223, 230, 235, 264, 325, 326
PAPACHNIA (*Colocasia* sp.)
PAPASH (*Felis wiedii*)
papaya (*Carica papaya*)
Paragonia pyramidata (TANISH NAEK) 164, 253
PARAPRA (unidentified narcotic plant) 163
parrot 95, 134; blue-headed (*Pionus menstruus*)
passerines/passeriforms 90
Passiflora sp. (MUNCHIJ), or granadilla 164, 253
PATU (generic term for the Anatidae)
PATUKAM YAWA (*Speothos venaticus*)
PAU (*Pouteria* sp.)
PAYAASH (*Piscidia carthagenensis* [?])
peach palm (*Guilielma gasipaes*)
peanut (*Arachis hypogaea*)
peccary, *see* Tayassuidae
PEE PEE PINCHU (*Chondrohierax uncinatus*)
PEESEPEESI (*Pitylus grossus*)
pencil fish (KUSUM), an Anostomid 95, 275
PENKA (*Rheedia macrophylla*)
PENKE JEENCHAM (*Desmodus rotundus*)
PENKE NAMAK (*Ichythyoelephas humeralis*)
peppers (*Capsicum* sp.)
Perebea guianensis (SUNKASH) 73, 164, 253
Persea sp. (KAI), or avocado, 161, 168,
Phaseolus sp. (MIIK), or beans 149, 161, 165, 166, 168, 174, 178, 179, 181, 320; nitrogen 341 n. 13
Phaseolus vulgaris 178
Philander sp. (KUJI), or woolly opossum; prohibited 338 n. 2
Phoebe sp. (MACHAPI) 225
Physalis sp. (YURANKMIS) 164, 253
Phytelephas sp. 58, 164, 167, 253 (CHAAPI), or Ilarina palm 51, 52, 73, 117, 164; (KINCHUK) 53, 58, 139, 224, 253
PIAKRUR (*Monasa atra*)
Pimelodidae (TUNKAU) 56, 58, 88, 94, 95, 273, 274
Pimelodus ornatus (JUUNT TUNKAU), or catfish 274, 343 n. 2
"pimento tree" (*Mouriri grandiflora*)
PINCHU (several species of Falconidae and Accipitridae) 87, 88
pineapple (*Ananas comosus*)
PINIA (*Calathea* aff. *exscapa*)
Pionus menstruus (TUISH), or blue-headed parrot 165, 166
Piper sp. ? (SHINKI-SHINKI) 164

Cambridge Studies in Social and Cultural Anthropology

Editors: Ernest Gellner, Jack Goody, Stephen Gudeman, Michael Herzfeld, Jonathan Parry

*available in paperback